Cheap Chic UPDATE

by
Caterine Milinaire
and Carol Troy

Revised edition by Carol Troy

Designed by Bea Feitler

Harmony Books
New York

Design Assistant: Carl Barile
Research: Martha Siegler, Diane Partie
Cover Lettering: Barbara Richer
Cover Photograph of Yasmine courtesy Pinky and Dianne Ltd.

Harmony Books, a division of Crown Publishers, Inc.
One Park Avenue, New York, New York 10016
Published simultaneously in Canada by General Publishing Company Limited.
Printed in the United States of America.

Library of Congress Cataloging in Publication Data

Milinaire, Caterine.
Cheap chic update

1. Fashion.   2. Clothing and dress.
I. Troy, Carol, joint author.   II. Title.
TT515.M59 1978   646'.34   78-4148
ISBN 0-517-53460-6
ISBN 0-517-53456-8 pbk.

TABLE OF CONTENTS

dedicated to

maurice   hogenboom

from caterine

RAGS

Mary Peacock

Carol Troy

For Mary and everybody who's worked so long and hard on Rags magazine!

And with love to Lucian K. Truscott IV
—Carol Troy 1978

7

INTRODUCTION

You might be interested in the story of this little pink book and how it came to pass. Since it was written for you, you have a right to know.

Three years ago, when *Cheap Chic* was first published, I really took it on the chin from Barbara Walters. The "Today" Show was the first time I'd ever been on television, and I was scared to death. She stuck it to me, and I guess I didn't hold up my end too well. *Cheap Chic*, she said, was written only for skinny young girls who didn't have jobs.

Well, it looks like Barbara Walters was wrong. Because three years later we're coming out with a new *Cheap Chic*. The pictures have changed here and there, but the words remain pretty much the same. Because despite Barbara Walters, this book had some basic truths in it. Some truths about finding out who you are and being faithful to that person. Finding out what *you* like and feel good wearing, and hanging on to it. To me, this is the *real* way to dress for success. To feel it from the inside. Because what is style all about but wearing your insides on your outsides? And if we can tell you in *Cheap Chic* some of the sly ways of looking chic on the cheap, all the better. The real bottom line here is not dollars and cents: it's how you feel about yourself. Sure, we know you can't wear jeans to the office. If you're a career woman, you're going to be more interested in the Classics chapter than the Wrapping chapter...but maybe you'll love tying on a pareo when you take a well-deserved vacation! So there's something for everybody—and everybody, young or old, rich or poor, tall or short, slender or hefty—can find something good and useful in this book.

You don't have to lock up your wallet when you go shopping *Cheap Chic* style. The stuff in this book applies to a trip to Bloomingdale's, Neiman-Marcus, or I. Magnin, as well as to a trip to Woolworth's. We're merely encouraging you to embrace your own style and express your own individuality with confidence. You have the freedom to sidestep designer dictatorship and make the clothes you spend your money on work for *you*, rather than making *you* work for your clothes.

—Carol Troy/1978

The most basic element of Cheap Chic is the body you hang your clothes on. Building a healthy, lively body is far cheaper than buying a lot of clothes to distract from it. And once you really know your flesh and bones, you'll find it easier to choose the clothes you really need and love.

Try standing in front of a full-length mirror some morning, not holding in your stomach, tightening your buttocks, or sticking out your chest. Take a look at your body—front, side, and back. Are you content with what you see? Is your skin clear and healthy? Could the muscle tone of your stomach, upper arms, and thighs be firmed up with a little jogging, swimming, or a ten-block walk each morning? It isn't important if your breasts, hips, or legs aren't those you would see in a fashion magazine or in the pages of *Playboy*. What matters is that you get acquainted with them as they are and treat them with care and respect.

There are no secret recipes for keeping your body together, but learning to take a certain pleasure in self-discipline is a first step... discipline in eating and sleeping habits that helps build good emotional and physical relationships. Once you decide to perk up your body, there are many ways to go about it: Invent your own exercises and treatments, seek advice from a friend who enjoys and studies physical movement, find a class you like, read body books, and keep trying different ways until you find a routine that really feels comfortable for you...one you can really stick with. Diana Vreeland, after almost forty years with *Harper's Bazaar* and *Vogue*, describes the secrets of a vibrant woman: "You have to have a sense of pleasure and a sense of discipline to look really well. You have to have a sound, athletic body, lead a busy life, and worry less. Live correctly and take risks."

Once you have a body program set up, start having fun with your clothes. Perhaps the best place to start thinking about the evocative nature of fabric, color, and clothes is with the senses:

Touch: the softness of washed cottons, thick velvets, tender cashmeres, bumpy corduroys; the harshness of raw wool.

Smell: the scent of a real leather bag versus imitation leather; a wet wool sweater versus a polyester knit.

Sound: the rustle of taffeta, the squawk of rubbers in the rain, the flapping of canvas, the whisper of nylons.

Sight: the harmonious blends of bright or subtle colors, rough and smooth textures, straight and curved silhouettes.

Now, with all your senses in full gear, let's take a look into the world of Cheap Chic.

FIRST LAYERS

There's one very good reason for stocking up on the basics: peace of mind. You'll *never* have to get up in the early morning darkness and stumble about looking for something to match up with something else. If you've got the basics, they're all interchangeable—T-shirts, turtlenecks, or cotton shirts; and with them several pair of jeans, green GI pants, white pants, and a wide skirt. It's rather like wearing a second skin, but more colorful! The reassuring thing about having a drawerful of these things is that you can stick any top with any bottom and it will look great. How can you miss with solid colors, basic quality, simple cut and time-tested designs? And what feels better than slipping into a freshly laundered cotton outfit in your favorite color, tying on a scarf, and giving it no more thought? If you hate to think about what you're putting on your back, and refuse to spend any time messing about with your "wardrobe," you're all set with the basics. You'll have all the more time to get down to what you really want to achieve in life rather than spending hours shopping in department stores and dressing up in a "fashion statement" or a "look for fall." In the basics, you can remain anonymous, observe and stalk the life you're after in a quiet and individual style.

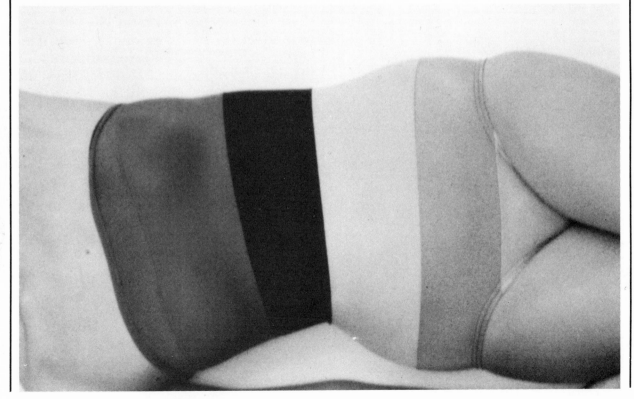

JEANS AND OTHER COVERINGS

One good friend of ours who dresses like a modern-day John Wayne professes to care nothing, or very little, about the clothes he wears. And yet he combs the city to find the precise pair of **jeans** he wants—Lees. Why? Because jeans, like almost everything else, have fallen prey to the fashion cycle. You can find bell-bottomed jeans, boot-leg jeans, even flared jeans. But just try to find a regular, trusty old pair of straight-legged denim jeans with no frills. Our friend has looked in Columbus, Ohio (Surely the farmers would have them!), in Chicago, Illinois, and in Binghamton, New York. His only dependable source: Kauffman's Riding Store in New York City. Jeans are such a totem of American culture that they inspire that kind of mania for the marginal differences, for the tiny details that will set you off from the crowd, set you apart from the blue-legged masses.

First layers: everything from leotards to Levi's can keep you going from morning 'til night with a minimal investment of time and money.

Forty-Niners at the Last Chance Mine, 1882, wearing riveted Levi's and sturdy boots that look like today's Frye boots.

In the fifties, jeans were good as gold behind the Iron Curtain: to the Russians they summed up all the romantic promise of the American frontier, the wildness of the West. Like nylons in World War II, jeans were great for bartering and bribing. The Levi trademark—that little red tab sewn into the side of the back pocket—is registered in sixty countries including Russia, where they don't even make jeans.

Originally, jeans were coveted in Paris, and then Yves St. Laurent came along and knocked them off in couture. The French have taken the basic idea of blue jeans, re-styled and recut them for that tight European fit . . . and now they sell like crazy in America at twice the original price. It's typical of the French to pick up basic American design and transform it with colorings and proportion into something quintessentially Parisian, something almost like a national uniform.

A good basic pair of jeans will last several years, mold themselves to your body, and fade with style. Like all good clothes,

Cher, wearing a pair of jeans that fit the way jeans should fit.

they improve with age. In the summer, you can cut them off into shorts; in the winter, open the seams of the legs, set in a piece of denim, and have a warm, long skirt.

The price of jeans is going up, due to world-wide demand for denim, but they remain one of the central American classics.

Once you find a brand of jeans that fits you the way you like to be fit, stick with it. Plan on the waist and inseam shrinking about 8 percent. Levi-Strauss boot-leg jeans are cut shorter in the front of the leg and longer in the back so they'll look good over Frye boots, cowboy boots, or any boots with

Sasson, like Fiorucci, Jesus Jeans, etc., is just one of the many European jeans cut tight, tight!

Levi-Strauss Company when it comes to putting together a totally functional, beautifully designed piece of clothing.

If you don't relish the thought of marching around looking like a Vietnam vet in jungle green pants, there's yet another alternative—white pants. You can buy white jeans, English or American sailor pants, or painter's pants.

Sailor pants have wide, straight legs and come in a tightly woven long-lasting cotton twill with buttoned closings. They should run about $6 if they're truly "surplus" and not some slyly manufactured imitation. And if they are the real thing, you'll find they take dye beautifully because of their pure cotton fiber.

The first time we saw white **painter's pants** was in a "street fashion" photograph in the Los Angeles *Times*. You can find them at Standard Brands Paints in Los Angeles for 69¢, or in boutiques for several times that. They're a great buy, with all

heels. Straight-legged Lees have an easy fit and fly front, whereas Wranglers come in a more malleable denim that takes less breaking-in but is less durable. You can choose a less sturdy, less expensive brand like Wayfarers or Landlubbers, which don't last a lifetime but are easily settled into. Once you've settled on your best size and brand, it's sometimes easier to buy them already worn at a swap meet rather than breaking them in yourself. Or, as John Burks noted in a book about jeans, "When you're rich you have them pre-bleached and pressed. Bleached Levi's: upward mobility."

Jeans come in all styles and colors these days, but beware! Stick with straight legs or pegged legs without cuffs, and avoid jeans cut very low on the hips. Even jeans can do you in with supermarket overchoice. Stick to the basics because that "fashion detailing," like industrial-zipper-fly fronts, is going to tire real fast.

If you've never been fond of jeans, consider buying a few pair of green **Army fatigue pants** with the pockets on the sides. All over Europe, fashionable girls are wearing them tucked into the tops of their high leather boots or with a pair of patterned socks and loafers. The fabric is the best, and the U.S. Army is easily the equal of the

Twenty years ago James Dean seemed stylishly alienated in well-worn denim jeans and a tattered cotton shirt. Today, jeans still have a whiff of the rebel about them ... not without cause.

realize how really nice they feel on the legs and how charming they look to others. A tight skirt isn't really practical in this era of constant movement, but is fun to wear in the evening with a big T-shirt or man's shirt

Designer Ola Hudson puts scissors, pins, markers and measuring tapes in the pockets of her sturdy white painter's pants and rotates different long-sleeved cotton T-shirts. With a drawer full of pants and T-shirts, she never has to worry about what to wear to work in the morning.

sorts of mysterious pockets, straps, and tabs designed for the house-painter's craft. A designer in North Hollywood, who could choose to wear any of her luxurious designs, seems to wear nothing but painter's pants and T-shirts under her forties-look velour jackets and coats.

Of course, now that everyone's been wearing pants as a daily routine, there's a strong feeling in the air for **skirts.** We're over the boring, burning issue of how long a skirt should be, and can lean back and

Peter Hujar's uniform: jeans, an army-surplus leather belt, and a crocodile shirt (without the crocodile).

18

Lauren Hutton's favorite style: jeans, a roomy man's shirt and a pastel Shetland sweater.

on top and high strappy shoes on your feet. And if pants make you feel uncomfortable, get several skirts. You can find gathered, circle, pleated, or soft A-lines, reasonably priced, at department stores and boutiques. Get two or three in the right colors and you're all set. (A warning: beware of linen if you don't like irons.)

COTTON T-SHIRTS AND OTHER WONDERS

The cheapest mate for your jeans and skirts is a plain cotton T-shirt, so be sure to keep a good supply. A T-shirt in solid colors and different styles can take you through all the seasons. Once you've got a few in your drawer, you'll see how useful and dependable they are.

When you do find your favorite T-shirt, be sure to buy several. Cheap chic doesn't necessarily mean really cheap—spend your money when you find the best style for you.

Buy in multiples, because this is one situation where less is not more. With five perfect T-shirts and three pair of perfectly fitting pants or skirts, you ought to stay happily clothed for quite a while.

There is the **cheap, short-sleeved T-shirt** or the undershirt-style T-shirt that comes in white and pastels from discount and dime stores. Often you can find three packaged for $4.98. If they are dyed they look terrific (a dusty rose, for instance, tucked into tight olive pants and high boots). The pastels, like pale sky blue and sunny yellow, are fresh clean colors for summer: they look fine as a skinny-minny T-shirt at the beach. There's nothing like a fresh pastel cotton T-shirt and a warm, mellow touch of sun to make you feel great.

One way to wear these freshly dyed $2 T-shirts is like New York's Puerto Rican kids do in Central Park in the summer: the girls buy extralarge sizes, grab a handful of fabric on either side of the chest, pull it supertight, and make a knot in the front, along the lines of a calypso shirt bodice. It

20 **A T-shirt, with a touch of lace at the neck, dresses up a softly gathered skirt.**

To dye your T-shirt, try Andrea Quinn's recipes with Rit dyes for smokier, sun-bleached colors:

- Burnt Orange: ¼ teaspoon each of Golden Yellow, Orange, Chestnut Brown, and Dark Brown.
- Plum: 1 teaspoon Wine, ¼ teaspoon Charcoal Grey, and ¼ teaspoon Cocoa Brown.
- Fuzzy Green: ½ teaspoon Dark Green and ½ teaspoon Charcoal Grey.
- Blue Smoke: generous ½ teaspoon Navy Blue and skimpy ½ teaspoon Charcoal Grey.
- Mocha Chocolate: generous ½ teaspoon Pink and skimpy ½ teaspoon Dark Brown.

To dye a clean white cotton T-shirt, put on a pair of rubber gloves, line a hand strainer with a paper towel, and put in the dye mix. Hold it under the faucet while you fill the sink with your hottest water, and mix up the water to help it all dissolve. (Undissolved bits of

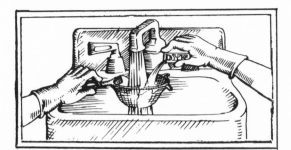

dye will spot your T-shirt.) Then put in a completely wet, clean T-shirt until it turns several shades darker than you want it. It will dry to the color you like (hopefully). The tiny undershirt bows take color faster so dye them separately.

If it comes out a color you don't like, buy some dye remover or stick it back in the basin for a darker color. You can also play with the mix of colors in the shade. To experiment with any colors, mix drops of dissolved dye in a bowl and test the shade with a white paper towel. To dye a skirt or white sailor pants to a matching shade, experiment to find the dye intensity that takes best on that particular fabric.

After you've finished dyeing, dip the clothing into half a cup of vinegar in a sinkful of cold water so the color won't fade. Always wash home-done dye jobs in cold water with a mild soap.

makes for a very narrow, high, tight bust. Cheap Chic! A man's large T-shirt also makes a soft dress to wear at a summer place over a bikini; they even come in handy as swimsuits when you've forgotten yours. Worn over a pair of brightly printed under-

Paul Newman didn't have to dye his undershirt to look like a real peach.

pants or Woolworth's brown $1 "string" bikini, a wet T-shirt can be terribly revealing while protecting you from the sun.

Sometimes you just can't get away with Woolworth's T-shirts, no matter how beautifully they are colored and camouflaged. And it's often very difficult to find plain T-shirts, either long- or short-sleeved. You can buy them with daisies on the front or a laughing cow, or in chartreuse and fuchsia stripes; but start looking for a plain, solid color, well-made cotton version. We once spent three hours doing just that in Chicago. And though it may be discouraging, the only plain T-shirt we came up with was a $12 French model at Jax.

Luckily, many manufacturers have realized recently that women like the idea of T-shirt dressing, and they are turning out new-looking T-shirts that can go to the office tucked into a skirt, then straight out to a dinner or date after work. These T-shirts are not as tight and often have a gathered or slit neck that can be worn untied after office hours. Loosen the neck, dress up your look with a favorite neck jewel or Woolworth's bangles, and a big hair comb. Blouse the T-shirt over your skirt (or slacks) with a narrow metallic belt, slip on high evening sandals, and you're off. (Just make sure your bag is large enough to carry all your presto-chango gear!)

23

Ingrid Boulting skips rope in Central Park and then bikes to lunch in her plain black T-shirt and pants.

One of the greatest bargains around is a plain old Fruit of the Loom man's T-shirt. In Europe, they're being worn with the label out. Here, they make the cheapest solution for that big top you're looking for to match up with a loose skirt or tight pants. Try dying them plum, fuzzy green, or blue smoke (see page 21) and wear them over layered, dyed petticoats from a dime store or ordered from a big catalogue.

When it gets chilly, **turtlenecks** are warmer than the basic T-shirt design. Army-surplus stores carry cheap long-sleeved turtlenecks in cotton knits, but they tend to bag, and sometimes the elastic in the cuffs and neck starts to give and curls out of the cotton knit like little worms after a morning rain.

A really sturdy turtleneck is more expensive, perhaps $15, and comes in a stretchy synthetic mix like nylon and Lycra. These fit beautifully, and the neck never gets worn out from all that on-and-off stretching. They're worth the price, but be sure to get

bound seams for your money. When they reach the end of their life, synthetics start to run at the seams, but this isn't for several years of almost daily wearing. A black T-shirt or turtleneck with a pair of black pants can take you almost anyplace, from jogging in the park to dinner at the finest restaurants.

When you're traveling, be sure to pick up a few **tourist T-shirts** for the folks back home. You can find the flashiest styles in the large discount stores of Florida, California, New York, and points between. They have a certain naive exuberance, with their Day-Glo oranges, state maps, and Hollywood fantasies, and they're always made up in cotton. Friends can wear them under or over other T-shirts, or throw out their old pajamas and sleep in a "Florida Sunshine State." A collection of twenty is more than enough to take a person through three changes a day for a week before hitting the washing machine.

For **dress-up T-shirts,** you can transform a scoop neck into a décolleté by gathering the front into a barette-shaped pin between the breasts. Or if you want to really get "steppy" (that's midwestern for fit to kill), buy some cheap, tattered twenties chemises or nightgowns at a thrift shop. You're looking for the lace edgings or beautifully worked pockets. Cut them loose from their old moorings and reapply them to your new T-shirt. With a pair of dusty blue sailor pants dyed to match the top, you've got a fairly delicate evening effect. Or you can stitch on an old piece of fabric or sew a few scarves around the hem of your T-shirt to create a loose and floaty dress.

We're not going to suggest you equip yourself with an embroidery outfit and start some five-hour home project with jeans and T-shirts. We're not getting into crafts, because the idea of Cheap Chic is to save on both the money and the time you invest. We figure that anyone who's sharp enough to buy this book isn't sitting around spending huge amounts of their time "saving money" with homey handiworks when they could be out making the money to save them the time. (Make the money, buy yourself time. *Then* you can dawdle with crafts to your heart's content!)

COMBINATIONS - MODEL JERRY HALL - MAKE UP & HAIR RICK GILLETE / INSTAMATIC PHOTOS BY PATAUD 75-

LEOTARDS
AND OTHER STRETCHY THINGS

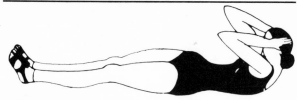

Leotards come in a close second to T-shirts for all-around wearability. They are lightweight, durable, crushproof, quick drying, and they really shape themselves to your body, giving a custom fit at noncustom prices.

A leotard can go under all your basic pants, shirts, and skirts. You can perk it up with a cheap cotton scarf. You can wear it by itself for dancing, exercise, and swimming. And you can pick one up just about anywhere—hosiery shops, dime stores, department stores. Sometimes you can even find a leotard on a rack next to the fruit stand in the supermarket.

A tiny nylon leotard can fit in your pocket for the first ray of sunshine and then take you off to a patch of grass or the seashore. In the summertime, leotards litter the streets of Manhattan. Both Capezio and

Liza Minnelli's outgrown her first Capezios but she still loves to wear leotards . . . even if they are by Halston!

Danskin Classics: the leotards that stepped out to the beach, the disco, the office . . . in shimmery, mouth-watering colors. 27

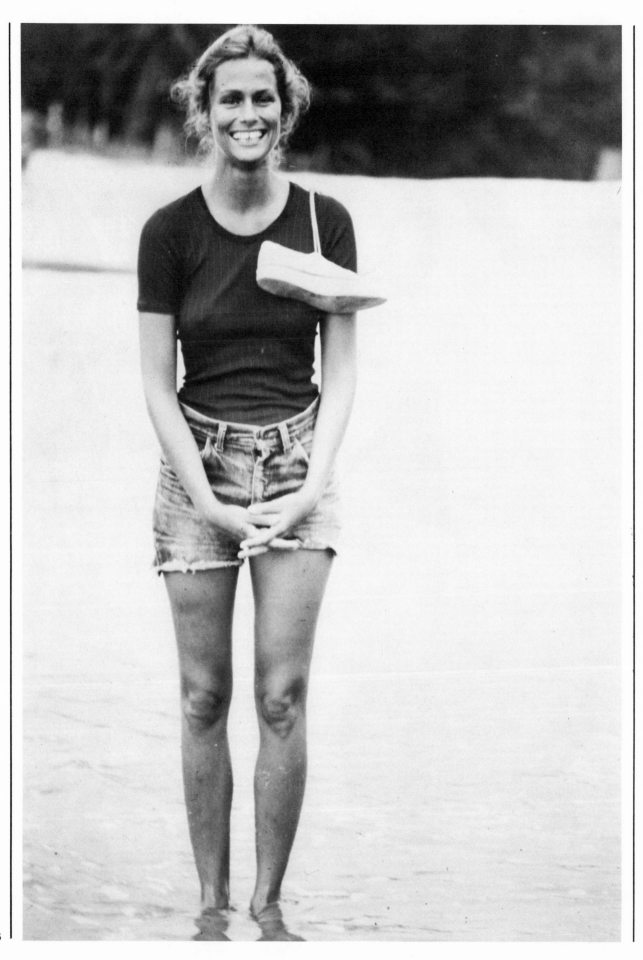

Danskin have been at their business a long time and are extremely knowledgeable in the ways of manufacturing a long-lasting, durable product. The locked seams hold together under the stretchiest of stretches. And they come in a great variety of shapes and colors. A recent classic is the Danskin wraparound skirt dyed to match their leotards, perfect for business travel and trips to and from an exercise class. (One small warning: Keep an eye on your layering when you wear a leotard without a snap crotch. The snapless leotards are smoother and healthier, but it takes forever to unpeel yourself in the bathroom!)

If you don't feel comfortable in skin-tight turtlenecks and T-shirts and leotards, gather up a collection of **loose cotton shirts.** A man's old shirt can look terrific tucked in at the waist over a turtleneck; or, if it's large and straight at the bottom, pulled tight with a wide belt at the waist. If the collar has seen better days, cut it off above the seam where it joins the shirt, turn it under, and sew into place. If the shirttails are too curved, cut them straight and then hem them. A lot of women sneak into the boy's department of Brooks Brothers, the crusty old men's outfitters in New York. When the owners found they were buying boy's shirts to wear, they made one conces-

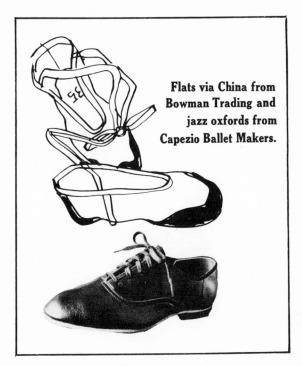

Flats via China from Bowman Trading and jazz oxfords from Capezio Ballet Makers.

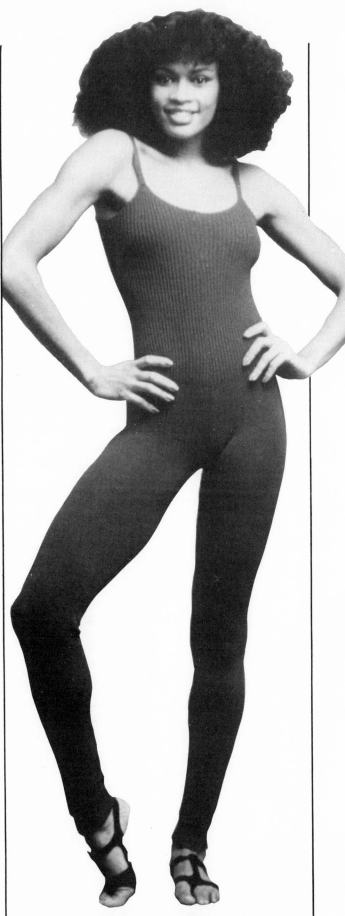

Capezio Ballet Makers' one-piece knit camisole jumpsuit—under skirts, loose shirts, long tunics, wide hip-belts, legwarmers—however it feels good on you.

29

Wendy Whitelaw—New York makeup artist—considers her face the real first layer of her style.

sion: they made up a cotton broadcloth button-down shirt sized for women. But for some reason, the boy's shirts are as popular as ever, perhaps because of that loose, low-arm-holed look and those pure cottons you'd pay four times as much for in other stores (if you could find them). And you can order them easily by mail.

So choose your skirts, pants, and tops very carefully. Now, sit back and relax. You can stop reading this book right here, and if you happen to live in a warm climate, you'll have enough clothes to take you through the whole year.

THE LAYER ESCALATION

One woman who has made a total discipline out of dressing around the basics is Helene Gaillet, a New York photojournalist. Her working day usually starts at eight sharp and keeps her running until six or often seven at night. Since she has little time to change from working clothes to evening clothes, she's eliminated dress-up clothes as much as possible from her wardrobe. She works at such an intense pitch that she has to be very careful about keeping both her body and her clothes in perfect running order. Her clothes are now so few and so honed down that when she travels, she takes only one duffel bag, which fits under the airplane seat in front of her. Here are her rules.

This gold and leather English cavalry belt has been worn with jeans every other day for over ten years and it looks better now than ever.

The monogrammed boy's shirt is a basic element in Helene Gaillet's special system of year-round layering.

"Ninety-five percent of my clothes are in navy blue, white, or khaki. I never go shopping, and when I do, I know specifically what I want. I have an $80 or $100 bill a year plus shoes, and that's it.

"I buy my jeans in shades of blue at the army-navy store. They're always Levi's, often in corduroy. The Levi cut is thinner—they seem to cut Wranglers for big asses and Levi's for almost nonexistent asses! Levi's are cut straight and never need to be tailored to fit me.

"I wear the same shirt all year round, even when I'm skiing. It's the layer theory: one, two, three, or four things go on top of each other. My cotton turtlenecks go under the shirt—they're $6 at the army-navy store, or $15 in an imported stretch acrylic fabric. I get the little-boy's button-down oxford shirt from Brooks Brothers in three colors—white, the blue stripe, and yellow—a dozen at a time every three years. They're $11 plus $5 for the initials, and that way it looks

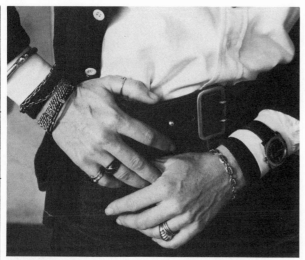

An inexpensive shirt, jeans, a belt and overshirt are complemented by Helene's collection of gold jewelry.

like you're wearing a $60 custom shirt. Then I have three good silk shirts, all in ivory white. My oldest one is eight years . . . I got it on sale for $50. But they usually only last two or three years, because they get yellowish with dry cleaning.

"Boots are one of my most expensive items because I literally live in them. I get one or two pair a year and wear them over three or four years. They're usually English or French. My pant boots are $90 from Veneziano, but I usually buy St. Laurent boots; one pair long, the other short to go under jeans, and they run around $150 a pair. I've found the trick to keeping jeans tucked into your boots—fit a pair of bright red 69¢ socks from Woolworth's over your pant legs with tights underneath. I love wearing bright red underthings!

"To go with the tops and jeans, I have just three belts that I bought in the sixties: an old leather army belt from the flea market in Paris, a Turkish metal belt from an antique store, and a gold-and-leather English cavalry belt from the Chelsea Antique Market that I wear about every other day. They were all under $20.

"My everyday winter outfit is my jeans, turtleneck, shirt, and T-shirt, plus a fisherman's sweater from the Fulton Street Fish Market, a belt, and usually a long, thrift-shop scarf. If it's really cold, I add a $6 safari jacket from the army-navy store. And

The ins-and-outs of the over-and-under school of dressing: Helene puts on a T-shirt, a boy's shirt, a denim overshirt, tucks it all into jeans and a pair of good leather boots and then relaxes.

always boots, a canvas camera bag (actually a game bag, which was a gift, because I think they're too expensive), a $2 denim hat from the dime store, and a pair of sunglasses.

"In the summer I wear cutoffs, Cloroxed $11 Wayfarer jeans, and T-shirts I can throw in the washing machine. If it gets cold, I put on a denim shirt.

"I just don't buy expensive things, except boots."

"For evening wear, I've worked out a 'tuxedo'—eight-year-old wool gabardine St. Laurent pants copied by Alexander's department store with a black velvet jacket from a boutique, plus a vest and cheap satin shirt. I wear it with strapped sandals and flaming red tights, and the red toes peek out from under all the black!

"I do sink money in accessories: I always wear the same ones, and I do spend on them. I've got a five-year-old brown suede pouch from La Bagagerie. All my gold things have been stolen twice, so I don't have much left: five rings, a Cartier tank watch with a clasp that cost $600 in Paris eight years ago, a Van Cleef and Arpels bracelet, and some gold chains. They're like good-luck charms. I even swim and sleep with them on.

"In the last year I've gone from 124 pounds to around 118 at five foot six. My secret is a small breakfast: a glass of orange juice, four cups of very strong espresso, and a toasted English muffin. I eat lunch less than once a week, and when I do, try to make it Japanese. And then I eat anything for dinner, but very little. That way I never diet!

"I go to an exercise class twice a week. I spend my money there and on having my hair streaked. And I've done the Royal Canadian Air Force exercises ten minutes every morning since 1962. I save money on cabs by doing everything on my bike or on foot; and year round I play tennis and ski. I'd love to be one of the great beauties, but, to make the best of myself, I have to radiate what I can get from inside: health. I think your mental attitude is based on your physical well-being."

Ballet clothes become fashion shows: Rudi Gernreich's "tunic" panelled leotard for disco dancing.

GILDA RADNER

Saturday Night Lively!

Gilda Radner, one of the Glamour Queens of "Saturday Night Live," talks about her off-camera fashion style. What does she base her particular taste in clothes on? "What doesn't itch."

"I think I've always been ahead of fashion. I tucked my pants into my boots years ago, mainly because they were usually too short. And I've always worn clothes in layers 'cause it seemed there was always something to hide. Now, in fashion, I think I prefer the classic, peasant, layered look: clothes that don't match that you could wear to any country on top of each other.

"In the morning I choose my clothes by what's clean . . . also, I think clothes should feel safe. I just like clothes you could want to go to sleep in. I sometimes stand in front of the mirror and change a million times because I know I really want to wear my nightgown. So I guess I associate clothes with home and comfort. I don't have a wardrobe. I have a history. Things that went through stuff with me.

"The clothes I hate are the ones that let me down. You know, the ones that are never the same after the first washing. I hate materials that retain perspiration that you know you didn't make yourself. The ones you always have to smell before you wear or pour a lot of perfume on. And I hated thigh chafe guards as a kid . . . I've weighed up to 150 pounds and I'm five feet six. I lost weight by being on every diet I've ever heard of or read about or had passed to me on a mimeographed piece of paper. I'm a compulsive eater, and the only way to stay thin when you're a compulsive eater is to be just as compulsive about losing weight.

"TV hasn't changed my life too much, but it's changed my hair. I used to wear it in a style . . . all curly around my face. I used to hide somewhere in there, but then they told me they couldn't see my face at all when I turned to the side on TV. So I started pulling it off my face. Then I stopped setting it and started rolling it into a little knot. That was the first time I actually got a good look at my face and decided it was a regular face, not beautiful, but at least I looked like a real person on TV. With all this new self-acceptance, it takes a lot less time to get ready in the morning.

"My favorite accessory? My contacts. Because if I didn't wear them I'd have to wear big, thick glasses. And I like shoes that make your feet look cute, like puppy paws. And high heels if they make your legs look long. A guy once told me I had long legs; so I capitalized on them by wearing high heels. Unfortunately, I also have a small head . . . the longer I make my legs, the smaller my head looks .

"Exercise? In the morning I do a hundred jumping jacks, then I do a hundred skip ropes. Then I make the bed, picking up the pillows off the floor without bending my knees. There are four pillows. Then I do thirty leg lifts and thirty bum walks, backward and forward. Then I take a bath and think about whether I should add another exercise to my regime."

CLASSICS

Sometimes Cheap Chic boils down to spending much more than you feel you can afford on the kind of classic, quality clothes we talk about in this chapter. We think it saves you money in the long run. If you're a real purist, Cheap Chic can become a matter of extremes: throwing your last $150 into a tweed riding jacket and riding out poverty in style. But if you don't feel comfortable investing in truly expensive classics, then consider buying some of the second-string classics we'll be talking about in the next chapter, like a lovely Shetland sweater or cowboy boots.

There are still certain things you shouldn't fudge on no matter how cheaply you dress: the very best boots, a sturdy bag, a glorious jacket or shirt. You can't afford cheap boots that will last a year and then crack across the sole. If you had loads of money you

could; but since you don't, spend your money where it shows the most.

If you look closely at a woman with a strong individual style, you will discover there is almost always something in her outfit that costs a lot. Perhaps it's a five-year-old pair of French boots or a simple, solid-gold chain around her wrist. Whatever it is, that one touch makes her look ten times better. The throwaway chic gives her an intriguing look.

It might seem impossible to think of yourself laying out $150 on a pair of boots. If so, start saving, even if it's only $5 a week. If you can't manage that, then stop smoking, and start eating soybean protein! In five years you'll still be wearing those boots (inflation will then have jacked them up to $300) and they will look beautifully, aristocratically worn and weathered. They'll save

A well tailored suit can last decades. Antonio Lopez's suit is made of black cashmere by Cifonelli in Paris.

your wardrobe with a cheeky touch of class even when you're really hard up and down to your last pair of jeans.

This is a very European way of dressing. French designer Emmanuelle Khanh thinks that the great thing about France is the *bon gout*, the good taste. "It's a process of refining that's been going on for centuries. We're more moderate and appreciate quality, so our clothes last longer. Since we don't exaggerate our appearance, we have more balance in choosing our personal styles. At first it may look as if we're wearing a uniform, but then you notice the subtle differences in shades, cuts, and quality of fabric. An older woman is often seen in what a girl of eighteen buys because it's all based on classic proportion."

You can keep a very small closet if you're careful, almost ruthless, in choosing your few classic investments. Tina Bossidy, a nine-to-five fashion editor in New York, has it down to a system. She believes in that old fashion-magazine idea of "setting up a wardrobe." It sounds terribly stuffy, because we haven't needed the discipline to think this way for a long time. But the results can be great—a group of clothes that are not faddy, that are not going to pass out of style, and that you can build up year after year. What this plan involves, again, is a much smaller, more thought-out wardrobe. Here are some of her tips.

• **Color** is the most important thing in dressing well. The whole point of looking good is feeling good, so find the colors that make you feel best and stick with them. Women often forget they look very good in soft colors, like a light turquoise. Try it.
• One of the big mistakes is buying **prints.** If you develop your sense of color and buy mainly solids, everything will work together.
• A big secret is to buy things in **multiples.** Once you find your favorite colors, the easiest thing to do is to set up a sort of *uniform* of top quality: For instance, buy six mens' silk shirts when they go on sale: blue, red, black, green, maroon, turquoise, and purple. Buy two identical skirts: purple and black. Department stores usually overbuy. If something falls into the uniform category, then it will probably go on sale in three weeks to a month, even at the designer boutiques. Then, if you can afford it, buy two good coats and two good jackets, since that's what you're seen in first.
• Supplement these investments with thirteen-button navy wool pants, cotton and velour pullovers, T-shirts, and cotton drawstring pants.
• Shoes and boots are some of the most important things you can have in your wardrobe. Spend money on styles like short pink boots cuffed at the top, brandy kidskin boots, ponyskin pumps—things that really set you off.
• All other shopping can be done from thrift shops and army surplus—here's where

you find your basics and special accessories, lots of bright belts, and jewelry.

The color, the quality, and the limited quantity of this wardrobe give you a luxurious style on a tight budget. Special accessories raise it from the rank of a working-woman's uniform.

You're always going to get the most out of your money by buying something really luxurious that makes you feel fantastic, wearing it to death, and paying absolutely rock bottom for the cheap things you can get away with. Draw the line at quality; don't skimp on the classics. And in ten years, who knows? You might even have an air of shabby gentility! Classics are clothes that last.

Soft wool sweaters over a loose classic skirt, silk shirt with the collar up, good boots . . . comfy classics.

ACCESSORIES

Sink your money into a very good pair of **boots.** Expensive European boots are a consistent favorite among snappy dressers who spend their money sparingly but buy things that last. You'll often find a pair of four-year-old St. Laurent boots making a very cheap turnout look terribly chic. It's not because they bear the name St. Laurent, though he does have a first-rate sense of classic design. It's because they're made in a European

A favorite felt hat with the perfect, small gold and enamel earrings are both classic investments.

artisan tradition with good lasts, hand finishing, the best leathers, and sumptuous colors.

Boots not only look good, they feel good. How far and how fast can you walk in a pair of high-heeled pumps? Boots look just as good, and you can really walk your heart out in them. The money you save on cabs and buses will pay for the next pair. But a European last is uncomfortable for some American feet, so never talk yourself into a pair of good boots unless they fit perfectly. A seamstress can do nothing about this particular problem!

Although it's perfectly sensible to buy black or brown, some girls go out and find just one pair of the very best boots in colors like gray, red, green, or burgundy. They figure it looks like you have lots more at home. So if acid green cheers you up, why not acid green?

Well dressed? Look down. Expensive boots and expensive shoes are worth saving up for. Not because of a designer label but because one good pair is the basis for a pared down, solid classic wardrobe. They age well, too.

The best quality, quietly conservative **men's shoes** can be found in the Brooks Brothers catalog. Peal & Company and the "Brooks English" line have wingtips with very thin soles, not those thick Big Mac numbers most guys walk around on, as well as simple oxfords and rakish tassel loafers. If you want to head for the very best, Lobb Bootmaker's representative takes orders in the spring and fall at a shop called Everall Brothers in New York.

Belts are worth an investment, since they will last a lifetime. A silver belt looks spectacular with anything from a tweed skirt to a pair of skintight leather jeans. Be sure any "investment belt" can fit in both places, at the waist or hip. You can occasionally find antique silver belts from Turkey at street markets and obscure shops, but they usually wend their way to the more pricey boutiques and antique stores. If you buy one of the large silver belts sold by weight, the heavier the better. (You can always hock it.) If you don't like silver, keep your eyes

open for that unique, one-of-a-kind belt that looks as if it had always belonged to you, and buy it on the spot.

A good basic leather belt, totally simple, can be worn with interchangeable buckles. The buckles can be your personal trademarks. For about $25 you can buy a fine lizard belt from Tony Lama at a western

The ultimate in custom— made shoes are these now forbidden, handmade, crocodile tasseled loafers worn by Richard Merkin.

Find jewelry you'll keep a lifetime at auctions at Parke-Bernet. Ask to be listed for catalogues, and bid by mail.

store to wear with a big oval silver-and-gold rodeo belt buckle. Steer clear of imitation-antique, imitation-brass buckles, because there are just too many of them around.

A concho belt in silver, turquoise, and worn brown leather is a collector's item, a good investment now that they are no longer at the height of fashion. If you prefer to wear your art around your waist rather than on a wall, here's your chance.

Real jewelry adds a quiet little touch of elegance. Perhaps the most beautiful and inexpensive gold jewelry comes from Thailand—simple, tiny gold chains bought by

the ounce, closed by a hand-soldered S. A plain gold chain looks perfect at wrist, waist, finger, or neck. Smooth hoops in pierced ears last a lifetime, and a gold band is almost nicer than a diamond. Gold can always be sold or bartered—it's much better than dollars.

If you wear a **watch,** you'll probably be seeing more of that than anything else you own. The nicest watches seem to be the most simple, not too tiny and "feminine," but something with a readable face and the best-quality brown or black leather band you can afford.

Today, the size of your **bag** seems to matter more than variety or expense. It used to be that you could always spot a "lady" by her shoes and purse. But now many of us are walking around in sneakers with portable offices in our purses—address book, note pad, appointment calendar, magazines, some letters, bills, makeup, Instamatic, small electronic calculator, checkbook, and wallet. With all this stuff to cart around, size becomes the primary consideration. The best place to find a sturdy leather or canvas bag is in the luggage department, in sporting goods stores, or at prestigious old-line leathergoods shops like Crouch & Fitz-

If you must wear a watch, choose one carefully so it will blend with all of your clothes and still be functional.

gerald in New York. A leather bag from a department store is going to cost too much: a simple legal-pad-sized shoulder bag is now up to $140, and the Hermès leather shoulder bag is a staggering $600 with tax.

If you can't afford a leather bag, it's awfully luxurious to use a leather-lined canvas bag, if you can find one. Some sly women-about-town buy the $30 Danish schoolbag by mail from Chocolate Soup in

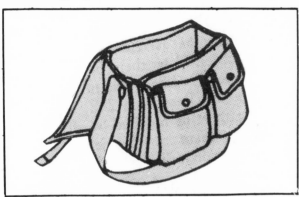

The Danish Souperbag has pockets for everything!

New York and sink the rest of their money into one beautiful, obviously expensive leather accessory like an address book or small monogramed diary from a place like Mark Cross. Whether you choose leather or canvas, it's always nice to have a clutch purse slipped inside for pared-down situations, like a business lunch at a good restaurant.

CLOTHES CLASSICS

Old etiquette books used to list the minimum wardrobe an impoverished gentleman of quality might collect. It is a system of dressing where less is more . . . of necessity! Transposing the rules for a man's wardrobe to a woman's can give you a fresh approach for a well-thought-out closet.

Three or four suits: a brown one, a gray pinstripe, a tweed or tan gabardine, and, in hot climates, a summer seersucker or white linen.

Jackets: One navy blazer and one brownish tweed sport coat.

Two or three pair of pants: gray flannel, beige whipcord, and perhaps white flannel for eccentricity's sake.

Three pair of shoes: brown single-sole wingtips, brown tassel loafers, and perfectly plain black oxfords.

A woman organizing her wardrobe on this minimalist principle would substitute a skirt here and a riding jacket there. Think of the ease with which you could dress. There would be absolutely no room to make a mistake (unless something didn't get back from the cleaner's in time for you to get to work in the morning!). Think of the beautiful, uncommon effect of such understated elegance—especially when mixed in with a few pair of Levi's and shiny boots. A couple of things from the classics lend presence and weight to all the clothes in your closet.

Before we run through some of the classic investments you might want to make, we offer a word of warning: In buying tailored clothes, steer clear of foppish effects like flapped and buttoned pockets, patch

Francois de Menil blends a classic St. Laurent blazer, a silk shirt, Levi's jeans and Lucchese boots from Texas. 43

pockets, contrasting-color overstitching on lapels, snazzy buttons, inverted pleats, epaulets, and gewgaws of all descriptions. You're going for well-tailored, expensive clothes that will not call attention to themselves and will not look out of fashion in six to eight years. Try to find an old-line conservative tailor whose judgment you can trust. Look at old pictures in movie books and magazines—there really are timeless looks that you can step right into today.

The **blazer** is one of the most elegant yet congenial designs from the classical repertoire. Navy blue is the traditional color; the cut is usually double breasted. If you have a blazer tailor made, it can be lengthened and shortened, made boxier or more shapely, according to the feel of the times. The blazer is ageless.

A black velvet blazer or lush green smoking jacket has become a dinner party classic. Wear it with cowboy boots, jeans, and an old belt. Put a flower at the lapel (gardenias waft deliciously as you walk down the street), put a wisp of silk at the neck or, if

Most classic wardrobes include a calf-length cape, a well fitted wool riding jacket and an all purpose raincoat. Left: Captain Bogart rides the waves in a timeless, navy wool crewneck sweater.

you can't get a fresh flower, make yourself a cluster of satin lingerie flowers from the twenties. And blaze.

If you must have a **suit,** it's best to get one that can go a million different ways— the jacket with jeans, the slacks with shirts and Shetlands. The owner of a men's boutique in New York suggests that a dark blue suit with a vest is the absolute minimum a man can have in his closet (along with a pair of Levi's, a drip-dry shirt, and a silk shirt). Another designer likes a navy serge suit backed up with a chalk pinstripe and a gray flannel—all paired with shirts of the same tone. A Prince of Wales glen plaid suit is the height of daytime elegance but trousers can't live a double life as easily as gray flannel or blue serge, but that's the price you pay for the sublime! Lauren Bacall wears a black, man's tailored suit with a polka-dot silk hankie and fuschia stitching on the lapel buttonhole.

You can dress a **riding jacket** up or down, over a Shetland sweater and jeans, or with a silk shirt and luscious brown velvet skirt.

George Stavrinos

Italy's Giorgio Armani: designs of subtle, refined simplicity brushed with the most elegant colors .

Dietrich's mysterious sexuality changed the tailored look.

The psychology of a riding jacket is fascinating, especially if it has a worldly patina. It seems to demand a stance of being in command, a certain swagger and controlled elegance . . . pure attitude. If it's difficult to find a riding jacket in your area, you can order from one of the riding stores in New York that stock English and French imports, and have it tailored once it arrives.

A good pair of pure wool **slacks** will last years. If you can't afford to have them custom-tailored, you can order something called made-to-measure, put together from a combination of existing patterns. Or you can order by mail from Brooks, Chipp, or Press. Women can find well-cut slacks in boutiques and good department stores. Gray is a good color if you can only afford one pair, as is beige gabardine. Navy blue wool has a very sober and bracing elegance and can take you anywhere. The best cut is very conservative, with small pleats and straight legs. If they start to get shiny, they can be deshined by a special cleaning process listed in the back of this book. Tailor-made slacks

cost little more than very good ones in department stores. If you find the right tailor, you can get them for $50–$80, and have everything exactly as you like it—pockets, watch pocket, cuffs, pleats, belt loops, zipper or button fly.

A **cape** is a necessary accoutrement for swirly, dramatic people. Look for a fluid, loose, ample fabric you can whoosh around in, drape over your arm, or throw over a shoulder like a scarf for the body. The black wool Spanish cape with its high collar is a good buy. The full-length wool Inverness cape from Scotland is especially dashing. And plain old cashmere makes the softest cape of all.

To wrap up the classics in the middle of

Never go anywhere without a trench coat. This is St. Laurent's; Burberry or Brooks Brothers are comparable.

a downpour, try a British **trench coat.** The Burberry is more than a raincoat—it can serve as a top layer year round, over a thick sweater in winter and a thin T-shirt in summer showers. The trench coat design is timeless, with its epaulets, knotted belt, slash pockets, and raglan sleeves.

We talk a lot about the **silk shirt.** A good one is hard to find. Some people dislike silk because it tends to feel clammy if you perspire. The secret to wearing a silk shirt is to buy it very loose, so that it is not cut in tightly under the armpits. Then perspiration is able to evaporate off your body and won't stain the armpit. The other problem with silk is that it takes an incredible beating at the cleaners. So the other secret to wearing a silk shirt is learning to wash it gently by hand in lukewarm water and then have it pressed at the cleaner's. Once you master the care and feeding of a silk shirt, there is nothing that will look so luxurious, wear so beautifully, and feel so incredible. Silk picks up everything you own, including your spirits.

Yves St. Laurent makes ample silk shirts in a wide variety of colors. One of his crepe de Chine shirts has full sleeves, a sheared back and front, a narrow collar band, and a front placket. It is soft and loose; the look is elegant lassitude. Tuck it in as a blouson, wear it out as an overshirt, wrap it with a wide leather belt, or knot it over a swirling skirt. Or wear one traditional shirt over another and layer the collars like the petals of a flower.

You can often find a better shirt in the men's line—the cut is bigger, the tails are longer, the stitching is closer. Turnbull & Asser of London will make them up in any shape you prefer for around $125, or in the very finest cotton for less. If you're not ready to spring a week's wages for a shirt, send for samples of the beautiful $10-a-yard crepe de Chine at Oriental Silk in Los Angeles and ask a seamstress to copy a friend's shirt. Or, again, you could be patient and do very well at a half-price sale. Silk shirts that have faded where they've been folded sometimes sell for $25 at St. Laurent (25 percent of their original price) but they need to be dyed a dark color or worn under

A classic silk tunic-length shirt by Pinky & Dianne, sleeves pushed up for a casual look.

a sweater so just the collars and cuffs show.

Richard Merkin dresses only in tailored clothes and thinks they are, indeed, heaven incarnate. Every morning Richard gets up in his apartment on New York's West Side, pulls on a battered old gray sweatsuit, and jogs through Riverside Park. When he gets back, he changes into his work clothes and goes into his painter's studio until three in the afternoon. Then, Richard turns toward his vast, overflowing closet and chooses the suit, tie, shirt, collar, suspenders, socks, and shoes for his tailor-made composition of the day. Richard Merkin, artist, becomes Richard Merkin, noted dandy, a man fascinated by dress, and especially by the aristocratic British tailoring which he affects to an extreme. Once you read and absorb Richard Merkin's views, you should be able to talk to any British tailor with ease. Tailor-made clothes are nothing more or less than a collaboration between you and the tailor; part fabric, part psychology. Here's what happens when a man (or woman, for that matter) develops a craving for The Real Thing.

| **Richard Merkin's classic dinner jacket is highlighted by a lavender carnation and a slick shoeshine.**

"I started having clothes made for me in the sixties, when my first show of paintings sold out in Boston. Before that I couldn't afford it! My suits from 1964 look as new as a suit I would have made today. But ten years ago, you could get a really good custom suit for $190 . . . now a good custom suit is upwards of $380.

"George Frazier was the most elegant man I've ever known, a columnist and journalist who wrote for *Esquire* and the Boston *Globe*. He didn't have very much clothing, but everything he had was impeccable. There was no room for any mistake. And it wasn't self-conscious, it was at one with him. Every so often I used to wear both a flower and a handkerchief, and George always chided me for it. He said it was disturbing to have put the two things together. He was right. It's just a spot of color that accents a whole totality. And it shouldn't be two spots.

"I like the idea of being able to take a classical form and punctuate it with invention so that you come up with something like a new color combination, or just using an unexpected collar with a suit. Most guys who were concerned dressers in the twenties wore flowers in their lapel. People come up to me and say, 'Where did you get that flower?' It's just a carnation. But the point of it is the concern, of course. I mean, a flower is really beautiful, it's very perfect . . . a beautiful flower and a good shoeshine. Nowadays most ready-made suits have no buttonhole. How sad.

"George Frazier always said, 'Wanna know if a guy is well-dressed? Look down.' The greatest degeneration of any particular garment is shoes. The nicest shoes you can find are those old Brooks Brothers brown ones. Outside of dancing pumps, they're the most elegant. I wear dancing pumps a lot in the summer when I'm not wearing socks. And I love tassel loafers.

"I think we live in a time when people are superficially more interested in dress than they ever have been. People today want approval for the way they dress, which is the kiss of death. You really can't 'do your own thing' unless you know who you are. I think there's a very delicate kind of merger between your clothes and your personality, a give and take between who you are and what you're wearing. When I get dressed, I do become a little bit more severe, more decisive. Actually, I think the most fashionable dressers are the nonfash-

Mr. Merkin, a perfectionist in his attire, likes to accent his grey pinstripe double-breasted suit with a British bowler and butter cotton gloves.

David Croland bought his one dollar tuxedo in a thrift shop, had it recut twice and is determined to have it copied if it doesn't hold up for another five years.

ionable dressers. Style really has to do with being able to perceive what's best for you; taking care to analyze just the way something really looks. For instance, a really big tie doesn't look good on everybody. I can't stand shirts with crippling patterns. You have to be very careful about things like lapels, which can get too big and fall into caricature and trendiness.

"The really great dandies devoted a major section of their life to dressing. Certainly in Beau Brummell's case it didn't lead to ostentation. It led to dressing that was perfect, just absolutely perfect, nothing off, not a hair!

"Obviously, that takes a lot of concern and a lot of time. If you need two hours to dress in the morning and you have to be at work at nine, then you have to get up at seven. Is that approaching insanity? No, it's approaching perfection, but then perfection is just a stone's throw away from insanity.

"I don't understand the passion for informality, the contemporary loathing for discipline. There's an absolute fetish these days about being comfortable, being loose. But I rather like the idea of a starched collar.

It's not as comfortable as an open-neck shirt . . . but it's beautiful looking! Why not put up with a little discomfort to achieve a more significant effect?

"When I say somebody dresses well, I mean cohesively. It doesn't mean just like me. For instance, I'm a fight fan and I've seen some pimp types who were fabulously dressed! Those guys really know what their *body* looks like.

"I'm terribly contrary, and if something becomes popular, it generally gets ruined, and I'll give it up like that! I never wear jeans. And I don't like costume, putting things together for an effect which may not be beautiful and may not have anything to do with your life. I like things that are ordered, the same kind of order I look for in a painting or in a supper or in a girlfriend or in a car . . . a blend of the function and the form of it.

"Art is exactly as important to me as the way I dress. When I choose a tie and a shirt in the morning it's no less important to me than going in and making a picture. It's the same.

"But I am an artist, so I really hate it when I buy a shirt and the guy says 'Would you like a tie to go with that?' It's the 'go with' syndrome. And if somebody puts his name on something, I don't buy it. I'll wear a tailor's name, but a designer's? Any person is a unique totality, and what does St. Laurent know about where I grew up and what I think?

"Unless something is made absolutely right, it bothers me, so I spend the extra money. But if I didn't have any money, I'd much rather go to a thrift shop and find some old English suit or jacket and bring it to a tailor than go buy something off the rack in a department store.

"You see, most people mistrust any kind of classical values or verities. I think there are certain articles of clothing that are absolutely the most impeccable: the summer Panama hat, a black satin tie with a clean knot, a navy blue blazer, the pink Brooks button-down, a double-breasted Chesterfield with a black velvet collar. I mean, all these things are just absolutely the *zenith* of gorgeousness. All you have to do is buy them! There it is!"

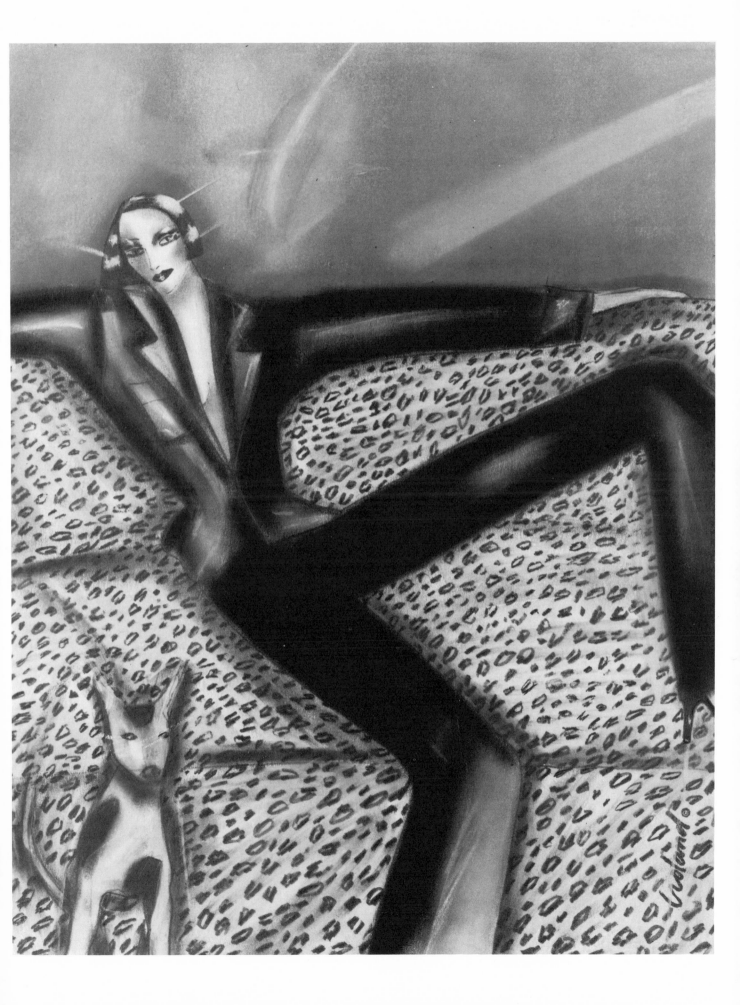

DIANA VREELAND

Eccentric Elegance from the World of Vogue

For more than thirty-five years, Diana Vreeland has been a leading figure in the international world of fashion, first at Harper's Bazaar and then as editor-in-chief at Vogue. Since October 1972 Mrs. Vreeland has been Special Consultant to the Costume Institute at the Metropolitan Museum of Art in New York. The world she has experienced ranges from the extravagances of the twenties in Paris to the creation of the

The super-pros at the Metropolitan's Costume Institute.

Beautiful People, a mix of society and fashion, in the sixties. Called "Empress Vreeland" in some papers, Mrs. Vreeland has completed her autobiography that is sure to intrigue fashion insiders.

A woman of great charisma and originality, Diana Vreeland speaks her mind about style, the importance of a fit body, and an element she still exudes in her mid-seventies, energy.

"I think everything is habit. Everything builds on itself. Energy builds on energy like love builds on love. Everything intensifies itself. This is habit. Energy and love are good habits, sometimes there are bad habits. Stimulation is happy energy. Then the energy produces itself and your excitement about whatever is going on.

"I think it's a very difficult moment to write a book on fashion. The first thing a girl's got to do is to keep herself together physically with any small amount of money she's got. However she does it, that comes before anything. This is a very vital moment. You have to be very healthy today—your skin, your eyes, your everything.

"Basically, people only look well if they have a very, very good foundation. You know what that means? You can't cover anything up with paint and powder. But I am tired of the natural look. I am fed up to the teeth. God Almighty, some of the girls who come into my office. Oh, how they look! For what is all this natural look? It must be for them, it certainly can't mean

Mrs. Vreeland's classic winter uniform: three black cashmere sweaters rotated with three black Givenchy skirts.

anything to anyone else. I am mad about artificial appearances beautifully done—the gilded lily is irresistible.

"The natural look is too colorless. Don't forget that the white person is not beautiful. Pale skin is not beautiful. It's very rare you see extraordinarily clear white skin. It's usually sallow. We are uneven owing to the many mixtures of bloods. So we've got to build ourselves up to something.

"You have to start with your face and hair and your body. Forget clothes until you've got these basics straight. Once you've got that in hand (if you're young you can do it very quickly), then you get with the clothes. I think clothes come second. Clothes are decor and you've got to have something to put them on. I'm not talking about expensive clothes. I don't see why clothes should be expensive. But don't forget I am talking about a girl with everything absolutely as best as she can do it . . . her hair, her eyes, her strength, her walk, her expression, everything. She's totally with it. That comes before clothes. Men the same. And for children too, but they have it naturally.

"First, I'd put money into shoes. No variety, just something I could wear with everything. Marvelous shoes and boots. Whatever it is you wear, I think shoes are terribly important. My shoe, that strap shoe, I had made again and again for about thirty years. Now I have pumps and boots made exactly as I want them.

"Style is everything. Style is the most important word. I think we've lost some of the sense of what 'fashion' means. But I'll tell you why I don't think fashion is over. First, I don't think any of us know now what we're talking about when we say fashion. If you mean dictatorship of fashion, no one at the moment has anything to dictate. But once they do, we'll be very pleased and excited to hear it. Fashion is a rhythm controlled by the economic and social conditions of the times, and neither our social nor economic condition is very good. But I do think that clothes today are very pretty. There is a repose, a charm about the new clothes.

"I believe I just really like clothes. Peo-

ple want to be a little too deep about the whole thing. But I think all charming women will always have a sense of the refined, a sense of delight, and a sense of themselves. I don't envision a somber world. One likes certain things. For instance, I never thought the style of the thirties was remotely interesting, and I was living in a full world in those days. There

was no war, there was no visible depression in Europe, and Paris was absolutely remarkable. The clothes were beautifully composed and shown but they were never, to me, really interesting. I don't understand today's fascination with the clothes of the thirties. If you only knew how really weak they were after the clothes of the twenties.

"Today, I suppose Pucci and Gucci is good because it stimulates people toward a status symbol, but it keeps people apart. When I was in Beverly Hills I went down Wilshire Boulevard on a Saturday afternoon and saw crowds of cars and people. Usually there are never many people—after all, it's not a big city. And I said to my son, who was driving, 'Oh God, I hope it isn't an accident!' And he said, 'Good God no,

Diana Vreeland visits Kyoto with the Couture Show from the Met: Do it right, do it big, give it class! 55

that's just Saturday afternoon at Gucci's.' I just couldn't believe what I saw. All these men bring in girls that want to shop. That's all they want. At the end of the week it's 'Baby, I'll take you to Gucci if you're good.' This makes a lot of people happy, so put it down as good for business.

"You need a sense of humor in fashion, you have to see where you are. For instance, I've never tried wearing synthetics. It just never came my way. But I do remember one experience very well. I was motoring up to Maine for the weekend. I went to Brooks Brothers and bought myself a Dacron shirt, the copy of the men's pale blue button-down shirt—all the English and Europeans who came over bought them by the dozen and said they were marvelous.

"We got through Boston and it was terribly hot . . . we were in a traffic jam and we couldn't move. And you know, I thought I was in a fire! I had to open the shirt completely, I had to get out of it, and my husband said, 'In the name of God, what are you doing!' But I really and truly was in flames locked in this synthetic thing.

"I wouldn't have felt a chemical fire if I had been wearing pure cotton. It just would have been damned hot. But this was what I call an experience. Synthetics, however, have simplified the life of all of us. I suppose polyesters and so on are marvelous. They make clothes stand up and out and all that, which is great . . . for people who like it.

"It's been very curious, moving from a magazine to a museum, because now there are no daily deadlines. But all of the shows I've worked on have been revelations. You think of the idea, and then of course, panic. Is it a good idea? Will it charm, pull and amuse the imagination? Can I pull it off? You don't know until you really work at it. But each show has been so marvelously revealing and wonderful. As you unpack the clothes coming from this museum and that, from Rome and Madrid, you look at them and you're so glad they're beautiful. It is never a letdown, never. It's always been just right! Now we have taken the couture show to the Modern Museum in Kyoto. It's the first time an Eastern museum has ever asked for a collection of European clothes.

"When I go through the Costume Institute at the Metropolitan Museum, one thing is more beautiful than the next, so well arranged, so well shown. Everything breathes, everything is free . . . they're alive, these clothes. You don't know how beautiful it is!

"Last year I used some Schiaparelli clothes from the thirties and we were very short of original hats. So we found some Southern Russian hats of the nineteenth century, all in solid silver embroidery, more or less the same shape, just like 'Schiap' used to make. I knew her collection well and these were absolutely suitable. It wasn't cheating in any way. You don't notice these things. You just see the effect and they're exactly correct.

"And for the Hollywood clothes exhibition, this dear gentleman asked, 'Would you be interested in Mary Pickford's curls?' He keeps them in a Baggie and I said, 'Where in the name of God did you get them?' He said, 'But she sent them to us for the Los Angeles Historical Museum.' Isn't that marvelous? After all, in all the world, those curls were the most special, just perfect . . . 'America's Sweetheart,' the first star, everything!

"In the beautiful gown from **The Bride Wore Red**, Elizabeth Lawrence, who works on all the costumes, noticed that the bugle beads are all shaded as it fits the body. It's fantastic—the highest, highest couture refinement. It's total. I told a French couturier, 'You'll never find better-made clothes than these Hollywood outfits in any Paris workroom in the last forty years,' which is as far back as I can go. The great thing that went out across the studios from Louis B. Mayer when a new movie was being made in Hollywood was, 'Do it right. Do it big. Give it class!'

"Those Hollywood designers knew how to dream up extraordinary clothes and dress beautiful women. You can always find great artisans. You can always get quality if you demand it.

"And what happens in five or ten years? Who's worrying? Every year I'm told it's the last Ball in Venice. All my life, the last Ball. But I've had a long life and gone to a hell of a lot of Balls. And life goes on very much the same."

YVES St. LAURENT

Sticking with the Classics

Yves St. Laurent is the top designer of our age. He is French, or rather Parisian: an elegant, understated perfectionist who makes it all look very easy, lazy, languid—and very sensual. His clothes for men and women are very special, very contemporary, but they always remain in style.

At forty-two, St. Laurent is still youthful. He has a strangely confident shyness, as if his slight smile is about to be captured by a flashbulb. After becoming the star designer of the House of Dior at twenty-one, he was drafted into the French Army, suffered a nervous breakdown, and came back to start his own couture house. St. Laurent is now part of a conglomerate, Lanvin-Charles of the Ritz, which backs his perfume. He himself has couture, jewelry, fabric, Rive Gauche ready-to-wear, accessories, perfume, and men's wear ventures. American retailers say, "St. Laurent is like money in the bank."

"It is good for me to come here, to New York. It is very exciting. The United States is going through the crisis we had in France after May 1968, like the consequence of the riots. Perhaps because they're not accustomed to this kind of crisis, this kind of depression, Americans are much more upset than in Paris, saying that life must change, that new things must come. On the street, I see only blue jeans. . . . This is the first time I have been in the United States when there is so little involvement in the fashion sphere. Perhaps it is because blue jeans give more confidence.

"This crisis, this depression, of course influences me in some way. More and more I believe in well-made, basic clothes with no 'fashion' that last many years without transformation—exactly like a blue jean. 'Classic' seems to be an old-fashioned word, but I think the contrary. A blue jean is a classic and I don't think it's old. I believe in basics,

LULU JOYEUSE

LULU TRISTE

LULU LUXE

LULU NERONE

LULU BATMAN

LULU DE BAR

LULU JUST A WOMAN

vilaine LULU MIDI-MINUIT

a wardrobe for a woman that is like a man's —exactly like a blue jean—pants, jacket, raincoat, not similar in details, but in mind. But if an amusing thing happens in fashion, why not try . . . but I don't like too much 'fashion.' Things must have a direction, a continuity.

"Now people are aware of their individuality more and more. To have style you must believe in yourself.

"The men's designs for St. Laurent Rive Gauche are exactly the same here as in France. I don't believe in special things for one country or another. Fashion is the same more and more. And more and more I don't think about the age of the woman or the man. There is no age to wear my clothes. They are basic. It is important to be yourself, not to want to look younger.

"Clothes are things that must last a lot of years without transformation. I like pure fabrics—cotton, silk, wool. I am unable to work with synthetics. Mixtures, yes, but synthetics have a contrary reaction for the body. I don't even like working with mixes, but what can we do? The time is coming in the world when a silk shirt will be a treasure.

"I find that prices are really too high. It's a question of the materials being so expensive. Everything is made in France. There are no workmanship problems, but to reduce prices I think the only thing to do is to be more and more specialized in a kind of clothes. Again, classics.

"The Paris woman in the past one or two years has been very exciting in fashion. Perhaps it was not so before. Recently Paris has taken a new vitality, new shape. There is a new woman with more sense of quality and refinement in life. A mixture of serious and giggle, a good balance in life for me. But the American woman has been the first image of the modern woman. It is a good experience to come here. In Paris perhaps, not to be pejorative, but because of all the continental traditions, they dress more seriously. France is full of traditions.

"A woman can feel very sexy in a chemise, as she can feel very sexy in jeans. It depends on the person. If she thinks she isn't sexy, she will not be sexy."

St. Laurent's cartoons of his mischievous little French character called Lulu.

SECOND-STRING CLASSICS

IVY LEAGUE AND WESTERN

Now that we've taken you through the never-never land of high finance and international tailoring, we want to tell you that it's all right: You don't have to spend all that money. If you want to look rumpled and tweedy without all the formality and expense of custom-made clothes and silk shirts, you can turn to the Ivy League look. Or if you want to look like the quintessential American, you can turn to Western classics.

THE IVY LEAGUE LOOK

Brooks Brothers has been called the Chanel of men's wear for sticking with the simplest designs year after year until they have become as classic and recognizable as a Chanel suit. The Brooks style provides a gently wrinkled old-money look in a range of subtle colors. These are the clothes you see on those mythic couples walking the deserted beach of Martha's Vineyard in early

Parisian Ivy Leaguer in a reversible poplin raincoat.

spring, sipping a summer drink in Southampton, sitting on the terrace of the Ivy Club after a Princeton game, or browsing for antiques at a Chicago auction gallery. It is a very precise way of dressing, almost like an unwritten code, and one item of clothing seems to require the corresponding item. So although you can mix a Brooks look with jeans, dressing it down, you would drive classicists crazy by wearing Brooks

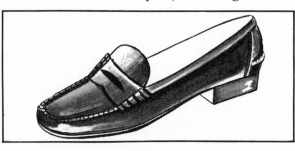

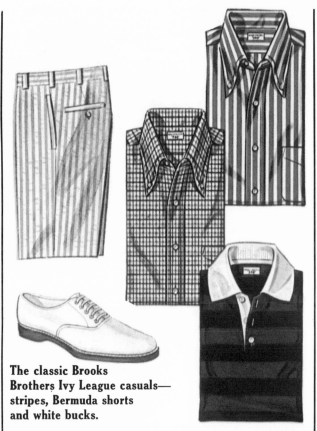

The classic Brooks Brothers Ivy League casuals— stripes, Bermuda shorts and white bucks.

slacks with a shiny red ciré motorcycle jacket. But that's just what you should do if you feel like it.

The Ivy League look for summer runs something like this.

Shirt: An English cotton lisle polo shirt by Solly for the guy, a simple French cotton T-shirt for the girl. A pale blue, pink, or yellow button-down shirt under a light cable-knit sweater for both on cooler evenings.

Wear the shirt or T-shirt with yellow, tomato, or beige chino straight-legged pants, midwale corduroy slacks (perhaps in a bright color), corduroy jeans, or blue jeans. Belt the pants with solid-color webbing finished with leather closings.

On the feet: Weejun loafers or Top-Siders worn without socks.

When it gets chillier, the Ivy League dresser pulls a Shetland sweater or off-white Irish fisherman's knit over the shirt, with cords or jeans. The guy tops this off with an old tweed sport jacket that is meant to look as if it was handed down from his father (but could just as well have come from the local thrift shop). The girl pulls on an old tweed riding jacket or single-breasted blazer. In blustery weather, the old worn

beige gabardine raincoat with reversible wool hounds-tooth check makes its appearance. These seasonal fashion changes are as dependable as the coming of autumn.

A modification of the Brooks look can be really stunning on a pretty girl. For instance, you could collect a few Brooks V-neck cashmere and wool sweaters in pale pastels and wear them big and baggy over tight Lee jeans and a pair of high-heeled, gray St. Laurent boots. Add some plain gold chains here and there and you have a look both boyish and sophisticated.

The rules of dressing in Ivy League classics can be almost as stiff and demanding as those of the custom-made universe. But this just gives you all the more room for innovation and invention within the basic form. Rules are made to be broken.

COWBOY CLASSICS

Cowboy clothes were once designed for survival on the range, but now they're our most popular home-grown classic. "Western clothes were originally survival clothes," wrote Jon Carroll in *Rags* magazine, "and

The essence of rodeo tailoring: country sequins.

Brooks Brothers supplies the Shetland sweater and cotton shirt; Lauren Hutton supplies the sneakers and smile.

these elementary jeans, according to *Rags*, "tucked into the tops of heavy leather boots. A red flannel shirt was worn outside the trousers and gathered round the waist with a scarf of Chinese silk or a leather belt, or both, with a holster for a heavy Colt revolver. And any sort of hat . . . except the stovepipe beaver. They didn't want any class symbols out on the Great Frontier."

The custom-made leather jeans of today may not be class symbols, but they sure look classy. Those of us who bought them five years ago in the "latest" bell-bottomed style made a big mistake. The leather is still in great shape, but that hip-slung flared-leg fashion just doesn't look right today. The safest way to order leather jeans is as an exact copy of whatever jeans you've been wearing since you first played cowboys and Indians. The best leather jeans (often costing over $100) are so sturdy they can be pummeled, scrubbed, and stomped in the bathtub. You save on those exorbitant cleaning bills.

Another staple in the Western repertoire is the cowboy shirt. It's cut tight to the body (so it doesn't flap while you're riding),

First class examples of "rodeo tailoring," both by Nudie of Hollywood. Right: Francois de Menil wears a conservative maroon and beige wool garbardine shirt tailored to fit the body. Above: a peach of a suit from one of Nudie's old catalogues. Add a buckskin skirt . . . that's cowgirl heaven.

their increasing relevance to our lives, along with the increasing relevance of the social and moral systems they symbolize, may say something about how close to the edge of the cliff of civilization we are."

Levi-Strauss jeans, as we've mentioned, are all-time classics. They began during the Gold Rush as sturdy trousers made of sailcloth, riveted with copper. The Americans and Europeans who headed west wore

yoked across the back and front, snapped on the sleeves and down the front, and flapped and snapped on the breast pockets. These shirts are especially handsome in plaids, ginghams, and solid colors, and take a bow tie or neck scarf with panache.

If you want conservative cowboy clothes, you can have them tailor-made by a "rodeo" tailor. We have seen beautiful wool gabardine shirts with contrasting yokes and white pearl snaps. One "formal" tailor-made jacket owned by a friend of ours has thirteen—count 'em, thirteen—buttons marching up the sleeve of the jacket, a sand and maroon gabardine trimmed with white piping on the yoke, patch pockets, and sleeves. It never fails to get a few conversations going during a stroll down Broadway. A really elegant way to wear these under-stated cowboy clothes is to put them together with jeans and a silk shirt for a party. It shows you care enough to make an extra effort to "dress," while letting you keep your own particular style of dress-up.

If you want even flashier cowboy clothes, send to Los Angeles for the catalog from Nudie the Rodeo Tailor. He does the rancher look as well as the gaudiest "parade class" around—electric colors, metallic trims, flashing fringe, sequins, and glittering jewels. If the Flying Burrito Brothers are your kind of rock group, Nudie's is your kind of store.

Cowboy boots are a well-heeled alternative to a pair of European "investment" boots. Although custom-made boots can easily run you up to $250, you can still find mail-order cowboy boots for under $100, custom-made to a drawing of your foot. The

Below: Cowboy Boots come in a dizzying array of colors, leathers and stitchings. What makes them a great investment is their rugged nature and timeless style.

prices are so reasonable because many Texas bootmakers use artisans over the border in Mexico. The design of the boot makes it good looking and sensible for the rider. The boot is shaped to give leverage in the saddle, the pointed toes get the arch into the stirrup fast, and the high heels catch the foot so you can't be dragged by the ankle. Genghis Khan and his Mongol warriors wore boots heeled with bright red to celebrate their fierce occupation and high status, but we can merrily outdo him. Joe Hall in El Paso

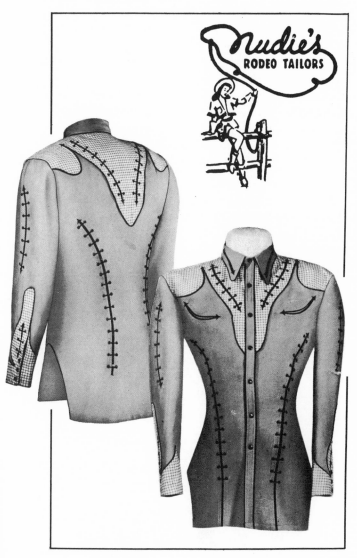

Today, just as in 1886, feathers and leathers have a classy look. Left: A timeless style, that fitted custom cut of a classic Western shirt.

makes up boots in cowhide, veal, steerhide, calfskin, horsehide, kangaroo, boarhide, sharkskin, ostrich, elephant, and snakeskin, with bright colors to match. Some of his best customers are professional wrestlers, men who really know how to put on a show; the boots he creates for them are real showboats.

Some Western boot connoisseurs think the most satisfying thing about their elaborately stitched and overlaid high-top boots is the fact that all that icing is never seen, except in the owner's closet. It's not exactly conspicuous consumption. But we think you should show them off. You can tuck jeans or jumpsuits into the tops of stovepipes. You can make a long skirt look different by wearing it with mid-calf boots, or alter the proportion of a big knee-length skirt with short boots. It takes a while to adjust to the look of it, but short or mid-calf boots look really new without being in the least bit nostalgic.

JEAN-PAUL GOUDE

Fashioning the Body Beautiful

Jean-Paul Goude is an artist and art director who lives in a combined working and living space high above Union Square in Manhattan. He grew up in Paris with a French father and an American mother, and now lives in New York dreaming up ways to lengthen everyone's image, if not body. A meticulous artist, he combines photography and painting in such a personal and precise manner that you often cannot tell if you are seeing a picture or an illustration. Jean-Paul carries his personal brand of estheticism into his daily life and personal movie making.

"I've always art-directed my appearance. Naked, I have short legs. When I was a kid, I was doing men's fashion illustrations for Le Printemps department store in Paris. I gradually realized that these drawings were actually a projection of how I wanted to look. On paper I was elegant, long legged, broad shouldered, slim, etc. One day I decided to make the fantasy real, so I visited John Lobb, the bootmaker in Paris. Being conservative, I wanted a traditional shoe with no high heel, so the only solution was to have lifts put in them. I was twenty then. I still go to Lobb's. Now I'm six feet tall!

"Lobb shoes can cost up to $600, even more. It's not expensive because you get to wear them for ten years at least. I like white bucks too, and sneakers, but only with lifts.

"The American men's wear look is summed up for me by Brooks Brothers. It's not what it used to be, but it's still good when not trying to be 'continental.'

"I used to wear 'high-water' pants; you know, tight pants too short so you can see your socks (like Lil' Abner) because I liked the look of the rhythm-and-blues singers who used to perform in the Olympia in Paris. (That was in 1965, long before I came to live in the United States.) They were country boys and had a special style about them. I guess they were just 'country,' but to me they had a great look. I tried to wear 'high-waters,' but one has to be built like those guys to make it work.

"If one is small, one is almost forced to wear tight-fitting clothes. (James Cagney used to; so did Adolphe Menjou, even Fred

69

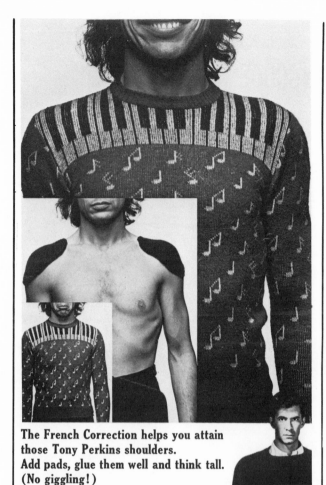

The French Correction helps you attain those Tony Perkins shoulders.
Add pads, glue them well and think tall.
(No giggling!)

Good, better, best: noses in Jean-Paul's pantheon are OK on actor Jean Paul Belmondo, but the boxer at right has the truly perfect nose.

Astaire.) Did you ever see South American diplomats in the fifties, the ones who used to have their clothes made in Saville Row in London? They used to wear real tight jackets, rather wide trousers, and all the accessories; stiff collars, club ties, carna-

The sizzling energetic style of New York Puerto Ricans.

tions in their lapel. They were a reduced version of the tall English dandies, only they had brown Indian faces and shiny black straight hair. They really looked great. Porfirio Rubirosa had that look, except he was tall.

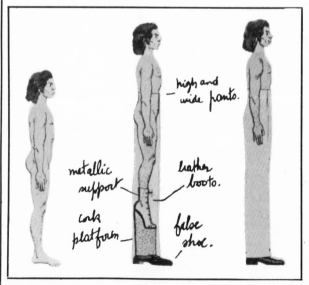

The French Correction II: To look like a fashion illustration, lengthen your lines with Jean-Paul's fantasy shoes. The normal shoe is buttressed with a towering cork platform, a metal support and lace-up boots and voilà, the designer's dream. (No wobbling.)

"In France, we have a certain idea of what Americans wear, and a lot of Frenchmen dress American when in fact Americans have stopped wearing these particular clothes, and are in turn wearing 'continental' clothes. Americans used to look great to us when they wore the Ivy League style. Now they wear Cardin suits which look like they are made of cardboard. It's a shame in a way, though I've seen some little French guys in their version of Brooks, and that can be sad too.

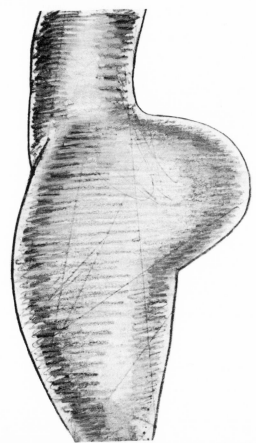

His ideal derrière is high, round, womanly and black.

"My tailor is Maurice Breslave. He used to be Eric Von Stroheim's tailor. Remember how great old Eric looked? Breslave still works for some of the best-dressed stars. He's the one who did those suits in the French movie *Borsalino*.

"Men are vain, but for some reason most of them think it's wrong to admit it. I guess they think it's not masculine.

"Tony Perkins used to look great in the late fifties before he started making films in Europe and tried to look French. He completely lost his style. He should go back to Brooks Brothers.

Sweatpants and white bucks with an impeccably tailored jacket, closed with an eccentric button at the neck.

The femme French Correction, or, Height is Pain.

"Don Robbie, St. Laurent's American men's wear designer, tried to capitalize on the way Puerto Rican teen-agers dress. He made them look like gangsters. I prefer to see those kids in their fifties thrift-shop clothes. They have such great taste and invention. It's funny, though, that it's the teen-age Puerto Ricans who have the taste. Through their influence Puerto Ricans have become the new ethnic stars.

"This reminds me of the 'Minets de L'-Étoile' when I was in my late teens. We were a whole gang hanging around the 'Drugstore' de L'Étoile in Paris. We wore blazers and flannel pants, trying to be very British. We came from the suburbs, not the elegant districts of Paris, but we looked more stylish than the rich kids. We were outdoing them with silk ties from polo clubs, monogramed shirts, cashmere scarves, and so on . . . I had a blazer made when I was about sixteen, and on the pocket was a gold embroidered emblem which I had copied from the golden eagle stamped on an American passport.

"My friends and I wanted to look like British clubmen and French race-horse owners. Consequently, I bought my first Rolls Royce when I was twenty-three, to complete the image; what I was doing actually was a softer European version of what black pimps are doing here. I never paid too much attention to physical characteristics at that time. I mean my face. But now, it's a different story. I always had a childish face because of my turned-up nose. The problem is, when you get a certain age and still have a kid's face you can easily look like an old

faggot. It's charming to have a kid's face when you're twenty-five, but I've just turned thirty-three, and I don't look so cute anymore. When I reach forty, I must have the 'face of a man,' a virile face. So I need a serious nose, not a kid's nose. If I had the nerve, I'd get a nose job. I'd have a boxer's nose done. But I don't trust plastic surgeons for myself because I'm too specific. I'd be scared they'd give me one of those obvious nose jobs. Too bad, I wouldn't mind looking like an ex-fighter when I'm forty.

"Mind you, I think plastic surgery and health spas will get so big they will be a threat to the garment industry. The better looking you are, the less clothes you need. In 1972, I started in Esquire the 'French correction,' in which I showed readers how to improve their appearance by wearing special shoes, shoulder pads in T-shirts, instant capped teeth, and so on.

"I still think it's a good idea, because people need advice before going into the hands of plastic surgeons who fancy themselves as modern versions of Leonardo Da Vinci, only they use a scalpel instead of a brush. I have seen so many rotten nose jobs done, I guess, by surgeons who could not draw. To become a truly great plastic surgeon, one should first win the 'Prix De Rome' in sculpture, then go into the medical profession.

"Sports are great to watch, not for the sport itself but for the way athletes move. I don't care much for ballet, but I've always liked dance and movement; that's why I'm a fan of Muhammad Ali. He's my favorite dancer. I think that most black fighters care more about looking good in the ring than actually winning a fight. Black people always dance whatever they do. I'm not a bleeding-heart liberal or a slummer. I like the esthetic of black people. Also, I think they are the most vital energy in American culture.

"Nowadays, my paintings as an illustrator tell anecdotes. I try to translate various assignments in the most sophisticated manner possible. But my stuff is sometimes too subtle, that obsession with style and good taste may hurt my career someday. For the time being, call me the 'Ernst Lubitsch' of illustration, and I'll be happy."

INGEBORG DAY

The Office Uniform with a System

Ingeborg Day is a thirty-four-year-old office worker in midtown Manhattan, mother of a twelve-year-old girl. She has devised a money-saving program called "Cost Per Wear" which she tells about here.

"In the winter I wear black. Two pairs of black pants, a black shirt, a black wool turtleneck, a fisherman's sweater, and a short-sleeved black sweater. I have a pair of black evening sandals and Italian boots.

"With all this black, the thing that I buy most often is tights. I never do comparison shopping for them, I just use the store that's closest to the office. I'm not going to stop wearing them if the price goes up, just like I'm not going to stop buying milk at the corner store. I get tights in special colors because it's the only color that shows in my clothes.

"In the summer I wear a pair of loose cotton pants in a purplish beige and a similar pair in blue, both two years old. This summer I bought some black drawstring pants. And last summer I went on a binge and bought three identical pairs of lined white slacks, two white t-shirts, and two white halters. They're all washable. In the summer I don't buy things that have to be

Plain pants subtly compliment an elegant dressing gown.

dry-cleaned. If you wear white and have three of each thing you can manage, even riding the subway and bus every day. I bought a white hat and a white skirt, and I wear white espadrilles. White is more practical than yellow, brown or even black, because you can use nurse's white shoe polish on the canvas—with any other color, there's nothing you can do if you spill something on them or someone steps on your foot.

"Summer and winter I wear a St. Laurent crepe de Chine skirt with narrow stitched-down pleats. I've had it since 1974, so I've worn it almost four years. It was on sale for $60, but the "Cost Per Wear" is small.

$$\frac{Price}{Number\ of\ times\ worn} = C.P.W.$$

$$\frac{\$60.00}{400} = 15¢\ per\ wearing$$

I've worn it at least 100 times a year over four years, so the CPW comes to 15¢ a wearing. In contrast, take what sounds like a cheap evening dress I bought on sale for $16 some years ago—I only wore it twice, so the CPW was $8. Compared with the 15¢ for my expensive skirt, that evening dress turned out to be a waste of money. Of course, people complain about my wearing black all the time—they say 'Has this become attached to your body?' or 'Didn't you sleep at home last night?'

"I don't dress up. No . . . that's not true, I do have three dress-up items: a Thea Porter dress, a Man Ray lip print a friend bought for me on sale for $30 that I've had since 1970, and a long black wool dress with a plain neck and no back which I bought because the designer and I both have the same first name. Recently my best friend gave me a long red velour wrap robe/dress from Betsey Johnson's.

"I always wear a simple ring given to me by my daughter, my mother's wedding ring, and a gold necklace with a guardian angel charm from my grandmother. It's all sentimental. In the summer I alternate two strands of pearls with the white T-shirts. I wear them so you can see them on the side and tuck them under the front. And recently a close friend gave me a scarab. 'It's like a pedigreed dog,' she said. 'It comes with a piece of paper, certifying that it's 3,500 years old, from such and such a dynasty.' It's now my favorite piece of jewelry.

"There are really only six areas of life you have to dress for. I've managed to get it down to three. The six areas are: bed, work, play casual, play elegant, sports, and social obligations. I've combined social obligations with play elegant. Sports, work and play casual have become the second category. Bed remains the third. If you also consider the time of year you can wear things, the clothes that fall into more than one season will give you the best CPW.

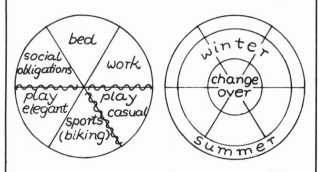

"On the east coast, winter would be the largest circle, but in other places, summer might be bigger. The French butcher's smock I just bought is going to have a low CPW because I can wear it in the summer with pants and espadrilles and in the winter with a turtleneck and boots, and all the times in between. I love it."

Uniform chic—the black T-shirt and pants with classic pearls and a Guatemalan bag.

FRAN LEBOWITZ

Grouchy Simplicity

Fran Lebowitz, author of **Metropolitan Life**, is a writer of great wit and imagination, but when it comes to her own clothes she follows a strict line of quality and austerity. She owns very few clothes, yet always appears in well-tailored, neat outfits. Fran insists on following her basic ideas in getting dressed, for fear of wasting her energy on frivolity.

"I have no colors in my clothes. The most colorful I get is with two pale-pink shirts. I get too hot if there is red around me. I'm so particular about what I wear that my parents have been afraid to buy me clothes since I was six years old. I'm so conservative I still wear clothes from high school, but I haven't worn a dress in five years. It comes down to the idea that I don't like my clothes to make me stand out. To me, if anyone gets remarked on because of what they wear, they are badly dressed.

"I can't believe what some people wear. A great majority of kids in their late teens are the worst dressed . . . incredible platform shoes, glitter, hideous fabrics . . . useless extravagance.

"The only thing I ever regretted buying was this pair of black patent-leather shoes for $65 at Charles Jourdan. They're ridiculous, but I'll wear them until they fall apart. My most precious possession is a terrific riding jacket that was made a century ago for the aunt of a friend. She was eighty when she died, wearing it, and it is still holding up impeccably. The silk lining by itself is a beauty. I wear it with $2 white cotton sailor pants.

"A fan sent me a T-shirt inscribed with all sorts of ugly lines. I hate gimmicks and it prompted me to write a few paragraphs in **Interview*** magazine."

* ©Fran Lebowitz

Clothes with pictures and/or writing on them—yes, another complaint. Now I'm not just talking about Vuitton bags. Or Gucci wallets. Or Hermes scarves. Designers and/or business concerns who splash their names and initials all over overpriced accoutrements of dubious quality are of course exceedingly distasteful, but I am not talking about the larger issues. Open-necked deco-ish shirts with repeating patterns of middle-sized silhouettes of sailboats. Blue jeans depicting the death of Marilyn Monroe in waterproof pastels. Dresses upon which one (but preferably two) can play Monopoly. Overalls which remind toddlers, through the use of small pink animals spouting comic strip balloons, to brush their teeth. T-shirts which proclaim the illegal sexual preferences of the wearer. Ectetera. Ectetera.

"While clothes with pictures and/or writing on them are not entirely an invention of the modern age, they are an unpleasant indication of the general state of things, which encourages people to express themselves through their clothing . . . I mean, be realistic. If people don't want to listen to you, what makes you think they want to hear from your sweater?

"There are two main reasons why we wear clothes. First, to hide figure flaws, of which the average person has at least seventeen. And second, to look cute, which is at least cheering. If some people think that nice, muted, solid colors are a bit dull, they can add some punch with stripes, plaids, checks, or if it's summer and they're girls, small dots. For those of you who feel that this is too restrictive, answer me this: If God meant for people to walk around in coats that have pictures of butterscotch sundaes on them, then why does He wear tattersal shirts?"

ANTIQUES

SHOPPING THE THRIFT STORES

Up until a few years ago, wearing some stranger's old clothes was something only the poorest people did when forced to. Can you imagine your mother buying used clothes, except in an almost-new shop with prices to match? But as everyone is discovering, it feels good to wear expensive clothes, especially when someone else paid for them the first time out. And today, it can be a positive joy to track down that one beautiful item of used clothing you have your heart set on. As chic antique clothing boutiques proliferate, even smart department stores are carrying antiques . . . and the quality never seems to run out!

Old clothes give you a sense of continuity with the past—an elegant way of life lived in luxurious fabrics of strict tailoring, a life of fluttering afternoon rituals and evening formalities. Solid old clothes give you a feeling that in this throwaway world

Tiny strips of cotton are folded, appliqued and made into this unusual jacket by Florida Indians.

there are still some things around that can last ten, twenty, thirty, forty years, or more, and remain beautiful. And if you have the instincts of a bloodhound, they can be in your very own closet!

BEING CHOOSEY

There are a few things to keep in mind when shopping for old clothes. When you come upon something that appeals to you, ask yourself if the design is timeless. Will you be able to wear a thirties dress in a comfortable, contemporary style, or will it resist all your attempts to take away its strong costume look? Unless you prefer to wear costumes instead of clothes, you will not be happy with it. A costume takes a lot of energy to wear. It's usually going to wear you; perhaps wear you out (and that's not what you're after).

Secondly, is this discovery of yours in first-rate condition? Will the fabric hold up? Will the beading stay on? Will it come back in one piece from your friendly neighbor-hood dry cleaner? And has it been cleaned often enough in its past life? Or does someone else's smell waft from the armpit of that glamorous but seldom-cleaned beauty? If it does, think twice. Perspiration may be chemically locked into the fabric, and each time you start to perspire in it, it will add its own unnerving scent—which won't be Chanel No. 5!

Third, if a piece of used clothing doesn't fit perfectly, is it close enough to your size to be fixed by a tailor or seamstress? Try it on. When thrift shopping, wear a leotard, tights, and a wraparound or button-front skirt. This way you can slip things on even if there's no dressing room. And if you like to wear high heels or boots, bring them along to get a sense of proportion when you try on dresses or pants. (Be careful with pants, because they often stretch to fit the ample aspects of just one person's derrière and can't be reshaped.)

Once you start collecting old clothes, line up a seamstress or tailor to help match up those brilliant discoveries of yours with the realities of your body. Because it seems that body shapes, as well as fashions, go in and

80 | **Jezebel is a top banana in New York's used clothing scene, specializing in droopy dresses and stiff Victoriana.**

out of style every few years. (Witness Marilyn Monroe's Nike-missile breasts versus Twiggy's flat chest. Yet you want to wear both fifties and sixties things, right?) Make a pact with yourself to put aside the money to *make it fit*. Fit can make the least expensive find look very elegant.

You need a sensitive, able seamstress to make an old dress look as tasty as it did back in the forties.

TYPES OF SHOPS

There are several kinds of stores that sell used clothing. In a descending level of price (though not necessarily quality), there are the antique clothing boutiques carrying exquisite hand-finished antique dresses and couture clothes; the almost-new shops that hold clothes on consignment; private-enterprise boutiques, flea-market stalls, and thrift shops that pick over other thrift shop racks and sell you their finds for a markup. The privately owned youth-oriented thrift shops are where most of the action is, since they're a trendy compromise between department store and junk shop. They're popular because we don't all have the time and guts it takes to comb through hundreds of musty old thrift shops. These shops take the worry out of being cheap.

Los Angeles is a used-clothing haven. For some reason, perhaps the high glamour quotient of living near Hollywood and a tendency to treasure things that remind one of past dreams, southern California has the most accessible, appealing, best-quality clothes around. There are stores like Anne's-Tiques in Santa Monica that sell prim hand-starched and hand-ironed Victorian-era wedding dresses in absolutely pristine condition at a quarter of their price in New York. There are hundreds of thrift shops hidden amidst the waving palms, both charitable and not, classy and not-so-classy, as well as a thriving private business in selected secondhand clothes. With practice you can shop these stores as fast as your favorite boutique.

Lesley, a tough-minded English girl who always wears used clothes, shops nothing classier than thrift shops when she's working in Los Angeles. She has the time and the practiced eye to come up with some beguiling clothes, and she really can't afford to buy any other way. One of her most prized possessions is a perfectly preserved red satin jacket with bias-bound buttonholes and tailored cuffs by Don Loper, a grand designer-to-the-stars of the fifties era. She found this treasure for 95¢ at the downtown

Angeleno Antiques: Paul Ruscha's wardrobe comes exclusively from thrift shops and friends.

Accessories . . . they're the things that can take a basic wardrobe and make it into something special, something unique. The perfect accessories are often found at thrift shops, like this fifties-style Scripto lighter—every time you light up, you make a "fashion statement"!

Los Angeles Goodwill store. By always checking the labels in clothes she has become something of an expert on the shopping habits of fashionable Angelenos of twenty and thirty years ago. There is an I. Magnin label in her early fifties red wool coat. It hangs straight from the shoulder and is cut full in back with deep, cuffed sleeves. She found it for $2 at a thrift shop in Pasadena, a once-palmy area of Los Angeles now fallen on hard times. The fabric alone in the coat would cost $20 a yard today. Her favorite buy was discovered at a Bekin's Moving and Storage sale that she saw announced in the paper. This knockout navy blue Marlene Dietrich-style blazer suit would have fit right in on a weekend with Marion Davies at Hearst's San Simeon. Inside the jacket pocket, where all custom-tailored labels are found, the former owner, date, and tailor are listed: Mrs. Tom May (of the family that owns the famous May Company department stores), 1936, Watson & Sons Tailors of Hollywood. The suit is totally lined with silk. To have it made today, at Bernard Weatherill Tailors in New York, would cost $400. It cost Lesley something like $3.

Lesley never fiddles with her clothes. "I never buy anything unless it fits. I like to keep the original length and proportion. I could never afford the quality I like in new clothes—that's why I buy old clothes. But I do spend a lot of time looking. It's the chase I love, the great discovery you feel when you're really struck by something!"

Artist/calligrapher Paul Ruscha is a neighbor of Lesley's who wears thrift-shop clothes as well as bits and pieces he trades around with friends or gets in exchange for his work. Artists who haunt thrift shops are always trying to one-up each other, and it leads to some very entertaining clothes! Paul's closet is hung on pipes, thrift-shop style, at one end of his studio. His prize is a monkey-fur coat given to him by an actress who got religion: she got a calligraphed Ten Commandments, and he got the coat. At night, Paul loves to go dancing in outfits like his white Tropicana Hotel pants with a blue silk, Isle of Capri, flare-collared, fifties shirt. Paul says you can always find Dior, Cardin, and St. Laurent shirts at the social aid societies ("like the Assistance League Thrift Shop on Fountain across from the Gas War"). Rich women have a quota of clothes they have to turn in to remain chummy with their friends at the league, so they bring in their hapless husband's almost-new shirts and go charge him newer ones. Paul figured all the young wives were doing this when he lived in Oklahoma City.

EXPERTISE

One of the reasons Susan Doukas moved to Los Angeles from New York was because of all the great thrift shops. Her taste leans toward unique, funny dresses with a lot of style, like her "Lauren Bacall" dress with gold studding on rust crepe and lots of sophisticated cutting. She's a definite believer in recycling, and says even when she gets rich she'll still go to thrift shops. "You can do really well if you have a little taste and not much money, especially if you look for beautiful things with a sense of humor. Certain clothes were really very silly, like the dresses of the thirties with all the intricate cutting and flaps and brooches. Dresses made statements of humor, and you could choose something you responded to because it was unique. Now fashion is just androgynous. Mass manufactured clothes have no individuality. Here are some of my pointers for shopping for used clothes:

1. Look for messy shops. A good one will have things like pants mixed up in the blouse bin. The very best bargains are in stores where you get really dirty, like the Volunteers of America in downtown L. A.

2. If you have a whole day and don't mind driving, hit the outlying areas, especially the old-guard suburbs, like Locust Valley out on Long Island.

3. Try to get an immediate sense of price. You can tell right off with shoes, first, then hats, picture frames, kitchenware. A glass for a nickel is cheap. Even though the stuff

Trucia Kushner found this beautiful Sulka silk man's robe at a used clothing store in New York City.

may seem depressing one day, remember shops really vary because they constantly get new shipments.

4. You must wash things to kill the bugs, and that bothers some people! If there's a smell or stain, I just scrub and scrub and send it to the cleaners. But remember, for $8 you can get the most absolutely gorgeous thirties or forties crepe dress. And if you take it in, you can make a drawstring purse from the leftover fabric.

5. If salesladies want to help you and follow you around, avoid the shop. It's not worth it. I prefer a place where I can barter. Say I find a $1.50 sweater with a couple of buttons missing or a hole in it. Usually it's okay to say, 'Can I have it for a dollar?,' especially if it's a Christian organization. In the Jewish ones they don't usually let you bargain—they just say, 'No, honey, the price is marked.' "

When a group of friends all thrift shop, they can help each other develop collections. Susan, for instance, has a closet full of bowling-league shirts and soft-drink-delivery-man's uniforms.

| **Susan insists her style is silly rather than chic, but she always pulls off an individual look with special moxie.**

Valentina has to put together a wardrobe on the small salary she makes as production assistant and receptionist on the Cher Show. She tries her best in the midst of all that Bob Mackie-designed Cher glamour to pull off a special look. She likes to mix the old with the new, and for her the private-enterprise used-clothing store is the best bet. In the funky Silverlake section of Los Angeles where she lives is a typical shop called Aardvark's Odd Ark. Used clothing chosen with an eye for the younger customer is arranged on racks by category: used jeans, plaid shirts, overalls, Levi jackets, forties and fifties tailored jackets, suits, beaded thirties dresses, bias-cut nightgowns, Mexican felt jackets, and a multitude of sins. The most outstanding and high-priced items are displayed on the walls above the racks, rather dusty, but often the only decor in this type of low-overhead operation. And where do the clothes come from? Shops ranging from Aardvarks's on up to the used chic of Yesterday's News near Beverly Hills buy their goods from out-of-the-way thrift shops or from the sinister-sounding "rag houses" in downtown Los Angeles. Ropa Usada is one of these rag house warehouses. Room-sized bundles of clothing from the Midwest are piled to the ceiling and sold in one-thousand-pound lots without being cleaned. A thousand pounds of clothes can run $200 to $500. The bundles then have to be sorted by the buyer and the best things winnowed out and cleaned. Some of the smaller dealers complain that the used-clothing business is getting so profitable it's being run like the Mafia, that Beverly Hills-style boutiques have a complete monopoly on the rag house bundles.

People in the West and down South hold outdoor swap meets year-round, while others have to wait for the summer months. One of the Angelenos' favorite gathering spots is the Hollywood Swap Meet, located in an empty corner parking lot on Santa Monica Boulevard in West Hollywood. It's a lively area filled with picnic tables, makeshift dressing rooms, and jerrybuilt clothes racks. Just plain folks as well as Zsa Zsa Gabor, Ruth Buzzi, Lena Horne, Shelley Winters, Sonny Bono, Carol Lynley, and

Valentina eyes the reindeer rack at her local L.A. store.

Cher drop by to try stuff on. The sellers rent space to display their wares and the lot is open every day of the week. We found an apricot, hand-sewn crepe de Chine bed jacket for $2; beautiful pure silk nightgowns with hand-stitching and hand-made lace appliqués (perfect for transferring to a T-shirt or dress if the rest of the fabric is frayed) for $3 to $10; hundreds of pairs of used jeans arranged by size for $4 or $5; Air Force flight suits for $25–$35; sailor tops, military uniforms, and safari jackets, and typically Californian standbys like kimonos, Mexican felt jackets, Oriental-theme satin baseball jackets, and Hawaiian print shirts. (The best-priced and most amiable stall is run by Ruthie, but she's only there on Fridays.) Another popular swap meet is the massive gathering held on weekends in the Hollywood Bowl. It's so big it can make you dizzy.

San Francisco is a tremendous place to find stylish used clothing because of the flashy transvestite and gay scene crystallized by the Cockettes in the early seventies. Stores that cater to this taste, like Casey's Faded World and the Flying A, have higher prices but very select merchandise. It's nice to have a gay friend—he can often steer you in the direction of the most chic, and the most cheap, shop in your town.

It's always smart to get shopping advice from people who make money from their clothes. Carrie White, who runs a beauty salon in Beverly Hills, rented out some things from her personal wardrobe for the film *Shampoo*, set in 1968. ("1968, can you believe it! They're already being collected!")

Carrie says to stake out five thrift shops rather than spreading yourself thin over fifteen. Whenever you travel, check the most remote places for shops (like Cathedral City, which is ten minutes out of Palm Springs), or at least go one block off the main drag. She looks first for colors and patterns that will ease her eyes when she sees herself in the salon mirror at work. She always checks the thrift-shop drawers, which a lot of people forget, and finds doilies, ribbons, scarves, bathing suits; napkins which make great skirts and pieces for lengthening jeans; and white lace to lengthen white pants. And since Carrie has four kids, she's always looking for children's hand-crafted clothes. Carrie loves the sport and the fun of it. "In nine years, no customer has ever seen me in the same thing twice!"

Another person who makes money by

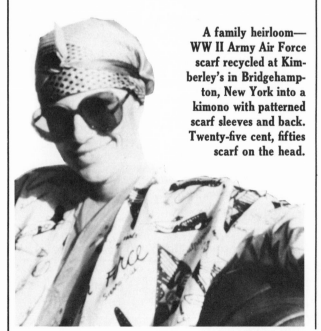

A family heirloom— WW II Army Air Force scarf recycled at Kimberley's in Bridgehampton, New York into a kimono with patterned scarf sleeves and back. Twenty-five cent, fifties scarf on the head.

The ultimate luck is to dig up a twenties extravaganza in a musty, old thrift shop. When luck strikes, spend.

collecting old clothes is Steve Starr. The Steve Starr Studio in Chicago is home for a truly spectacular collection of period clothing, some for sale. Steve says he collects "art deco, art moderne, art ultra, and twentieth-century costumes and accessories." Every year he stages the Steve Starr Vanity, which stars his clothes, decade by decade, worn by an all-singing, all-dancing, cast of clothes freaks and models parading through a series of elaborate production numbers and film clips. It may well be the most entertaining event of the year in Chicago, a home-grown *That's Entertainment*. Since he has so many first-quality dresses and accessories, he is often reluctant to sell his favorites, which he keeps for the Vanity and

Wendy Whitelaw in a favorite brown crepe antique dress with inset velvet bows, teeny-tiny buttons, and a beige silk sash tied at the waist.

uses in producing and styling photographs, many for *Playboy*. He's now working on a full-color collection of these photos, which should be a tremendous source book for period clothes.

In London, the painter Duggie Fields and about twenty or thirty friends put on their own "jumble sales" by hiring a church hall and bringing things to sell. "The rental goes to the church charities, and what we make we keep for ourselves. We advertise the sale in the local papers, list it in *Time Out* magazine, and design posters to put in neighborhood shops. Hundreds of people come. It's fun, and it's a good way to get rid of your old stuff and get new from your friends. It's good recycling, and at the same time you can make $100 in an afternoon just for cleaning out your closet.

"The clothes are all piled up—our first jumble sale was chaos—and as soon as the doors open, people run in, grabbing. It's like being in a chicken coop. But it's a nice afternoon, and it's fun to see who turns up. I even see people stealing. They know I know they haven't paid, but I'm not going to say a thing . . . things gotta go!

"I only buy clothes in stores if I need something I can't find here. They're not necessarily fashionable stores. My favorite is called 'Sex' in the World's End . . . bits of furs, porno embroidered T-shirts, and humorous clothes. My idea of wearing clothes is to make myself smile. I like that in others too. I don't think clothes should be serious."

In New York, the used clothing prices

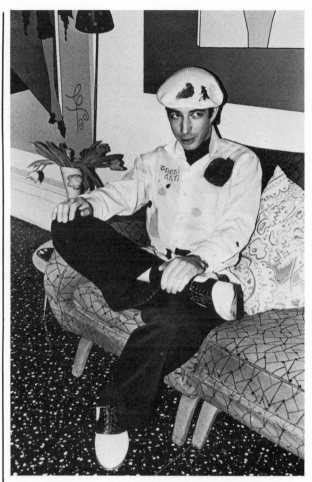

Duggie Fields' sensibility is born of jumble sale chaos.

are much higher than they are in Europe or on the Coast. Some of our favorite stores in New York are Everybody's Thrift Shop, Jezebel (on the West Side), Cherchez!, and especially Harriet Love's in the SoHo district south of the Village. Harriet's been selling antique clothing for years, and now her specials run from beautifully embroidered turn-of-the-century white petticoats, slips, and camisoles to Annie Hall-style men's pleated pants for women.

One of the best places to find rich New Yorker's castoffs is where they vacation, like the Palm Beach Thrift Shop in Florida. Beautifully tailored three-piece suits can be found here for $10, and with tailoring, a suit for the office can cost only $35. One New York businessman has three $10 English-tailored suits he bought at the Palm Beach Thrift Shop: two formerly lived in New York, one in Chicago. Along with a navy cashmere coat from Saks, also used, they make up his entire office wardrobe, and no one is any the wiser.

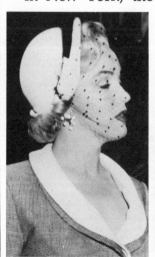

Blondes do have more fun, especially when they're hiding behind an old-fashioned mysterious bit of veiling.

Garbo put this outfit together forty years ago, but by smart antiques shopping, you can put it together today.

ANTIQUES

For some fashionable women, the ultimate chic is dressing in couturier clothes of the past. An eccentric editor at Italian *Vogue* dresses entirely in antique Poiret couturier originals that are terribly elegant yet contemporary in feeling. Who could make a more glorious dress than Schiaparelli, or a more elegant suit than Chanel? If you set your sights on originals like these, you have to be extremely lucky (of course, the first step to "luck" is to learn as much as you can about the couture), and it helps to cultivate rich relatives or friends, unless you are prepared to spend your life's savings!

Most of the truly classic couture clothes are now being donated by estates to museum collections for the inevitable tax write-offs. Thousands of beautiful things are locked away in the climate-controlled storage rooms of the Chicago Historical Society, the Metropolitan Museum, and the Museum of the City of New York. Entire wardrobes, right down to the needle-toed, stiletto-heeled Charles Jourdan black faille pumps, arrive by chauffeured limousines and are carried into these grand museums, never to be worn again except by plaster mannequins. Some designer clothes are still at large, though they are increasingly rare. The owner of an antique clothing shop in New York has two St. Laurent couture dresses, because, she says, "they are a lot nicer than the things that are being made now. I bought them for a good price and can resell them at a reasonable profit. I've been collecting clothes for about ten years, going to places like Canada and south to Georgia, but now it's costing too much to go out and look." She has sold a Chanel, a St. Laurent, and a Fortuny dress. If you don't have hundreds in disposable income, your best bet is to try Canada and Georgia yourself!

GREAT FINDS

When shopping for used clothing, whether you are in a pricey on-consignment store or a dirty old thrift shop, be sure to keep your eyes peeled for the following:

Luscious fabrics, like pure **silk,** in nightgowns, slips, loose undershorts, chemises, bed jackets. All sorts of scarves, especially the $1 bias-cut, long, thirties silks (now selling at around $30 in antique clothing shops). Well-cut silk shirts. Lovely silk

Expert thrift-shoppers keep their eyes peeled for pure silks like this arty-looking, loose-cut blouson.

neckties, silk squares, and neck scarves.

Cotton petticoats, lace shirts, Victorian dresses with tight bodices, men's and women's shirts, straight nightgowns, cowboy shirts, cotton flannel plaid shirts, pedal-pushers, slacks, and safari outfits.

Pure **wool** is found in women's tailored suits, coats of gabardine, melton, cashmere, tweed, and challis, tight or big mid-calf skirts, and sweaters. If you're looking for a sweater, be sure to look through the children's bin, because the French size their sweaters 1, 2, and 3, and the ladies who work in volunteer thrift shops aren't going to know this, but you are. In fact, it helps to familiarize yourself with European sizing.

The French sizes 1–2–3– for T-shirts run a bit tighter than American S–M–L, because the French prefer shirts to be a bit more clinging. English dress sizes usually run one size smaller than American. A size 10, for instance, would be the equivalent of our 8. And continental sizing for dresses, blouses, pants, sweaters, and so on runs 38–40–42–44, roughly the equivalent of 6–8–10–12. For slips and bras, 80–85–90–95 is 32–34–36–38. European shoes don't have the range of widths ours do, and the sizes 36–37–38–39–40 are roughly 5 – 6 – 7 – 8 – 9 . Of course, as with anything you find at a thrift shop, try it on.

Men can look for beautiful wool overcoats, tailored suits, sport jackets, formal evening wear, fifties Eisenhower jackets, letter jackets, and pleated slacks. A tailor can make you feel like a million bucks for an investment of $25 and a morning spent digging through likely looking shops. A

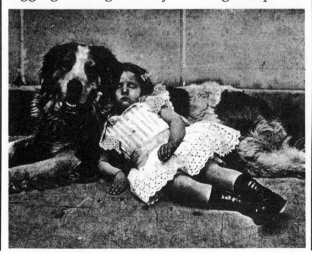

True costumes like this demand a self-confident stance and a bit of discipline, qualities exuded by the two sisters, above. Such old clothes were once cared for by a battery of seamstresses, laundresses, dressmakers and ladies' maids. Delicate antique clothes still demand very special hand care and a slower, self-contained manner of moving. Start dancing, and precious old fabrics rip and shred and seams reach the breaking point.

A fifties jewel-encrusted, beaded cardigan with matching knit skirt—both from Macy's antiques corner—flashed up with Woolworth's bangles and skyscraper sandals!

slim woman can look beautiful in a man's suit if she has it tailored to fit perfectly and wears it with the humor of Bianca Jagger: walking stick, hat and veil, a crisp cotton shirt or a bright silk blouse unbuttoned practically to the waist, with a tiny gold chain underneath.

Another material to look for is beautifully worn **leather,** which can always be relined; tent-shaped trenchcoats for men or women, suede jackets and sport jackets, brown or black motorcycle jackets with a diagonal zipper. Some people have good luck with shoes, like worn brown English oxfords, expensive old high heels, and weatherbeaten riding boots.

And for extraspecial evenings: fur boas, pleated or gathered taffeta skirts, soft velvet dresses or smoking jackets, all sorts of fancy cocktail dresses and ball gowns, and men's velvet evening jackets. One friend of ours found custom-made tails with a label from Barcelona for $5, including the

A terrycloth bathrobe wrapped with a long knitted scarf becomes a spring coat for boutique-owner Dianne Schools.

starched front. His tailor fit it to him for $30, and the couple of times he's worn it to formal parties he's had great fun imagining the stiff and rather large Spaniard who inhabited the tails before he did.

So, if you want to be cheap and stay terribly chic, remember that your best allies are thrift shops, used-clothing stores, antique clothing boutiques, swap meets in empty lots or out-of-town drive-ins, European flea markets (like Portobello Road in London, the Thieves Market in Amsterdam, or the Marche aux Puces in Paris), street fairs, block parties, and individual garage sales. If you're still unfulfilled, have your own "jumble sale."

A little-known bit of forties chic: The "captain's dinner jacket" in a light wool gabardine, from the collection of Chicago's Steve Starr Studio, worn by Mr. Starr himself.

If you have to go white tie, try the thrift shop route. A fifties spaghetti-strap gown is the perfect companion.

DISCOUNTS

Aside from all these used-clothing resources, smart dressers have always known that you can finish off a look very cheaply at mass-market discount and five-and-dime stores. Great bargains are there for the finding at chains like Woolworth's: smock tops;

Thrift shops are a godsend for parents on a tight budget. You can always find kids' wonderful hand-made things here.

An antique Philippine tea dress Larissa found at Harriet Love's in N.Y. Without an underslip, it's a party dress.

printed, pleated, or visored scarves; armloads of beads, pearls, and plastic bracelets; hooded sweatshirts and pants; bikinis or $1 Rio-style pants; short shorts; plain and souvenir T-shirts in cotton and terrycloth; country bandanas; summer shifts; and lots of interesting shoes, like the plastic, fisherman's Mary Jane, a ballet slipper flat you can wear on the street, the Japanese rubber-and-straw-soled shoe with a velvet thong, and the canvas cross-strapped old ladies' shoe. The drawback these days with the discount chains is that they are trying to merchandise "looks," which means that the quality of the fabric and construction is going down while you pay more for a "fashion" that will probably bore you next

Sofi Bollack and little Eleonore created the lush look of Victorian teatime with the help of a friendly thrift shop and plump pillows made of fancy remnants.

The formal social dance of the past has been bypassed by the hustle of today. But by outfitting ourselves in luxurious antique clothing, we can afford to partake in the old rituals. Here, Pierre Clementi in Steppenwolf approximates fin de siecle seriousness.

year or even next month. Too bad, but you can still snoop around and find classic designs if you persist.

Big-volume department stores, like Alexander's, Ohrbach's and Macy's, often carry the newest ready-to-wear looks from Europe at very low prices, but you have to shop carefully and know just what you're looking for so you don't get swamped by all the merchandise.

Ethnic shopping areas will often yield great buys. In New York, Jewish merchants sell their wares in crowded stalls on Orchard Street, and a lot of almost-whole-sale buys from Seventh Avenue manufacturers are mixed in with the cheap merchandise. Also on the Lower East Side are the Russian shops around St. Mark's Place, which carry about the same merchandise as the government-run tourist shops in the capitals of Eastern European countries—peasant blouses, challis scarves, carved wood boxes, painted eggs. On Fourteenth Street there is a vast hubbub of Puerto Ricans shopping discount stores with bins

The jacket: Chinese silk brocade. Era: pre-Communist. Point of purchase: Palm Beach Thrift Shop, $10 (plus tax).

along the sidewalk, and way uptown is La Marqueta, the enclosed Puerto Rican market area with stalls running under the elevated tracks of the New York Central Railroad. These street markets are not limited to clothing and household goods—you can always pick up some compatible food, like blinis on St. Mark's or Caribbean plantains in La Marqueta.

Some people stroll by Fifth Avenue department store windows for entertainment, but shopping older urban areas can be a much less expensive pastime. No matter what city you visit, seek out the old neighborhoods with their thrift shops and discount stores. You can spend a fine afternoon looking for wonderful bargains, and finish it off by devouring an adventurous local meal.

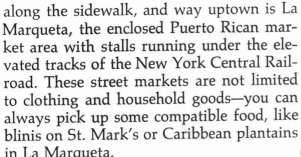

Genevieve Waite loves her
soft apricot crepe de Chine bed
jacket for summer parties.
Totally hand-stitched,
it was $2 at the Hollywood Swap Meet.
Her son Tamerlaine is less fond
of his new school uniform.

DONNA KARAN

Designing Woman

Donna Karan has been designing at Anne Klein since 1971 and she's now reached the venerable age of twenty-nine. She's a smart cookie with a real feel for the Anne Klein customer . . . a woman who likes to dress in fine designer sportswear. Donna ought to know the customer. At fourteen she was selling up a storm in a Long Island dress shop. Her passion for making women look better never stopped. Three years ago Donna said she thought a woman could get away with a pair of good black

Donna giggles with a model before a show.

pants, a good black skirt, black turtleneck, a pair of boots in a neutral color, straight-leg jeans, and a fabulous belt. "The big word is function," she said then. "Everything has to work together." And today? She's still all for neutral colors. How does she feel about tailored classics like the blazer when the fashion code word is soft? And what about the rules in the Dress for Success book: a woman will move on the job if she wears a sort of uniform made up of a conservative, blue three-piece skirted suit, a light or white

blouse, and plain, low-heeled pumps. With an executive's briefcase, gold pen, and attitude. And never, never boots....

"The tailored blazer I did a few years ago isn't out. But fashion would be boring if it didn't change. Today there's much more inventiveness in fashion. Finding that one accent that changes how you look. Pulling clothes together you usually wouldn't pull together. Not looking as matched. Yesterday, for instance, I was wearing a pair of 'Garbo' pants that I did four years ago. I wore a different shirt—crepe de Chine, unbuttoned, with the sleeves rolled up— then tied a softer sash belt around it and wore my ballet slippers. I was working with a soft look. One day I might wear big . . . a big pair of corduroy pants and a bulky sweater and the next day, go slim. That's why I don't think there's any dictation of a proportion in fashion today. It has to do with how I feel today. Ladylike, sporty, sexy.

"I never want to go back to feeling con- 99

stricted in clothes, putting myself together uptight, like in an A-line skirt with no movement to it. If you can't get your hands into a pair of pockets and move around in your clothes, it's not worth it! I can wear a piece from my collection year after year, but I'll change the way I wear it, the attitude. Like the big suede skirt I did three years ago; that was the biggest investment of anything! It's not that there's a major change in fashion now, it's just how you're wearing your clothes. Like taking a sleeve, pushing it up, wearing a shirt more open, sexy.

"I was approached to write a book like Dress for Success. But I believe that a woman's professional clothes have to come from the inside out. The clothes are never going to make the woman. To be successful today a woman has to be professional, have a clean-cut head. Keep her body and mind in shape. Stay clean and kempt. And be smart enough to look in a mirror to judge for herself what's right and what's wrong on her. Clothes have nothing to do with success. But I guarantee you that if a woman's together, she's going to know enough about herself to look outta sight!

"I believe that feminism comes through a woman's body, from the inside out. A woman who is uptight is never going to get free. Her movements . . . her body should be toned up, able to move, not stiff. Then she puts on clothes that work for her, that move with her. The uptight woman is just too afraid to look in the mirror. You've got to experiment and not be afraid. The European woman, for instance, works at it. A lot. She's not afraid of change. With change you can find out about yourself and what your style is. Believe me, when a woman puts on that thing that looks right on her, she's going to feel great! And when you have an assurance about yourself, honey, you can walk into any room and command anything. But you've got to work at it. It doesn't come easily."

Above: designer's table . . . sketch, box of Biba cosmetics, Rolodex, ashtray, WWD, coffee mug.
The sketch is just one of dozens that will end up swatched with fabrics like those on the wall behind Donna.

EWA RUDLING

Ragpicker Deluxe

Ewa Rudling is a deluxe ragpicker. She directs and paints her life in muted tones. In her large white-and-silver Paris photography studio everything is mobile. Ewa uses all of her furniture and her own clothes as accessories in her detailed and refined photographs.

"I want to be like a mop of quality. Nobody can ever say I look dirty, because I dress on purpose in dirt tones. I dye most of my clothes dust brown, dust gray, and so on. A few years ago I saw the film Trash and was shocked to see someone furnishing their house with things retrieved from garbage and getting dressed out of rags. At that time I was really living in luxury with a wealthy husband in a three-floor house surrounded by a garden.

"When I left, it was total poverty and a long struggle. When you are, or when you become, poor, you also become very inventive. You find yourself taking in things you normally would not have looked at before. Like an ant, you gather other people's discards that, with a little thought, they could put to use themselves.

"After a while I accumulated so much stuff that I started making money from it to pay for my photography. I would hold 'chiffon parties'—I would take all the things I thought were good to sell: clothes, jewelry, objects, suitcases, shoes, hang them all over the studio, and let everyone know that a sale was going on. People would bring other people and I would get rid of all the clothes in one go, and often also acquire new ones or simply exchange. It's the best way to clean out your closet and make money.

"Of course, by that time you have left your pride far behind you . . ."

SPORTS

At one time, sportswomen looked precisely like sportsmen—there was no room for good looks in competition. But now we can have our cake and eat it too. Style is so free we can look as feminine in a man's football jersey as we can in a ruffled tennis dress. Today, more and more women are wearing professional athletic clothes as an almost day-in, day-out style of dressing. There are several reasons for the popularity of authentic sportswear, but their main attraction is functional, unchanging, unflappable design. Sports clothes are built for speed, endurance, power, and winning. And who can't use a little injection of that in everyday life?

With the advent of color TV, pro sports picked up electric acrylic colors—the Oakland A's suited up in Fort Knox gold, trimmed with Pacific Ocean green; and everyone acquired a taste for nice, tight-fitting, stretch uniforms over well-muscled, shapely bodies. Professional athletes say that looking good makes them play better; their uniforms give them that winning feeling.

Also, some sports clothes offer the cheap thrill of discovery. A Cheap Chic adept is going to go out and find the ones that haven't been discovered by Seventh Avenue because they offer economy with true style.

Last· year a friend of ours was driving through Ireland and stopped at an out-of-the-way sporting-goods shop in Galway hoping to discover some new well-designed uniform. The soccer things looked rather promising—those great T-shirts and striped socks—until she got back to London and visited Biba's department store, where the soccer motif had been so thoroughly run through the fashion grinder that little 75¢ soccer-ball-shaped change purses were up for sale next to the cash register. She decided there was nothing left to discover on God's green earth. But then came the import of the sport of motocross, still relatively unknown outside southern California and the Northeast, where the major events take place. She discovered a whole new world of clothes—high, sturdy leather boots with bright contrasting panels in the front, and beautifully cut pants with diagonally quilted leather pads along the sides of the hip and thigh. She was ecstatic. Since she was tall and skinny, the motocross pants looked great, despite the padding.

The cheapest places to find authentic

athletic clothes are sometimes out of the way, but it's worth bypassing your expensive local pro shop or tennis boutique. The best way to buy professional athletic wear is to look up sporting-goods stores in the Yellow Pages and give them a call. If they don't have what you're looking for, it's almost as convenient to order things by mail. You'll have to ask a male friend for a size approximation if you're sending for boys' or men's sporting uniforms, but if they don't fit, most mail-order houses will usually exchange them. Try the big mail-order catalogs, and for the less-popular uniforms, like rugby or soccer, send for information from the manufacturers listed in the back of this book.

The good feeling you get from honest-to-goodness sports clothes comes from their purity of design. They haven't been through the fashion mill of Seventh Avenue, and they still have that legitimate feeling. They're not yet made into the processed

American cheese of sportswear, bristling with unnecessary buttons, flaps, cuffs, and seams. Sports clothes still have the magic of childhood game clothes.

FLEET OF FOOT

Warm-up suits give you that fast-on-your-feet look even if you don't jog or play tennis every day. What thief would risk snatching your purse if you look like a champion sprinter? **Warm-up suits** are being manufactured in more styles and brighter colors. If you feel conservative, buy yourself a high-school-style warm-up suit in gray, fuzzy-lined sweatshirt material with a front-pocketed top. It's as comfortable for sleeping on cold nights as for shopping on crisp afternoons. The gray sweatshirts can also be dyed in darker colors to fit your mood. A $7 sweatshirt can be ordered from J. C. Penney's catalog in pale blue, yellow, red, or green, with matching $7 snug-fitting sweatpants, which won't look or feel as floppy as the loose, baggy, sixties style. Oleg Cassini makes a jersey warm-up and competition set with jacket, pants, sleeveless T-shirt, and tiny shorts, all in bright colors. The women athletes wore them for the ABC-TV Women's Superstar event at the Astrodome. Suzy Chaffee looked especially snazzy in her acid-yellow short-shorts combined with multicolored Peruvian-style patterned knee socks and black professional warm-up shoes.

Tennis whites are so popular these days that demand is rumored to be more than

the manufacturers can churn out. In the suburbs, many women have taken to wearing inexpensive, easy-care tennis dresses as their everyday uniform. If you have nice legs, a tennis dress gives you a good excuse to show them off. One problem with tennis dresses these days is that they have become a fashion item, and dashing, simple design has given way to all sorts of "cute" motifs and silly details. Tennis stars like Billie Jean King and Françoise Durr wear these flashy dresses because they consider themselves, quite rightly, to be in show business. Are you?

Sneakers are basic Cheap Chic footwear. It used to be that fashion started at the top and worked its way down; the feet were just an afterthought. But here we are in an era of tight money, and we don't have that much to spend on body coverings. To save money, we can displace our fascination with the minutiae of style and status to the foot—a foot dressed in a very expensive permutation of what was once a cheap shoe, the sneaker. Sneaker demand is up almost 25 percent this year. Of course, the sneaker is not only stylish, it's Good for You, like chicken soup on a cold day. Sneakers bring you back to childhood, high spirits, and magically high leaps.

In the haute monde of sneakerdom there is a competition of status symbols which easily rivals the Fifth Avenue battles of Gucci, Hermès, and Mark Cross. Sneakers don't have designers' names, they have signs: stripes, wedges, chevrons, and stars of status. And they have endorsements by the new media stars, athletes like Billie Jean King and Walt "Clyde" Frazier.

It started with the war between Adidas and Puma, companies owned by feuding German brothers. *Sports Illustrated* did an exposé on their buy-out of the athletes at the Mexico City Olympics, and for the first time, Cheap Chic students were exposed to the full stylistic possibilities of $30 leather-and-suede athletic shoes. Wrestling shoes, boxing shoes, high-tops, training shoes, track shoes, football shoes, soccer shoes, officiating shoes, tennis shoes, handball shoes! It was a mere hop, skip, and a jump from track and basketball shoes into tennis shoes and out onto the streets. Now you can choose from the Converse star, Pony chevron, Adidas triple stripe, and the Puma flying wedge. Somehow, those $11.98 Levi's feel a lot livelier when a pair of $30 wear-forever leather sneakers is peeking out under the cuff! If you want a man's sneaker, buy them 1½ sizes smaller than women's sizes.

SPEEDSTERS

Grand Prix drivers have highly romantic images. Just think of Paul Newman, Jackie Stewart, Steve McQueen, or Mike Hailwood. Yet the actual competition uniforms for speed are terribly uncomfortable and

The precision of a chronometer when seconds count.

hot. Their function is to protect the racer from contact with the ground at speeds hovering around one hundred miles per hour; and, in the case of Formula cars, to protect the driver from fire in case of an accident. None of these uniforms really breathe, which is one reason, along with fear and excitement, why professional racers often sweat off six pounds driving a two-hour race. But if you want to look like a Grand Prix driver without all the sweat, you can find Nomex-style, one-piece, mechanics' jumpsuits like the drivers wear. Bright orange is the sexiest color. Tight is the sexiest fit. (You'll need a seamstress to get it tight, unless you're a sewing-machine genius.)

Motorcycle gear, no matter how hot or uncomfortable, is still an evocative style of dress. "Leathers" have symbolized anger,

Racy jumpsuits built with style for speed and adventure.   109

Terry Melville: a plain gray sweatshirt and sweatpants. She wears them weekends, working, even out at night . . . watch!

Sweatshirt in the office? Sure, over a white cotton man's shirt, with a soft wool riding jacket, hankie in the pocket. Terry turns up the collar of her shirt and ties an old bowtie, just so.

Far right,
Weekends? The sweatsuit again. With a 59¢ cotton farmer's scarf knotted around the neck. A man's patterned silk vest from a used-clothing store, taken in by the neighborhood tailor. A plastic stuffed-olive bracelet (her favorite) with an art-deco bangle in olive green. The cowboy belt comes from Uncle Wally, who works for the railroad in Ohio. The three-tiered, light cotton gauze skirt comes from India. The cat comes without pedigree, and is known as Sam. And the finishing touch is bright red athletic socks (99¢) with metallic copper flats from Shoe Biz.

Disco sweatsuit? John Travolta might not approve, but Terry does it up with a hot-purple fur boa from Macy's, fluff from New York's flower district, expensive ankle-wrapped evening sandals, and a tiny Oriental brocade evening bag. Plus a beautifully embroidered silk kimono found in an antique clothing boutique.

Snowy flirting in stylish wools from the local sports store.

you are "molding your body to the terrain in a lyrical fashion. Freestyle is basically a feminine sport, intuitive and developmental, as opposed to pure, competitive, rational, aggressive male sports."

Of course, you can wear the uniforms of these aggressive male sports without competing, and if you're interested, here are a few team sports possibilities.

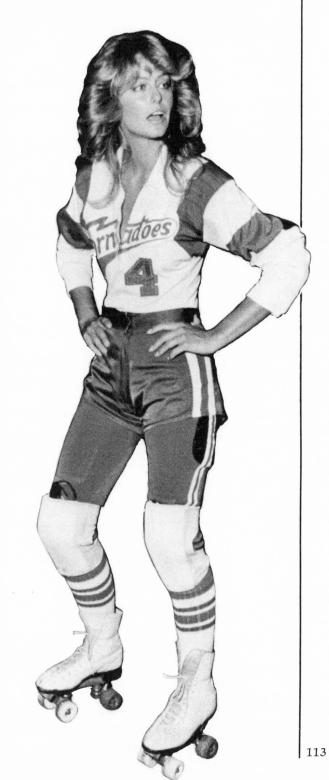

meanness, speed, and rebellion ever since Marlon Brando and the Hell's Angels. Leathers are particularly effective in black if you want to look tough! And they wear forever. A classic leather motorcycle jacket can take you through many cold winters in warmth and style—and if you happen to own a motorcycle, so much the better.

If you tire of black or brown, you can have a set of bright racing leathers custom-made by Bates in soft, thick leather with a zip-front jacket, contrasting zip sleeves, and black piping trim. To go full speed, get tight matching pants with a contrasting racing stripe up the side. It's hard for a motorist to miss you in Kawasaki green!

Ski clothes have always been very expensive; but behind the high prices lay good fabrics and excellent construction. Unless you live in a terribly cold climate, it is rather difficult to wear ski clothes as everyday wear except for the accessories like little knit caps and long johns. The beautifully stretchable one-piece ski outfits are like a second skin in freestyle skiing, where, according to Olympic skiier Suzy Chaffee,

113

TEAM SPORTS

Team uniforms can be raided to yield colorful jerseys, knickers, shorts, socks, and mini beach covers. Use your imagination—combine Rollie Finger's socks with Walt Frazier's shorts and an Yves St. Laurent silk shirt (or even jockeys' silks)!

Basketball players wear great rayon jerseys with contrasting binding on a low-scooped neck and cut-in armholes, or sleeved versions with a contrasting neck and set-in sleeves. Either style is in a supple, silky weave. Some men think a cut-in basketball jersey makes a woman look like a jock. But that's their problem! Swimwear designers have picked up on basketball trunks and copied them for men's trunks. The originals are synthetic satin boxer shorts with wide, stretch waistbands and stripes around the bottom or up the sides. Why buy a French designer's "tap pants" when you can get basketball shorts that have twice as much sass?

Basketball socks have contrasting stripes mid-calf, and some are built to have a "self-stirrup," which means they look like a pair of baseball-style socks: the foot and heel are cut out over a pair of contrasting, full-foot socks.

Hockey has a violent aura. If you're feeling particularly mean someday, you might want to suit up in a hockey jersey with a classic lace-up neck, inset saddle shoulders, and long sleeves with a white stripe inset above the elbow. A rayon-cotton fabric

The quick feet of Pele, the most famous soccer player in the world, move with the speed of the Puma he wears.

gives the jersey a good combination of silkiness and absorption, and they're very effective as minidresses. Heavy cotton socks reach mid-thigh, with stirrups under the feet and wide stripes above the ankle. The pants themselves are unwearable. They're just a visual cover-up for side, tail, thigh, and crotch guards, an assemblage of pad pockets. But those socks are wonderful.

Football pants with the laced fly and web belts are nice in white duck, but like hockey pants they tend to be designed more for protective pads than for the body. Football jerseys are an American classic with their double shoulders and yokes, striped arms,

The padded shirt softens the blows of rugby.

and gusseted armpits, and they are long and loose enough for summer dresses. Small sizes from the boys' department are nice for layering. One of the new fabrics they come in is a nylon mesh knit.

The psychological importance of color in competitive clothes is seen in the old home-team rule—a high-school team playing on their home turf was allowed to wear white uniforms. They felt white made them appear gigantic to their opponents and gave them the winning edge.

Soccer is becoming more and more popular in the States. Although it's equally as bone crushing as football or hockey, soccer jerseys have lace-up necks, short or long sleeves with contrasting collars and stripes, short shorts, and brightly striped socks with turnover cuffs which pull over the knee on women. Rugby jerseys in cotton with drill collars and button-placket front openings are very sporty in solids or stripes. Goalie pants for soccer players come with padded hips. (If you want to look even more curvaceous in shorts, check out Frederick's of Hollywood's padded girdles!)

Baseball uniforms are made of several layers. The raglan-sleeved, braid-trimmed, cotton flannel top snaps over a baseball undershirt which has solid-color sleeves and a white body. The knicker-length pants are worn over high-cut, striped stirrup hose and contrasting inner socks. You should check out the layered socks. Add a snappy high-crowned baseball cap and everyone will get hungry for hot dogs, mustard and Beer Day at Wrigley Field.

Letter jackets are a traditional "civilian" counterpart to all this competitive regalia. Like *American Graffitti*, they epitomize the hot-rod era of the fifties and sixties. Sporting-goods supply stores that carry uniforms

Skateboarding is great for the body!

Get healthier and happier jogging your way around the city or country as Sue Murray and Ingrid Boulting do.

115

Japanese designer Issey Miyake likes to "shock people with ideas."
Study these clothes and you will find motocross-style knee pads
on the leather pants, flat English riding boots and football-jersey-sized
tops over tights. All rather stunning ideas .

Waiting for the right moment—leather clad, ready to go.

often carry letter jackets. They have been the rage in Paris for sometime now and sell for $100 over there. The classic letter jacket comes with leather sleeves and slash-pocket trim; a reprocessed wool body; stretchy striped collar, cuffs, and waist, and a snap front. If you don't want to spring for a jacket, a letter sweater is always stylish around the Beach Boys and the Dell Vikings. And a cheerleader's heavy sweater with crew neck is the cat's meow.

INDIVIDUAL SPORTS

Fencing jackets are usually too stiff to wear comfortably, but they have a unique, time-worn cut and come in pleasant cotton fabrics.

Judo is a more promising area for Cheap Chic: a judo ghi is made of pure cotton duck with a wrap front and dropped shoulders. We have seen them made in a diamond-quilted cotton duck with triple stitching on the sleeves. They look beautiful over soft white pants, but be careful about picking the color of the belt you wear! You don't want to get challenged on what you thought was merely a point of fashion.

Golf is the sport responsible for introducing those bright, bold colors into weekend sports clothes. Professional golfers like Carol Mann always look terrific in their bright mini golf skirts and matching tops, socks, and gloves. But that's because they have contracts with the manufacturers and can afford all the mix and match, since the clothes are free. Golf clothes are really rather difficult to put together with others, because the trim of the skirt is usually quite strong and demands a matching top. If you can't afford several sets of golf clothes, perhaps the best item from the golfer's repertoire is the visor, which looks especially striking over a crisp cotton scarf tied peasant-style at the back of the head. Golfers' fingerless gloves are rather interesting, and the classic fringed golfing shoes look beautiful (without the cleats) for city or country walks, sort of like saddle shoes with an extra spin on them.

If your self-image tends toward **hiking** into the sunset with a copy of *Field And Stream*, the L. L. Bean catalog from Freeport, Maine, is a must. They have everything from the puff-ball eiderdown ski jackets you see on every school kid to all the woodland fantasies: an Australian bush hat with built-in mosquito netting, Lees Frisco corduroy jeans, wading shoes, fishing jackets, hiking boots, rain suits, suede musette bags, leather and twill haversacks, and a virtual wonderland of roughing-it paraphernalia which translates perfectly to city living.

The personal twist that makes active sports clothes amusing to wear every day lies in taking them out of the context of their particular sport and customizing them to your whims. Mix a baseball shirt with a wide seersucker skirt and wrap it with a soft leather belt. Wear an oatmeal wool tunic over bright hockey socks and a turtleneck in the winter. Wear satin boxer shorts with nothing else. And put a tough but well-fitting leather motorcycle jacket over a skimpy silk Halston dress. Use these clothes with a certain disdain for their original function but an appreciation for their functional style, and they will inspire you to keep a lean, lithe, lanky body and an aura of nonchalant sexuality.

HELENE DE BARCZA

College Clothes on $150 a Year

A college student on a tight budget, Helene has nevertheless managed to work up her own personal style. She's nineteen and a freshman at Hunter College in New York.

"There aren't as many jeans and boots around school as there used to be. I think people want to look nicer. So you see more espadrilles and longer skirts, dresses made of that Indian muslin with big belts around the waist.

"Since I only have a budget of about $150 for the school year, I have to be really careful with everything I buy. Most of my clothes are in solids; I have only a few stripes and prints. I wear a lot of boys' shirts, Eagle Brothers shirts from my old school uniform. I have six- and seven-year-old hand-me-down turtlenecks, a couple of sweaters that are two or three years old, lots of jeans from the army-surplus store and a longish dress I found at a department store for $20. But I always wear scarves, which makes things look special. A lot of my money went for my boots—the leather ones cost $60 and the denim ones were $30 at Chandler's. Then

I've got some leather espadrilles and a similar pair in cloth, and a pair of dressy shoes, but never for school.

"In the winter I wear this black thrift-shop skirt almost every day, with a shirt, a scarf around my neck, and a chain with little charms on it from friends. Or I'll wear jeans rolled up over my denim boots, a shirt with a thin sweater over it, and a scarf knotted at the neck.

"The black and Puerto Rican girls in school really pulled a look together that is sharp and very inexpensive. They'll wear earrings, a bracelet, a little hat, an inexpensive Indian cotton skirt, or rolled jeans with a thrift-shop jacket . . . and they look fabulous! It's not the budget, it's the imagination.

"On the weekends, I wear old school sweatpants with cowboy boots and a shirt. It's cheap, and it looks different!

"Sometimes I wish I had more money. I'd love to have clothes, but I don't want to own the same kind as the kids with money. Some of my things may look similar, but I think I always wear them differently."

ETHNIC

Ethnic clothes are in a certain disrepute these days. Lips curl at the mere sound of the word, and it's easy to understand why. Mass manufacturers have cheapened, bastardized, knocked off, diluted, and wrung the juice out of ethnic looks. And on top of all that, ethnic clothes have the gall to be bright and colorful in this depressed era of ours. But so what! Ethnic clothes can make you feel like a million bucks if you pick out the styles congenial to you. You can feel as if you're traveling to the Peruvian Andes as you set off for a business appointment; feel like you're off to a Hawaiian pig roast when you're actually en route to a leftover supper.

There's something about wearing a garment that's the product of another culture which is adventurous, even daring. If you have a beautiful printed silk kimono, for instance, you have to acclimate yourself to the bright, contrasting colors, to the sensual feel of the silk lining against your bare skin, the looseness of the sleeves and slit sides over a bare chest. You even have to move differently, because if you storm about a room in a normal Western way, your kimono will fall open. It gives you more body awareness—you quickly sense where your elbows are or you soon find the long, hanging arm of your kimono draped in the soup, in the salad, or up in flames.

The really special thing about ethnic

clothes is the fact that they are totally original. And when you blend in some exotic garment with your own well-worn and well-loved wardrobe, something interesting is bound to happen. (Just spend half an hour in your room with the radio blasting and start acquainting your new ethnic purchases with everything in your closet. You're sure to come up with a special look.) Ethnic clothes can be worn in a subtle way. They can be as classic as a tweed skirt if you think of them as individual garments rather than as parts of some exotic costume—if you take them out of context.

The trick of buying ethnic is to get a sense of the garment's inherent style and feel, independent of the rest of the outfit with which it's usually associated. Do with it what you will. Ethnic clothes seem to lose their vitality when foreign manufacturers move into a country and set up shop for mass-marketing designs that once had a very personal feel. After several years of these mass-manufactured imports, we have reached the point where we can select only the best. People are learning to look twice before they buy something with an ethnic air to it. It has to be a very special item; otherwise, you will be branded a hippy, and no one wants to look that dated! Selectivity pays off. In a few years, you won't be able to find true ethnic clothes anymore.

Sometimes it is easier to find national dress in the shops of America, like the Old Country stores along Clark Street in Chicago. A friend of ours was driving through Czechoslovakia several years ago and wanted to buy some typical Eastern European peasant scarves. There were none to be found in the bustling department stores of Prague. Yet, you can find them easily in New York. It seems that immigrant groups in the United States have held onto their national dress as a means of asserting their national identity; in the host country everyone rushes headlong into the future.

Lesley Jean Goldberg has made an art of the way she dresses, managing to put to-

The most elegant nomads of the Sahara desert are the Touareg tribe in Niger. Their loose robes, head wrappings, silver jewelry, embroidered money pouches and garments are all purchased at the market in Agades.

124

gether a very luxurious ethnic look without having the money to travel around the world. Lesley is an artist who works in soft sculpture, creating strange, attenuated people with looks of bland astonishment and plenty of sexual paraphernalia.

She assembled her beautiful wardrobe in San Francisco, where she haunted flea markets and used clothing shops, and cultivated friendships with the dealers who make trips to Africa, Asia, and the Near East. She has

Emmanuelle Khahn designed this graceful handkerchief skirt, the trim patiently embroidered by deft Roumanian artisans. Venitia finds it an ideal outfit for the squash court.

amassed so much jewelry that some hangs as decor in her house and the rest spills out of a big, beautiful Japanese mother-of-pearl chest. She has big, heavy Russian pieces, necklaces and coins, and silver and amber from Morocco, Ethiopia, Afghanistan, the Berbers, Turkomans . . . rare coral and enamels, carnelian, turquoise and jade rings, mammoth opalescent Dutch beads, African trade beads, Peking glass, ivory, carved blood-red cinnabar, bone and coral. She spends a lot of time at her collecting but pays very little for these very special pieces. She knows the value of things and has paid her dues learning where to get them.

Lesley has, she admits, more jewelry than clothes, but her favorite dresses carry out the ethnic style: a beautiful quilted-cotton Russian coat that she wears lining-out; a kimono found at a flea market that she recut into a loose V-necked dress because the edges were frayed. She loves soft silks and panne velvets, and when she's not wearing one of three extraordinary robes, Lesley puts her tops and dresses on over a long black velvet skirt and expensive boots, or mixes ethnic pieces with Victorian antiques. Lesley always looks like an exotic vision, a traveler back from Timbuktu loaded down with luxurious booty.

Martine Sitbon does travel. She says that dressing well is not a question of money. She doesn't buy ready-to-wear but looks for the special items that really please her. For about ten years she's dressed in old clothes from her grandmother's attic and thrift shops, but now she's turned her attention to antique ethnic clothes. "They're colorful and not sophisticated. I like a prophet look, large white Moses robes! I dream of Cecil B. DeMille movie clothes walking around, beautiful wool burnouses and big cotton djellabas. And I think makeup and kohl is important to accentuate a mood. I see it as an exaggeration, a kind of daily theatrics. Every day you wear a different mask. You put your mood on your face with makeup, and it, in turn, affects you and the people around you."

If you or one of your friends is about to take off on an exotic journey, here are a few observations and hints about the special finds you can discover while traveling.

126

Markets Around the World

Long before there were shopping centers and supermarkets, specialty stores and boutiques, goods were being traded in open or large covered markets. People gathered at regular intervals to buy, sell, trade, and gossip. The marketplace was the center of town as it still is in most country villages outside North America. Village markets in any country always seem to generate excitement. They are a feast for the eye as well as the place for cheap finds.

The first buy is a local **basket** or bag. The Majorca/Ibiza straw basket is now an essential international summer carryall. Everyone who visits these islands off the Mediterranean coast of Spain buys one. The shape and flexibility of the basket are so practical that stores all over the world carry it as a steady item. In some countries the basket may turn out to be a net (like the *filet* in France), a knotted square of cotton from Japan, a stiff, round basket reinforced with metal shipping bands from Jamaica, or the goatskin bag of southern Morocco.

Make sure to find a light basket for long-distance trekking.

Markets are usually divided into stalls, and most of the time you will find the fruits and vegetables in one area, the meat and fish in another, and then an area for clothes, kitchen utensils, and crafts. The fabric and clothing sections are very different from market to market, depending on the abilities, ingenuity, and needs of the local people.

Each country and each province within that country has a set of traditions and clothes which by now take a trained eye to spot, since the whole world is becoming increasingly Westernized. People who like unusual clothes are quick to discover the find that is not imported at an enormous markup. Clothing sold at the marketplace may look attractive and colorful to the foreign eye, but it is there primarily because it is functional, durable, cheap, and usually made of local raw materials.

What to Look for in

EUROPE

Europe is the Old Country where fabric and color know-how originated. To learn how to recognize quality sweaters, for instance, step into a truly British shop and finger all the cashmere sweaters until you appreciate the difference between synthetics and the finest of wools. In France, Switzerland, and Italy, buy a yard or two of the most luxurious fabrics—crepe de Chine, georgette, or peau de soie—make a shift or wear it as a head scarf. If possible, always buy fabrics in the country of origin, where you get the advantage of local prices.

BRITAIN is famous for its quality sweaters. Shetland and lambs' wool can be found all over the country in chain stores and Woolworths at decent prices. Tweeds at all price levels are also a perennial item, particularly in Scotland, where weavers have a way of blending earthy colors that take your imagination back to the highlands. In Scotland the multitude of clan plaids sell by the kilt or by the yard.

IRELAND knits some of the warmest white wool sweaters on any side of the Atlantic Ocean. They are worn by everyone, whether they work the land, do office work, or simply pub crawl in Dublin. These sweaters are also perfect for the ski slopes of the Alps and Colorado, wintry campuses, and city streets.

SCANDINAVIA has all the best local clothes in the back country. The northern countries still have a strong folklore tradition which keeps local costumes dancing through the villages. In Norway, Sweden, and Finland, the country women wear white embroidered shirts with wide, embroidered, handwoven wool skirts over petticoats. They usually add a white apron and a bonnet (which we can do without today), but the tight, little, laced-up bolero completing the outfit is appealing. New ones can be found in the general stores and at local dressmakers, used ones in the secondhand shops. In Norway the best buys are the colorful sweaters with plain backgrounds and geometric patterns that start at the neck and expand toward the chest. They are sold as cardigans or crew necks, and if you have the time, they can be knitted for you in your own choice of colors if you can find a willing pair of hands.

Sweden excels in contemporary sports clothes, found in most of their department stores. There is a Swedish army coat which strikes many men visitors as being very practical. It's white canvas lined with sheepskin, with large pockets, and is cut, like all military clothes, with great classic proportions. The Swedish army coat can be found used in surplus stores or made new for a reasonable price at any military tailor. It looks good soiled, but if you like it white, wash it often in lukewarm water and let it dry away from direct heat.

GERMANY makes sturdy and efficient items without frivolities. The styles are often stiff, the colors muddy. Walking shoes are strong and well-made, but the Germanic forté is leather—coats and jackets that last a lifetime.

HOLLAND has its share of sailors' outfits, and Amsterdam has a "thieves' market" (or flea market) with a lot of good antique clothing.

BELGIUM: In no other place in the world are the women so agile with their fingers as the lacemakers in Ghent. Try replacing a worn collar with a dash of exquisite Belgian lace, or buy it by the yard to blend with other fabrics for a dress.

FRANCE, like the rest of Europe, has great local weekly markets where you can find things not sold in stores: slippers, wooden clogs with straw outside and sheepskin inside, large calico aprons, peasant blouses, long cotton underwear, head scarves, and fabrics that reflect the temperature of the region. Brittany has lots of rain; therefore you can be sure to find good sailors' raincoats and navy sweaters. The Riviera basks in the sun and produces the tiniest, best-cut bikinis in the world, as well as a whole array of light cotton sportswear in warm colors. Markets, small shoe stores, and department stores all carry the marvelous walking shoe known as "l'espadrille." It originated as a peasant shoe made with a canvas top and a light flexible straw from Algeria, ideal for weaving into a most comfortable sole.

French people have a knack for redesigning functional wear into appealing, must-have-it-in-your-wardrobe pieces of clothing. The espadrille became the most sensible footwear to own for men, women, and children. At first you could buy it only with a flat sole. Then Yves St. Laurent spotted a Basque shop near his first ready-to-wear store which handmade the shoes with an elevated wedge and laces to tie around the ankles. He contracted the Basque workshop to turn them out exclusively for his boutique. Flowers were embroidered on the canvas, and the colors became wilder until everyone caught on that the espadrille with an elevated heel was really the happiest and most comfortable shoe around. Now they are manufactured throughout the United States and Europe in a great variety of shapes and sizes. Chances are that you will not find a cheaper shoe except for the weird, functional sandal known as the "shrimping sandal," made of molded plastic.

SPAIN AND PORTUGAL both are a delight for people who have the patience and imagination to have their clothes custom-made. Ask around and someone is bound to recommend a good seamstress who will copy your favorite old shirt or whip up a skirt with hand finishing in the exact style you desire. Madrid was once famous for its suede and soft-leather shops that could custom-tailor anything you wanted in a few days. Now, as foreign manufacturers monopolize the market, there seem to be fewer shops like these. Yet the quality, color, and fit of the work of the small workshops and craftsmen found in Spain are very rewarding for people who love the feel of suede and leather. The Barrio Chino in Barcelona has the strongest boots (inspired by Frye) for a mere $25.00. In Majorca, ingenious cobblers make custom boots and shoes. Ordinary lace-up boots can be specially made with a small patch of Moroccan carpeting. If this costs more than your purse can afford, you can always pick up the best Spanish walking shoes—part canvas, part suede, with a sole made from recycled tires. Several people we know have been wearing them for four years or more. Pollensa in Majorca is one of the towns that specializes in this shoe. A similar style of sandal, locally called "Tijuana retreads," is available throughout the American Southwest at a very modest price.

ITALY is also crazy for shoes. There are shoe stores on every corner, and even the cheapest have great styles and colors, particularly in Milan. There seems to be more emphasis on men's wear in Italy. Good, cheap, and stylish suits can be found in many department stores.

CZECHOSLOVAKIA, HUNGARY, RUMANIA, AND POLAND are the places to look for hand embroidery on white cloth, meticulously sewn by diligent female hands. The tradition of hand embroidery began for filling trousseaus, but today these beautiful peasant clothes can be purchased in government stores and tourist shops.

YUGOSLAVIA still has a lot of folk crafts at fairly cheap prices which the local people take for granted. A good selection can be found in folklore stores and high-class souvenir shops similar to the shops in New York's East Village. These stores carry jewelry, costumes, luggage, and assorted crafts brought in by the peasants on market day. Farmers come from the villages surrounding the cities with sacks of knit socks, sandals woven from leather strips, vegetables, and cheeses for sale or trade. Mixed with all these goods are beautifully embroidered robes and intricate filigree bracelets that they regard as mere old clothing and trinkets. Bartering and trading between visitor and peasant is quite popular, especially when done with a smile and for the pleasure of the exchange.

Large cotton muslin peasant scarves can be worn many ways: babushka style, wrapped as a turban, tied as a halter or beach skirt. From Greece or Greek stores.

GREECE has, from time immemorial, seen its people dressed in shirts and dresses made from the off-white gauze that is woven on the islands. In the days of Socrates, the cloth was worn as a toga, and today it seems that summer clothes are returning to these loose, comfortable styles. Once again the mills are

weaving the white cloth that is so perfect for wrapping and draping. After you have covered your body, choose an open pair of sandals which slip around your toe. The Greeks really know how to make sandals that last, as well as using the prettiest colors for decoration. Jewelry found in Greece is particularly attractive and can run from the simple bronze cross of Mikonos to the bright blue glass beads taken from donkeys' saddles and strung into necklaces.

Russian peasant clothes: the woman's dress of the Ryazan province; the man's traveling coat is from central Russia.

RUSSIA is one of the few countries where amber is in abundance. Necklaces, bracelets, and rings can be purchased very reasonably at Beryoskas in the government shops catering to tourists who will pay in foreign currency. Another sound buy is the Chapka, that famous Russian hat with the ear flaps. Made of mink tails, fox, astrakhan, or rabbit fur, they will keep any head warm even in the coldest of Siberian winters. If you do go as far as Siberia, track down the secondhand shops—with luck you may find a local policeman's sheepskin coat in off white or brown. The superb tailoring, the fitted chest, and large collar make them very special.

The most Russian of all garments is the side-fastening, collarless, bloused shirt worn in khaki wool by the army and in beige/brown by the country people. The festive version of these shirts is made in white or black satin with embroidered ribbons at the cuff and neck, held loosely at the waist with a wide leather belt or a simple cord. The image of traditional Russia is that of a country woman wearing a long jacket over a loose dress with heavy boots, her head covered with a babushka or floral scarf of wool challis with pink and red roses mingled in among green leaves.

AFRICA

This is a continent where you can sit for hours at the marketplace with the robe maker and discuss at length the blue of a cloth, the zigzag designs his machine can perform, and describe what you want for yourself by indicating what you like on the people passing by. Most of the population in countries like Algeria, Morocco, Tunisia, Mali, Niger, and Egypt have been wearing the same basic type of clothing for the past two thousand years: pre–New Testament classics such as woven woolen capes that double as blankets, gabardine caftans, and large cotton robes for both men and women.

NORTH AFRICA is one of the least bastardized of all regions as far as clothes are concerned. The *souk* is the old open market of the large towns. You're well advised to take one of those self-appointed guides that crowd the entrance, because the place is like a labyrinth. These guides are usually young boys full of tricks and enthusiasm. Select the calmest one you can find since they can drive you crazy trying to make dizzy deals with their store-owner companions (to whom they will no doubt lead you at triple speed). You can wander in alone, but you'll find that all along the way young boys will walk alongside of you whether you like it or not. Once you see

These Moroccan women adorn themselves with their finest amber and silver jewelry. The huge, inlaid metal triangles add beauty but also secure veil and robe against the mountain winds. Silver kohl accents their eyes.

something you really want, you might as well get it right there, because you are going to see hundreds that look pretty much alike, and the few pennies you might bargain down are not worth the energy. Or, you can choose your cloth and trimmings for a *djellaba* (a long house robe) and go over all the details with the tailor: length of sleeve, side slits, etc. All this usually takes place over a cup of sweet mint tea. Shopping in Arab countries is considered an agreeable pastime; you meet, sit, chat, and exchange views. It is not an impersonal

Ever wonder how all the ethnics come together? Here's an English wool cap, Scotch cashmere sweater, tightly woven and patterned African bag, worn with traditional American blue jeans, legwarmers (they date back to the Ballet Russe), and snazzy midcalf cowboy boots!

supermarket or department-store operation where you dash in, grab, pay, and dash out.

EQUATORIAL AFRICA has body coverings, for the bush and cities alike, that are even more basic. The wide, loose shirts for men let the air through and can be bought at the market in a great variety of prints. The women wrap their heads with a large piece of cotton batik and wrap their bodies from bosom to ankles in a similar print. At the market you can get typically colorful African batiks with cameos of the local president or the late President Kennedy, General de Gaulle, and other political personalities.

In any country, check what the local people are wearing on their feet; it's usually the cheapest and most durable regional footwear. In this part of the world shoes are called *samsaras*, and can be found at the stall of the man in charge of leather at the general market. The same vendor will also have leather pouches worn around the neck or diagonally across the chest, which serve as a money purse for both men and women. These hand-sized pouches are worked in different-colored leathers and have many concealed compartments to store amulets, money, medicinal herbs, and photographs.

Venetian beads used centuries ago as bartering pieces, and no longer available in Venice, pile up in little mounds of swirling colors among the heavy silver bracelets in the alleyways. The blanket vendors sell carefully woven narrow strips stitched together to form assorted-sized blankets with geometric patterns and dazzling colors. If you arrive early at the bush or city market, you can get everything at almost half price —a friendship discount. Ideally, one should not require any other entertainment, because the open markets are so fantastic. As the heart and life of any region, they give you a real feeling for the country. In Nigeria and Ghana the heavy-work laborers wear a cotton patchwork sleeveless tunic that sells for less than 50¢.

All over Africa, the most venerated man next to the local chief and the medicine man is the blacksmith. He not only makes horseshoes but also fashions silver jewelry out of coins by melting and casting them in sand.

Henna-mud designs, lasting for two weeks to a month, both decorate and antisepticize. These designs took an entire day of skillful and ancient craftsmanship.

In Agades, Niger, we saw a European woman, amazed at the timeless, precise work of the blacksmith, give him one of her favorite Navajo bracelets to copy. The result was all the more interesting since it combined two very distinct and distant cultures.

A great part of the Niger population consists of the Tuareg or "blue people," who wrap their heads in a navy blue fabric that looks like carbon paper. The color from the fabric rubs off on their heads, which is the reason why they are called blue people. They are a nomadic tribe who roam the area carrying goods to inaccessible regions. A rugged people, they have for centuries worn loose, wide robes and turbans to resist heat, wind, and sand. The women gracefully wrap yardage of azure blue cloth above a long robe of white lace. When they have children, the long robe is cut at the waist so the baby can be breast fed. These people have become such masters at artfully using fabric that during the dawn dance they manage to make their headgear resemble a cock's comb, the animal they want to imitate.

Another nomadic tribe of that country are the Fulani. The men and women wear little pouches around their necks that contain small mirrors and a pair of tweezers to remove both the thorns from their feet and the hair from their foreheads and beards.

All over Africa, there is an endless variety of beadwork and the use of grass or straw for skirts, hats, and bags. Besides the marketplace, there are talented craftspeople who work in small huts tucked away in villages. If you can express what it is you are looking for, the local people will lead you to the artisans.

THE MIDDLE EAST

This area has a very limited selection of women's wear, except for the big white sheet exposing only one eye. (But you just might go for an Arafat type of head wrap.) Men are equally uniformed, in their long white robes and muslin turbans.

TURKEY has deep red velvet jackets and dresses which have gotten even better with age. They are often embroidered with gold or silver threads and can be retrieved from masses of smelly clothes in Ali Baba-type secondhand shops. Turkey is also well known for beautiful silver belts which, depending on the source and workmanship, run from about $40 to $300. Local shops in Istanbul and in many little villages display crinkled cotton shirts in a natural egg-shell color, with or without red stripes. The same garment can be found in knee or ankle length and are all very cheap.

JORDAN AND ISRAEL have the Bedouin woman's dress with the embroidered yoke, one of the most sensible long robes on earth. It comes in either heavy cotton or black velvet and is tucked under the breast all the way to the waist. When a woman reaches the middle of a pregnancy, it is untucked for extra room.

PAKISTAN AND AFGHANISTAN have been over-exploited for their mirror-embroidered

Baby stays snug in this little Afghanistan mirrored coat straight from the market-place in the mountains.

skirts and shirts, and the strong-smelling goatskin coats. Yet the women who live in the northern regions wear a type of clothing very different from that seen in the south. They are difficult to see because the women hide themselves behind a black veil with only a net insert at eye level, but underneath they wear large black cotton dresses with silver embroidery of great beauty, worn with heavy silver bangles. If you love boots and want to have a pair made that will be inexpensive but very special, see the cobblers of Afghanistan, who work in leather and make soft riding boots that can be ordered with or without embroidery.

INDIA has such a huge selection of cheap clothes that one really has to examine carefully before buying. The rush was so great on all the long cotton skirts, vests, Nehru type shirts and such that little attention was given to the quality of the stitching or the

134

cut. However, the people of India who still care produce some of the finest clothes such as the very popular *kurta* (white voile shirts with simple drawstring pants). Each province of India has an individual style—the state of Baroda, the state of Madras, and so on, each with particular colors and prints for the saris in which the women wrap themselves.

———————————

KASHMIR, the fertile and lush valley at the top of India, is a paradise for market lovers. It is the kingdom of papier-mâché—beautiful jewelry and jewelry boxes, painted with intricate miniature floral designs and then varnished to sparkle in the sun. Fur coats abound, but again, if you have one made, select the skins with someone who is knowl-

edgeable. The hides should be supple, the fur shiny. Work closely with the tailor so that the seams are not half done with weak thread and the length is correct, as Americans in general are considerably taller than the local inhabitants. Wolf, fox, and other skins can be made into coats for about $100. Embroidered shawls made of the finest wools come in subtle shades and are covered with hand-stitched paisley designs.

———————————

NEPAL, the small country that begins where India rises to meet the Himalaya Mountains, has quilted coats of heavy hand-woven fabrics that can be dyed and/or made to order. People there have a wonderfully unique way of layering colorful woolen garments when the cold sets in.

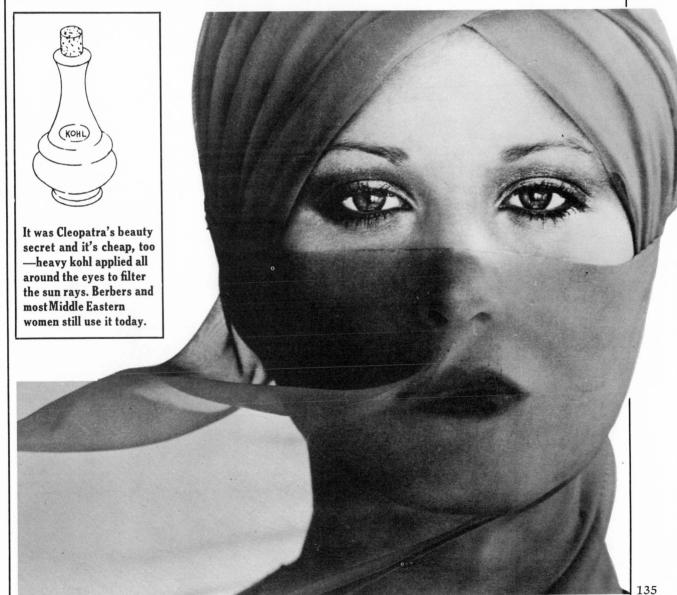

It was Cleopatra's beauty secret and it's cheap, too—heavy kohl applied all around the eyes to filter the sun rays. Berbers and most Middle Eastern women still use it today.

135

ASIA

As you will discover in the wrapping chapter, INDONESIA has developed maximum simplification in its clothes. Men and women wear a sarong or length of waxed batik wrapped around the hips as a long skirt. For women it is topped with a sheer voile, loose blouse edged with flower embroidery.

In BALI, the graceful and magical island, the young boys walk along the beaches with dried seaweed bracelets, delicate shell necklaces, and tortoiseshell rings. To find the best bargains in batiks, go deep into the market, as the peripheral vendors are out to get the hurried tourist for as much as they can. (For those who like pipes, the Balinese are also great carvers of ebony or bone pipes, chiseled with great love and artistry.)

When we think of Bali, we think of Dorothy Lamour, revealing sarongs, and the irresistible lure of strong, tropical perfume. We can't provide the Lamour or the perfume, but here are a few hints about the cotton sarong or pareo wraps. Cotton is the best natural fiber in a hot and humid climate because it allows the body to breathe freely. The best cotton now seems to be coming from mainland China. The most beautifully batiked designs are layered by hand, using one color at a time. Hot wax prevents it from going where it isn't wanted (thus the term *wax resist*). The delicate, sophisticated patterns are created layer by layer in a slow painstaking process. A very complex and fine piece of work can take as long as a year, just like the creation of a fine, hand-woven Japanese obi. Some of the typical patterns are Kawung (simple geometrics that look like colliding amoebae); Parong (diagonal squiggled stripes); Three Countries (a patchwork); Magamundum (the Chinese Cloud of Life); and Pekalongan (an exotic floral design incorporating the most complex wax-resist process).

The Chinese influence on European dress is spreading fast. Stylish Parisian Sofi Bollack picked out this old black and gold brocade and had it transformed into a classic coat-dress.

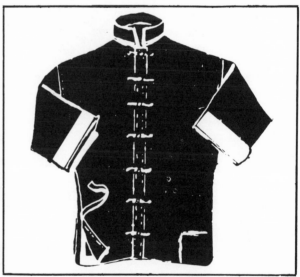

This basic kung-fu attire can also be an everyday jacket.

HONG KONG, Taiwan's neighbor, requires looking beyond the typical tourist traps to discover the really cheap and useful finds. There is a five-story building on the main street of the island called the China Em-

Kansai: Euro-Japanese design at its most exuberant. 137

Designer Betsey Johnson (read about her on page 185) goes to Hong Kong regularly on designing trips. Advice from her last visit? Almost everything is gone! Yue-ha is the best store—a department store chock full of mainland Chinese goods. The zappiest custom-made shoes and boots can be had for $30 to $60 if you know what you want!

porium which sells a great assortment of quality goods made in mainland China. It is an outlet for them to collect foreign currency, and the prices on most things are extremely reasonable. A friend of ours bought a backpack embroidered with funny animals which was a solid combination of silk and cotton. For her boyfriend, she brought back a navy blue quilted jacket which is as warm as a fur coat.

The "Chinese blues" are everywhere, of course. Both men and women wear those loose pants and straight jackets with frog fastenings. Depending on your inclination, you can get them either ready-made there or in any Chinatown in your own country. In Hong Kong you can pick up a smooth navy blue velvet jacket with silk lining and give it to a local tailor, who will quilt and custom finish it with special frogs in just a few days for about the same price as a jean's jacket and dungarees at home.

In China the regime of Mao brought about a sobriety in fashion which is very much in line with the Cheap Chic utilitarian idea. Yet there is a great deal of beauty and charm in the ancient Chinese robes, long skirts, and pajamas that are still worn today by older people in Hong Kong, Taiwan, and Chinese communities abroad. The amazing fact is that a lot of these decorated coat dresses can still be purchased at reasonable prices all over the world; they make most attractive at-home or party wear.

JAPAN

JAPAN is a treasure trove for anyone who appreciates refinement and delicacy in color and print. All the energy concerning clothes has gone into the same basic form for hundreds of years, the kimono. The only difference in kimonos lies in the fabric. The very formal way for a Japanese woman to dress is first to wear a knee-length white cotton kimono belted loosely with a length of dyed silk. On top of that goes a kimono of thin silk or rayon in a pastel color (usually printed with cherry blossoms) tied with an even more elaborate sash, then the final kimono of a color and embroidery dictated by the occasion. The formal kimono is truly an art form in itself, with paintings depicting an aspect of nature stitched in a world of glori-

Japanese designer Kansai Yamamoto's dramatic cape.

ously colored threads. The large sash or *hobi* securing the top kimono is carefully considered and almost as costly as the kimono because of the handwoven brocade from which it is made.

For everyday wear, the outer kimono for both men and women is of a flat woven cotton or wool in earthy tones, often with a geometric pattern discreetly running through the fabric. For our money, the *yukata* is the most accessible and practical kimono. It is worn by the Japanese either at home or for traveling to and from the bath house. It usually comes in white cotton printed with natural or abstract motifs in navy blue or mauve. In a spa town you will see everyone walking around in these robes, and it is a refreshing sight. The *yukata* can be purchased for about $10 in any Japanese department store or for slightly more in the Japanese stores in our country.

A variation of these house kimonos is the *hoppi* coat, most often seen in black with a good-luck symbol or dragon on the back. Another very practical Japanese invention are *zoris*, or thong sandals, which come in every form—flat, on stilts, with straw soles, with a cork platform, with velvet or plastic padding. The *tabi*, or white cotton foot covering that fastens on the side, completes the traditional wear. It is fairly inexpensive, but not very practical. Nippon ingenuity also includes beautiful but cheap waxed paper umbrellas priced so that you don't mind losing it.

A Nippon oil-paper umbrella serves well in America to protect this southern belle from the sun.

SOUTH AMERICA

Throughout South America there is a general feeling for simple hand-woven cloth that has multiple uses. The Indians turn out the most interesting combinations of colors and textures.

MEXICO, the sad and singing country that touches its white cotton clothes with vibrant colors, still produces a lot of attractive, cheap clothing. The market of Toluca, not far from Mexico City, sells a huge assortment of shiny, multicolored scarves.

Natural cotton is egg-shell colored. The shirts of this material that most men wear on Sundays in the villages are sold in the markets. They have long sleeves, narrow

This Mexican jacket of embroidered white wool goes for $25 in Paris, which is probably triple its price in Mexico.

pleats, and tiny bone or plastic buttons. In the south of Mexico, where it gets hotter, women's dresses are looser, like chemises, with large flowers embroidered on the shoulder straps and front to resemble big necklaces. Walking for long distances in the dusty heat is a part of life there, and the famous *huaraches*, leather-strip sandals, developed out of that need. Their flexibility and airiness have also made them very popular abroad.

Each country in South America has its distinct, almost national, sweater. In Mexico, the most appealing and classic is of thick natural wool with a shawl collar that comes up to your ears to protect your neck from the cold at night. Silver jewelry is cheap and looks it, but it is fun and imaginative. There are all sorts of brooches in butterfly or bird shapes, outlined in silver and inlaid with iridescent abalone shells, and small perfume bottles covered with cut-out silver flowers that let you see the remaining level of the liquid. You may find a *mariachi* leather belt studded with shiny nails, or an armadillo bag, which is both a curious and rather sad object.

GUATEMALA follows much the same line of clothing as its Mexican neighbor, except that the ponchos and shawls are even more common and often become a skirt, a scarf, or a head wrap at the twist of a wrist. You'll discover that each town has its own distinct weaving colors.

BRAZIL is so widespread and varied that it is difficult to pinpoint the many local specialties. The general markets are called *feiras*. In the cities they move to a different section every day. In the beach towns like Rio, you can purchase mercerized cotton thread at one stand, hand it over to be crocheted at the next stand, and have a bikini the next day for approximately $8. As an alternative to T-shirts, you can get some of those skimpy, spaghetti-strapped undershirts; they are made of cotton and take well to dyeing. A tougher look is that of the *cangaceiros*, the cowboys of Brazil, who wear all-leather chaps and tight jackets worn with wide sombrero hats. The saddle makers also produce large bags of different kinds of leathers. The prettiest and least expensive hot-weather clothes come from the region of Bahia. Men of all ages wear white cotton trousers and loose white blouses in the Macumba region. Women's skirts are long, extremely wide, and often trimmed with lace.

People in Brazil pay a great deal of attention to superstition, and many will carry a few charms to ward off evil spirits. The most popular one is the *figa*, a carved hand with the thumb stuck between the index and the next finger. You can find them for very little money, made out of the semi-precious stones that abound in Brazil.

The Amazon Indians have a way of weaving fine straw and dyeing feathers to create tickly necklaces. They also alternate beans, dipped in earthy colors, with little stones and tinted feathers, as is done nowhere else in the world.

BOLIVIA AND PERU have very colorful ponchos, gloves, and bonnets, knit with childlike designs, which keep the mountaineers warm and free in their movement. Whenever a traveler starts talking about the markets of South America, the conversation always comes back to the multitude of patterns in weaving. It is also an amazing sight to see women at the market wearing hats that closely resemble bowlers or businessmen's hats.

More booty from Mexico is this handpainted sequined skirt. Only sixteen dollars across the border!
Right, The South American Mix: A Mexican blanket skirt, Bolivian sweater and a coat from a Peruvian poncho.

CATALOGUE HITS

In the last few years, there has been a virtual explosion in the shopping-at-home field. There are catalogues for every occasion; items for every persuasion. The big three, J. C. Penney, Sears Roebuck and Company, and Montgomery Ward, offer an exciting new array of both fashionable clothes and transformable goodies like old-lady slips you can dye and make into summer dresses; painter's pants; and all sorts of work clothes. Each catalogue has a different requirement for getting on the mailing list, but often, if you order by mail from one, you will find yourself suddenly receiving catalogues from all the others. This can be either a blessing or —if you're on a tight budget—a curse. Some of these catalogues offer such enticing items it's hard not to send right off for them. Also, technological innovation has reared its lovely head among catalogues,

and there are many, including staid L. L. Bean, that offer 800-code (toll-free) long-distance calls. You simply pick up your phone and dial in your order. Charge it, of course. Many take Master Charge, VISA, and American Express. And since merchandise is returnable, shopping by mail can be a real convenience for working women who like to spend weekends relaxing (and don't consider shopping on Saturday a mode of relaxation).

THE BIG ONES

Since all catalogues change each season (or, in the case of the smaller ones, every few months) the specific items shown on these pages may no longer be available as you read this book. But we show them to give you a taste of the

kind of clothes—both fashion, and fashion-in-disguise—you can turn up in the pages of these catalogues. . . .

Here are some tempting items from **J. C. Penney's** catalogue. As mentioned in the first chapter, it's smart to buy clothes in multiples, choosing solid colors that make sense with what you already have in your wardrobe. Penney has interesting tank tops in strong solids like green, yellow, blue, ivory, and orange, at approximately $6. They come with matching drawstring pants. Classic T-shirts in pastels with cap sleeves go for the same price. They're good with skirts, or match them up with sports shorts with elasticized waists.

For wrapping, you can even get a pareo from Penney, with a matching bikini. Tie it at the hip or, to make a strapless dress for evening, around the bust.

Get their really sexy bikini (with top and bottom sold separately) and suit the style perfectly to *your* figure.

The leotards are shiny Antron and Lycra. They make nice maillots for swimming or exercise leotards when worn with tights.

Penney has a classic man-style shirt with a turn-up collar that looks great belted over a skirt—and it's machine washable as well. Or order directly from their men's pages for a really loose fit.

The "Savvy" section of the Penney catalogue says "you understand that understatement is elegant." If understated elegance is *your* understanding of style, this section might be for you.

And when you want to get away from it all, you can order a great big beautiful bed with linens designed by Cathy Hardwick—a terrific clothing designer—in soft watercolor pastels with lots of feminine flounces.

Night-time fashions from Penney's: you can sleep in the nude and still be well-dressed.

Montgomery Ward's Rita Perna, assistant vice president and national fashion coordinator, says "the dress is having its day. It's bringing the leg out of hiding with one continuous flow of fabric or matching skirt and top." Ward has a pretty, crystal-pleated dress in Arnel for under $40—the neckline can be worn either on or off the shoulder. This dress, like many of the big three catalogue clothes, comes in talls, and many come in half sizes as well.

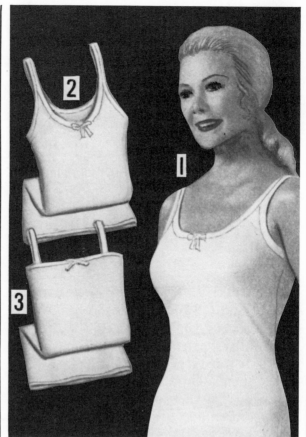

Ward's old-time undies: fabulous finds.

Also available is a beautiful shimmering Lycra four-way bandeau-look maillot bathing suit in a peacock blue that will knock your eyes out.

Ward's has equally enticing lingerie, but Cheap Chicers will enjoy rooting around in the back pages for items like the "straight-top vest" with a drawstring around the neckline and ribbon straps, just right for dyeing. (They also come with matching bloomers. In pink only.)

There are also cute "cuff panties" in pink acetate that must have been first offered around 1933.

The one-piece underwear is always comfy for wearing around the house, and the enterprising accessorizer could, undoubtedly, wear it around town with impunity, once dyed and disguised!

Rockford socks are classics and look great with mules: their little red heels show on the tweedy brown and beige ground of the socks. (They also look awfully nice with traditional pink ballet slippers on sultry summer weekends in the country, perhaps with an old slip dyed a dusky pink.)

You'll go ape over these socks. Cool, comfortable cotton with bright red heels to perk up your footsies.

"Cotton utility hose" are another Ward's find. They're *seamed* fine cotton in beige or taupe, three pairs for under $8. Just the thing for the Virginia Woolf look.

The men's work clothes section has a lot of intriguing items, like the fourteen-pocket canvas apron and the leather, two-bag carpenter's apron. The fourteen-pocket canvas apron might be just the ticket for free-lance photojournalists who cart around lots of cameras and film.

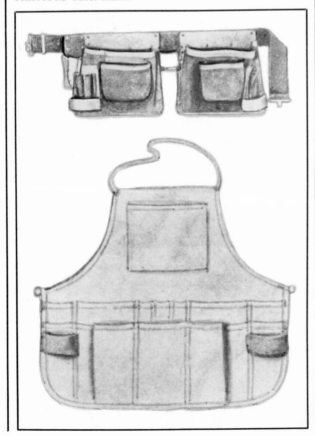

Sears Roebuck offers "designer groups" where two or so pieces work together as classics, like the outfit shown above. This soft lamb's wool, angora, and nylon sweater, tattersall shirt and tweed jacket, worn with pleated pants or skirt and handsome boots.

Their man's "shop coat" makes a perfect white summer coat with three big pockets, a snap-front closing, and side slits, all for around $12. You can also find "shop aprons" that are great for cooking.

If your look is more feminine, try their camisole and petticoat of eyelet embroidery. They're not 100 percent cotton, so you'd have to consult your local dime-store expert to see if Rit Dye will take.

Sears Western Catalogue has things like leather thongs, handwoven Indian-style blankets of reused wool (they make great rugs), and wide, mohair girths you can make into huge belts. They also sell handsome straight-leg chaps made of cowhide, buckstitched in white with a fringed trim.

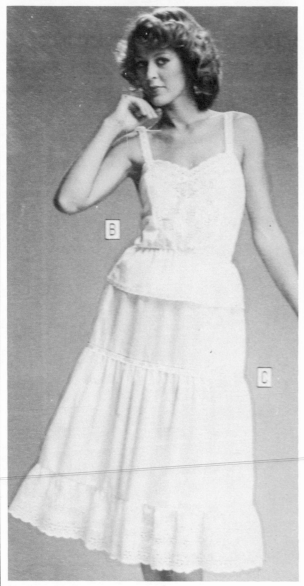

From super-macho leathers to super-feminine lace, Sears has got the goods.

The smaller catalogues range from the outdoor chic of L. L. Bean in Maine, Fulton Supply Company in New York, or I. Goldberg & Company in Philadelphia, to the high style of store catalogues like I. Magnin's or Bonwit Teller's. Here are just a few examples. Again, they're only representative of the kind of thing you might find. By the time you read this, most of the merchandise will have moved on. . . .

Trifles is a new catalogue from Horchow. For example, a soft gray dress with white collar and cuffs works any season, over a turtleneck, under a vest. They also have all sorts of lovely gifts, an enticement to give *yourself* gifts!

Viva Magazine Products sells really sexy lingerie through the mail, in case you'd rather not buy it in person, like this tiny Antron bra trimmed with scroll lace and matching bikini with teeny satin bows.

Frederick's of Hollywood has fabulous marabou-trimmed stilettos, springolator-style, in black, white, candy pink, powder blue, hot pink, red, or champagne. They're called Glamour Doll, and they're hard to find on Main Street!

Brownstone Studio offers classics especially useful for the working woman. We found this nice Anne Klein belt there, in good basic colors.

147

Sakowitz has a cunning catalogue that makes you feel you're about to read a fascinating magazine. Since their store is based in Houston, you'll find lots of things good for a warm climate, like a gorgeous raw silk, rolled-sleeve shirt with a shirred yoke, and gathered dirndl-waist pants with a narrow leg . . . both in a creamy ivory.

Chris-Craft is for the sporty life, offering lots of electronic gear as well as athletic gear. Their warm-up suit is in sweatshirt gray with bright red at the neck closure, and it comes in men's sizes as well. You can also find their rainbow-bright Chris-Craft Maine-style moccasins and boots, great for the out-of-doors, and hot sellers in Manhattan's most fashionable stores.

Adam York offers a heavy-duty tool bag of ten-ounce natural canvas with leather handles, straps, and reinforcements. You could probably get it cheaper by tracking it down at a supply store, but the catalogue offers the convenience of ordering by mail or toll-free call . . . and charging!

Kaleidoscope, out of Atlanta, offers special clothes suited for warm climes and very special gifts. These tank-watch faces are in white, red, or green acrylic with real lizard straps. They look great with sportswear.

Crafty Chris-Craft warms up the gray warm-up suit with a touch of red at the neck.

Norm Thompson promises an "escape from the ordinary," and offers all sorts of Oregonian outdoor delights. Classic tailoring, subtle colors, and high-quality natural fabrics make these a sure bet. They may not be cheap, but they'll last you a lifetime.

The Talbot's, from Hingham, Massachusetts, is instant Ivy League by mail. Where else could you find these monogrammed scalloped-collar blouses shown above in bright, innocent white with bluebell, hot-pink, green, red, navy, or yellow trim? Or the monogrammed crewneck Shetland sweater? You can find the sweaters for men here also.

The chic-est initials are your own, when they're monogrammed on this sweater from The Talbots.

The Horchow Collection was the first catalogue to merchandise a collection of exclusive, big-city status possessions like Rigaud scented candles, Cartier tank watches, Tiffany key rings, or Givenchy loungewear, and make them available to every U.S. citizen by mail. Definitely the catalogue for the sensuous shopper. And that toll-free number! You can call up until 10:00 P.M., Texas time, so those late-night impulses can be instantly gratified. You could call right up and order something like a $325.00 Georg Jensen 17-jewel watch with a totally blank chrome face. For an extra $16.50 you can get a one-inch-wide brown pigskin band. Otherwise, you'll just have to settle for the flat black, which isn't bad. . . .

Sportpages is outdoor chic all the way. For winter, terrific suede after-ski boots; for summer, all sorts of nifty terry and velour bikinis, robes, and overshirts. Plus tennis gear up one side and down the other, like a Diane von Furstenberg velour knit sweatshirt in glowing sapphire.

Propinquity, from Los Angeles, had our favorite lamp, Gladys Goose, for everyone who is still a child at heart! And for those of you who still smoke (shame!) a classic WWI oval-ended lighter that buyers always end up giving away to admiring friends.

So . . . have fun with the catalogues, and try to watch that 800-hot-line-itch.

President of Henri Bendel

"Everyone has an individual style. It can be born of all things, including necessity," says Gerry Stutz, the only woman president of a major fashion department store in the U.S. Necessity, in this case, is Henri Bendel, New York's most chic specialty store for women. Gerry Stutz's magnificent and unique feel for the look that's just beyond now encourages her special blend of individual styles to coexist at Bendel's.

"Fashion says, 'me too,'" says Gerry Stutz, "and style says 'only me.' It's your way of saying HERE I AM. . . ." At Henri Bendel, the only "look" you'll find will be your own, because Miss Stutz wants it that way. She saw today's woman coming years ago, and that woman was herself. Bendel's reflects Gerry Stutz's special attitudes about style.

"The way it was before with fashion, you really felt that to look right, you had to move to the new 'look' each and every season. What happens now is that a woman gets tired of wearing the same thing, and she moves, by herself, to change it. What we're involved in now is a time when women are becoming more self-conscious, thinking about themselves as special, unique, one-of-a-kind . . . and that's got to be how they look, too.

"What were once the focal points of fashion, big things like skirt lengths, are now only a matter of proportion. Pants, for instance, may seem more interesting narrow, but only because women become bored. Not because the fashion press or some designer says, 'JUMP,' and snaps his fingers.

"Do you know how a designer designs a collection today? By asking around about what women are going to want. They try to get inside women's heads! That explains the emergence of so many more interesting women designers, who are really reading their own minds. They design for themselves, and they pick up fans the way guys cannot. Because women who are that style identify with the designer's image of herself. As it moves toward less fashion and more style, women designers are more apropos. Sonia Rykiel designs not just for style, but perfectly for shapes: her body is shaped like mine. There's Rykiel, Chantal Thomass, Norma Kamali, Mary McFadden, Carol Horn, Donna Karan, Harriet Winter, Pinky and Dianne, and lots more!"

"So while a woman wants to be herself, she's immediately drawn to a style that's like her own self-image. She looks at the dame and says, 'Eh, that's like me!' And if the designer is good, she moves along and keeps up the momentum. Women are moving fashion today, not the other way around!

"I'm in the process of putting together my four 'uniforms' for the year. It takes time and energy. Effort is the sine qua non in dressing yourself. Style, even if it doesn't seem to, demands effort. A person with style and no effort can look just dreadful. There are people with a really clear, sharp sense of communicating themselves. I think

Barbra Streisand was the first contemporary watershed for looking like yourself. Style is talent, like writing or performing, and the more training, the more polished the style becomes. It improves with exercise. It takes work.

"Each season I pull together four things —two remakes from my closet, and two new ones. I put all my attention, effort, and energy into altering them so they fit me perfectly, together with the right accessories. I'm a perfectionist about details. I've never believed that anything goes . . . never have . . . never will."

WRAPPINGS

Wrapping the body is the simplest form of clothing and the most sophisticated. Some people consider the clothes of classic Greece to be the height of elegance. Today, millions of people around the world wear pieces of cloth draped and knotted and folded about the body. In Southeast Asia, men and women wear identical sarongs. In Africa, Masai tribesmen throw a large piece of orange cloth over their shoulders like a dashing cape. Desert robes and intricate turbans protect the Arabs from heat, wind, and sand. On the Indian continent, women wear a long length of fabric wrapped about their body, a sari. In South America, Indians only twenty miles from large cities still wear the simple loincloth. In America, Zuni women wrap fabric into skirts.

The art of keeping a piece of fabric on your body shows in the way you pull it, tie it, and work with the tucks and folds and bias . . . there are no buttons or zippers. For those of us who grew up knowing nothing but fastenings and more fastenings—zips, buttons, hooks, eyes, snaps, and laces—it

All it takes to gift-wrap yourself is a certain assurance about preventing that piece of fabric from slipping off your body. Christiana's discovery is to make a triangle out of a large Indian silk scarf, then with the long edge up, cross it in back and knot the points in front. Add a silver belt to determine the waistline, a whisp of point d'esprit tulle at the neck for drama and you have ingenious evening wear for next to nothing.

may be rather difficult to relax wearing just a flimsy piece of fabric wrapped between our bodies and the cold, cold world. But once you start playing with the idea of wrappings, it can become very exciting. All you have to work with is:

The fabric
The body
Your imagination

A combination of these three things can become the most sensual thing ever! What painting is more sumptuous than Ingre's *Turkish Bath*? How sparse it would look without the full, intricately wrapped turbans on the heads of the naked bathers. Draped fabric offers a soft, charming look in this world of stiffness and neatness.

Wrap up a skirt and halter, if you find yourself really down and out. You'll be back on top of the world looking totally unique. No one will mix patterns and colors the way you do, no one is going to wrap their body just the way you do, and no one has a

For a sexy summer skirt, take a large fringed shawl, hug it tight around the hips and knot it below the belly-button. If the fabric is slippery, add a safety pin underneath for security (and peace of mind).

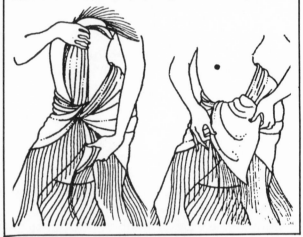

A sarong is traditional for men in Southeast Asia. It's as simple as a wrap around the hips, pull and tuck.

During her pregnancy, Marcia found the most comfortable covering around the house was a loosely held length of sari.

body to reveal that is quite like yours. You can't make a mistake. Wrapping is totally individual.

A girl who lives in Los Angeles makes full use of the warm weather—she pulls a long piece of peach jersey out of her drawer, wraps it once or twice around her body, plays with it this way and that, and finally settles on one style of draped gown for the evening. She has a talent for it, yes, but it's something we can all develop.

If you grow fond of this gentle, feminine look, you can buy yards and yards of silky jersey, Indian cotton muslin, antique scarves, Liberty of London prints, Provençal cottons, and Balinese saris; fabrics that stick to the body and don't slide around.

When you travel, pack a few folded lengths of fabric to soften modern motel lamps, change the color of the lighting, cover ugly bedspreads, hang as wispy curtains, and double up as beach towels and bikini covers. A few pieces of fabric can

The Bikini

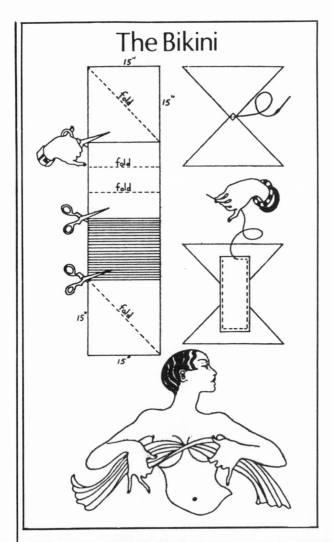

transform the mood of the grimmest institutional room—suddenly it looks personal and creative. You can do the same thing at home for a quick change of mood.

Inventive European models with little money soon develop a knack for finding bits and pieces to make into little, wrapped creations to express their very personal esthetic sense. Christiana Steidten always carries scarves to wrap into a strapless dress, a little bandeau top, or a floaty skirt, as you can see in the photographs.

There are endless ways of doing yourself up in fabric. To start, you might buy a three-yard length of light Indian cotton gauze, the best size for beginners. Take a look at the pictures in this section and start right in, twisting, tying, and tucking. One of the easiest skirts to create is copied from the Balinese. A three-yard length is wrapped

It's silly that the tiniest bikinis fetch ridiculous prices when it is so simple to create your own. It's just a twist of a wrist and two scarves. The ones shown here are 58 by 15 inches. For the bottom, cut the scarf on the solid line and fold on the dotted lines to make the back and front triangles. Fold the remaining material in thirds to make a long rectangle which is stitched in as the crotch; tie the corners at the hips and you have bikini pants. For the top use a similar scarf, same size, twist it in the center and tie snugly in back or at the neck.

What do you do when the occasion calls for a dress and all you've got is jeans? Christiana, like most models, doesn't even bother with dresses. But she has developed the secrets of wrapping. With three yards of fabric, she envelopes her body as if draping a column. She ties a little knot at the top, turns the fabric down like a narrow cuff and accents this simplicity with extra-special accessories.

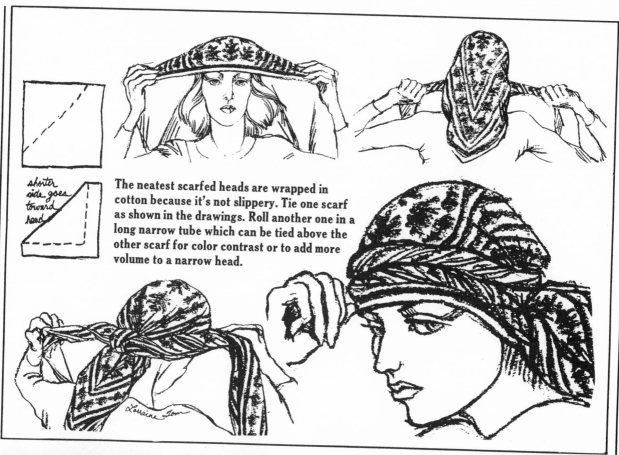

The neatest scarfed heads are wrapped in cotton because it's not slippery. Tie one scarf as shown in the drawings. Roll another one in a long narrow tube which can be tied above the other scarf for color contrast or to add more volume to a narrow head.

shorter side goes toward head

Acetate or silky jersey lends itself best to elegant wrapping. A skirt is a twist of the fabric and a tuck at the hip. Or use long yardage and invent variations on the same theme: Slip one end between the legs, shaping a halter top and strapless pantaloons.

Once in a while you may find yourself near water, wanting to swim but lacking a bathing suit. It's wonderful to go naked, but most places are still uptight about nudity outside the bathtub. With wrapping, you can always roll up your dress, pull the back through your legs, tucking the gathered fabric in the belt. Now you're ready to hit the waves!

around the waist or hips, the extra fabric is folded on top of itself in an accordion pleat at the front, then the material around the waist is folded over on itself to hold the skirt in place.

Rayon or nylon fabric is another inexpensive fabric to experiment with. You can cut yourself a sari length and still have lots left when you buy an $11 nylon georgette sari from an Indian import shop.

If you're uncertain with your knotting and tucking, add some insurance—a belt, tight at the waist, a brooch, or a big solid pin. In Bali they don't use buttons—the standard Balinese blouse is just held together in front with two or three safety pins. Most of the people use standard safety pins; the wealthier have more elegant models based on the same theme. You can put a security safety pin at the waist, the shoulder, or the center of the bosom and emerge with the cheapest chic on the beach!

Although it's quite difficult to get around a big city in wrapped clothes, you can still play with fabrics and patterns by wrapping lengths of cloth around your head. In the winter, nothing feels better than a nice tight head-wrapping. During the day, you can use bobbypins to set your hair in tiny pincurls and wrap it tight with a babushka. At night you may emerge with a superfluffy head.

One long scarf looks great knotted at the back of the head with the ends hanging down. Two Russian peasant flowered wool challis scarves look exotic wrapped and twisted over each other so that the patterns and colors contrast. Several scarves look fantastic folded and tied in the middle as a ponytail at the back of a scarfed head. That way you can have your "hair" and set it too.

Don't just stick to your neighborhood Singer Sewing Center. Polyester double-knits won't do. Try to track down the pure cotton and silks that make the best fabrics for wrapping. The range of silks carried at a little cubbyhole of a shop in Los Angeles called Oriental Silks is breathtaking. This listing hints at the wondrous variations of

The Halter

Another multi-purpose piece of cloth to own is this long rectangle of fine cotton or chiffon. For an instant top, put the scarf around your neck, pulling the ends out equally at arms length in front. Cross one over the other to tie in back. Depending on the length of the piece, you may even be able to bring the ends back around to tie in front.

fabric that still exist in the world: silk pongee, Poa Shan pongee, chefoo pongee, ya kiang pongee, pure silk chiffon so light it floats, China silk, Honan silk, spun silk for lingerie, Soo Chow brocade, silk satin, raw silk shantung, palace silk brocade, silk crepe brocade, Kuan Lo Siok crepe brocade, printed silk crepe, printed twill from Shanghai, silk satin tapestry, tinsel-mixed silk satin (said to be the most exquisite silk exported from the mainland), silk marquisette, silk brocade matting, crepe de Chine, Habotai silk, nubbly white silk, silk gauffer, and Po Po silk crepe.

Wrapped in white fox mixed with yards of tulle, Edita Sherman knows how to make that "grand entrance" and liven any party!

ZANDRA RHODES

Pushing Fabric to Extremes

Zandra Rhodes is an English designer whose chic is not cheap to her customers. But to her, and to anyone willing to work and push their imaginations to the utmost, the results can't be anything but individual and rewarding, whether one is designing clothes or just getting dressed for the day.

Zandra has been doodling, snipping, cutting, dyeing, sewing, pleating, and feathering clothes for almost a decade. Yet, today they sell in the hundreds of dollars, but she started with nothing other than her imagination, perseverance, and a totally fresh approach to what can be done with fabrics. Each new Zandra Rhodes collection becomes more personal, startling, and refined. Zandra's clothes are unlike anything you have ever seen or imagined. Solarized lilies, luminous pinks, ripples of silk jersey, an octopus of chiffon, yard upon yard of squiggled labyrinths unfurling to the tune of a mad samba, and now the grand elegance of minuscule pleats on long burgundy silk, and lace-entwined pastel chiffons.

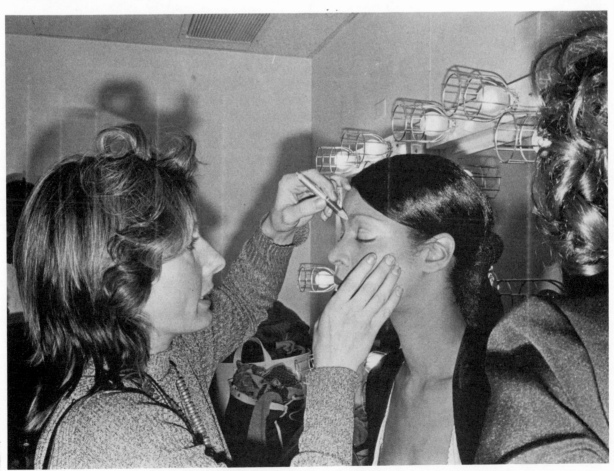

Far from trying to lead the same life as her moneyed customers, Zandra can often be found slaving away in her overcrowded London workroom wearing patched jeans and a silk jersey top over a black turtleneck, or driving around the States in a sleep-in van.

"I come from a very middle-class family near Dover, you know, sort of your average person. Well, I suppose my mother was rather extraordinary; she worked as a fitter in Paris for the couture house of Worth. She met my father, a truck driver, at one of those typically English ballroom dancing contest evenings. She would wear incredible multilayered bright tulle dancing dresses.

"Later, my mother taught at the college where I studied, so I never learned pattern cutting and practical sewing because that was the class she taught! Instead I studied textile design and went on to the Royal College of Art in London, where Mary Quant and a lot of people with new ideas were studying. That was in the pre-Carnaby Street days of London, and when I started taking my textile designs around to be executed, manufacturers kept saying, 'We can never sell these.' So I set up my own print workshop with a friend. And then when boutiques started springing up everywhere, I opened one with another girl, but we fought like crazy because she didn't like my designs. So I thought I better try my luck in America.

"I had to take a crash course in pattern making and then learn how to fit on a stand. I had no idea what the grain in fabric does. I made some terrible mistakes, but at least I had no preconceptions of how a dress was constructed. It was so lovely for that reason . . . bodices falling all over the place! I'm still learning, and it's only been a few years since I've actually sewn pieces of fabric together.

"Now when I show the collections, I stage a spectacular. For the first one I wanted a great Brazilian carnival feeling, mixed with a masked ball. The people who wear my dresses want to stand out in a crowd, not look quiet and secret.

"The more I try to analyze the kind of

clothes I make, the more I find they stand on their own without precedent. People are buying an original—it's what I see that particular year. Those funny dresses I made one year with holes cut in them might not have sold very well when I did them, but

165

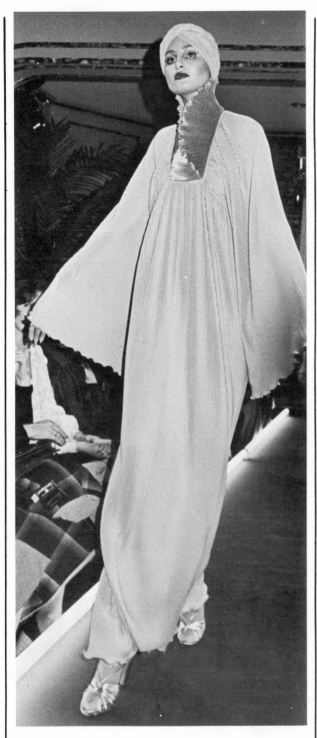

me. My partners used to say, 'For money's sake, Zandra, tone yourself down. You are frightening the buyers away!' But I don't do my makeup to spook people. It just feels fine to me to have fun with colors on my face.

"As long as you are prepared to make mistakes and have other people laugh at you, you can wear and create what you please. I have worn weird things and six months later looked at photographs of myself and thought, 'Oh God, how could I ever have looked like that!' There was one phase where I wore my hair pulled back and painted my face red on the sides. When I look back, it looked terrible, but somehow it was right for me because it pleased me first. I like to pursue ideas that amuse and surprise me, even if they are considered cheap and vulgar by most standards.

"A lot of people I know don't have any money and yet they look very special. It often has to do with the fact that you cannot define the value of what they are wearing, so their personality comes through. Tie a little chiffon handkerchief around your ankle and then wear something completely plain, or add a colored cord for a ring. Why be so status conscious with designer letters all over the place? It's sheer waste. There are plenty of good things everywhere. My bag, which I bought at a London department store five years ago, has gone through everything with me. So what's the point of spending a lot of money on owning a small 'status bag' if I have to carry three paper shopping bags around with it?

"I have to work extra hard because I am always going along my own way. It's not easy; I don't find the act of designing easy at all. I have to shut myself away to do it, even though I like people around. The actual creating part is hell, but the glossy part is easy. When you've done the clothes and you see people galloping around in them, then you're inspired. And you can get back to the locking-yourself-in-the-studio bit. Sometimes I am terrified! My mind becomes a total blank. Actually, I am glad when that happens, because when you get stuck you have to rethink and relook. Then I move along and don't fool myself with the same old ideas."

somewhere along the line they are going to make their mark. I believe my dresses never date. People will wear them ten years from now because I am not involved in trends.

"As far as my own way of getting dressed and made up is concerned, I feel totally immune to what anyone says. That's probably why I sometimes go around with green hair, red cheeks, and iridescent blue dots here and there. It's not that I have a fear of being anonymous. It's something else that drives

Some of Zandra's sketches from her earlier days, above and left, and a 1977 sketch, right . . . all fantasy!

WORK CLOTHES

The easiest style for working women is quiet uniformity punctuated with a special personal touch. If we're disillusioned with the high cost of up-town basics, we can track down lovely, inexpensive army-surplus and work clothes. Work clothes were built to fill a need. Since they were never designed to be in fashion, they can never go out of style. And though they are intermittently taken up as fads, whenever a manufacturer tries to knock them off, the imitation comes out looking silly and inept.

Some of the work clothes' colors are a drawback—who wants to look like the school janitor? But if the colors don't match your mood, you can dye them or punctuate them here and there with bright accents. While rejecting fashion, you needn't reject a look of individual charm.

SURPLUS PARADISE

The army-surplus store is the place to head for cheap status. "One might think that status and recession don't marry too well," wrote Enid Nemy in *The New York Times*, "and one might be wrong. The recession is here, but it hasn't driven away status—it's merely reversed it. It's no longer how much one has paid for something, it's how little."

In a time when it's almost impossible to afford top-quality construction, stitching, and fabric, you can find it surplus for low prices. For the person with a tight budget and an aversion to thrift shops, army-surplus stores are a cheap way to dress. The armed services, unlike department stores, do not take delivery on goods that do not meet the strict specifications of their contracts. The stitching is close and tight, the seams are often bound, and buttonholes don't unravel.

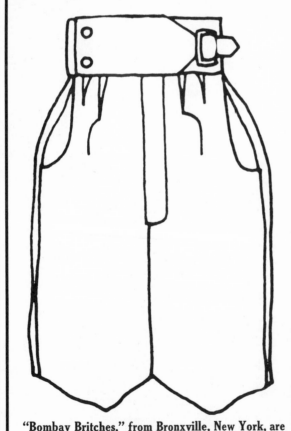

"Bombay Britches," from Bronxville, New York, are typical of classic English army-surplus gear.

In a world of synthetic blends and plastic ultrasuede, military clothes are almost the last inexpensive sources of pure cottons, wools, and leathers. And they last *forever*. Army-surplus means never having to say you're sorry.

For those who are still entranced by new silhouettes, perhaps the freshest look is short boots and the bloused pant, dropping to mid-calf or around the ankle, pants a bit big, pulled in at the waist with a knotted belt. This "look" can be seen in Israeli training camps and on the drill fields of Fort Hood, Texas, as well as in fashionable world capitals. It is ironic that a new silhouette is evolving from the regimentation of the military. If you play with these clothes you can develop an individual look. Khaki needn't belong exclusively to the military, just as red isn't the exclusive province of firemen. A regulation army raincoat becomes a nice background when you add a brilliant purple scarf or a fluffy fox collar. The dash of color and the softness of the fur destroy the military character the coat once had.

People were understandably reluctant to go to Vietnam in the sixties, but it seems now that everyone on the street has zipped into the **army field jacket.** For under $10, it's about the cheapest covering around. It's not rainproof, and it isn't too useful without the system designed by the army to go with it—the liner and hood. The field jacket is the hardest popular military design to wear in an individual way. But it does have mystique for some, perhaps it carries the romance of the invisible urban guerrilla.

Fatigues are made of green khaki and once functioned as the army's great equalizer. Within the service an elaborate status system evolved around this basically drab uniform. (Fidel Castro, after all, elevated fatigues to the status of black tie for formal occasions of state.) All military uniforms in America are designed at the U.S. Army's Natick Labs outside Boston. They are meant to work in an ordered system, possible when recruits wear only what they are issued, exactly as issued. But of course, no matter how functional the fatigues were, a soldier had to tighten up on the basic theme, embroider it, embolden it, upset the army's

Making work clothes work for you: black jumpsuit with angled zippers; bright red webbed belt with a brass buckle; knitted watch cap angled on the brow; red snap-closed nylon windbreaker. (And bright red lips and nails!)

Above: in sunny Southern California, where the body reigns supreme, they take their T-shirts tight . . . this one's with a surplus web belt and army pants dyed red, and comes from Camp Beverly Hills, where all those film types   get the surplus-look together without trekking to the army-navy store (aviator glasses . . . very important.)

Left: an army-surplus beige cotton shirt spiffed up with a beautiful old belt and necklace from the Middle East.

order—for his personal dignity if nothing else. When recruits cut down and tailored their fatigues for that tight, sexy fit, the Natick "life support system" was shot to hell. The system was based on layering, but there was no way these soldiers could squeeze their winter sweaters and socks under tight fatigues. Luckily, we're not in the army and don't have to go on winter maneuvers or listen to the rules from Natick, so we can get our fatigues in any size, dye them any color, wear them loose or tight, or even chop off the sleeves or legs . . . systems be damned!

The army **fatigue shirt** is like a shirt and jacket rolled into one, with nice big pockets over each breast and sturdy welt seams. You can wear it tight as a glove over a turtleneck, unbuttoned to a knotted waist over a tan, or as a summer jacket with the sleeves rolled up over a T-shirt and drawstring-waited cotton muslin skirt.

Fatigue pants are designed to be bloused over boots. The army rule is that trousers are not to hang above boot tops, a holdover from World War I leggings which protected against mustard gas on the battlefield.

The aviator's companion, a durable navy blue nylon, fur-collared blouson jacket, which comes with a detachable quilted lining is made all the more attractive by this pilot.

Natick came up with **jungle fatigues** for the war in Vietnam, with roomy, snap pockets on the thigh and bloused drawstring legs that tied mid-calf at the boot to intercept insects and bugs.

It's best to buy fatigues that are older, because the modern "new army" has done away with pure cottons. Starched fatigues used to be a point of pride in the sixties—"breaking starch" meant putting on a nice crisp pair of fashionably faded fatigues—but now the army is designing things for washing machines rather than breaking starch. Fatigues are now of wash-and-wear synthetic blends.

You'll find it's difficult to get both a tight fit in the crotch and enough length in the leg in almost any military uniform, so consider taking them to a seamstress. Tuck the short pants into high boots or under a pair of crazy socks. (Take a look at the chapter on sports clothes: hockey socks? Baseball gaiters? Soccer stripes, perhaps?)

Several schools of blousing developed in the army over the years, and you might as well know what they are.

1. The George Washington School. The pant's leg is folded around the ankle, wrapped with 3-M® masking tape to hold the fabric tight, and then inserted into the boot.

2. The Blousing Rubber School. The blousing rubber is a big green fabric-covered elastic band similar to a ponytail holder. The band is snapped around the ankle, the trouser leg is tucked up under the inside of the rubber band, and *voilá*, a simple blouse.

3. The Blousing Ring School. The one person in ten who seeks true perfection inserts a heavy metal blousing ring, about six inches in diameter, down the leg of the trousers before using the blousing rubbers. The weight of the metal ring gives the bottom of the blouse that perfect, rounded shape. In theory, the blousing ring refinement is rather like the tiny golden chains Coco Chanel placed in the lining of her suit jackets to make them hang perfectly.

4. The Tin Can School. A number-ten vegetable can with both ends cut out and

taped is slid down the pants leg to give a smooth, even, blouse above the boots, but tends to clank while walking. Some blousing experts prefer a *Time* or *Newsweek*-sized magazine slipped inside the pants to give a stiff look to the leg. A magazine is much quieter than a tin can, and you can read it if you get stuck in line!

Once you've mastered the arcane art of blousing, you might as well top it all off with an olive drab cotton cap. Don't go too all-out with fatigues, or men will turn from you with horrible memories of mosquito-spattered training at Parris Island. Tuck in a blue pack of Gauloise cigarettes in the waist, put a pumpkin-bright T-shirt under the top, tie on a long, multicolored silk jersey scarf, turn up the collar and sleeves,

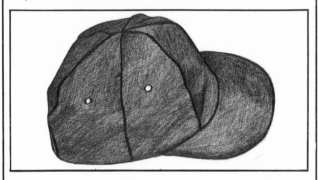

blouse the pants into your favorite boots, and you're Cheap Chic. The surplus outfit basics shouldn't cost more than $13–$15.

If you're one of those purists who search high and low for **pure wool socks,** we have it on good authority that the army issues the finest socks of the world's finest wool. Of course, they come in olive drab, but you can't have everything! At Brooks Brothers they would cost $5. Some surplus stores carry the British army sweater of thick-ribbed wool with canvas shoulder patches.

The **army-issue undershirt** is made of wool and cotton with a big crew neck and a long, long, knitted cuff on the sleeves. In a big size on a thin girl, it looks like a drop-shouldered beach dress, especially when tied up with a brass-buckled web belt or a classic silver antique or conch belt. Also nice in summer is the $1 khaki cotton undershirt. The quality is much better than comparably priced discount-store undershirts.

What a way to go to work—practical, loose and protected.

The big, mid-calf **army raincoat** is a fashionable alternative to getting wet. Over a sweater or two, it can function as a year-round raincoat. The designers of this coat weren't stingy: there is lots of room here for layering, because the cut is really ample. Not bad for $6.

A pilot's one-piece **flight suit** looks like a dashing coverall, with a zipped front and two diagonally cut zip pockets on the chest, and pockets here and there for maps and things. They come in brown or olive, cotton

Elaine Grove, illustrator and a star of the popular daytime soap opera, "Love of Life," in her off hours: she's wrapped a little boy's Western-style belt around the waist of used Walls Master Made coveralls from Texas, and she's peering at us through army-issue style tinted glasses, popular with everyone from McGeorge Bundy to Mick Jagger to Elaine Grove!

or wool, and at $15–$20 could be a year-round uniform over a silk shirt or turtleneck, or under a leather vest. (But remember that the jumpsuit and coveralls were designed for men. Like the leotard, it can be difficult to unlayer yourself when you have to run to the bathroom.) If you grow inordinately fond of the airman look, sink some money into a weathered leather flight jacket lined and collared with fluffy wool shearling. This jacket develops a rich and romantic patina with age and proper care.

For a more conservative effect, look for the below-the-knees classic blue wool **air force officer's overcoat.** They really knew how to make these right, and if you set a tailor to work on it, you can wear this coat from Wall Street to Walden Pond with ease. In quality and design, the officers coat is equal to a made-to-measure overcoat.

The dark blue **navy pea coat** is another almost-luxurious military classic, beauti-

Pants that take forever to unbutton but last and last.

fully designed in quality wool. Yves St. Laurent copied it almost line for line in his couture collection a few years ago and is returning to it again. You can get the original design for much less at your local army-navy store.

The navy blue **thirteen-button wool sailor pants** with black lacings can take you

A navy captain's coat is fine protection against winter wind.

through many winters, but beware of length because they are often too short to wear with heels.

The U. S. Navy also makes the very best **100 percent wool sweater** in a flat dark-blue knit that will keep you toasty warm and good looking. The navy sweater comes with long or three-quarter length sleeves for under $10. To keep your head warm, pull an inexpensive knitted navy watch cap down over your ears. (Your hair gets brittle, and over half your body heat can be lost by an uncovered head in the bitter cold, so cover it! Ears too.)

Navy surplus is also a rich source for perfect pale blue cotton **workshirts.** Sak's, Bloomingdale's, I. Magnin's, and Macy's all

WORK CLOTHES

American work clothes have been around in one form or another since the country was built, working on the railroad, down in the coal mines, busting sod, putting up skyscrapers, and digging subways. Their functional style evolved from a long line of anonymous designers and the demands of hard work. They've got integrity, stamina, good looks, and oh you kid!

Coveralls are worn by mechanics, freaks, artists, and just plain folks. Antonio Lopez, one of the most original fashion illustrators of New York and Paris, wears $20 khaki coveralls every day: "They're so comfortable and made so well that I live in them!" It is intriguing to think that Antonio—who

This is a cape made out of a flare parachute, with white British gurkha shorts, and suede and canvas ballet slippers (imported from China by Bowman Trading). The rest of the surplus comes via Camp Beverly Hills, where cheap is definitely chic.

sell dippy imitations in polyester-and-cotton blends, but the navy makes the real McCoy. Starched and pressed and teamed up with a fine silk tie, some men wear them daily to the office to give a tongue-in-cheek note to the suit-and-tie tradition.

More high style that can sometimes be discovered at army-surplus stores: Beige twill **shorts** with buttoned cartridge pockets and epaulets; khaki cotton pleated **walking shorts;** the classic **safari jacket** with epaulets, breast and hip pockets, back pleat and belt. The safari jacket is another military classic that has made its way from the streets to the couture houses of Paris. It's $80 at Abercrombie & Fitch, under $15 at a surplus store. Take a look in First Layers (Chapter I) to see how one woman uses the safari jacket as the year-round top-layer in a flexible clothing system. The U. S. Army Natick clothing labs would be ever so proud.

Carol Troy's outfit cost $9: $1 for the Boy Scout pants, $1 for the matching khaki shirt, $7 for a T-shirt with the Cheap Chic logo color-Xeroxed on the front. (And then there are the boots . You can bring them in at under $100.)

The French waiter's jacket ($12) from La Samaritaine in Paris, is available in similar styles at uniform supply houses in the States. Take a look at how well it works as a jacket (dressed up by grandmother's lace handkerchief in the pocket) by comparing it to a real waiter wearing it as a uniform on page 182.

discovers and styles some of the most beautiful and eccentric fashion models in the world—is fond of going around town in the lowly coverall.

Can't Bust 'Em brand coveralls have a multitude of pockets and are meant to withstand grease and grime and heavy washing, so a little city dirt doesn't faze them. Sweet Orr overalls in brown hard-hat style make you feel like a construction worker, with their bib front and suspender back. In gray pinstripes, they make you want to ride the rails; in denim you can tame the West or wrassle a commune to its knees.

What's blue, denim, and very baggy? **Carpenters' pants,** with a fascinating array of pockets down the side and mysterious loops and fasteners for hammers, chisels, rules, and flat pencils. Find them in white and dye them any shade you like. **Painters' pants** are another cheap, stylish way to dress.

Checked wool **lumberjack shirts** from

Janitor's wear, the beige twill shirt, gets all dolled up.

army-surplus stores are a handsome, sturdy classic, and the more expensive Pendleton soft wool plaid shirts are a worthwhile investment. Wear one under a riding jacket with a butterfly bow tie.

European work clothes offer all the good design and construction of the American breed, and give you that extra ripple of pleasure from finding something cheap, stylish, and really unique that no one has yet. Looking for work clothes is one way to see more of what a country's all about. A friend of ours brought back a pair of pinstriped gray overalls from Prague just after the Russians had occupied Czechoslovakia. The saleswoman couldn't understand a country where rich students preferred wearing work clothes, and our friend couldn't understand why the Czechs didn't see the inherent beauty of a well-designed pair of overalls. It was an international standoff, but the Czech overalls were a big hit back in Boston.

La Samaritaine, the biggest department store in Paris, has several floors full of some very unexpected, beautiful work clothes. Their oatmeal linen **jewelers' smock** makes a very chic dress, with ample fabric gathered from an overstitched neckband and loose, gusseted sleeves. La Samaritaine also carries well-tailored overalls, black coal-man's suits, ciré fishmongers' tops, nuns' aprons, painters' smocks, dress-length sculptors' smocks, blue cotton electricians' jackets, butchers' smocks, and medical uniforms; all unchanged for a hundred years.

Cheap protection against the rain is a simple beret along with a basic private's raincoat found at the surplus stores.

La Blouse des Halles is another Paris work-clothes headquarters. Here you can find bright orange polyester zip-up coveralls, a butchers' jacket in a small hound's-tooth check, the white garçon de café waiters' jacket in prices ranging from $15 to $20. The long doctors' coats are cool and crisp for summer, and cheap at $13; or you can fashion your own white "linen" suit by getting a $9 medical jacket to wear with sailor pants and a bright scarf.

The shop Sotovol in Paris caters to race-car drivers and aviators. The special Numero Uno **jumpsuit** opens with dual zippers from neck to leg, so you can put it on over everything you're wearing. This design has a stand-up officer's collar, chest and hip pockets, and two map pockets on the side of the leg. All this intricacy costs $50. It comes ready to wear or made to measure in poplin or gabardine of slate blue, mouse gray, chestnut brown, taupe, beige, or white. Or choose the parachutist's camouflage piebald coverall for $32.

There is also an extremely stylish shop in Paris called Globe, so severe it looks like a

| **Take this white cotton jacket out of context, and you have comfortable, chic summer wear.**

locker room. The owner sees work clothes as the only logical way to dress after the thirties-to-sixties revivals with all their kitsch overtones. In the midst of these riotous shapes and colors, Globe leans toward a sober chic which can look rather somber. If you wish to pass quiet and unnoticed, Globe will outfit you with work clothes imported from all over the world: French, English, and American army/navy uniforms from around the world, Chinese padded jackets, and Japanese street-workers' pants

By gosh, Osgood never tires of his Osh-Kosh.

A uniform, dyed a favorite color, could be a favorite dress.

and kimonos. "You say khaki looks sad," says the owner, Gerard Decoster, "but is shocking pink as gay as all that? I've been wearing khaki for six years now, and I've had a ball every day. And besides, for the quality of cut, stitch, and fabric, you can't find a better bargain."

PROFESSIONAL UNIFORMS

A Japanese painter lives in New York, buys medical uniforms, dyes them, and sells them to expensive department stores. She uses a particularly Japanese palette which ranges from dusky roses to deep violets that take beautifully on white cottons. Her most popular uniforms are the short surgical gowns and long wraparound patients' gowns with loose raglan sleeves and little ties in the front, short wraparound operating jackets, button-front cotton short-sleeved nurses' uniforms, and three-quarter-length duck lab coats. Other specialties are hand-dyed 50¢ cotton petticoats with eyelet-trimmed

hems found on Fourteenth Street and sold for summers at the beach with an undershirt of a similar shade.

Hotel and restaurant supply houses carry perfect white waiters' jackets, kitchen pants, and big wraparound aprons to color for summer covering and winter jumper

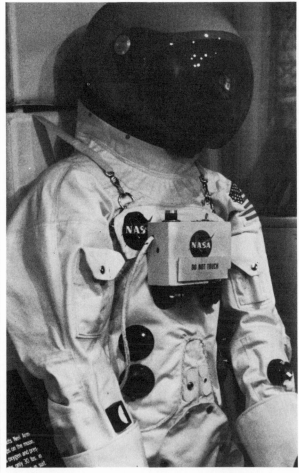

The most perfect and advanced of all jumpsuits or work clothes is also the most useless garment for earth-wear!

wear. You can find large **canvas totes** at supply houses such as the All-Steel Scale Company in New York. They sell mail totes and leather-trimmed canvas bank-note bags that you can have monogramed and made to order in the size you like for $30 to $50.

If you're looking for an inexpensive yet classic blazer, track down the department store that carries uniforms for the most exclusive girls' or boys' school in town. One friend of ours in San Francisco bought a single-breasted navy wool school blazer which was actually the uniform for Miss Burke's School, added special English buttons, had it shaped by a seamstress, and has been wearing it on and off since 1962. It now needs only a new lining—not bad for $30. While you're in the uniform department, see if you can dig up a crisp little nanny's dress, a school's cotton shirtwaist, or sturdy brown walking shoes. School clothes are rather appealing once you're not forced to wear them. The best places to find

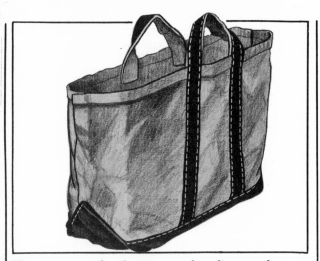

The canvas tote for shopping, week-ending, or whatever.

used school blazers are the exchanges run by the private schools to raise money for charity and scholarships. The Spence-Chapin Exchange in New York occasionally has uniforms on its racks, and once in a while an absolutely breathtaking couture debutante gown will make an appearance.

If you have a little girl, ask friends going to France to buy the adorable little button-front, long-sleeved school uniform called a "tablier," which can be found in most hosiery or haberdashery shops for $1. The older the store, the bigger the chance of finding an old stock of these pure cotton uniforms.

Wendy frolicks in her "le tablier" school-girl dress.

184

BETSEY JOHNSON:

Fanciful Young American Design

Betsey Johnson sizzled onto the fashion scene in 1965 as top designer for Paraphernalia, where she kept churning out unique styles—the skinny T-shirt dress, tiny undershirt tops, miniskirted A-lines—pop clothes that were a jumping reflection of those heady days of the "youth revolution." Betsey was our own homegrown Mary Quant, a designer of immense talent and energy. She went on to Puritan, Alvin Duskin, Alley Cat, Capezio, I. Miller Shoes, and during the "baby years" (Lulu was born in '75) "free-lanced all over the place, but basically I went back and forth to Hong Kong for a junior manufacturer. Now she's got her line, "Betsey Johnson," "very sexy, modern, graphic, 'look at me,' almost like Paraphernalia come full circle, but my taste and my lines are just more grown-up. It took me eight

SUN + MOON IN LEO...TAURUS RISING.

MAYBE CHILDREN'S PATTERNS ...NEXT: TOY CLOTHES!

ME. AUGUST 10, 1942. WETHERSFIELD, CONN. THE ONLY THING I KNEW WAS THAT NOBODY COULD GET ME OUT OF MY HAND-ME-DOWN LITTLE RED WOOL DRESS.. WITH REAL PEARL BUTTONS!? MAYBE MA MADE IT. WHEN I HAVE KIDS I'M GOING TO MAKE THEM EVERYTHING THEY PUT ON.

months. Nobody wanted to take the risk of backing me. 'We don't know what the new direction is,' they'd say, and I'd say, 'I AM the new direction! Why wait!'' She continues her involvement with Betsey, Bunky, and Nini, a New York boutique that serves as a laboratory of ideas for top designer Betsey Johnson.

"All my work is really a good time. I approach it thinking 'would I want to wear it?' But I don't want the manufacturers to think the way that I look is the way my work looks. I want to get them to think of my work as separate. So I wear my housedresses or old jerseys up to their offices. After leaving Alley Cat I realized that I had this terrible freaky Junior Designer image, and it's hard negotiating with businessmen who are trying to play dumb and pretend that they think you can't design anything else. But these stupid jobs become challenges! It's a challenge to use cut chenilles and mohairs and the colors I want. Despite the problems, I love mass-market and inexpensive stretchy stuff. I like to work in an isolated way—a private clientele would involve a lot of socializing.

"My ideas come from everywhere—I guess you'd say I'm eclectic. I get ideas from the costumes I used to make for dancing school as a kid; from those T-shirty kinds of baby clothes. I go to the textile library at the Metropolitan Museum—but if they see you doing anything more than looking, they rush out with big sheets of plastic to protect the fabric! And I visit the Philadelphia Museum, which has a great collection of old American work clothes. In terms of countries, I get most ideas from South America, India, and Turkey. I used to make fabrics and clothes out of India, Turkey, and Hong Kong. And colors—in Burma, those saffron-robed monks in the middle of all those shades of green—that registers later, when you're designing.

"I'm so tactile that when I teach for free I blindfold the kids so they can really feel things. I think that the tactile sense is the most important thing to have in your work, being able to feel how something is going to fit on your body.

"My ideal would be to sell one item a week on a corner, Saturday afternoons. The people would know I'd be on the corner with pants one week, then matching tops the next . . . that way I could do what I wanted in any colors that I wanted, and they wouldn't be marked up. I know women I'd love to have here in my loft just sewing, sewing. If you keep it to one style a week a lady can make it quite fast. Of course, you'd have to guess at the fit. You couldn't try my things on, just like Biba T-shirts. But I think the person I sell things to has a sense of holding things up to her body and seeing if they fit. I never try things on when I shop. But that's my dream—a street-corner operation—because I never have an outlet to do exactly what I want. I know I'm more proud of the T-shirts and pants and drawstring skirts than of all the expensive, overdone things at Betsey, Bunky, and Nini, where I know the prices are too high but don't have any control!"

MAYBE CHILDREN'S PATTERNS... NEXT. TOY CLOTHES! MAYBE

OH...I REALLY WANTED TO BE A DANCER..... MY GREAT TEACHER WOULD LET ME DESIGN ALL MY SOLO COSTUMES. MY MOTHER MADE THEM. I STILL HAVE EVERY ONE. I'D MAKE DOLL CLOTHES OUT OF THE VERY UNUSUAL FABRICS, SEQUINS, CHINA SILK, TARLETAN, LAMÉ + GLITTERED NETTING.

TOO BAD...NOTHING AS FANTASTIC AS PARAPHERNALIA COULD LAST.

+ HERE'S ME IN A TV STUDIO IN NEW YORK... THE ALL TIME "CITY OF MY DREAMS". AFTER GETTING AN ART DEGREE, WINNING MLLE. G.E. CONTEST... WORKING AT MLLE MAG...GOT A JOB AT THE MOST FANTASTIC "DESIGN WORKSHOP" (1965).....I COULD ALWAYS SEW + MAKE MY OWN PATTERNS...+ FOR 3 YEARS MADE ANYTHING I WANTED TO.... I LIVED IN SILVER TAP SHOES, TEENY TINY SKIRTS + REALLY STARTED DOING MY BODY-BASIC T-SHIRT STUFF.

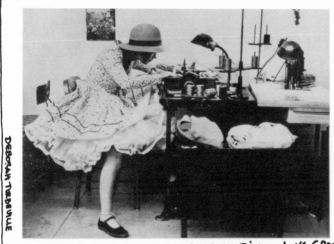

SO...HAPPILY ON TO "ALLEY CAT" + BUTTERICK...A.C'S GROWING UP...BUT BUTTERICK IS GETTING MORE + MORE FUN. LOTS OF "CRAFTY" STUFF...LIKE THE IRON-ON DRAWINGS "APRON-KIT"...I LOVE TO MAKE THINGS THAT. NO MANUFACTURER COULD TURN OUT IN MASS-PRODUCTION. VERY PERSONAL...CREATIVE THINGS. MADE WITH CARE + PRIDE. FOR BUTTERICK I'M GOING TO STICK WITH "CRAFT" THINGS...

INDIA WHERE I LIKE TO GO MOST.

OH DEAR....MY "BRAID OFF THE BOAT PERIOD"- (JUST OVER.) I'M A LITTLE SWEDISH + LIKE TO WEAR PEASANT CLOTHES BEST. THE EARLY 70'S-I WAS DOING MY "OWN THING" NOT WANTING TO LOOK LIKE ANYONE OR ANYTHING.

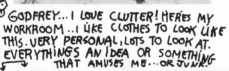

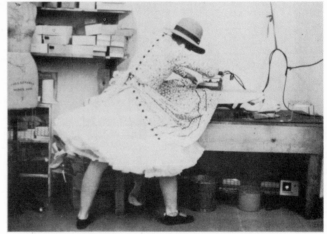

GODFREY...I LOVE CLUTTER! HERE'S MY WORKROOM...I LIKE CLOTHES TO LOOK LIKE THIS. VERY PERSONAL, LOTS TO LOOK AT. EVERYTHING'S AN IDEA OR SOMETHING THAT AMUSES ME...OR JUNK.

I THINK ITS BEST TO SAY HERE....THAT YOU CAN DO ANYTHING YOU REALLY WANT TO....THERE'S NO "SECRET" WAY...JUST LOVE + DESIRE...I THINK....+ AS A FRIEND JUST TOLD ME...REMEMBER....YOU CAN NEVER HAVE TOO MUCH FUN......

+ YES...MY DEAR WORKROOM "LADIES" THAT MAKE MY DAYS PEACEFUL + HAPPY. WE'VE ALL BEEN TO-GETHER FOR YEARS. CHELENA, EMMA, MAGDA + CHERRY ALL WORKING TOGETHER...OUR FAMILY. APART FROM THE "RAG" BUSINESS.

+ TODAY....HENNA IN MY HAIR...STILL BASICALLY IN T-SHIRTS + FUNNY BOTTOMS. I'M MOVING INTO A BIG LOFT DOWNTOWN + FEEL LIKE I'M STARTING FRESH. THAT FEELS GOOD. XOXO LOVE, BETSEY.

LUCIAN K. TRUSCOTT IV

Playing the Market

Lucian K. Truscott IV is a journalist and author of The Complete Van Book *and the novel* Dress Gray. *He is a graduate of West Point, where four years in the cadet uniform taught him to appreciate the freedom of expression clothes give the individual. He now lives in New York and is at work on his second novel. "I wear my old army T-shirts when I write," he says. "I guess I still equate sweat with work, so those T-shirts are the bottom line of my wardrobe.*

"When I was seventeen I worked in a men's specialty shop in Alexandria, Virginia. Those were the days of Bass Weejuns and Gant shirts, and rebellion was defined by the boldness of your madras plaid. That year I learned about clothes. I watched ties widen from 2⅜ inches to 2⅝ inches, lapels creep toward the shoulder seam of your sport coat. I spent a year watching the men's clothing marketplace at work. I discovered this: they work on you, and if you want to be

different, you've got to play the market.

"This is how it shakes down. Levi's were hip for about a year, then the marketplace absorbed them and turned the cultish arrogance of jeans into a garment version of fast food. It's happened to every break-away style that's come along since. Right now, it's almost impossible to achieve sixties-style individuality with clothes.

"Me? I just keep playing the market. If you can't stay one step ahead in style, then beat them on price. I buy everything I own at ½-off list, nearly wholesale. I pick up 'out-of-style' suits and sport coats and shoes and salt them away for a couple of years and wait for the market to circle around; then I jump on, pull out the old stuff, and ride the curve. After inflation and the dollar jack-up of the 'latest style,' you end up saving about 75 percent by simply biding your time. Things move so fast these days, everyone forgets you can play the market at your speed."

The 50 percent solution: Lucian's jacket was half-price from Alan's Apparel in Albuquerque, designed by Ralph Lauren for Chaps. His Jaeger 100 percent cotton shirt with a striped body and white collar? Also half-price. The pants, by Yves St. Laurent for Men, one-third off at Bonwit Teller. And the shoes? From the Gucci factory, and sold off-season at half-price for $35 at Shep Miller's in Southampton. The car? $700.

THE MIXES

Once you have set up your basic uniform, a few special classics, and some thrift-shop finds, how do you go about putting them together for the way you live, be it in Portland, Oregon; Albuquerque, New Mexico, or Buffalo, New York? This chapter will show you the different ways people put themselves together. They can be quite extreme, but we think you will find hints, ideas, and inspirations from all of them. We want you to see the kinds of individual styles that never make it to the fashion magazines. Ultimately, the crux of Cheap Chic is learning to put things together for the person you imagine yourself to be. Some of you may want exotic evening fantasies; others may go for a sexy but ladylike elegance; and others, just that special accessory that lifts the basics out of the uniform category and gives you an individual stamp. The way you put things together tells others and yourself that you care about feeling good, which is, after all, the point.

LINGERIE

Those night-sparkled seamed stockings give us a hint as to what lingerie has become in recent years, more an accessory than a necessity. It wasn't until the early seventies that the full range of underwear stopped selling: the half-slips, full-slips, panties, bras, girdles, or garter belts with thigh-high stockings.

Once these items went out of favor, brains started to percolate, and stylish girls realized that these once-utilitarian items can be put to the nonutilitarian uses of enticement, seduction, and humor. Seamed stockings with a garter belt are downright sexy, especially with a pair of marabou-trimmed satin mules. You can even pull off the effect of seamed stockings when wearing pantyhose. Biba makes seamed pantyhose in a mind-boggling array of colors for under $1 a pair. If a friend goes to London, ask her to buy some for you in the one-size-fits-all.

Tight panties and bikinis can be rotated with silky, open-leg, lace-trimmed shorts, like the ones worn in the twenties. These floppy pants allow the body to breathe, and look surprisingly sexy, both naive and knowing. Fernando Sanchez designs the sensuous underwear that shows up in the fashion magazines and is being copied by all the manufacturers, but thrift shops still hide the most luscious pure-silk styles. Even if your underpinnings never show, you get a charge of erotic energy just knowing you're wearing the most beautiful, silkiest lingerie imaginable under your plain T-shirt and jeans. Or, on the other hand, you may get the same effect knowing you are wearing the tackiest, hardest sex-queen lingerie ordered directly from the catalog master himself, Mr. Frederick of Hollywood.

192 | **A sexy, feminine, classic design by Fernando Sanchez.**

Janet Reger's filmy concoctions from Beauchamp Place, London: all silk and all heaven.

Antonio's antic sketch of legs, legs, legs, chock full of ideas you can adapt to your life. Look across these pages: here are ballet-slipper type soled flats with tights and legwarmers, men's argyle socks you might wear under slacks, flat, comfy Mary Jane's with anklets under long, baggy slacks.

LOTS OF LEGS!

Leg dressing is one game you can really play on a low budget. You don't get too many tips from fashion magazines, because, after all, how much do socks cost! But they can give you more bang for your buck . . . from textured pantyhose to shocking-pink legwarmers . . . than almost any other element ·in your wardrobe. And this is especially true if you keep your wardrobe pruned to one or two basic colors.

Jacque McCord, an editor at *Modern Bride,* says they're doing all sorts of things with legs all of a sudden. They're shooting pictures of brides in midcalf or ankle-length dresses, for instance, wearing ivory point d'esprit or textured stockings so their legs look more delicate.

Modern Bride, she says, has a whole closetful of ribbons. "They're from Hendler's, *the* ribbon store in the garment center,

on West Thirty-eighth Street. So you can decorate your ankle with a ribbon, maybe with a flower knotted on it, like an ankle bracelet. You can even thread sneakers or any lace-ups with long ribbons, then tie them up around your ankle over a pair of ankle socks to get that fat blousy look with pants—say, midcalf—or a tight-wrapped look with pegged pants." She also suggests that pants in a light fabric might be pegged tight, to make a new shape out of old, at the dry cleaner's or tailor's. These look great with very high heels.

Jacque herself wears men's socks under her boots in the winter. First, she says, you don't run your nylons unnecessarily. Second, you get good insulation, especially with cotton socks. She feels men's socks come in both a better quality and range than those available now for women. And she often wears mules, both summer and winter, because her shoes get a lot of wear and tear. Once these leather slip-ons begin to stretch, she starts wearing them with her

194

Soft ballet slippers with a satin bow at the throat, elastic across the arch, and feminine little white anklets . . . for the young at heart! Midcalf cowboy boots with men's work socks; and flats worn under a petticoat with the stockings rolled down around the ankles, fifties style.

favorite men's (or women's) socks, as both a color accent and to keep the shoes on her feet!

Polly Mellen, the fashion editor of *Vogue,* is known for putting together beautifully patterned and textured outfits in neutral tones and then sparking them with a flash of color at the ankle . . . like peach-pink angora socks with a pair of really good heeled moccasins (and *everything else* beige). There are incredibly wild things to be done with socks; but subtle touches like this are the unexpected glints that really pull an outfit together and give it flair.

Ki Hackney Hribar, who covered the top American designers for *Women's Wear Daily,* is now editor of the new Sunday-supplement *Style Magazine.* She's a self-confessed conservative dresser but still has lots to say on the subject of legs.

"I wear socks to rejuvenate my old shoes," says Ki. "Good, expensive Gucci-style moccasins with heels—I usually buy mine at Shoe Biz or Charles Jourdan—al-ways seem to *stretch.* But you can get the heels and soles fixed, keep them nice and polished, and keep them your size with socks. Then you can still wear them week-ends with pants." Ki also prefers men's socks, because they are often higher, but finds women's manufacturers are starting to make good socks now too. "Men have interesting argyles," she says, "plus 'preppy' colors like red, yellow, lime-green . . . with all-black or all-navy clothes I like the psychological lift of bright-colored socks. Last summer I got bright red socks from the boy's department of a store in Southampton. Conservative men's stores are always dependable places to shop . . . for women! Now, I might even wear subdued argyles to work if I'm wearing all black. Or even a pair of pink or metallic turquoise socks!

"When you're wearing jeans, play around with your legs. It's fabulous to have these colors and patterns sticking out. It's a relatively inexpensive way of having fun . . . and I'm basically *conservative.* I always

195

Granny's high-heeled lace-ups with baggy legwarmers; high-heeled backless springolator stilettos with wrapped ankles, and ankle-fastened boots with slim pants tucked into them . All ideas . . . all rather stunning!

keep a supply of black and brown knee-highs on hand to wear with pants. But you need a little color sometimes. What's fun is to wear neutrals and then play around with your legs because it's so cheap!

"For the office," continues Ki, "I always keep a stock of black, brown, and sometimes gray and burgundy opaque pantyhose on hand. They can even be a bit sheer if they show good color. Buy one pair to check on their size and opacity, then six at a time for black and brown, three at a time for your two other basic colors.

"Recently, I've started to fool around with the opaque striped and textured pantyhose for the office and I love them! I always like it, even with a tweed. There's nothing wrong with a patterned leg." Ki also wears the textured legs when there's something going on in her shoe, like perforations or a two-tone leather like a spectator pump. "A lot of women might be nervous about wear-

ing patterned hosiery with anything but a simple moccasin," she says, "but you shouldn't be afraid to go ahead and wear textured hosiery . . . it looks good!

"Bendel's in New York carried the point d'esprit pantyhose for the winter of 1977. It was so chic in black! By this winter, hopefully, all the stores should be carrying them." The big, inexpensive department stores like Mays in New York are *good* resources, she finds. They keep stride with fashion and are now carrying textured and patterned pantyhose. They needn't cost a lot of money: Keep an eye open at the volume stores, the bargain basements. Ki's burgundy striped pantyhose were $1.59 at Mays. And it's certainly more fun to play with a cheap striped leg than sticking to the basic $1.39 nude sandalfoot. You certainly don't have to pay $4 or $5 to get fashion diamond-patterned pantyhose—you can get something similar for $1.59!

Antonio's favorite slim leg and high, high heels again, next to flat, crushy soft leather boots with a bright shot of legwarmers over them . . . comfy and warm for the winter, but only for the very coldest days.

In the evening, Ki wears men's gangster-style striped silk or rayon socks in black. The problem? They're often too short. And in the summer, when it's hot, what can you do but get a tan and go without stockings to the office, or play around with textured sheers. And it's always good to have a supply of knee-highs in nude to wear under slacks if your shoes are uncomfortable without socks.

If you're going to go without stockings in the summer, Ki recommends leg waxing for some women. "It's such a relief, it's like a tranquilizer! You just don't have to worry; it's worth every single penny. Depending on how many years you've been doing it, you can go about every three weeks in the summer and every six to eight in the winter." Elizabeth Arden salons around the country are supposed to be excellent, if this proves to be your summer treat.

And of course there are toenails . . . paint them some color you'd *never* consider wearing on your fingernails, like firehouse red, burgundy, mauve, metallic anything! Check out the dime store for the loudest colors you can find.

What about the fashion of wearing short cotton anklets? They look great on Gilda Radner on "Saturday Night Live" (she decorates them herself with little rhinestones and stuff), but Ki Hackney doesn't think they're really *her!* "I'm 5'10½", so the idea of me putting all that height on little white anklets doesn't appeal to me! But you do have to be more willing to experiment. We just did a Ralph Lauren fashion shooting for *Style*, and he sent over these blond woolly knee-socks for the model to wear with a bare, suede high-heeled sandal underneath a simple, classic cashmere sweater dress. It *sounded* so bizarre to me, but it looked terrific when the model put it on!"

THE BARGAIN HUNTER

Sophie uses her face as the strongest, most extreme aspect of her appearance. She will never go out in public without having her face done in the palest foundation, her eyes heavily outlined in a smoky gray, and her mouth painted a dark, shiny plum. On other days it will be other colors. Accentuating her strong face will be another strong color, the rich henna shade rinsed into her thick hair. Sophie is known in Paris as one of the most extravagantly dressed women around. Whatever she wears is an original Sophie concoction. She always looks extraordinary on very little money, with a lot of imagination, experimentation, and practice. By trade, she designs textiles and sportswear, and when she's not at the office she's home, compulsively decorating and redecorating her apartment.

Sophie's secret is a willingness to push a look as far as it will go, trusting her eye to find the prize yardage hidden in a stack of mediocre fabrics on sale at the big department stores; trusting her luck to dig up the perfect bits of fur to transform simple cloth into rich exotic gowns, and knit caps into romantic Russian fur clouds floating above her brow.

She always tries to buy everything wholesale, telling manufacturers she's in the trade and hoping they'll sympathize. You can try this in New York or other large garment manufacturing cities on the weekends, or find a friend who has an in with a manufacturer. Clothes are usually half-price, if not less, when bought wholesale.

Sophie makes a masterful use of bits of **fur trim,** adaptable to almost any climate. For instance, in Los Angeles, where it is seldom bone-chillingly cold, a designer cuts striped Mexican serapes into bright, long, conch-belted coats, hangs raccoon tails

198 | **The secret shopper: Sofi puts together the most extravagant creations from bits and pieces of sale goods in Paris.**

Simple and elegant: plaid on the bias, hanging in large triangles, topped by a babuska and strong makeup.

along the sleeves and the yoked cowboy-style back, then fluffs a fox collar around the neck. There are all sorts of ideas here for transforming a thrift-shop find into a deluxe western look.

The contrast of fur with extreme combinations of fabric and patterns is really arresting, like fur on a soft-flecked wool jersey lined with a check-tablecloth plaid. A seamstress in Paris called Galiana makes odd use of fur by draping the skin of the animal around the front of a coat and down the sleeve, wherever it lands, then stitching it in place. It looks as if some pelt fell out of the sky and just happened to land on the coat. The very primitive treatment of the fur on the tailored wool coat is an odd sight.

One young fashion editor in New York feels you should always take fur to ex-

tremes—use it to further your fantasies rather than just to keep you warm. So she plunked down all her money on a royal blue fox neckpiece on sale at a top furrier instead of opting for a sensible used fur coat from the Ritz Thrift Shop. No one ever forgets those crazy blue foxes nuzzling her neck, and somehow she manages to keep warm. Exaggeration is its own reward.

Larissa Jarzombeck is another New York City fur freak. After coming to New York from Europe, she said, "I had to cope with the overheated apartments and freezing streets. The logical solution was to dress lightly in silk chiffon and wear fur close to

The contrast of fur against day clothes: a bowtie bristles against a warm, puffy old raccoon coat.

the body. Nothing like that was available, so I bought some lamb skins in the fur district and put them together like a jigsaw puzzle. The result was so shocking that for two weeks I dared only to wear it at night!

The first day I ventured into the sunlight, I ran into Miles Davis, who ordered a white one, and later many more. This started a word-of-mouth clientele, mostly musicians and artists." Larissa's coats are sensible, durable, and handsome. Like the royal blue foxes, they are not cheap.

STREETWISE

Marcia approaches a stylized look from the other direction. Instead of furs and luxuries, everything she wears is from a thrift shop, but layered flippantly and combined with ethnic favorites in a really in-

Colette livens up a discreet beige outfit with Indian silk.

Marcia's street chic mixes well-worn thrift shop buys, exotica from abroad, and unexpected layers, then adds a scarf at the neck to tie it all together.

genious way. Everything she wears is tiny, tiny, tiny. She'll wear a miniskirt, for instance, but
• Sling a belted Peruvian bag around the waist, and
• Add silver-trimmed hand-tooled cowboy boots.
To get a couple of lengths going, she'll wear

a mid-calf coat with a tiny waist over the short skirt, and tie a shiny yellow 59¢ Woolworth's scarf in a practiced knot at her neck. Marcia is not trying to tell people she is a lady of luxury; she's telling them she's an independent soul with enough imagination to pull the most disparate bits and pieces into a very personal look. This streetwise look says she's an artist of the first order.

If you study photographs of people who have a finely tuned sense of style, almost invariably you find a **scarf.** Knotted at the neck, draped over a coat, twisted around the head, tied at the waist—scarves show up everywhere. Since fashion magazines often have to show some rather uninspiring dresses manufactured by their major advertisers, they have developed the skill of transforming the ordinary into the exceptional through the use of scarves, belts, and other accessories. Nearly every page of *Vogue* is a lesson in the uses of scarves.

Start up a collection of scarves from thrift shops or Woolworth's and add the cheap cotton squares sold in summer. Try to get different sizes in your favorite colors. Experiment until you feel ready to sink some money into a crepe de Chine square for head wrapping, a silk muffler for the neck, or whatever it is that will give you the most pleasure. The same goes for **belts**—they can change the look of almost any outfit. Try to get as many inexpensive belts as you can find: wide cinch belts in your favorite colors, narrow leather bands that can be worn singly or three at a time, plus an investment belt or two (see Chapter II, Classics).

Perching a **hat** atop your head every morning is a sure way of creating an image. We're not talking about wearing a lot of hats that are in, like a stiff new gaucho hat tied under the chin. We're talking about hats that look better and better as they become more and more you. Some people grow so attached to their hats and their hats to them that they become virtually inseparable; look at Congresswoman Bella Abzug. One of the most original and talented stylists in New York is never seen without his

Hats can create and extend an image...in John Wayne's case, it's rough, tough, and very, very tall.

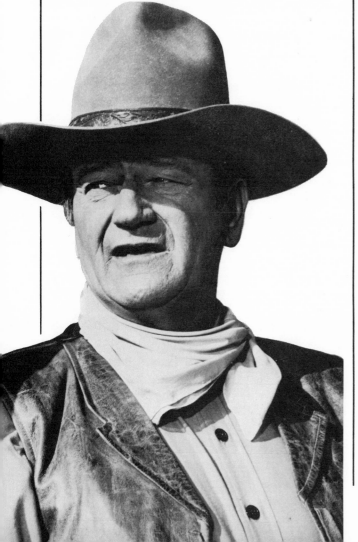

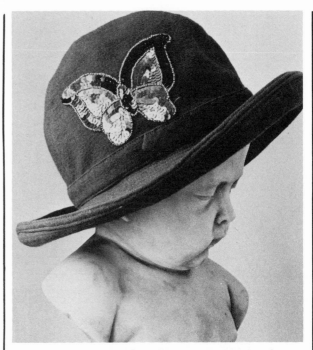

Make a hat your own by adding a personal touch.

trademark Japanese student cap festooned crown-to-brim with the charms of a decade of friends and travels. He is always dressed in black. All his decorative impulses go into his work and into that extraordinary, glittering, charm-laden cap.

CONSERVATIVE MIX

Andrea Quinn, a beauty editor at *Seventeen*, is another person seldom seen without a hat, a man's battered old felt hat with a slouched-down brim. Andrea is as selective and consistent about the other clothes she wears as she is about her hat. She wears a very toned-down mix of the classics, work clothes, cowboy things, and thrift-shop finds. She prefers old, well-worn clothes to the mania of seasonal fashions she sees covering the market in the showrooms of Seventh Avenue. Her apartment on New York's East Side is a reflection of her understated style: pared down, almost severe, with classic American quilts and bare wooden floors.

Andrea's basic working uniform is jeans and gym T-shirts with two shifts of jewelry, either ethnic things in silver, or gold antiques and family hand-me-downs. "I don't like new clothes very much," she says. "I

201

Conservative Mix: To one oatmeal linen dress, Andrea adds worn St. Laurent boots, an antique knit vest, beat-up riding jacket and a battered hat from a flea market.

used to O. D. on fashion all the time. When I was first a fashion editor, I got a lot of stuff because I could get it half price. But it gets to be too much. Now, if I'm expected to look like a fashion editor then I do, but most of the week I wear very simple things." These are the things that get the most wear in Andrea's closet: Frye boots, St. Laurent boots, cowboy boots, a $6 army-surplus raincoat, an old riding jacket, T-shirts and jeans, a French jeweler's smock, thick sweaters to pile on under the unlined raincoat in the winter, and a collection of old patterned vests she slips on over everything. "It's really weird," says Andrea. "I'm a fashion editor, but I just don't dress myself up much anymore. I've found I like wearing very simple things."

Dalila wears her best fur jacket with second-string classics, gold jewelry, a Cartier watch, and a tight pair of recycled Lee jeans.

Holly's sensuous jerseys: the dirndyl pants are a day and night constant. Here, a silk crepe de Chine head-wrap, antique fur, and her dyed jersey bandeau.

NAUGHTY BUT NICE

Holly Harp has probably never worn a Mr. Frederick's original, but she doesn't have to. Her designs have been described by customers as "naughty but nice," just the kind of thing for the sexy, body-conscious, but upstanding ladies of Los Angeles. Clothes that bear her label are expensive, but Holly's style doesn't have to cost a lot. It's a system of simple, sometimes whimsical, clothes centered around her basic silk jersey dirndl pants and, quite often, her exercise leotard. The mix will take her from her factory to exercise class to a party in the Hollywood Hills. Because of the free and open way people dress in southern California, Holly never worries about looking overdressed. She just wears what pleases her.

The Holly touches that enliven her basics are:

These pants are Holly's "jeans." Here she wears them with an old belt, capelet, and Lycra exercise leotard.

• A scalloped capelet that was a *Ladies' Home Journal* home sewing project in the forties, decorated with mysterious drippings she has not been able to re-create.
• A piece of chiffon made into a belt for the twenties diamenté belt buckle she found at a thrift shop.
• A silk crepe de Chine scarf wrapped around her head, peasant-style.

All her colors are in a muted range of smoky violets, grays, and greens, so everything mixes with everything else. The strong, simple impact of Holly's style leaves little room for showy jewels or accessories. Cheap Chic comes in knowing when to subtract from a look as well as when to add to it.

ECLECTIC ELEGANCE

rançoise Kirkland is a lady whose clothes energies go into tops and shoes. Her look is totally eclectic, with an international ring to it. She grew up in Paris and eloped with an American. That was ten years ago, and Françoise still shows that kind of headlong daring in her life and style. Having recently moved from New York to the Hollywood Hills, she is studying journalism at UCLA and developing a new set of thrift-shop contacts.

A typical Eclectic Elegant outfit might combine a bit of everything: wrapping, sports, thrift shops, classics, ethnic, work clothes, basics. Pegged jeans from France with that special tight cut, well-worn suede boots, a $2 Hawaiian print shirt from a rag house bundle, an Isotonic Lycra leotard, and traveler's jewelry: a single earring made from a child's silver bracelet hung with feathers, beads and bits of leather; a silver-studded bracelet from New Delhi; bangles from Morocco; a Cartier tank watch with a

Francoise sports the look of an Angeleno Mixer. Her heavy wool coat is made by Barbara Hokonson of New York's Copper and Decay.

Jazzy day-into-night clothes, left, by Norma Kamali. The suit teams up with anything from drawstring pants to a ruffled evening skirt or all-out Chinese robe glamour. Francoise, above, wears her go-everywhere top.

204

brown leather band; a bolo tie from Arizona; and a gold chain hung with *figas*, charms from friends, and a childhood St. Christopher's medal.

All this stuff piled up on one person could court disaster, but Françoise puts it together with a practiced eye and a sense of humor:

• The jeans are rolled up over the boots.

• The Hawaiian shirt is knotted in front over the leotard like a calypso dancer's,

• and all the heavy jewelry just seems to fall into place, perhaps because it's all of such quality.

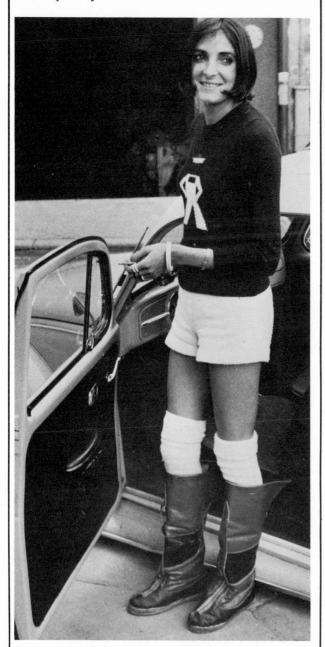

Short, short-shorts, georgeous Tibetan boots (available by mail order), over-the-knee socks: that's imagination.

Tune into Soul Train when you're running low on ideas!

And Françoise loves wraps. "I make a turban out of this huge piece of tie-dye you just wrap and wrap, whatever way you can manage to keep it on your head! You can also wear it as a sarong skirt. One night I went to Claridge's in London in knickers with the scarf wrapped around my head. The headwaiter said I wasn't allowed in the dining room because I wasn't wearing a skirt. So off I went to the ladies room, took the scarf off my head, and wrapped it into a skirt. They had to let me in!"

Women between eighteen and thirty-five are said to spend over $10 billion on clothes each year. Some of the women in this chapter spend a bit more, and some make a point of spending much less than average. But whichever camp they fall in, they get ten times the mileage and ten times the fun out of their clothes because they've developed their unique talents for making chic from cheap.

THE CHIC SHOPPER'S GUIDE

A directory of stores, flea markets and mail order houses in the U.S., England and France.

Our listings could never be all-inclusive, and regrettably we have missed many excellent stores. Also regrettably some of the store listed may no longer be in existence as you read this. The purpose of the listings was to give you an idea of what to look for. With this in mind we suggest the following:

Check your local phone book for the address in your town of Goodwill, Salva-tion Army, Volunteers of America, Catholic Charities, and charitable thrift shops.

Check your newspapers for church, school, and charity rummage sales, flea markets, yard sales, and the like.

Don't overlook the Five and Ten in your town. Woolworth's, McCrory's, and other large chain variety stores offer a wealth of Cheap Chic.

United States and Canada

ARIZONA

How Sweet It Was
636 North 4th Ave.
Tucson
Vintage clothes, an assortment of original designs, and recycled denims.

Phoenix Art Museum Shop
1625 North Central Ave.
Phoenix
Ethnic folk patterns.

ARKANSAS

The Left Bank
One McIlroy Plaza
Fayetteville

Lois Gean's
109 South Jackson
Magnolia

CALIFORNIA

LOS ANGELES AND SOUTHERN CALIFORNIA

Aardvark's Odd Ark
Los Angeles
(3 locations)
Tremendous selection of used clothes, generally under $10.00.

Anne's-tiques
Main St.
Santa Monica
Antiques at excellent prices.

Bazaar de Mundo
2754 Calhoun St.
San Diego

Bun-Ka Do
340 East First St.
Los Angeles
Amazing selection of Oriental trinkets.

Camp Beverly Hills
9640 Santa Monica Blvd.
Beverly Hills
International surplus antiques and creative used clothing. Army-navy gone chic.

Copeland's Enterprises, Inc.
233 Madonna Rd.
San Luis Obispo

Dasu-suda
614 North Doheny Dr.
Los Angeles
A sassy boutique.

Eclectiquaria
8939 Santa Monica
Hollywood

Eric & Company
6915 Melrose Ave.
West Hollywood

Fiorucci
Los Angeles
Italian design shop with American panache.

The Flying Emery Board
Beverly Hills
A real investment for fingernails.

Harold's Place
420 North Bedford
Beverly Hills
Classy antiques.

Headquarters Army-Navy Store
131 East 6th St.
Los Angeles
A local favorite.

Holly's Harp
Sunset Blvd.
West Hollywood
Sexy, ladylike clothes.

Julian's
3716 Sunset Blvd.
Silverlake, Los Angeles
Underground ethnic, gorgeous Chinese jewelry.

Junk Store
Wilshire Blvd.
West Hollywood
Good used clothing.

Kobo
1446 Camino Del Mar
Del Mar

Lame Deer Indian Store
8009 Santa Monica Blvd.
Los Angeles
Western apparel.

Los Angeles Museum of Art
Museum Shop
5905 Wilshire Blvd.
Los Angeles

Los Angeles Uniform Exchange
5239 Melrose
Los Angeles

Manchee
334 First St.
Los Angeles
From lovely, tie-dyed double
comforters to geta sandals on stilts.

Maxfield Bleu
9091 Santa Monica Blvd. and
Doheny
Los Angeles
Terrific European imports, expen-
sive but choice stuff.

Mehitabel
3716 Sunset Blvd.
Silverlake
Scarves and cottons from India,
exotic beads and amulets—all at
reasonable prices.

Miss Amber
Los Angeles
6640 Hollywood Blvd. Hollywood
Beverly Hills too.
Flash and dazzle; first with English
scarf dresses.

Ola Hudson
Melrose
West Hollywood
The funky forties feel, custom
designed.

The Orient
6626 Hollywood Blvd.
Hollywood
Real finds; cotton and silk kimonos
hidden among the standard tourist
items.

Oriental Arts
325 First St.
Los Angeles
Antique Orientalia in brass,
bronze, and cloisonne.

Oriental Silk Company
8365 Beverly Blvd.
Los Angeles
Beautiful silk fabrics, robes,
scarves, crocheted tops.
Send for catalog.

Pasadena Flea Market
The Rose Bowl
Pasadena
The biggest.

Pierre La Jond & Co.
516 San Ysidro Rd.
Santa Barbara

Pillars of Eagle Rock
Eagle Rock (near East L.A.)
The Loehman's of the West—
designer clothes at less than half
price.

Pleeze
708 North Curson Ave.
West Hollywood
Antiques.

Post Exchange
18433 Plummer St.
Northridge
Surplus.

Rainbow Resource Co.
1048 Hermosa Ave.
Hermosa Beach

The Red Balloon Ltd.
168-63 Algonquin St.
Huntington Harbor

Repeat Performance
7621 Melrose
Hollywood
Antique clothing.

Right Bank Clothing Co.
Beverly Hills
Now has snazziest shoes, too.

The Supply Sargeant
631 Santa Monica Blvd.
Santa Monica

Surplus Marts
6263 Santa Monica Blvd.
(corner of Vine)
Los Angeles
Army-navy surplus.

The Surprise Store
Los Angeles
Like New York's Unique Clothing
Warehouse—in Culver City and
other locations, too.

3 Plus One
219 Manhattan Beach Blvd.
Manhattan Beach

Topanga Threads
110 North Topanga Canyon Blvd.
Topanga
Macy's and the big stores find
things here.

The Trunk Salon
8701 Santa Monica
West Hollywood
Antique clothing.

Vanity
704 North La Cienga Blvd.
Los Angeles
Franklyn Welsh's beauty
emporium.

Wylan Gallery
9619 Brighton Way
Beverly Hills

Zaca
Los Angeles
Carries Lily Bleu—fabulous shoes.

NORTHERN CALIFORNIA

Abbe's
1420 Clement St.
San Francisco
Antique and secondhand clothes.
Most look new and barely worn.

Bary
125 Geary
San Francisco
Stylish boutique.

Bizaare Bazaare
5634 College Ave.
Oakland
Lots of antique finds in clothing,
hats, jewelry, feathers.

Carousel Resale Shop
1642A Irving St.
San Francisco
Used clothing with sensational
buys from the thirties.

Casey's Faded World
2265 Upper Market
San Francisco
Embroidered kimonos and satin
acetate lingerie.

Chicken Little's Emporium
1108 Polk St.
San Francisco
Crazy gifts and clothing; great
shoes and accessories as well.

Coastside Corral
Oddstad Blvd.
Pacifica
Full line of Western gear.

Cottonworks
137 Forest Ave.
Mill Valley

County Fox
10821 North Wolfe Rd.
Cupertino

Dark Horse Trading Co.
Mill Valley

Divina
60 Maiden Lane
San Francisco
To eyeball Fernando Sanchez,
Ralph Lauren, Dorothee Bis, New
Man Jeans.

East-West Leathers
Sausalito
Also at Grant Street in San
Francisco.
Leathers that last.

Far and Few
1510 Walnut Sq.
Berkeley
Quality antique clothing at fair
prices.

French's Hitching Post
1205 Third St.
San Rafael
Shop for Western wear.

Good Measure Fabrics
322 Miller Ave.
Mill Valley

Green's Boot & Saddle Shop
12153 San Pablo Ave.
Richmond
Another "don't miss" for Western.

Janan Resale Fashions
1432 California
San Francisco
Buys on secondhand designer
clothes and shoes.

Kaplan's Surplus & Sporting Goods
1055 Market (near 7th)
San Francisco
Check for army-navy surplus and
utilitarian looks.

Lost Horizons
2003 Fillmore
San Francisco
Up-to-the minute styles, cheap to
expensive, in a fantasy setting.

Lucette
77 Bridgeway
Sausalito
Original things no one else has.

Macy's
Union Square Shop
San Francisco
Go to the shop—fantastic.

Miki
Ghirardelli Sq.
San Francisco
(also on Telegraph in Berkeley)
Select boutique.

Ming Quong
1517½ North Main St.
Walnut Creek
Ethnic, handmade clothing,
jewelry. This store has quite a
history. It was named after an
orphanage and means "Radiant
Light."

Nasi
1156 Taylor
San Francisco

Next-To-New Shop
2226 Fillmore St.
San Francisco
Operated by the Junior League—
terrific for classics.

New Ideal
1336 Grand
San Francisco
Clothing for men and women, all
organized by racks. No fitting
rooms; good buys.

New York Fabrics
245 Tamal Vista Blvd.
Corte Madera

Obiko
3924 Sacramento
San Francisco
Expensive, unusual jewelry; unique
designer clothes; satin shoes from
Hong Kong.

Oui Oui
1529 Shattuck
Berkeley
Children's shop—everything from
French flea market to hand-dyed
Oshkosh overalls.

The Outdoorsman
197 North Main St.
Bishop

Painted Lady
Divisadero
San Francisco
Antiques.

The Palace Museum
1546 Polk St.
San Francisco
Elegant funk, specializing in
recycled clothing made from old
jeans.

Panache
Sacramento St.
San Francisco
Nice taste for a limited budget.

Pauli's
Broadway
San Francisco
Nice old clothes.

Poppy Fabric & Trim
1845 Solano Ave.
Berkeley

Pretty Mamma Inc.
1012 Pacific Ave.
Santa Cruz

Robert Kirk, Ltd.
150 Post St.
San Francisco
Tops in men's classics. Send for
catalog.

Ron Richards Saddlery
2510 Telegraph Ave.
Oakland
Wide selection of Western wear.

Satin Moon
14 Clement St.
San Francisco
Wide variety of fabrics: cottons,
silks, wool, Dutch wax, Liberty
House prints, crepe de chine,
gabardines, old buttons.

Second Hand Rose
3326 23rd St.
San Francisco
Fantastic emporium where you can
find racks of antique and period
clothes.

The Street Shop
4100 19th St.
San Francisco
Best for used men's wear—lots of
quality at bargain prices.

Tail of the Yak
2632 Ashby
Berkeley
Even more Oriental than San
Francisco's Thousand Flowers.

Thousand Flowers
311 Grant St.
San Francisco
Unusual, fantastic clothing and
gifts from all over the world.

COLORADO

The Deb Shop
123 West 4th St.
Pueblo

Denver Army Store
Denver
Here's the place to shop in Denver.

La Boca Ltd.
2412 East 23rd Ave.
Denver

La Piuma
Aspen

Last Tango
Boulder
Wonderful dress shop, stylish,
splashy.

The Lotus Eaters' Boutique
27 East Platt Ave.
Colorado Springs
Make most of their own things,
carry European garments, all
natural fibers and recycled drapery
fabrics.

Marcy's
203 South Galena St.
Aspen
Although geared more toward
women, tends to be fairly unisexual
with a range in style from fatigues
and plastic to silk. Prices range
from $1.50 to $350.00.

Uriah Heep's
P.O. Box 1362 Jerome Hotel
Aspen
Snazzy as the Jerome Bar! And you
can send for mail order too.

CONNECTICUT

Gorden's Bootery Inc.
936 Chapel St.
New Haven

Revival
213 Main St.
Westport

The Seraph
Good Speed Landing
East Haddam

DISTRICT OF COLUMBIA

Deja Vu Antiques & Objets d'Art
1675 Wisconsin Ave.
Georgetown
Vintage clothing 1900-1950s: hats,
purses, furs, fans, jewelry,
collectibles.

Sunny's Surplus
3342 M St., N.W.
Georgetown
Georgetown headquarters for
army-navy surplus. Sunny's first
gained fame in Baltimore,
Maryland, where they still have a
store.

Vernon's
1055 Thomas Jefferson St., N.W.

FLORIDA

Adam's Rib Boutique Inc.
Santa Rosa Mall
Mary Esther

Army-Navy Surplus
700 West Broward Blvd.
Ft. Lauderdale
Dash in for a khaki T-shirt to wear
as a hot-weather tank top.

Edge City
1017 Park St.
Jacksonville

Palm Beach Thrift Shop
Palm Beach
Beautiful tailoring, sumptuous
beading . . . the impeccable castoffs
of the luxury trade.

GEORGIA

Razzle Dazzle
2823 Peachtree Rd.
Atlanta

ILLINOIS

Ann Taylor
Michigan Ave.
Chicago

The Blue Parrot
217½ South 6th St.
Springfield
Buy, sell, trade men's and women's
old clothing, accessories.

Bottega Glaseia
49 East Oak
Chicago

Fiberworks
2364 North Lincoln Ave.
Chicago

Sami
3755 North Freemont St.
Chicago

Stanley Korshack
Michigan Ave.
Chicago
The Windy City's special specialty
store.

Steve Starr Studios
2654 North Clark St.
Chicago
Art deco, art moderne, jewelry,
furnishing and accessories.

Ultimo
114 Oak St.
The ultimate European boutique
look. The ultimate prices, too.

IDAHO

Boise Art Gallery Shop
Julia Davis Park
Boise

Yellow Brick Road
Ketchum

INDIANA

The Bootlegger Inc.
1016 Broadway
Fort Wayne

L. S. Ayres
Indianapolis
Look for Unique Clothing
Warehouse department.

IOWA

Crest Bootery/Coach 'N Four
104-106 North Maple
Creston

Things, Things, & Things
130 South Clinton St.
Iowa City

KANSAS

Collage Ltd.
1008 Main St.
Goodland

LOUISIANA

The Front Run
1305 Dublin St.
New Orleans

Jeans
2707 Williams Blvd.
Kenner

Rivet, Haute Coiffure Boutique
236 Metairie Rd.
Metairie
Hair, cosmetics, fashion.

MAINE

House of Logan
Booth Bay Harbor

MASSACHUSETTS

Armadillo of Boston
134 Newbury St.
Boston

Central War Surplus
433-435 Massachusetts Ave.
Boston
The place to look for army-navy
surplus finds.

Dorothy Dodd
57 Suffolk St.
Holyoke

Earthwares, Inc.
103 North Pleasant St.
Amherst

GB Ltd.
115 Newbury St.
Boston

Glad Rags
76 Church St.
Lenox
Fills 5 rooms on the ground floor of
a beautiful stained-glass-windowed
Victorian house. Stock: new
imported, domestic, and handmade
clothes. Also recycled and antique
"Little Rags," a kid's version.

Honey Suckle Rose
Winter St.
Edgartown
Fancy old women's clothing and
reproductions. Open summer only.

Song of the Road
Union St.
Vineyard Haven
Wearable folk art and handwork—
Central and South America.

Take It Easy Baby
Circuit Ave.
Oak Bluffs
Funky old clothing, mostly from
Europe. Open through December.

MICHIGAN

The Red Flannel Factory
Cedar Springs

MINNESOTA

Depth of Field
405 Cedar Ave.
Minneapolis

MISSISSIPPI

Dixie's
Starkville

Fashion Station
2131 24th Ave.
Meridian

MISSOURI

Famous–Barr
St. Louis
Look for Unique Clothing
Warehouse department at all 3
branches.

Macy's
Kansas City
Look at their junior clothes.

NEBRASKA

Hitching Post (men's)
Wooden Nickel (women's)
144 North 14th St. Lincoln
333 North 72nd St. Omaha
15 West 23rd St., Kearney
Specialty apparel and shoes. Fast
moving.

NEW JERSEY

The Cellar
Woodbridge Center
Men's and women's clothing.
Antique and new designs. Hand-
crafted clothing and jewelry.

Fly By Night
18 North Washington Ave.
Bergenfield
Items from over the rainbow and
around the universe. In a mall, but
customers are made to feel at
home. Imports and originals.

Island Shop-Man Stop
4205 Long Beach Blvd.
Brant Beach

The Last Straw
317 Glenwood Ave.
Bloomfield
Fine handcrafted jewelry,
distinctive clothing, gifts,
decorative accessories and
paraphernalia.

Little People Clothing Company
12 South Fullerton Ave.
Montclair
Fantasy in a brightly colored
gingerbread house over 100 years
old. Merchandise for children.
Handmade toys and imported
clothes, getting away from pink
and blue.

Marcia's Attic
213 Main St.
Fort Lee

NEW MEXICO

Alan's Apparel
57 Encantada Sq., N.E.
Albuquerque
Only store in 400-mile radius with
classic menswear—no doubleknits.

Gallery One
620 Sierra Dr., S.E.
Albuquerque

Kidstuff
230 Park Ave.
Raton

Wild Rose
2916 Central S.E.
Albuquerque

NEW YORK

NEW YORK CITY

ABC Antiques
122 Prince St.
Antiques, bargains.

Albert Hosiery Stores
Eight branches in Manhattan.
Full line of Danskin leotards and
tights.

Alexander's
731 Lexington Ave. (at 58th St.).
Department store with little-
known areas of designer copies and
inexpensive European imports: the
"Next Shop."

A. Altman
204 Fifth Ave.
French Imports, Calvin Klein,
Stanley Blacker; tailored suits.
Reduced prices.

Ann Taylor
15 East 57th St.
(also in D.C., Conn., Mass., N.J., R.I., Chicago)
Career-oriented clothes with great style that you can build on from season to season.

Arden's
1014 Sixth Ave. (near 38th St.)
Knit clothes, broad-brimmed velours in many colors, and broad-brimmed straw hats—all at low prices.

Artbag
735 Madison Ave.
Mail in your worn but classic bag for an estimate for repairs. They give a one-year guarantee on all work.

Atabex Boutique
243 East 53rd St.
Custom copies in wool, silk and silk/polyester blends—Calvin Klein, etc.

Azuma
415 Fifth Ave., and branches
Cotton scarves, straw hats, cotton skirts, blouses, dresses.

Bargains Unlimited Thrift
1429 Third Ave.
Guccis and Puccis alongside junk as low as 25¢.

Barney's
111 7th Ave.
Classics for men and now women. Special Italian and French designer imports.

Beckenstein Woolens
125 Orchard St.
Fine woolens, men's suits.

Henri Bendel
10 West 57th St.
Train your eye with the best of European and American ready-to-wear. Shoe Biz has the best, most stylish shoes in New York. The "Street of Shops" is a free amusement!

Bloomingdale's
Lexington & 59th St.; Bergen County, N.J.; Garden City, N.Y.; Short Hills, N.J.; Stamford, Conn.; White Plains, N.Y.; and D.C.
The hottest merchandisers with the hottest merchandise. Instant boutiques with runaway looks.

Bogie's Antique Furs
201 East 10th St.
Antique furs and clothes, with new bundles arriving twice weekly.

Bonwit Teller
721 Fifth Ave.
Someting special to train the eye in Missoni Boutique, Valentino's Piu, the Hermes shop and Turnbull & Asser menswear.

Bottega Veneta
655 Madison Ave.
Silk squares of crepe de chine from Milan; beautiful leather goods and bags for people who don't need designers' initials.

Brooks Brothers
346 Madison Ave. (at 44th St.) and branches
The store for American classics. Send for catalog and for the location of store near you.

Budget Uniform Center
110 East 59th St.
Lab coats, nursing, and waitress uniforms. Large selection of hospital "scrub" clothes for dyeing which can only be purchased by the dozen.

Buffalo Weavers Clothiers
203 East 60th St.
Smashing young Italian imports; great for ideas of what European trendies are wearing. Also Kensai imports from Japan. (Check this whole block of 60th Street: boutique paradise.)

Camouflage
141 8th Ave. (at 17th St.)
Men's classics and sportswear.

Camp & Trail
Park Place (near City Hall)
Clothes for the *Field and Stream* effect.

Center Thrift Shop
120 East 28th St.
Some things priced, some not. If you're in the neighborhood, it's worth a stop.

Charles Jourdan
700 Fifth Ave.
See it here first for the footsies.

Charleston Market
21 Second Ave.
A huge selection of thirties clothes.

Cherchez
864 Lexington Ave. (at 65th St.)
Beautiful Victorian camisoles, slips, dresses for summer; in perfect condition.

Chinese Emporium
154 West 57th St.
Utilitarian Chinese workers' jackets, other items from China.

Chipp
14 East 44th St.
Full line of traditional, English-oriented men's clothes.

Chocolate Soup
249 East 77th St.
Darling children's clothes; also, the mail-order Danish schoolbag that's a great carryall.

Chor Bazaar
801 Lexington Ave.
A wide selection of cotton, muslin, scarves, dresses.

Cora and Laura
369 Canal St.
Early antique clothes; Edwardian lights; silk stockings; doodads; pretty lacy stuff. A Wendy Whitelaw favorite.

Diamond's Secondhand Clothes
42 Hester St.
Every day but Saturday. Caters to men only. All suits are marked "fair," "good," or "excellent," and range from $1 to $30.

Dianne B.
729 Madison Ave.
Imports from France. Issey Miyake, Cygne, and Dorothee Bis designs. Very *Elle* magazine, very chic. Not very cheap.

Double Dealers, Ltd.
1364 Lexington Ave.
Children's resale store.

Dudley Eldridge
39 West 32nd St.
Custom-made shirts.

Early Halloween
180 Ninth Ave.
They carry a wide selection of old clothes, old shoes, and wonderful suspenders.

Echo Scarf Co.
485 Fifth Ave.
(682-5430)
Write or phone for store near you.

Eddris Shoes
314 East 78th St.
Secret source for the shoes for the yearly Madison Avenue boutiques co-op fashion show. Very reasonable original designs.

Emotional Outlet
91 7th Ave.
Young designer clothes at excellent prices ($8-$40).

Encore Resale Dress Shop
1132 Madison Ave. (at 84th St.)
Where the local upper-East-Siders take their year-old designer clothes.

Equator
79 Wooster St.
Antiques.

Everybody's Thrift Shop
324 East 59th St.
Some of the most well-heeled New Yorkers donate their clothes to the ten charities represented at this shop.

Farkas and Kovacs, Inc.
1187 Lexington Ave.
The most exquisite custom-made shoes for men and women.

Folio
888 Madison Ave.
All sorts of little books and notepapers. Beautiful Susan Suble calling cards made up with your choice of fifty designs.

Fiorucci
125 East 59th St.
American designs reinterpreted with Italian panache.

Fonda's
168 Lexington Ave.
Designer clothes (Marta Salvatore, Cacharel, Carol Horn, Cygne, Kenzo, etc.) and antique clothing at wholesale or discount prices.

Forty's Wink Antique
Fashion Boutique
1331A Third Ave.
Good assortment of antiques and children's clothes.

Freshwater Mfg. Inc.
716 Broadway (at 4th St.)
Used blue jeans, fatigues, sailor pants, army-navy overcoats. Old dresses, coats, scarves; and new T-shirts in a rainbow of colors.

Frugal Frog
1707 Second Ave. (near 88th St.)
Clean, very cheap. Thrift shop for children with amusements for the children while the mothers shop.

Gladstone Fabrics
16 West 56th St.
Carries many fabrics from the forties and fifties. They will match a color swatch for $7, no matter how much fabric you need.

Greenwich House Thrift Shop
273 Bleeker St.

Grizzly Furs
7 St. Marks Place
Military surplus, navy blue winter coats from England. Furs.

Gyro Surplus Corp.
Broadway & Bleeker St.
Large supply of work clothes.

Halina's Beauty Shop
160 West 55th St.
A seventh heaven of antique combs and hairpins...ivory, sterling, gold, amber, from the 1850's to the 30's.

Happiness Thrift Shop
1444 Third Ave.
Run for the benefit of the United Cerebral Palsy Associations of New York.

Harriet Love
412 West Broadway
Classic antiques from a lady who really knows her business.

Havona
110 Thompson St.
Contemporary and antique clothing.

Herbert Dancewear
1657 Broadway
Full line of Danskin dance supplies and Herbert Economy leotards, tights, and skirts.

Herman's
15 West 38th St.
Well-made hats at reasonable prices: velour, beaver, straw, or fabric from about $10 to $15. Ribbons, flowers, and feathers to choose for a personal touch.

Herman's Sporting Goods
42nd St. and Sixth Ave.
Sweat chic; top to bottom and back.

Hornblower Antiques
Canal St. & West Broadway
A good place for used clothing.

Hudson's
Third Ave. at 13th St.
Army surplus but often jammed, and grouchy salesmen. Brown leather motorcycle jackets and a large stock of jeans and work clothes.

Ina
105 Thompson St.
Soho shop, special lingerie, shoes, scarves, one-of-a-kind Soho artists.

Jackie Rogers for Men
27 East 67th St.
Men's clothing, many imports, excellent taste, rather expensive.

Jenny B. Goode
1194 Lexington Ave.
Mini department store. Inexpensive and unusual clothes and accessories with dash.

Jezebel
265 Columbus Ave.
Antique clothes in top condition. Good shopping area around this store.

Julie Artisan's Gallery
687 Madison Ave.
Art fashion from America's traditional craft techniques: weaving, knitting, painting, crocheting.

Julio's
867 Madison Ave.
One-size-fits-all concept in the most exquisite fabrics and exquisite prices...good for ideas.

Kamali
6 West 56th St.
Brilliant disco dressing, sexy draped jerseys and tight leggings. Norma Kamali is an endlessly inventive designer.

Kasoundra Kasoundra
(777-9851, by appointment)
One-of-a-kind, handmade, patchwork clothes of unusual fabrics. Crocheted Art Nouveau-ish handbags in antique frames.

Kaufman Surplus & Arms
Broadway & Houston St.
Jeans, army surplus, and work clothes.

Kaufman's
139 East 24th St.
They carry everything for the rider and Midnight Cowboy.

Kip's Bay Boy's Club Thrift Shop
1577 Third Ave.
Worth a stop as you tour the Third Avenue thrift shops.

Lady Madonna
793 Madison Ave.
The breakthrough merchandisers in stylish maternity dressing.

Larissa Designs
118 Forsyth St.
Fur coats, worn inside-out so the fur is next to your body. Phone first: 431-4295.

The Leader
305 West 125 St.
Army surplus and work clothes uptown.

Lee Ann Thrift Shop
215 East 59th St.
Handpicked, funky clothes & jewelry.

Le Gaspi
743 Madison Ave.
Jewelry by Richard Erker. From doing LaBelles costumes in the village, Larry's moved his fantasia uptown to Madison.

Le Grand Hotel-Tales of Hoffman
471 North Broadway
The classy Soho look defined—downtown elegance. Shoes, too.

Fred Leighton
763 Madison Ave.
The best deco, 40's and 50's jewelry in white, yellow, and pink gold.

Life Style Antiques
46 East 57th St.
Collectors of the very best antiques drop in here.

Loehman's
9 West Fordham Rd.
Bronx
The prototypical designer discount store—surely you've seen it in fifties movies. Take the IRT Lexington Avenue #4 to the Fordham Road Station. It's there on the corner of Jerome.

Lonia
55 W. 55th St.
Fashion forward, one-of-a-kind items, quality-conscious, natural fibers. Lots of personal attention.

Macy's at Herald Square
The world's largest store: if you can't get it here, it probably doesn't exist. Juniors on Four is like walking through *Cheap Chic*!

Mater's Market
237 East 53rd St.
Maternity shop.

Medusa
1207 1st Ave. (at 65th St.)
All kinds of adorable accessories: French and English hair combs, barrettes, bracelets, pins, necklaces, boxes, little purses, scarves, masks, at reasonable prices.

Memorial Sloan-Kettering Cancer Center Thrift Shop
1410 Third Ave.
The best to the worst: furs, clothes.

The Merchant of Venice
159 Prince St.
Italian clothing. Crazy!

Michael's Resale
1041 Madison Ave. (at 79th St.)
Great buys on designer clothes; all in excellent conditon.

Miller's
123 East 24th St.
Horsey-set central. Jeans, jodhpurs, riding boots, everything.

Miso Clothes Ltd.
416 West Broadway
Sparkly clothing—Cathy Hardwick, the young designers, very Soho chic.

M.J. Knoud
716 Madison Ave.
Ivy league, horsey shop: riding clothes, books.

Montenapoleone
789 Madison Ave.
Lingerie exclusively from Florence: silk nightgowns, hand embroidered silk delicacies.

Moroccan Fashion & Art, Ltd.
818 Third Ave.
Importers of Moroccan and Tunisian classics, such as solid black capes, cotton hooded jackets, leather gold-embossed slippers.

Mythology
370 Columbus Ave.
A shop of wonderful surprises behind the Museum of Natural History. Great for gifts!

The Nearly New Thrift Shop
54th St. at Ninth Ave.
A well-heeled group gives donations here, so keep trying.

Neighborhood Thrift Shop
449 Second Ave. (near 25th St.)
The last Monday of each month is sale day—half price for everything on the racks.

The New World Gift Shoppe
906 Madison Ave. (near 73rd St.)
and also at
1131 Amsterdam Ave. (near 116th St.)
Oriental garments, jewelry, and gifts.

Odyssey House Thrift Boutique
861 Third Avenue (near 52nd St.)
Shoes are the hottest item right now, both used and new. There are also a number of new clothes that sell for about 40 percent less than they would in typical boutiques.

Ohrbach's
5 West 34th St.
Department store with copies of designer clothes and inexpensive European imports, as well as masses of inexpensive merchandise.

O Mistress Mine
143 Seventh Ave. S.
New and old dresses, always changing. It's their policy to underprice.

Ophelie
673 Madison Ave.
Imported French jewelry; the tiny earrings make the store special.

Opportunity Shop
46 West 47th St.
Perhaps the largest thrift shop of all, with two selling floors, and four storage floors that add new items every day.

Opportunity Shop of Community Service Society
(oldest charity in New York)
46 West 47th St.
Quantities of nice stuff.

Palma
77 Wooster St.
Some Soho-designed antique and handmade clothing, plus antiques.

Paragon
17th St. and Broadway
Sporting source.

Paris Fashions
270 West 38th St. (17th fl.)
Designer fashions, wholesale prices, suits, separates, raincoats, blazers, capes, and more.

Pentimenti
126 Prince St.
Antique clothes, in Soho.

Planned Parenthood Thrift Shop
324 East 59th St.
Good variety of children's clothes. Theatrical and antique clothes are another feature.

Plymouth Shops
Fifth Ave. & 52nd St.
A good place to find inexpensive accessories.

Propinquity
243 Third Ave. (near 20th St.)
Pretty antique costumes.

Resale Shop
802 Lexington Ave. (62nd St.)
High quality, low quantity, pleasant help.

Richards Army-Navy Authentics
233 West 42nd St.
Army-surplus classics in an exciting area.

Ridge Antique Furs
33 West 8th St.
(and the Warehouse at 55 Great Jones St.)
For years a favorite of chic New Yorkers with little money. Their fur coats range in quality from tattered to flawless.

Ritz Thrift Shop
107 West 57th St.
Use your old fur as a trade-in. If it's in good condition, Ritz will fit, process, clean, and glaze your purchase free.

Runner's World
275 Seventh Ave. (near 26th St.)
Head to toe for sweat clothes.

S & W
165 West 26th St.
All designers, 1/3 to 1/2 off.

St. Laurent Rive Gauche Boutique
855 Madison Ave.
YSL's ready-to-wear shoes and accessories.

Saks Fifth Avenue
The name says it all—perfect for strolling and spending . . . judiciously!

Salvation Army (main branch)
536 West 46th St.
This is thrift-shop central.

San Francisco Clothing
975 Lexington Ave.
Annie Hall forever—men and women.

Second Act
1046 Madison Ave. (near 80th St.)
Children's resale shop with a good selection, more for girls than boys. Shoes, boots, records, and books on sale, too.

Selva and Sons Inc.
1776 Broadway
Dance shoes, leotards, etc.

Sermoneta
740 Madison Ave.
South American market goods at low prices. Wicker and clothes.

Simons
67 Third Ave. at 4th St.
Work clothes of all manufacturers.

Small Business
101 Wooster St.
Darling children's clothes.

Soho Canal Flea Market
369 Canal St. (near W. Broadway)
An indoor and outdoor market, open year round, seven days a week from 11 A.M. to 6 P.M. Antiques, clothes, and collectables.

Sona
11 East 55th St.
East Indian clothing.

Spence Chapin Corner Shop
1065 Lexington Ave.
Unique beauties such as cashmere overcoats, turn-of-the-century embroidered Chinese coats.

Stitching Horse, Inc.
156 East 64th St.
Frye boots and handmade Stewart cowboy boots from Arizona. Send for free catalog .

Stone Free Kids
124 West 72nd St.
For children: original British antique christening gowns, functional American workwear, full cowboy and girl outfits. The owner, Sheila Gholson, travels the world to find children's unusual things.

Stuyvesant Square Thrift Shop
1430 Third Ave. (at 81st St.)
Big, airy sales floor, good supply of furs and better women's clothes.

Sun Hi's Gift Co.
126 7th Ave. (between 17th and 18th Sts.)
Oriental gowns, lounge robes, Hoppi coats, and bright padded cotton jackets from China.

T. Anthony
772 Madison Ave.
Leather-trimmed canvas baggage in classy colors.

Thrift House
39 West 57th St.
Offers delicious outfits at prices well below many of the other thrift shops.

Tibetan Arts & Crafts Ltd.
693 Madison Ave.
Tibetan shoes and wonderful pointed-toe boots; fur and wool hats with earflaps; fabrics, sweaters, coats, and more.

T. O. Dey
509 Fifth Ave. (near 42nd St.)
8th Floor
Shoe and boot remodeling. Will blunt or round off pointed toes, change closed shoes to sandals, change heel height and width.

Union Shirt Company, Inc.
915 Broadway
Makers of the West Point uniform shirt.

Unique Clothing Warehouse
718 Broadway
One of the original Cheap Chic hotspots, that now has branches in department stores all over, including Macy's.

Vandyke Hatters
848 Sixth Ave. (near 30th St.)
Westerns, berets—theatrical to folksy. They can also block, clean, and restore favorite hats.

Victoria Falls
170 Spring St.
White Victoriana: from wedding gowns to sleep shifts in delectable eyelets, embroideries, lace. Nice blouses.

Weiss & Mahoney
142 Fifth Ave.
Almost every imaginable army-surplus item down to women's dress uniforms. The best all-around assortment at the lowest prices.

Wendy's Store
1046 Madison Ave.
Everything for the chic small one.

Woolworth's
34th St. (near 6th Ave.)
How about some cheap accessories? Cartier-style tank watch for a price anyone can afford.

NEW YORK

OUTSIDE OF NEW YORK CITY

Gauze & Effect
19 Middle Neck Rd.
Great Neck

The Graduate Boutique
269 Main St.
Oneonta
Jeans, tops, jewelry, gifts, baskets,
lingerie, fur coats, jackets.

Hapiglop
Woodstock

Kimberley's
Main St.
Bridgehampton
Wonderful antiques, imports, and
scarf-kimonos.

Marsha's Mood Ltd.
470 Central Ave.
Cedarhurst

Old World Imports
21 Tinker St.
Woodstock

Three Eleven Shop
Walt Whitman Shopping Center
260-1 Route 110
Huntington

Zoom
10 Job's Lane
Southhampton
Some real Cheap Chic. Jan
Cushing's bikinis; Lee Radziwill's
T-shirts. Simple.

NORTH DAKOTA

Touch of Class
614 Kirkwood Plaza
Bismark

OHIO

Creative Fashions
2869 Chagrin Blvd.
Woodmere

Earth Rose
221 Xenia
Yellow Springs
Gifts and clothing from all over the
world. Hand-hammered Persian
copper jewelry from Greece. Indian
clothing (cheap).

OKLAHOMA

Cyrk & Company
50 Penn Pl.
Oklahoma City

Life Style Unlimited
3311 East 11th St.
Tulsa
Pure silk, cotton, and wool clothes
from China, Afghanistan, India,
Indonesia, and Africa, and jewelry.

Ms. Salon Hair Care Center
6221 East 61st St.
Tulsa
Linda James, makeup artist.

OREGON

Sinu's
9526 Washington Sq.
Portland

Sophisticate
917 S. Walden
Portland

PENNSYLVANIA

Bob Henicle & Company
534 Spruce St.
Scranton

Gimbels
Pittsburgh
Look for the Unique Clothing
Warehouse corner.

I. Goldberg's
8th & Chestnut Sts.
Philadelphia
University of Pennsylvania
students with army-navy surplus
for years.

Penn Center Army-Navy
20th & Market St.
Philadelphia
Standard army-navy supplies in the
heart of Philadelphia.

Scoop
227-233 Fifth Ave.
Pittsburgh

Stoney End Boutique
7608 City Line Ave.
Philadelphia

Straw Flowers
8138 Germantown Ave.
Philadelphia

TEXAS

Backstage Designs
802 W. Alabama St.
Houston
"For the woman who knows
fashion," personalized designs.

Beacon Company
4538 McKinney St.
Dallas
Check them for utilitarian clothing.

Big Tex Army-Navy Store
215 W. Jefferson St.
Dallas
Army-navy surplus items.

Contagious Clothing Co.
5362 Westheimer St.
Houston
Surplus and primo antique
clothing.

C.R. Adkins Army Store
5800 Maple St.
Dallas
And yet another army-navy store
to peruse for finds.

Las Manos, Inc.
12215 Coit Rd.
Dallas

Maharani
270 N. Anderson Lane
Austin

Neiman-Marcus
Main & Ervay Sts.
Dallas
To experience the best, as Stanley
Marcus envisioned it. Also in
Houston.

Stelzig's
Houston
Old, established store carrying
Tony Lama boots, Lucchese boots
made in San Antonio since 1883.
Basic Western clothes and
accessories.

Tootsie's
5350 Westheimer Rd. (near the
Galleria)
Houston
Basic European tops and bottoms;
unique accessories.

VERMONT

Phase One, Inc.
Waitsfield

Wings
38 Elliot St.
Brattleboro
An oasis of clothing consciousness:
silks from the Victorian times to
the fifties, jeans, accessories,
jewelry; natural fibers; custom-
made; small-time designers.

Yankee Notions
41 West Rd.
Bennington

VIRGINIA

Pennyante
Bragg St.
The Plains

Sautar Brothers, Inc.,
Department Store
629 Mercer St.
Princeton

WASHINGTON

Waitesmith's Photographic Styling
and Design
14 West Comstock
Seattle

WISCONSIN

Goldfish-U.S. Surplus
2103 W. North Ave.
Milwaukee
One of Milwaukee's favorite stores
for army-navy surplus.

PEX-U.S. Military Supply
533 West Wisconsin
Milwaukee
Another place to shop for army-
navy needs.

CANADA

Marni
55 Avenue Rd.
Toronto, Ontario

Northwest Handcraft House
110 West Esplanade
North Vancouver, B.C.

Robin
37 Hazelton Ave.
Toronto, Ontario

Tiangius
2505-1850 Lomax St.
Vancouver, B.C.

Valley Fibers Ltd.
51 William St.
Ottawa, Ontario
Folkwear.

England and France

ENGLAND
LONDON

Pick up a copy of Kaori O'Connor's
Fashion Guide (Coronet Books,
£1.25) at Janet Reger's on
Beauchamp Place or at a local
bookstore.

Antiquarius
135 King's Rd.
Flea market extraordinaire.

Badges & Equipment
Real English army-navy-RAF
surplus including flying suits,
paratrooper trousers, jungle hats,
and more.

Beauchamp Place
Check out the whole street:
Cannibal; Caroline Charles;
Deborah and Clare; Emeline;
Graffiti; Janet Reger; Janet Wilson;
Lucienne Philips; N. Peal; Piero de
Monzi.

Bill Gibb
138 New Bond St.

Bochamba
104 Fulham Rd.

The Body Shop
King's Road punk.

Brother Sun
171 Fulham Rd.

Brown's
27 South Molton St.

Burberry's
18 Haymarket

Bus Stop
3 Kensington Church St.
Cheap chic.

C & A (Marble Arch)
505 Oxford St.
Fastest with the latest at the
lowest.

Captain OM Watts
45 Albemarle St.
For yachtsmen.

Carolyn Brunn
4 South Molton St.

Chelsea Cobbler
54 King's Rd.
Not to be confused with the store
in New York. This is the original.

Elle
92 New Bond St.
...if you're not going to proceed to
Paris.

Fiorucci
15 Brompton Rd.

Fortnum and Mason
181 Piccadilly Circus

Gibb's
38 Floral St.
All sorts of fascinating shops.

Harrod's
Knightsbridge
You can buy the English edition of
Cheap Chic here, along with just
about everything.

H. Huntsman and Son
11 Savile Row
Made-to-measure clothes,
including riding, hunting, and
jockey clothes.

Jaeger
204 Regent St.
Sweaters.

Janet Reger
Beauchamp Place
Lingerie.

Jap and Joseph
20 Brompton Rd.
Kenzo et al.

Joseph
13 South Molton St.

Kickers
66 South Molton St.

King's Road: Look for Ace; Joanna's
Tent; Ladies Habits; Meeny's.

Kurt Geiger
95 New Bond St.
Italian shoes and boots. Expensive.

Laurence Corner
62 Hampstead Rd.
Genuine army-navy surplus.

Liberty
210 Regent St.
The classic Liberty prints.

Lobb
Tops for men's shoes.

Marks & Spencer
458 Oxford St.
Large department store, great for
sweaters and children's clothes.

Mary Farrin
9 South Molton St.

Mrs. Howie
138 Longacre
Covent Garden area.
New shops constantly pop up.

N. Peal
54 Burlington Arcade

Piero di Monzi
70 Fulham Rd.

Portobello Road Market
Street market open Friday and
Saturday (Saturday is the best).
Antiques, clothing, and lots more
to see.

Scotch House
2 Brompton Rd.
Knightsbridge

Seditionaries
King's Road punk.

Stirling Cooper
94 New Bond St.

Thea Porter
8 Greek St.

Le Trousseau
64 Blandford St.
Sexy lingerie (all the way to
38DD!), plus handmade sewn-to-
measure delicacies.

Turnbull and Asser
21 Jermyn St. or
23 Bury St.
Fine, classic British men's clothing,
custom-made and ready-to-wear.

Zapata Shoes
49 Old Church St.
(off King's Road)
Shoes designed by Manolo
Blahnik...always one step ahead
of the game.

FRANCE

PARIS

Department stores

Galeries Lafayette
40 Blvd. Haussmann

Marche Aux Puces
(street markets in Paris)
Marche St. Pierre—good selection
of fabrics, old and new
Montmartre
Porte St. Ouen
Mairie de Montreuil—good
bargains; arrive by 7A.M.

Printemps
64 Blvd. Haussmann

Prisunic
109 rue de la Boetie

Samaritaine
18 rue de la Monnaie

Boutiques: Right Bank

A la Blouse des Halles
140, rue de Faubourg St. Martin
Coveralls, jewelers' smocks, and
butchers' jackets—plus more.

Azzaro
65 Faubourg St. Honoré
For fancy, fancy evenings.

Caracalla
95 rue de Longchamp
Silky underthings.

Charles Jourdan
5 Blvd. de la Madeleine
10 Faubourg St. Honoré

Dianne B.
Les Halles
Also a boutique on Madison
Avenue in New York.

France Andrevie
2 Place des Victoires

Indian Trading Post
Passage Choiseul
For American Indian-Western gear
in Paris.

Issey Miyake
38 Place du Marche St. Honoré
Domaine of the supercreator.

J.C. Castelbajac
31 Place du Marche St. Honoré

Jean Dinh Van
7 rue de la Paix
Gold jewelry.

Jungle Jap
3 Place des Victoires
Kenzo's domaine.

Madame Cadolle
14 rue Cambon
Fine example of French lingerie.

La Maison Bleue
1 rue du Marché St. Honoré

Les Nuits d'Elodie
Avenue MacMahon
Sexy lingerie.

Pablo and Delia
30 Place du Marché St. Honoré

Poiray
8 rue de la Paix
More gold jewelry.

Pulcinella
10 rue Vignon
Old jewelry.

Repetto
Place de L'Opera
French equivalent of Capezio.
Ballet supplies, leotards, etc.
Excellent "off-color" selection.

Roger Vivier
24 rue François 1er
Where Diana Vreeland's shoes
come from.

Soldes magazine
3, Place Malesherbes
Send for this—every month it lists
the best bargains in each of Paris's
twenty districts, with emphasis on
unique, quality items.

Sotovol
125, rue du Faubourg St. Martin
Ideal for jumpsuits. They cater to
racing car drivers, aviators, etc.

Thierry Muggler
10 Place des Victoires

Yves St. Laurent
38 Faubourg St. Honoré
(shoes at 58)

Boutiques: Left Bank

Andrea Pfister
56 rue du Four

L'Autre Jour
26 Avenue de la Bourdonnais
Antique clothing.

C.A.A.
45 rue de Rennes
Chinese imports, period clothes.

Carola
27 rue du Four

Centre Maine Montparnasse
3 rue de l'Arrivée

Chacok
18 rue de Grenelle

Exactement Fauve
5 rue Princesse

Fabrice
26 rue Bonaparte

François Villon
58 rue Bonaparte

Globe (The Khaki Rush)
12, rue Pierre Lescot
Army clothes, Chinese and
Japanese workers' pants and
kimonos; newest looks from old
favorites.

Jardins d'Orient
11 rue du Dragon

Jeanne d'O
Antique jewelry.

Maude Frizon
83 rue des St. Peres
Shoes (also in NYC).

Mezzo Mezzo
21 rue du Dragon

Mic Mac
13 rue de Tournon

Missoni
79 rue du Rennes

Moons
48 rue de Verneuil

Nuage
7 rue du Cherche Middi
Old clothes.

Sabbia Rosa
71 rue des St. Peres
Lingerie.

Sasha
24 rue de Buci
Shoes.

Sonia Rykiel
6 rue de Grenelle

Tango
26 rue de Rennes

Ter et Bantine
5 rue de Vieux Colombier

Thea Porter
15 rue de Tournon

UFO
8 rue de Grenelle

La Vie en Rose
27 rue de l'Abbe Gregoire

Western House
23 rue des Canettes

Shopping by Mail

Acadian Crafts Association
P.O. 29
St. Catherine St.
Madawaski, Maine 04756
Hand-crocheted French-Acadian
crafts—ladies' wear and infants's
clothing. Well priced.

Adam York
340 Poplar St.
Hanover, Pennsylvania 17331
Gifts, clothes, jewelry. Everything
from colorful hard hats to stuffed
dolls with the face of your choice.

American Express Gift Catalog
P.O. Box 754
Great Neck, New York 11025
Unusual items: Japanese screens,
small heart-shaped diamond
necklaces, canvas bags.

A. S. Cooper & Cons, Ltd.
37 Front St.
Hamilton, Bermuda
Classic shetland crew-neck
sweaters in fifteen colors. Other
classics.

Austin-Hall Company
P.O. Box 12368
El Paso, Texas 79912
Custom western boots. Good
quality, cheap price.

Belgian Shoes
60 East 56th St.
New York, New York 10022
Soft hand-turned moccasins for
men and women.

Bergdorf Goodman
754 Fifth Ave.
New York, New York 10019
Exclusive items, fine designer
clothing, and accessories.

Bloomingdale's Home/Living
Catalog
1000 Third Ave.
New York, New York 10022

Bombay Britches
Box 637
Bronxville, New York
(914) 961-4553
Money back guarantee on Bombay
britches, French army surplus,
authentic journeyman mason's
book bag, imprinted sushi tins from
Japan. "Good goods at a good price"
is their credo. All postage, tax, and
handling included.

Bonwit Teller
721 Fifth Ave.
New York, New York 10022

Brentano's
586 Fifth Ave.
New York, New York 10036
Books, games, gifts, jewelry.

Brooks Brothers
346 Madison Ave.
New York, New York 10017
Ivy Leaguer's delight.

Brownstone Studio
342 Madison Ave.
New York, New York 10017
Classic fashion items and
accessories.

Budget Uniform Center, Inc.
1613 Chestnut St.
Philadelphia, Pennsylvania 19103
Sixty-page color catalog mailed
three times a year. Uniforms in
white and colors; jackets, lab coats.

Camalier & Buckley
1141 Connecticut Ave.
Washington, D.C. 20036
Gift items: leather shopping bag,
hippopotamus planter, pig-shaped
cookie jar.

Capezio Dance Catalog
1841 Broadway
New York, New York 10023
Full line of dance clothes and
accessories. Ask for the store
nearest you.

Castello
836 Broadway
New York, New York 10003
Send for fencing equipment catalog, or combative sports catalog...judo coats, Kung Fu suits, etc.

Caswell-Massey Co., Ltd.
320 West 13th St.
New York, New York 10014
Hand-illustrated, old-fashioned toiletry catalog. Rare imported soaps, hair & scalp care, potpourri, and aromatics, etc.

Chris-Craft
Algonae, Michigan 48001
"Good life" equipment: from sailing attire to jewelry, suede tennis shoes to binoculars.

The Chocolate Soup
249 East 77th St.
New York, New York 10021
The Danish Souperbag in gray, chocolate brown, or bright blue waterproof canvas.

Danskin, Inc.
1114 Avenue of the Americas
New York, New York 10036
Tops, bodysuits, hosiery, and dancewear for men, women, and children. Ask for the store in your area.

Dunham's of Maine
20 Castongway Sq.
Waterville, Maine 04901
Classic designs for men and women in pure cottons, silks, linen, and wool.

Echo Scarf Company
485 Fifth Ave.
New York, New York 10017
(212) 682-5430
Write or phone for store near you that carries their 27-in. square, white, thin handkerchief; cottons.

Empire
443 Broadway
New York, New York 10013
Fifties leather jackets, chenille emblems, all sorts of uniforms.

Everlast Sport
750 East 132nd St.
Bronx, New York 10454
Boxing equipment, including shorts and robes.

Folkwear Ethnic Patterns
Box 98
Forestville, California 95936
Catalogs.

Frederick's of Hollywood
6608 Hollywood Blvd.
Hollywood, California
Longtime mail-order leader in "sexy chic"...worth reading, even if you don't order. Had perhaps the first "string" bathing suits; lots more.

Fulton Supply Co., Inc.
23 Fulton St.
New York, New York 10038

Gatsby's
P.O. Box 11723
Atlanta, Georgia 30305

Greek Island, Ltd.
215 East 49th St.
New York, New York 10017
Cotton voile or gauze scarves; cotton tops, skirts, and caftans.

Hammacher Shlemmer
147 East 57th St.
New York, New York 10022
Gifts: espresso makers (chrome or gold-plated); cordless, portable telephones that run on batteries. Not cheap.

Haucraft from Europe
P.O. Box 372
Sausalito California 94965
Folk wear.

Holubar
Dept. 4-119H Box 7
Boulder, Colorado 80302
Down jackets and parkas; also, duffel bags.

Honeybee
2745 Philmont Ave.
Huntingdon Valley,
Pennsylvania 19006
Classic, fancy, casual, and loungewear.

Horchow Collection
P.O. 34257
Dallas, Texas 75234
A collection of exclusive big-city status possessions. A must for the sensuous shopper.

Hunting World
16 East 53rd St.
New York, New York 10022
Safari central; great canvas.

I. Buss Uniform & Co., Inc.
50 West 17th St.
New York, New York 10011
Mid-calf slicker with corduroy collar.

I. Goldberg & Company Army-Navy
902 Chestnut St.
Philadelphia, Pennsylvania 19107
Scarlet wool French beret $4.25.

I. Magnin
P.O. Box 7660
San Francisco, California 94120
High style—designer clothes by mail!

J. Capps & Sons, Ltd.
1180 Sunrise Valley Dr.
Reston, Virginia 22091
Body- armor disguised as vests, sport coats, T-shirts, etc. Just the thing for revolutions.

J.C. Penny Co., Inc.
1301 Avenue of the Americas
New York, New York 10019
Big fall and spring catalogs. Very stylish too.

Janet Reger
2 Beauchamp Pl. SW3
33 Brook St. W.2
London, England
Catalog $4. Beautiful pure silk designer lingerie, night wear.

Joe Hall Boots
P.O. Box 17971
El Paso, Texas
Fine Western boots made to order, with custom details.

Kaleidoscope
2201 Faulkner Road, N.E.
Atlanta, Georgia 30324
Gifts! Unusual ivory jewelry; clock with personalized message on its face; leisure clothes and kitchen accessories.

Kaufman & Sons
139 E. 24th St.
New York, New York 10010
To keep your feet dry—elastic-sided jodphur boots. All riding clothes.

Kreeger & Son
16 W. 46th Street
New York, New York 10017
Outdoor clothing. Good deal on wool rag sweaters; heavy cotton "chamois" shirts. Good-quality down jackets.

L. L. Bean, Inc.
Freeport, Maine 04032
100 percent wool-plaid shirts, wool jackets, everything you'll ever need for the outdoor, sportive life.

Land's End
2317 N. Elston Ave.
Chicago, Illinois 60614
Sailing clothing and equipment.
Good-quality rainwear, duffel
bags, rain boots.

Macys
Herald Square
New York, New York 10001
You know what Macys has—well,
they have catalogs, too!

Mark Cross
645 Fifth Ave.
New York, New York 10022
Mark Cross totes, belts, and
luggage. Home of "Living well is
the best revenge."

Mark, Fore, & Strike
P.O. Box 640
Delray Beach, Florida 33444
"Resort Fashions" for the second-
string classics look, like sailing
slickers for $10.

Parke Bernet, Inc.
980 Madison Ave.
New York, New York 10021
Newsletter ($3. a year) lists all
auction sales. Write subscription
department for jewelry catalog for
each auction. With the catalog, you
can even bid by mail!

Pennsylvania Station
340 Poplar St.
Hanover, Pennsylvania 17331
Glorious gifts.

Propinquity
8915 Santa Monica Blvd.
West Hollywood, California 90069
Catalog worth having! Unusual gift
ideas; works of art. Things to treat
yourself to. Very "El Lay."

Recreational Equipment Inc.
Call toll free for free catalog
800-426-4840
Good outdoor equipment at some
of the cheapest prices. Down
parkas, ski jackets, sweaters, jeans,
hiking boots, etc. REI is a co-op;
optional $2. membership for 9½%-
10% dividend upon each purchase.

Right Bank Clothing Co.
313 North Rodeo Dr.
Beverly Hills, California 90210
Chic imported clothes and
accessories; shoes and make-up·

Robert Kirk, Ltd.
150 Post St.
San Francisco California 94108
Tops in men's classics.

Sakowitz
1111 Main St.
Houston, Texas 77002
Appealing clothing and lingerie.

Sears, Roebuck and Co.
Chicago, Illinois 60684
Comprehensive shop-at-home
catalogs; big fall and spring books.

Sears Western Catalog
Square-dance petticoats, saddle
blankets, cowboy boots, Western
shirts—low prices.

Shopper's Guide to Museum Stores
The Museum Shop
Baltimore Museum of Art
Baltimore, Maryland 21218
For $8, tour the nation's special
museum gift shops.

Shopping International, Inc.
Norwich, Vermont 05055
Imports from Peru, Iran Sweden,
China—to name a few. Baskets,
jewelry, clothing.

Sierra Designs
4th and Addison
Berkeley, California 94710
Good down clothing.

The Slipper House
1450 Ala Moana Blvd.
Honolulu, Hawaii 96814
Over one hundred slippers, thongs,
gaza straw thongs, Lauhala
slippers, and more. Most under $10.

Sperry Top-Sider
18 Rubber Ave.
Naugatuck, Connecticut 06770
Topsider moccasins for boating,
etc. Even after wetting, the elk hide
dries to its original softness.

Sportpages
137-19 Welch Rd.
Dallas, Texas 75240
Tennis, swimming, and golf
clothing accessories. Lots of shorts
and fishnet pullovers.

Miller Stockman
Box 5407
Denver, Colorado 80217
Comprehensive shop-at-home
catalog of men's and women's
western wear.

Miller's
Mail Order Division
P.O. Box 720
Canal Street Station
New York, New York 10013
Western and English riding clothes
and equipment; beautiful riding
jackets classic boots. Catalog, $1.

Montgomery Ward
Chicago, Illinois 60607
You must place an order first to get
the catalog. Good buys in sports
and work clothes.

Montgomery War Catalog Desk
393 7th Ave.
New York, New York 10001

Neiman-Marcus Co.
Dallas, Texas 75201
Christmas catalog is the big one—a
rich man's "wish book."

Norm Thompson
1805 Northwest Thurman
Portland, Oregon 97209
First-quality, outdoorsy classics for
men and women.

Nudie's Rodeo Tailors
5015 Lankershim Blvd.
North Hollywood, California 91601
Ultimate in flashy Western wear.
Custom tailor to the stars of the
Grand Ole Opry, as well as rock 'n
roll. Extraordinary boots, too.

Out Door Traders
Box 1608A Boston Post Rd.
Greenwich, Connecticut 06830
Classic "east coasty" outdoors wear
and accessories, sweaters, pants,
skirts. Afghanistan "opanks,"
which are leather-soled slipper
socks—knee-high and colorful!

Stitching Horse
156 East 64th St.
New York, New York 10021
Frye boots and handmade Stewart
cowboy boots from Arizona. Free
catalog.

Sweaters 'N Things
713A Brooklyn Ave.
Baldwin, New York 11510
More than sweaters! Coquille-
feathered neck pieces (covers the
shoulders with iridescent green
feathers). Silk and feathered
thongs to use as belt or necklace.

The Talbots
164 North St.
Hingham, Massachusetts 02043
Classic sportswear for men and
women.

Tantra
Box 489
121 Union St.
Providence, Rhode Island 02901
Cotton imports from India,
inexpensive and comfortable.

Tibetan Arts & Crafts Ltd.
693 Madison Ave.
New York, New York 10022
Tibetan shoes and wonderful
pointed-toe boots; fur and wool
hats with earflaps; fabrics,
sweaters, coats, and more. Hard to
obtain items available.

Tony Lama
P.O. Drawer 9518
El Paso, Texas 79985
Write for the name of a store in
your area. Extraordinary line of
cowboy boots in all leathers and
styles.

Trifles
P.O. Box 44432
Dallas, Texas 75234
New catalog from Horchow's.
Gifts, clothing.

Tuhi Latis Perfumes Ltd.
146-36 13th Ave.
Whitestone, New York 11357
Copycat perfumes—pseudo-"Joy"
by mail.

Victoria's Secret
P.O. Box 31442
San Francisco, California 94131
$1. for luxurious color lingerie
catalog.

Viva Products
909 3rd Ave.
New York, New York 10022
or call: 800-223-7763 (toll free)
New York residents: 593-0334.
Sexy, satiny, lacy lingerie.

Webco
Box 429
Venice, California 90291
116-page catalog for $1.50. Padded
denim motocross jeans, full range
of motorcycle gear.

Weiss and Mahoney
142 5th Ave.
New York, New York 10011
Ultimo army surplus catalog!

Western Brands
P.O. Box 1880
Estes Park, Colorado 80517
Mail-order Levi's, moccasins, scout
boots, buckskin trousers and shirts,
leather shoulder bags, and all sorts
of unusual leather items.

Wrangler
c/o Blue Bell
1411 Broadway
New York, New York 10018
Write to them for the store in your
area that carries Wranglers.

PHOTOGRAPHIC AND ILLUSTRATIVE CREDITS

Remember: style is about 5% investment and 95% illusion.

THE CARE AND FEEDING OF FABRICS

	COTTON	WOOL	SILK	SYNTHETICS
DESCRIPTION:	Natural fiber that's versatile, durable—launders well.	Natural fiber with insulating capacity—can be warm or cool.	Natural fiber that is expensive but dyes well, has natural luster and strength.	Many varieties that duplicate natural fibers, some are unique.
VARIETIES: (Types listed are but a few, those most mentioned in this book.)	Batiste, Calico, Cheesecloth, Corduroy, Denim, Gauze, Flannelette, Lawn, Madras, Muslin, Oxford, Velour, Velveteen.	Camel hair, Cashmere, Cavalry twill, Challis, Flannel, Gabardine, Herringbone, Melton, Mohair Tweed.	Chiffon, China silk, crepe de Chine, Georgette, Satin, Mousseline de Soie, Shantung, Velvet.	Acetate, Acrylic, Nylon, Polyester, Rayon and Spandex. Generally known under brand names as Orlon, Dacron, Fortrell, Kodell, etc.
CARE:	Hand-launders well. If pre-shrunk may be machine washed (depending on type). Iron with hot iron or not at all, i.e., terrycloth, seersucker.	Dry clean most items but may be washed in cold water with special detergent such as Woolite. Protect against moths.	Dry cleaning is recommended for most items but some can be carefully hand laundered in cool water. Protect from long exposure to light.	Care requirements vary, so for best results follow manufacturer's instructions carefully.

STAINS:	MACHINE- AND HAND-WASHABLES	OTHER FABRICS
BLOOD	Soak in lukewarm water and enzyme-containing pre-soak or detergent. Launder.	Treat with cold water plus 2 tablespoons per quart table salt solution. Rinse and blot with towel.
CHEWING GUM	Remove gum from surface with a dull knife. Soak affected area in cleaning fluid. Launder.	Same as for washable fabrics, but do not launder.
CHOCOLATE OR COFFEE	Soak in warm water with enzyme-containing product. Launder.	If fabric is colorfast, sponge with lukewarm water.
GREASE AND TAR	Place towel under stain. Pour cleaning fluid through stained area. Launder in hot water.	Take to dry cleaner. Identify stain for dry cleaner's information.
MAKEUP	Soak overnight in warm detergent solution containing 4 tablespoons household ammonia to each quart of water. Rinse. Launder. Bleach if necessary.	Take to dry cleaner. Identify stain for dry cleaner's information.
MILDEW	Launder with detergent and chlorine bleach if color and fabric permit.	Take to dry cleaner. Identify stain for dry cleaner's information.
PERSPIRATION	Launder with detergent in hot water. Bleach if necessary.	Sponge with water if fabric is colorfast.

Note on Linen: Once widely used for summer apparel because of its high moisture absorption, linen is fast being replaced by synthetics. A garment of real linen would classify as an investment today. To its advantage, linen is smooth and therefore does not lint and can be washed or dry cleaned, depending on dye, finish, design application, and garment construction. To its disadvantage, linen wrinkles very easily. For best results, it is wise to iron with a very hot iron and avoid pressing into sharp creases.

Race, Class & Struggle

Essays on Racism and Inequality in Britain, the US and Western Europe

Louis Kushnick

Rivers Oram Press
London and New York

First published in 1998 by
Rivers Oram Press
144 Hemingford Road, London N1 1DE

Distributed in the USA by
New York University Press
Elmer Holmes Bobst Library
70 Washington Square South
New York, NY10012-1091

Set in Sabon by
NJ Design Associates, Romsey, Hants
and printed in Great Britain by
T.J. Press (Padstow) Ltd

British Library Cataloguing in Publication Data
A catalogue record for this book is available from the British Library

ISBN 1 85489 096 4 (cloth)
ISBN 1 85489 097 2 (paperback)

This book is dedicated to the memories of Bessie and Meyer Levin and Evelyn and Al Kushnick who taught me by example that it wasn't necessary to be a racist in a racist society, and to Patricia Kushnick for her commitment and partnership in the fight against racism.

Contents

Acknowledgments

The essays in this collection have been written over a twenty-seven-year period. These years have been marked by struggle and progress and by reactionary and racist politics and resistance. I hope that this book captures these developments and struggles. If they do, it is because I have been informed and influenced by those struggles and by the work and lives of many individuals.

The education, comradeship and support I have received over the past three decades from my colleagues at the Institute of Race Relations has been the most important influence upon my work. Their willingness to work with me and bring me along, and to turn my convoluted prose into readable English, has been exemplary. The political and intellectual leadership provided by A. Sivanandan has not only informed my work but been a model of committed scholarship, linking research and writing with struggle, based on the understanding that the function of knowledge is to change reality.

The political commitment of my partner, Patricia, has informed her work as an educator and neighbourhood worker in inner-city Manchester. Her involvement with, and commitment to, inner-city, multi-racial working-class communities has helped to anchor me in the realities of the British class and race-stratified society — and to the need to change it.

I would like to thank the large number of activist scholars whose work has informed mine and whose commitment has been a model to me, and whose criticisms and suggestions have helped me develop my analysis. Among them are: Abdul Alkalimat; Huw

Beynon; Benjamin P. Bowser; Lee Bridges; Mary Ellison; Evelyn Hu-DeHart; James Jennings; Simon Katznellenbogen; Manning Marable; Jacqueline Ould and Melanie Tebbutt.

I would like to acknowledge the financial assistance provided by the Nuffield Foundation Small Grants Scheme in the Social Sciences and by the University of Manchester Fund for Research in the Humanities and Social Sciences.

I would like to thank Kristin Armstrong, Dave O'Carroll and Laura Turney for their sterling work trying to organise me and ensuring a high standard of finished work and my publishers, Elizabeth Fidlon and Katherine Bright-Holmes, for their enthusiasm, support and hard work to make this book possible, and for their confidence in me.

I want to thank Alex and Simon and John and Delia for their love, support and encouragement.

Introduction

The plight of the white working class throughout the world today is directly traceable to Negro slavery in America, on which modern commerce and industry was founded, and which persisted to threaten free labor until it was partially over thrown in 1863. The resulting color caste founded and retained by capitalism was adopted, forwarded and approved by white labor, and resulted in subordination of colored labor to white profits the world over. Thus the majority of the world's laborers, by the insistence of white labor, became the basis of a system of industry which ruined democracy and showed its perfect fruit in World War and Depression.[1]

The unifying theme of the essays in this volume is the centrality of racism in the creation and reproduction of hierarchical and unequal class-based societies. The research has focused primarily on Britain and the United States, but also includes a study of racism and anti-racism in contemporary Western European countries. These studies are based on the understanding that *race* is a social and political construct rather than a scientific category.[2] Racism does not require different physical characteristics, such as skin colour, to justify the distribution of resources in favour of particular groups at the expense of others. At different points in European history, for example, groups have been defined in racial terms without having different skin colour. It was developed as part of the triumph of England over the Celtic periphery, which Michael Hechter calls 'Internal Colonialism', over the Irish, the Scots and the Welsh.[3] The ideology which accompanied and justified this new world system was in part based on the construction of racialised categories and explanatory systems of thought established on these categories — as well as upon the validation of expropriation, enslavement and exploitation.

In the case of the conquest and expropriation of the land of the Catholic Irish Celts, Rolston argues that

> By the time the Elizabethan planters (settler-colonists) were moving into Ulster, they were carrying the legacy of almost half a millennium of racist beliefs with them as cultural baggage. In addition, they had their own contemporary reasons to denigrate the native Irish and thus reduce the likelihood of guilt in dispossessing them of their land and rights. Given the intensity of the Elizabethan thrust to plant Ireland, the old stereotype was given a new and more sinister lease of life.

He adds that

> the view of the Irish as ignoble savages took on an intensity under the Elizabethan conquest that it had never had before. Previously, it was reason for segregation; now it became the justification for genocide.[4]

> Elizabethan adventurers wrote of the Irish as a 'wicked race' which could only 'be subdued by force'. As 'pagans', they were a legitimate 'sacrifice to God'. They were a lower order of humanity who 'live like beasts, void of law and all good order ... brutish in their customs'.[5]

Such beliefs not only justified displacement and slaughter, it absolved those who carried out such actions of 'all normal ethical considerations' — and became part of a strategy of slaughter which was being carried out against Native Americans at the same time. There was a high degree of ideological and structural intertwining of actors and ideas in creating this new world system. Nicholas Canny is quoted by Rolston on this interconnection:

> The same indictments being brought against the Indians, and later the blacks, in the New World ... had been brought against the Irish .... Both Indians and blacks, like the Irish, were accused of being idle, dirty and licentious.[6]

The development of this system of 'Internal Colonialism' provided the structural basis of the ideological racism which continued as the unequal relationship between England and the Irish Catholic Celts proceeded, and as that relationship came to include the migration of the Irish to Britain as cheap labour. One crucial point is that seemingly obvious differences in secondary racial characteristics, in physiognomy and skin colour were not, and are not, necessary for the construction and reproduction of racism. The construction of the 'Irish' as a distinct racial group with specified racial characteristics did not require the Irish to be of a different colour. It is interesting to note that many of the stereotypes applied to Africans, and used to justify their enslavement, had first been used against another European group of people. Thus, the common-sense arguments about 'natural' responses, fears, antagonisms and the like of members of one *racial* group to members of another *racial* group do not accurately explain the processes through which racism is constructed. Race is a social construct — not a biological one — and how people are defined is the result of the interplay of structures, interests and ideology.

In the twentieth century, however, skin colour and its presumed associated traits have been, because of the history of colonialism and imperialism, in the words of Susan J. Smith, 'particularly salient'.[7] Plantation economies based on slavery in the New World provided for the development of manufacturing in the centre of the world system, particularly in Britain. The triangular trade was a stimulus for British manufacturers and for economic development in the British settler colonies in North America. Africans were bought with British manufactured goods. Those who survived the middle passage in British ships had to be clothed and fed by British firms and the crops they produced on the plantations provided both the raw materials for industry and capital for investment in new plant and equipment in the South and New England.[8] Winston Churchill identified the trade's importance in the following terms:

> The West Indies, two hundred years ago, bulked very largely in the minds of all people who were making Britain and making the British Empire. Our possession of the West Indies, like that of India — colonial plantation and development, as they were then called — gave us the strength, the support, but specially capital, the wealth, at a time when no other European nation possessed such a reserve, which enabled us to come through the great struggle of the Napoleonic Wars, the keen competition of the commerce of the eighteenth and nineteenth centuries, and enabled us not only to acquire this worldwide appendage of possessions we have, but also to lay the foundations of that commercial and financial leadership which, when the world was young, when everything outside Europe was undeveloped, enabled us to make our great position in the world.[9]

The importance of the slave trade can be gauged by the following quotation from a Liverpudlian authority writing in 1797:

> This great annual return of wealth may be said to pervade the whole town, increasing the fortunes of the principal adventurers, and contributing to the support of the majority of the inhabitants; almost every man in Liverpool is a merchant, and he who cannot send a bale will send a bandbox. It will therefore create little astonishment that the attractive African meteor has from time to time so dazzled their ideas that almost every order of people is interested in a Guinea cargo.... People used to say that 'several of the principal streets of Liverpool had been marked out by chains, and the walls of the houses cemented by the blood of the African slaves'. The Customs House sported carvings of Negroes heads. 'It was the capital made in the African slave trade that built some of our docks', wrote a late Victorian Liverpool essayist. 'It was the price of human flesh and blood that gave us a start'.[10]

Professor H. Merrivale, who delivered a series of lectures at Oxford in 1840 on the theme 'Colonisation and Colonies', asked two important questions and gave an equally important answer:

> What raised Liverpool and Manchester from provincial towns to gigantic cities? What maintains now their ever active industry and their rapid accumulation of wealth? ... Their present opulence is as really owing to the toil and suffering of the Negro as if his hands had excavated their docks and fabricated their steam engines.[11]

Bailey quotes the view of a mid-eighteenth century British merchant Malachi Postlethwayt, which provides support for Merrivale's conclusion:

> Is it not notorious to the whole World, that the Business of Planting in our British colonies, as well as in the French, is carried on by the Labour of Negroes, imported thither from Africa? Are we not indebted to those valuable People, the Africans for our Sugars, Tobaccoes, Rice, Rum, and all other Plantation Produce?[12]

The only 'black' spot on the horizon of this profitable economic system was that it was based on slavery. This was potentially particularly dangerous at that point because capitalism in its struggle against feudalism was evolving an ideology, alongside the political dimension, of liberation based on individuals. In this new system, individual transactions in the market place formed the basis of economic activity and societal progress — with each individual 'free' to sell his or her labour to any would-be purchaser. People were to be freed from their previous feudal ties to the land and, in their drive to maximise profitable use of the land as a commodity, landowners would be free to displace labour no longer required. How, then, is it possible to create a new economic and political and philosophical system dedicated to individualism, freedom and profit on the backs of slaves? James Walvin addresses this question in the following way:

> It was one thing to concede the economic importance of the African, it was quite another to justify the treatment to which he was subjected and yet the relevant literature tried constantly to fulfill both tasks .... Whenever varied interest groups sought to advance their own claims to a share in the African trade they generally presented their case not as a simple economic proposition, but as a moral enterprise, justifiable on the grounds of an alleged inferiority of the Negro. The distinctive qualities of the African, noted in the sixteenth century, became the hallmarks of inferiority by the eighteenth century. Even by the late sixteenth century British commercial practice, and the legislation defending that commerce, was actually treating the African as a form of subhuman; a species of property, or a simple commodity. Alongside this commercial fait accompli, through a multitude of tracts, pamphlets, handbills and books whose purpose was to defend and justify that commerce.[13]

These 'tracts, pamphlets, handbills and books' provided a 'solution' to the moral questions posed by Equiano and Montesquieu, among others. Equiano, an ex-slave and one of the leaders of the anti-slavery movement in eighteenth-century Britain, posed the problem: 'Can any man be a Christian who asserts that one part of the human race were ordained to be in perpetual bondage to another?'[14] Interestingly enough, on the other side of the Channel, the French philosopher Montesquieu articulated the problem in similar terms when he wrote: 'It is impossible for us to suppose these creatures to be men, because, allowing them to be men, a suspicion would follow that we ourselves are not Christians'.[15]

The resolution of these problems lay in the ending of slavery and of the slave trade only when economic change and the resistance of the slaves made the ex-slaves' free labour a satisfactory alternative. In a development similar to that adopted earlier *vis-à-vis* the Irish

Catholics, whose land and freedom had been taken by England, all of the victims of these processes, whether Irish or African, were defined as ape-like, less than human, savage. This 'solution' — slavery — has had fundamental and continuing consequences. It facilitated these barbaric practices by justifying their use in terms of the superior civilisation of the British and other Europeans. The rationalisation was subsequently used to justify imperial conquest of Africa at the end of the nineteenth century and has been a constant theme of British education and in popular culture since. Significantly, in 1983, when Prime Minister Margaret Thatcher, in full glory of her victory over the 'Argies' and of her putting the 'great' back into Britain again, was revelling in 'Victorian values' during one 'Question Time' in the House of Commons, a Labour MP challenged her by asking which Victorian values was she referring to: poor houses and gin-soaked mothers? Thatcher responded immediately and with vigour that it meant bringing civilisation to countries of the world which would not have it without Britain. It is equally significant that she included this assertion in her famous Bruges speech, where she asserted Britain's sovereign right to limit further integration.

Racism has functioned to legitimise inequality and hierarchy in class-based systems by rationing scarce resources in a racialised fashion. In this way it legitimates both rationing itself and the way available resources are defined, gaining the acceptance and loyalty of the majority of the dominant group on the basis of their receiving, 'deservedly', more than members of the dominated group. The key issue, then, becomes not the high degree of inequality among the members of the dominant group but the distinctions between lower-level members of the dominant group and members of the dominated group. Black sociologist Charles S. Johnson has argued that institutional racism is a response to the contradictions inherent in a society based upon 'capitalistic liberty', that it is 'a commitment to exclude the Negro from power in order to protect the limited expansion of equal rights to others'.[16] The following quotations will help facilitate an understanding of this dynamic in operation.

> I wonder the working people are so quiet under the taunts and insults offered to them. Have they no Spartacus among them to head a revolt of the slave class against their political tormentors? *Cobden*[17]
> ... it was 'our ignorance of society and of government — our prejudices, our disunion and distrust' which was one of the biggest

obstacles to the dissolution of the 'unholy compact of despotism'.
London Working Man's Association[18]

Ignorance, disunion and distrust are central components of and also the consequences of the dominant racist ideology into which successive generations of British and American people — and people in other race-centred societies — are socialised and which serves to maintain the capitalist world system.[19] As John Stanfield has written: 'Race-centred societal members are socialized in mundane ways to presume certain populations are naturally inferior or superior due to social and cultural attributes attached to physical features.' He identifies the two dimensions of racism 'as a central aspect of human development in America and in other race-centred societies ... racialism and racial discrimination'. Racialism is a product of developmental and everyday socialization; and racial discrimination 'occurs when a dominant population creates, legitimates, and reconfirms its superiority through labelling outsiders as inferior races and through dehumanizing them through withholding crucial resources such as property ownership, gainful employment, investment capital, and human dignity'.[20] Thus, this is not an argument about dumb workers, dumb whites being manipulated in a way that they are too stupid to understand but which is clear to white intellectuals. Neither is it an argument which asserts the primacy of ideology over material forces, nor, we hope, an argument which is so deterministic and instrumentalist that it constructs inevitable outcomes and ignores struggle. The dominant ideology and the extent of effective democracy that exist in any society at any point are the results of previous conflicts between classes and other forces, conflicts which have produced reforms, changes, concessions. Therefore, ideological and psychological processes, on the one hand, and material forces on the other are engaged in the dynamics of class relations. Concessions won by working-class militancy in one historical period may not be secure in another period characterized by a lower level of consciousness and militancy.

The organisation of power and distribution of resources along racial lines determine the conditions and chances of people in these societies. Therefore, the shape of class relations in these societies are the consequences of state power and action. State racism (that is, racism which is sustained in a variety of ways by state action) underpins and legitimates popular racism, itself transmitted by institutions under the control of the state and of capital. The dominant ideology — regularly reinforced by the political institutions and the media — can 'explain' events and provide an agenda for action, no matter how wrong-headed and contradictory to the material reality and interests of white workers. Thus, for the white working class in the metropole, racism, in both its material and ideological aspects, provides privileges at the cost of the continuation of a system which exploits its members, limits human development, maintains insecurity, and largely leaves the working class powerless to contest for power or even to maintain the material privileges won in previous periods. For the metropolitan ruling classes, however, racism has provided greater, and more sustainable, material benefits. Through their ability to set agendas, determine what is natural or normal and to define common sense, they have been able to establish a degree of control over the minds and consciousness of the metropolitan working class. This advances the bourgeoisie's political control of the state and society. Racism has enabled the bourgeoisie to establish the race-stratified labour forces in the metropole, which facilitates the super-exploitation of racially oppressed workers as well as the continuing exploitation of white workers.

One of the clearest examples of the operation of state racism, its role in constructing race-stratified societies and legitimating the common-sense racist ideology, together with creating 'the facts on the ground' which then structure future relations between people, is the forging of what D.S. Massey and N.A. Denton in the 1990s called 'American Apartheid'. Detailed studies of the construction of the first and second ghettos found the local state and the national state integrally involved, along with banks, savings and loan institutions, insurance companies and real estate and property development interests, in constructing those ghettos.[21] Hadjor identifies the role played by the 'property buyers' bibles' — *Babcock's Valuation of Real Estate* (1932) and *McMichael's Appraising Manual* (1931) — which indicated that the presence of 'undesirable elements' was 'sufficient grounds to refuse a loan'. He argues that this policy 'was not only an effective sanction against prospective black buyers, but was also a good way to put pressure on white homeowners to help keep blacks out and so protect the value of their property'.[22]

Hadjor also identifies the role played by the Home Owners Loan

Corporation (HOLC), created by the Roosevelt Administration, which institutionalised 'red-lining'. It instituted a system of grading for neighbourhood factors, which determined mortgage-granting decisions. The grades ranged from 'A' — 'areas in demand in good times and bad and were homogenous, i.e., American business or professional men' — 'B' — 'still desirable' — 'C' — 'declining' — to 'D' — 'declined'. Black areas were invariably put in 'D' while those areas 'within such a low price or rent range as to attract undesirable elements' were put in 'C'.[23] The Federal Housing Administration (FHA) and the Veterans Administration (VA) fuelled the post-World War II suburbanisation programme which led to the construction of over $120 billion worth of private, owner-occupied housing by 1965, 98 per cent of which was owned by whites. The FHA's *Underwriting Manual* (1939) emphasised the importance of keeping out 'inharmonious racially or nationality groups' and recommended the use of 'subdivisions, regulations, and suitably restrictive covenants' to achieve their exclusion.[24]

The result, along with racially segregated high-density public housing in the inner-cities, was, for Massey and Denton, 'Black reservations, highly segregated from the rest of society and characterized by extreme social isolation'.[25] Hirsch identifies the role of racism in allowing competing class interests among whites to be resolved at the expense of blacks and identifies public housing to become an officially sanctioned 'second ghetto ... solidly institutionalized and frozen in concrete' where 'government took an active hand not merely in reinforcing prevailing patterns of but in lending them a permanence never seen before'.[26]

Hadjor concludes that

> suburbanization has taken place within a social environment and political climate that have ensured that this moment took on racial overtones. With economic and political discrimination ensuring that blacks were concentrated in ghettos, it was not difficult to attack racial implications to the mass movement of white people away from those areas. Black neighborhoods were associated with deprivation and crime in the public imagination. For most whites, self-improvement became closely linked with putting distance between their family and the places where black people lived.[27]

With jobs and public services following the whites to the suburbs, it is not surprising that politicians cultivated the suburban white voters and that these voters used their suffrage to ensure the continuing flow of public resources. The inner-cities, meanwhile, continued to be starved of public resources and to be defined in racially derogatory terms. Crime, welfare and social dislocation were racialised and became the basis of a politics of scapegoating and of destroying the legitimacy of 'big government', while Military Keynesianism — the system of pump priming the economy via massive military spending rather than spending on civilian physical and human infrastructure — continued unopposed. Public policies continued throughout the Cold War to privilege the giant corporations, the 'industrial' component of what President Eisenhower called the 'military-industrial complex' and the largely white strata of well-paid professional, scientific and management elites employed by these corporation. The political Right in the US in both its 'Old' and 'New' forms, attacked income transfer programmes benefiting the poor as examples of wasteful governmental expenditures which coddled the shiftless and lazy poor and increased the taxes on the hard-working, decent people.

As African-American families were increasingly faced to rely on programmes such as Aid for the Families with Dependent Children (AFDC) because of the operations of structural racism in the labour market, in housing and in education, these attacks increased in ferocity. As economic restructuring began to erode the benefits which had accrued to white politics appealing to white working-class and lower middle-class people, particularly men, from the operation of this racialised system, the racialised attacks became even more central to white politics, appealing to white suburban voters and to divert the attention of those large groups of white working people from the real causes of their declining standard of living on to appropriate scapegoats.[28] These racialised attacks on 'dependency, welfare queens', and the underclass thus fed into the right-wing and corporate strategy of dismantling large parts of public provision and the Social Wage by scapegoating the black and Latino poor. It would thus allow Reagan and Thatcher to focus the attention of white working people on 'legitimate' enemies and gain their votes while carrying out an agenda constructed by, and for the benefit of, corporate capital.[29]

In Britain, the continuing definition of Afro-Caribbeans and Asians as 'the Other', as 'outsiders', as 'them' rather than 'us' served to enable Thatcher, Major, et al. to play the 'race card' in successive elections and facilitate the same restructuring. One of the most obvious examples came in the run-up to the 1979 General Election, when, in 1978, Thatcher declared her belief that 'the British people had a legitimate fear of being swamped by an alien culture'. She obviously had a limited definition of who constituted the 'British People' and of an 'alien culture'. Clearly, the latter was made up of Coke, Pepsi, McDonalds or Kentucky Fried Chicken and the former equally clearly constituted whites. The language of 'swamping', 'floods of immigrants', etc. were emotive and threatening. On election night, 1987, former Conservative Prime Minister Edward Heath said that immigration was one of three key reasons for the third consecutive Tory victory. How accurate was this assessment and, more to the point, what exactly did Heath mean when he spoke of immigration? Immigration had come to mean black immigration in the most specific sense in the British political system, certainly since the late 1950s. But there had been virtually no black primary immigration into Britain since 1973, when the 1971 Immigration Act — passed by Heath's own government — came into force. Further, between 1965 and 1972 there had been only an average of 6500 black primary immigrants entering Britain a year as a result of the Labour Government's 1965 Immigration White Paper. Thus, if the former Prime Minister were correct, and I believe he was, both he and a significant proportion of the white British public and political elites must have meant something beyond black immigration when they spoke and wrote about immigration. That term had come to mean the very presence of black people in Britain. Thus, a more accurate statement would be that racism was one of the key factors ensuring a third successive Conservative victory, much as it was in the victories of Ronald Reagan and of George Bush.

The fourth consecutive Conservative victory, on 9 April 1992, provides additional support for an argument that racism played a central role in late twentieth-century British politics. In the year before the General Election, the Conservative Government and its allies in the press again raised the issue of immigration — or in their terms the spectre of Britain being flooded by bogus asylum-seekers. The Prime Minister, John Major, the Foreign Secretary, Douglas Hurd, the Home Secretary, Kenneth Baker and myriad of lesser Tories all warned of the threat of millions of economic migrants flooding into Britain and Europe and calling for more and more restrictive immigration controls both on the European level and on the national level. Britain began more openly co-operating with the Schengen Agreement nations within the European Community — France, Germany, Belgium, Luxembourg, the Netherlands, Portugal, Spain and Italy — which have agreed on the abolition of border controls, a common visa policy, common rules on which country should decide on asylum applications and the creation of the Schengen Information System, a powerful database which will hold details on several categories of individuals of interest to the police and other agencies, including foreign nationals deemed 'undesirable'.[30] On the British front, the government introduced the Asylum Bill on 31 October 1991. The Bill, designed according to the government, to deal with an increase in applications for asylum from 5,000 in 1989 to over 20,000 in 1990 — although there is no evidence to support the Home Office claim that the increase is owing to 'bogus' refugees — provided for compulsory fingerprinting of all refugees, fast-track removal of 'bogus' applicants, stiffer credibility tests on refugees claiming asylum — failure to apply immediately on arrival, failure to make prompt and full disclosure of the facts, and lack of a proper passport or travel document — refusal on the basis of the applicant's getting involved in political activity in Britain which might upset the authorities in their own country, removal of rights to legal aid and lawyers of applicants' choice, and removal of family right to council housing until case decided. Frank Krenz, the London representative of the United Nations High Commissioner on Refugees, said the new rules were 'tendentious and biased against the applicant' and could damage the chances of *bona fide* refugees who needed protection under the 1951 UN convention. The Commission for Racial Equality informed the Home Secretary that the plans to remove eligibility to legal aid was illegal under the Race Relations Act. Human rights and welfare organisations, such as Amnesty International, the British Refugee Council and the Medical Foundation for the Care of Victims of Torture, as well as the Archbishop of Canterbury, George Carey, and the Roman Catholic Archbishop, Basil Hume have condemned the measures proposed in the Bill. The government withdrew the bill just before the 1992 General Election because there was no time to complete its legislative processes — but used it, as did the Tory papers such as the *Daily Mail*, the *Daily Express*, the *Sun*, the *Daily Star*, as a weapon against Labour in the election. Labour was accused of planning to allow into the country thousands of bogus refugees. Only a Conservative victory would save Britain from being swamped with undesirables, that is non-white people. Both Foreign Secretary Hurd and Home Secretary Baker played this card during the campaign.

An interesting parallel to the Tory Press playing the race card in this way can be found in the Southern United States near the end of the nineteenth century when there was the 'danger' of poor white and poor black farmers and labourers coming together. To stir up racial discontent, the *Advertiser* on election day fell back on its tried and tested formula — race-baiting. The front page of the *Advertiser* was filled with reports of assaults by blacks on white women. 'The Negroes', reported the *Advertiser*, were 'getting very troublesome' in Mississippi. 'Several Negro women of Tuscumbia' were reported to 'have addressed a very insulting letter to several respectable white ladies.'... The 'white men of Lawrence County' were urged ... to 'do' their 'duty' to 'protect the white race from this animalism'.[31]

The same processes were apparent in the run-up to the 1997 General election with similar Conservative expectations of success. The Home Secretary, Michael Howard, introduced yet another Immigration and Asylum Bill in 1996, designed to tighten still further regulations denying entry to asylum-seekers. The Government and its friends in the media continued the process of labelling asylum-seekers as bogus and denying their legitimacy. Howard was joined by the Social Security Minister, Peter Lilley, in this attack and Lilley introduced measures to deny all benefits to asylum-seekers who failed to apply for asylum at the port of entry. In September 1995, Andrew Lansley, a Conservative Party official, wrote in the *Observer*, that the Conservatives had successfully played the race card in the 1992 General Election and in the 1994 European Parliamentary elections, and would do so again in the next General Election.[32]

The continuing centrality of racism in Britain, the United States and in Western European countries is striking. This racism in found in the disproportionate number of African-Caribbean youngsters being expelled from British schools; the disproportionate number of African-American men and women imprisoned in the United States; the disproportionate number of African-Caribbean men and women imprisoned in Britain; in differential access to bail hostels in Britain; in the refusal of Congress to accept the recommendations of the Sentencing Commission to end the massive disparities between crack and powder cocaine possession levels before mandatory sentencing commences — a difference of 100; in differential levels of deaths in custody and at the hands of the police; in differential funding of public services; differential location of investment and in location of toxic waste dumps and incinerators; in continuing racial discrimination in employment; in continuing and increasing differential levels of illness, disease and mortality; in differential levels of unemployment, underemployment and poverty. In the United States in 1996, tapes of a meeting of senior executives of Texaco Inc., exposed racist contempt for the firm's black employees and a willingness to destroy documents demanded in a Federal lawsuit. Executives were heard referring to black employees as 'black jelly beans' and 'niggers':

> This diversity thing, you know how all the black jelly beans agree ....
> That's funny .... All the black jelly beans seem to be glued to the
> bottom of the bag.[33]

From the late 1980s, the Reagan/Bush Supreme Court, under Chief Justice William Rehnquist, has undermined the effectiveness of measures taken by the Second Reconstruction designed to provide racial justice to the victims of institutionalised racism. David Kairys concludes after analysing the Court's decisions in this area that:

> The Court has reversed the social roles that shaped the history of
> American racism: whites have become the presumed victims and
> African-Americans the presumed racists. To rationalize this reversal of
> social roles, the Court has employed the history, language, and moral
> force of the progressive struggle against racism. Thus, while
> challenges to discrimination against minorities or women are greeted
> with scepticism, deference to government officials, restraint and an
> obliviousness to reality, affirmative action is an occasion to 'smoke
> out racism' and remedial redistricting draws a charge of
> 'segregation'.[34]

> .... Perhaps the hallmark of our time is the use of the ideal of color-
> blindness as a non-racist symbol and rationalization for halting and
> reversing the process of integration of African-Americans into the
> economy and society. In the cruelest of ironies, color-blindness has
> become a code-word not for inclusion or integration — words and
> ideas not heard much lately — but for the separation and segregation
> that increasingly characterize American society as we move toward

what looks like a developing American apartheid. This is not a reaction or response to equality that has gone too far, but to the first substantial entry in our history of African-Americans into the economy and social life of the nation.[35]

Throughout the European Union there has been both increasing state racism and an escalation of racist violence and support for far-right parties. The connection between these two phenomena in Western European countries is similar to that identified in the United States and in Britain. The combination of economic and social dislocation following attempts at restructuring and in the face of cheaper imports from other areas of the integrated and transnational, corporate-controlled world economy, plus the failure of the left organisations in the workplace or in the polity to challenge the increasingly dominant free-market ideology, has led to an escalation in the scapegoating of immigrants and settlers from the periphery. They are blamed for the loss of jobs; for the loss of secure jobs; for cuts in the social wage and consequent insecurity; for the growing fears for the future; in short, they are blamed for the consequences of globalisation and the collusion of national elites in the process and for the resulting increase in income and wealth inequalities caused by these economic and political forces. The national elites using their dominance of the state and the media have been constructing new definitions of national and European identity, identities which are racially constructed and oppositional to the constructed Other. Europe is, therefore, Christian rather than Muslim, white rather than black, civilised rather than backward and primitive. Europe must defend itself against Islamic Fundamentalism and from Economic Refugees posing as political refugees or asylum-seekers. Within this framework, the European Union has been constructing Fortress Europe to keep the hordes of 'racially inferior' on the outside. Among the measures taken, which in practice mean a betrayal of international agreements and United Nations charters on rights of refugees, are: the Schengen Agreement, the 'Safe Third Country' rule and fines imposed on airlines bringing refugees or asylum-seekers into EU countries without proper papers and visas — even if it is impossible for such people, fleeing from repressive regimes, to obtain visas or to leave their countries using proper papers.

This racism is becoming one with a common, European culture, 'which defines all Third World people as immigrants and refugees, and all immigrants and refugees as terrorists and drug-runners, [which] will not be able to tell a citizen from an immigrant or an immigrant from a refugee, let alone one black from another. They all carry their passports on their faces.'[36] As Sheila Allen and Marie Macey have written of British blacks in the New Europe:

> Formally, these people will enjoy all the rights of free movement as befits their British citizenship. But in a climate which equates race and ethnicity particularly with being black, and being black with being an immigrant (and a potentially illegal one), it is difficult not to foresee an increase in racial harassment and control not only at Europe's external borders, but internally as well.[37]

The experience of those at the cutting edge, the migrants and refugees, provides further validation of this crucial analysis. The Refugee Forum and Migrants Rights Action network found that it is no coincidence that countries such as Italy which did not experience racial attacks on its North African workers, began to see vicious attacks at the time when its government began imposing immigration restrictions. '*Unlike wealth, racism does 'trickle down' from the top, and when governments define peoples as unwelcome and undesirable, their populations follow.*' [Italics added][38]

Given such leadership towards racism from elites and the state, it is not surprising that support for the far right is growing. The *Front National* in France, for example, has won a growing number of town halls and is increasing its membership in areas of previously strong Communist Party membership. They are increasing their membership among police, prison officers and among college students and are seeking seats on housing association councils. The *FN* has recently launched a 'campaign against globalisation' and have supported demonstrations against cuts in defence industries.[39] They are attempting to fill the void left by the Left after the Mitterrand years. In Germany, the Social Democrats have not only supported the restrictive legislation proposed by the Christian Democratic Government of Chancellor Kohl restricting rights of entry and asylum but have tried to play the anti-immigrant card themselves. Throughout the Union, and in non-EU countries such as Switzerland, such political measures have been followed by increasing police violence against migrants and settler communities; increasing levels of imprisonment of young people from these communities; increasing levels of racial violence against these communities; and increasing activities by far-right organisations and parties.

The fundamental argument, therefore, is not only that racism has blighted the lives of tens and hundreds of millions of people of colour all over the world, but that is has also functioned worldwide to maintain class-stratified societies.[40] This racist system has, however, been contested terrain for its entire history. Individual whites, as well as people of colour, and organised groups of whites and groups of people of colour, and integrated groups have resisted the imposition of the racist ideology and the racialised organisation of society.[41] It is important to study that resistance and to understand the conditions within which whites opted for a more inclusive, not racially limited identity — as opposed to the racially exclusive basis of identification which has been the dominant mode for most of the period under review.

Summary of Themes

The chapters in this collection have addressed issues of racism since 1969. 'Race, Class and Power: The New York Decentralisation Controversy' was a study of the interconnections of race and class in the nature and outcomes of the New York City school system. It focused on the struggles around desegregation, decentralisation and community control which pitted parents of colour against the bureaucracy of the school system and the bureaucracy of the teacher's union. It analysed the centrality of racism in terms of the rationing of educational resources; in terms of an ideological justification for the racialised outcomes of the educational system; and in terms of the vested interests of a section of white society, particularly educational professionals and administrators in the maintenance of that racialised system. It also analysed the struggles of the African-American and Latino communities and of whites who had political identities and practices separate from racial privilege. This analysis was based upon an understanding that poor people, and people of colour and anti-racists are protagonists in their own history and make their own history, but not under terms and conditions of their own choosing. This chapter was recently recommended by James Jennings as one of three articles providing an understanding of this episode in the history of Puerto Rican activism.[42] I chose it for this collection because, unfortunately, the central issues I discussed in 1969 are still shaping the educational experiences of a large proportion children of colour throughout the United States. The patterns of racial segregation, constructed and maintained by state action short of a legally required system of segregation, not only continue but are being reinforced. Recent research carried out by the Harvard Graduate School of Education found that schools in the US are more segregated in 1997 than at any time since the 1950s, with children of colour increasingly confined to low-achieving classrooms in poor areas. State action is as integrally involved in the production of these outcomes as it was under the pre-*Brown* v. *Board of Education of Topeka* decision of 1954 which declared the 'separate but equal' system of *de jure* segregation unconstitutional. The researchers found that federal court rulings in the early 1990s which allowed schools to abandon busing — taking children by bus to schools in other racial/ethnic areas — have limited black and Hispanic pupils to these segregated, low-achieving schools. They found that after busing was introduced in 1971, 63.6 per cent of black students were in schools where less than half the pupils were white — the latest figure is 67.1 per cent. For Hispanics, the current position is that three out of four Hispanic pupils are in schools whose pupils come mainly from an ethnic minority background. The report concludes that:

> For both black and Latino students, the contact with whites is going down .... We are at a historic turning point in terms of the access to opportunity in American schools.[43]

The issue now, as it was in New York City in the 1960s, is not primarily whether children of colour sit at the next desk to white children. The issue is the nature and quality of education these children receive. The differential funding regimes continue to favour grossly suburban, white middle-class children [of course, the privileges of the children of the elite are taken as given] and to equip them to succeed in the 'meritocratic' race and to have greater and greater amounts of resources spent on their education and to ensure their success in the competitive labour markets. We either recognise this reality and the need to challenge it — as has social commentator and researcher Jonathan Kozol who has documented the extent of these differentials and their educational and personal, attitudinal consequences for both the privileged and the deprived youngsters in his book *Savage Inequalities*[44] — or we blame the victim using a variety of forms of scientific racism. The mainstream media's uncritical acceptance of the deeply flawed and victim-blaming, *Bell Curve*.[45] One of the major academic critiques of *The Bell Curve* analysed Herrnstein and Murray's basic premises and concludes that none of them 'can be established utilizing any approximation of the scientific method, their program reduces itself to only right-wing ideology, a right-wing ideology whose pre-scriptions need to be taken very seriously'.[46] Therefore, the choices facing the society about equality and education I discussed in 1969 in the first essay in this book are even more starkly facing the society in the post-Civil Rights era.

The next article, 'Race, Class and Civil Rights', also deals with issues of race and class in the United States. The development of the Civil Rights Movement CRM is examined and the analysis relates that development to struggles of African-Americans — and their allies among other groups in society — for racial justice and to ideological and structural and economic forces in American society at the time. The ending of the re-established plantation system and its dependence upon labour-intensive production was a major factor in the successful struggle to overcome the Jim Crow system of *de jure* segregation; the increasing diversification of the Southern economy and entry of new economic forces from the rest of the country brought new players into the game who understood that institutional racism could successfully replace Jim Crow in maintaining racial hierarchy and a weakened working class; the 'good war' against fascism had removed the moral justification for Jim Crow; the determination of the United States government to create and dominate a new world system created foreign policy imperatives to remove legal segregation from the statute books so as to deny the Soviets an ideological weapon to use against the United States in the two-thirds of the world which wasn't white; the anti-Communist politics of the post-war period silenced voices, black and white, which wanted to address issues of race and class, and legitimated those which focused on the removal of *de jure* seg-regation and which demanded incorporation into the existing liberal democratic institutions. This analysis identified the limita-tions inherent in such a set of demands and such a strategy in terms of the maintenance of structural racism and the consequences both for the majority of African-Americans, particularly for working class and poor African-Americans, and in terms of the reproduction of ideological and structural racism and for white working-class people.

I chose this essay for the collection because the continuing centrality of racism is apparent in everyday life: in the nature of the political process; in the imprisonment statistics — with an African-American male being five times more likely to be imprisoned in the US than an African male in South Africa; in continuing and escalating levels of class inequality and the increasing scapegoating of affirmative action and 'special interests' by both Democrat and Republican politicians; by the ignoring of the needs of the people living in the inner-cities; by the racialising and feminising of poverty so that the safety net becomes shredded and we end 'welfare as we knew it'.[47] These characteristics of contemporary US society illustrate the need to go beyond formal legal and constitutional rights to a more encompassing definition of rights and freedom and the inescapable need to link economic and political democracy.

'British Anti-Discrimination Legislation', was published in 1971, as an analysis of the passage of the 1965 and 1968 Race Relations Acts in Britain. It formed part of a collection of essays entitled, *The Prevention of Racial Discrimination in Britain*, which was sponsored by the United Nations Institute for Training and Research and the Institute of Race Relations. It was an attempt to study the response of the British state to the contradictions inherent in the recruitment of people of colour from the former colonies of the Caribbean and the Indian subcontinent to fill vacancies as cheap labour in the post-war period. It analysed the social and political costs of the popular racism which had rendered such labour cheap in the first place and the state racism which had historically created that popular racism and reinforced it through failing to challenge stereotypes. The situation was worsened by resource-allocation decisions that created and escalated infrastructure shortages which then became racialised. The chapter analysed the limits of the state response and the dominant ideology shaped in part by lessons drawn from state action in the United States.

I chose this essay because it illustrates my misguided optimism at the time about the *bona fides* of the British state. Since it was written it has become more and more apparent that structural racism has been shaping the experiences and opportunities of black British people, including the children and grandchildren of the post-war migrants, and that the British state was unwilling to forego the advantages of racial stereotyping and scapegoating. The politicians continued to define black people as outsiders, as 'the problem' and to play the 'race card' in election after election and to refuse to provide the agencies established to implement anti-discrimination legislation with the necessary powers to make a fundamental change in the operation of racialised labour markets. These factors were addressed in essays written after this one and which are included in this volume. [See Chapters 4, 6 and 7.]

'Parameters of British and North American Racism' was published in a special issue of *Race and Class* on the 1981 uprisings in British inner-cities. It analysed the causes of the uprisings and related them to the uprisings in the United States in the 1960s. The article studied the official responses in the United States, in particular the administration's establishment of the Kerner Commission and its responses to the Commission's recommendations. It identified the priority given to the implementation of those recommendations to do with policing and intelligence-gathering and the failure to address seriously those dealing with structural racism. It was in this context that the Scarman recommendations were reviewed and likely British governmental responses were identified.[48] Lord Scarman made a number of recommendations about recruiting more members of the ethnic minorities into the police; the establishment of consultative machinery between the police and the community; more community policing; more effective complaints procedures to deal with complaints against the police; and urgent actions was required if the social conditions which underlay the disorders in Brixton and elsewhere were to be corrected. He did not, however, accept that institutional racism was present in Britain.

I chose this essay because of its continued relevance in the face of repeated urban uprisings in both Britain and the United States and the political struggle over the meaning of these uprisings. The most dramatic of these uprisings was, of course, that of Los Angeles in 1992 following the acquittal by the suburban jury, made up of 11 whites and one Asian-American, of the four police officers who had been videoed severely beating Rodney King, an African-American. There were recent examples of urban unrest in

Britain in December 1995, following the death of the second black man at the hands of the police in Brixton within three months, and in a predominantly black area of St Petersburg, Florida in October 1996, just days before the presidential election, after police shot and killed a second black young man in a week. In these instances, in both countries, as in the US following the 1992 LA uprising, the dominant discussion ignored the fundamental issues of structural racism, police violence and injustice and focused on the supposed shortcomings of the rioters, their violence, their unwillingness to work, and on looting. One commentator on these developments concluded:

> The main point to come out of all the arguments and opinion exchanges that unrest such as the Los Angeles riots of 1992 is now considered to have far more to do with morality than with poverty. The real evil is, therefore, the act of riot, not the degradation of human life in the ghetto. While playing brief lip-service to the structural problems of the inner-city, the post-liberal consensus plays down those social factors that create poverty and emphasises instead that the cause of the problem is the breakdown in the moral code among individuals.
>
> The reorientation of the post-riot discussion in this fashion helps to divert attention away from a critique of the way in which American society is organised and run, and pile it on to a moral condemnation of the urban poor. The fact that the conservative opinion-makers have been able to achieve this so successfully despite the glaring weakness and vulgar prejudices underlying many of their own arguments, demonstrates the extent to which traditional liberal ideas have not been marginalised.[49]

In 'Revocation of Civil Rights' there was an analysis of the repeal of large sections of the Second Reconstruction through actions of the Reagan and Bush administrations and through a series of Supreme Court decisions by the Reagan/Bush Court. The limitations in the gains of the CRM, which I identified in Chapter 2, were examined and found crucially to have allowed this process of revocation, seen by many analysts as similar to the repeal of much of the First Reconstruction. The failure of both Reconstructions to challenge the economic organisation of society, a system of racialised capitalism, meant that the political gains could not be protected when the coalitions which had come together, under pressure from African-Americans, to institute the reforms broke apart. When the goals were achieved of those for whom the changes were tactical, designed to maintain the unequal hierarchical system they dominated, the change-oriented movement divided and a significant portion of its leadership was coopted.

I chose this article because I feel that it correctly identified these processes and raised questions about the implications for race and class inequality. The triumph of the 'post-liberal consensus' has meant that the election of a Democratic President in 1992 and his re-election in 1996, the first time a Democratic President has been re-elected since 1944, has not meant a fundamental challenge to the deteriorating position of large parts of African America.[50]

'Racism, the National Health Service and the Health of Black People', which was given 'top priority' for publication by the referee, was published in 1987 in the *International Journal of Health Services*. It analysed the nature and consequences of racism for black people as patients and as employees in the National Health Service and identified the interconnections between structural and ideological racism shaping their experiences in both categories. Racism in education, employment, housing and the criminal justice system all have health consequences and consequences for employment within the NHS and racism in the popular culture and state racism all affect the treatment of black people as patients and consumers.[51] I included this article because the issues I raised have continued to shape the experiences of black people. It is interesting and disturbing to note that a recent investigation by the Commission for Racial Equality has found patterns of racial discrimination in the appointment of consultants and senior registrars similar to those discussed in this article.

> Although almost every respondent had an equal opportunities policy covering the recruitment and selection process, in almost every case there was a big gap between policy and actual practice .... Taken together with the consistently low success rates for ethnic minority applicants for senior medical posts, the selection practices found among health authorities and trusts can give little confidence to ethnic minority applicants that their applications will be treated fairly.[52]

There is concern about racial harassment of black health workers and a lack of consideration and support by managers and supervisors; about the large gap, as described above in the case of consultants and senior registrars, between equal opportunities statements and implementation; and widespread discrimination in the allocation of training and promotion of nurses.[53] Recent research by the MSF union has found that there has been a short drop in the number of black nursing, midwifery and health visiting staff. This is particularly apparent in the numbers employed in the under-25-year-old category, 0.8 per cent, compared with those between 55 and 64, where the figure is 8.7 per cent,[54] the authors of this report conclude:

> Racial discrimination operates at all levels in the NHS, right from the processing of application forms through to top jobs. It presents a concrete ceiling which keeps many talented and qualified ethnic minority staff from the positions they could be filling. Racism operates also on other levels, be it racial harassment and abuse from patients or unequal disciplinary measures applied to ethnic minority staff. No statistic can ever measure the resulting waste of talent and opportunity, nor the indignities balk and ethnic minority people are experiencing daily.[55]

The need to place equality at the heart of the new, decentralised NHS has thus become ever more apparent. The problem of forcing institutions to prioritise equal opportunities and to move beyond mere symbolism is a major one and the experience in the area of the health-care delivery system is not an encouraging one. Similar issue need to be addressed in other areas of public life, such as education, policing, housing and employment. In each of these areas, black people are being denied equality in terms of employment, treatment and service delivery. As the power of democratically elected Local Education Authorities is eroded in favour of local management of schools, the problem of how equal opportunities policies are to be administered and monitored in such a multiplicity of locations is one that has not yet been seriously addressed — but clearly needs to be.

The last three articles in this collection, published in 1995 and 1996, take the analyses developed in the previous articles and apply them to explain contemporary race and class relations. They are based upon an understanding that in the years since the Civil Rights Movement in the United States and since the passage of the 1965, 1968 and 1976 Race Relations Acts in Britain — and more crucially, since the passage of the Immigration Acts of 1962 and

1971 and the Immigration White Paper of 1965 and the Kenyan Asian Act of 1968 — there has been a massive increase in racial polarisation in the United States, Britain and the rest of Europe, both East and West. There has been an increase in racial violence in these areas and increasing scholarly recognition of the centrality of racism in the organisation of modern Western societies.[56] The successful playing of the race card in election after election has been accompanied by a rightward shift of mainstream political parties and a narrowing of the parameters of legitimate political discourse in the United States and Western Europe.[57] This rightward shift in political and governmental action has led to an increase in popular racism. Politicians then used this increase as a justification for further racist state actions, which in turn exacerbated popular racism .... This growth of racism has accompanied, and made politically possible, greater class inequality and a restructuring of the political economies of the advanced capitalist countries at the expense of the working classes. All these events were anticipated in the earlier articles and are central to the analysis in 'Racism and Anti-Racism in Western Europe', published in 1995; 'The Political Economy of White Racism in the United States', published in 1996 in the Second Edition of *Impacts of Racism on White Americans*; and 'The Political Economy of White Racism in Britain' — published as an Occasional Paper in 1996 by the Trotter Institute.

The challenge facing our societies is the construction of social and economic justice. without racial justice, it will not be possible to create just societies. Without justice there will be no peace, Nor will there be effective democracy. Without effective democracy, there will be no control over the activities of the transnational Corporations and their Political Allies in power in the national state and in the international agencies such as the IMF, the World Bank, the World Trade Organisation, and in the impending European Monetary Union. The choice facing us is a stark one, I hope that the issue raised in this collection will have moved the debate forward and help in the chose of justice over barbarism.

1 Race, Class and Power
The New York Decentralisation Controversy

Racial and religious tension and conflict in New York City dramatically increased in the latter half of the 1960s. Charges of 'black anti-Semitism' and 'white racism' abound, while meaningful communication between the races is less than it has ever been. The general context within which the situation has developed has been that of the growth of the Black Power concept and the resulting black challenge to the white economic, political and educational power structures. This challenge, so different from the glorious days of the civil rights decade of the 1950s when blacks and whites marched together in the South, represents a realisation among black leaders that the basic problems of jobs, housing and education in the urban ghettos of America have to be solved before there can be any real progress of black Americans as a group. This, however, brings them into conflict with whites with vested interests to protect, and the resulting controversy has been bitter. An example of the break-up of the old civil rights coalition following the presentation of a challenge to white self-interest can be seen in the mobilisation of the majority of Reform Democrats of the FDR-Woodrow Wilson Club to defeat plans to pair PS84, a predominantly white elementary school, and a nearby black and Puerto Rican school. David Rogers, in *110 Livingston Street*, quotes one disappointed club member saying: 'All their old liberalism went by the boards. They are liberal in the abstract, and when the problem is far away, say in Selma, Jackson or Birmingham, but not for their children or their schools and neighbourhoods.'[1] The same, as we shall see, could be said of the 'liberal' United Federation of Teachers.

The latest round in this battle, and perhaps the most significant, has been the fight over the attempt to decentralise the New York City school system into between thirty and sixty school districts, each with a locally elected system. The conflict which resulted from this plan has received very wide press coverage not only in the United States but in Britain and the rest of Europe as well. Much of the coverage has concerned itself with the dramatic events of the confrontation blacks who are reported to be anti-Semitic; Mayor Lindsay being hustled out of a side door after intense barracking at a Jewish Community Centre by Jews irate at what they considered his surrender to black militants; and a series of teachers' strikes which virtually closed the city's school system for three months from September 1968. The interesting questions raised by this conflict are not merely over the types of, or control of, New York's educational system. The importance of this particular issue lies in its relationship with the broader fight for power of a previously powerless group in society. Rhody McCoy, the unit administrator or supervisor of one of the experimental school districts, that of Ocean Hill-Brownsville in Brooklyn, cogently declared that 'if anyone walking the streets of New York is under the impression that the teachers are on strike over an educational issue, he is grossly misinformed. The issues are politics and labour.'[2]

This attempt by the powerless to obtain power is part of a wider problem facing not only the United States but Western Europe as well. It is the growing sense of individuals that the bureaucrats who run the large units of government are too distant from them and that they are not really accountable to those they are supposed to serve. There is a pressure throughout the developed world for some form of devolution of power to bring control close to the individual and the region or community. This involves a revaluation of the expertise of the professionals and a decline in the previously almost automatic deference to that expertise. There is a class element in this attitude — a feeling that the middle-class professionals do not understand or value the way of life and aspirations of working-class people. But it is not restricted to any one class. For example, the President of the American National School Board Association said recently: 'The average citizen feels he's getting further away from influencing anything ... the schools have not found many effective ways to relate to the community.' *Education News* went even further when it declared that 'the invisible people also inhabit the wealthy suburb and the dusty farm town. And whether and when and how they will influence their schools is a national issue.'[3]

But imagine how much more invisible and powerless most urban black ghetto residents are. They are faced with an educational system which is segregated, inferior and, most of all, unresponsive to their legitimate demands. They live in segregated, overcrowded, substandard and expensive neighbourhoods, pay more for inferior merchandise and have twice the national unemployment rate. Their votes are solicited and then taken for granted and their wishes constantly ignored in favour of those of more powerful groups or in favour of administrative convenience and economy. They have been able to bring their grievances about the failures of the educational system to the fore, and to be in a position to have a say in the operation of the system in at least three areas, because their alienation from the present system coincided with the rejection of that system by outside white and powerful groups. It was this combination of previously powerless blacks, fed up with the system's failure to respond to their needs, and of foundational political figures, concerned about the failure of the education system, which led to the decentralisation controversy of the past two years in New York City.

II

It is important to sketch in the background to this controversy if we are to understand the form it took and its implications. Probably the single most important factor underlying the black demand for decentralisation and community control was the almost complete failure of the New York City school system to educate the majority of its black or Puerto Rican pupils. David Rogers, in his penetrating study of the system, concluded that the New York City schools have failed in ghetto areas, in most desegregated communities as well. 'One out of three pupils in the system is a year or more retarded in reading and arithmetic .... Public education was for previous ethnic groups a prime means for social mobility, but for the Negro it tends to block mobility and to increase socio-economic and racial segregation.'[4]

The schools that black children attend are overwhelmingly segregated. In 1969, fifteen years after the United States Supreme

Court declared that school segregation based on law was unconstitutional, *de facto* segregation in the North generally and in New
York City in particular is the norm. Sixty-five per cent of New
York City's black children attend schools which are over 90 per
cent black, while 80 per cent of the city's white school children
attend almost all-white schools.

Despite almost ten years of effort, civil rights groups were
unable to move the city's educational institution to integrate the
schools. There were, to be sure, a multitude of agreements in principle, policy statements and declarations of intent, but there was
little actual mixing of bodies in the schools. Most white groups
and school officials did not want the various desegregation plans
to succeed and these programmes were subverted by acts of omission as well as of commission. Not only were children not, in any
significant way, moved from black to white schools, but new
schools were consciously built in the heart of white and black
neighbourhoods so as to perpetuate segregated schooling.[5]

The importance of this failure to take positive zoning decisions
cannot be overestimated, for, as Rogers argues:

> A conventional interpretation of school and city officials, and of
> social scientists and urban planners, is that housing segregation is the
> primary cause of school segregation. It is assumed that school
> segregation was not deliberately planned, but just came about as a
> result of residential patterns. My evidence suggests that this is not
> totally the case in New York City and that the Board of Education's
> own actions contributed to the tipping of some residential areas that
> had previously been integrated. I am suggesting that school
> construction and zoning practices of the board were a cause not only
> of increased school segregation but of housing segregation as well.'[6]

> The educational system came up with a number of desegregation
> plans, such as Open Enrolment, which were sabotaged. The following
> comments are illustrative of the techniques which were used to
> sabotage these programmes. A Brooklyn civil rights leader said, 'In
> almost every school I have anything to do with, Open Enrolment was
> not only not pushed but talked against. Parents got lectures about
> how hard it is to travel and go to school far away.' A human relations
> staff person in the Bronx reported 'Open Enrolment proposals were
> always announced at the last minute, with a notice sent home the last
> two weeks of school with an invitation to visit new schools. They
> know that the parents don't have time on two weeks' notice to get
> involved. So in a way, it was doomed to failure before they started.'[7]

Not only were black parents thus discouraged from enroling their children in the programme but if they did attempt to transfer their children further difficulties were put in their way. Forthcoming pupils would often be placed in slow and/or segregated classes or streams, more disciplinary measures would be used, and often little attempt was made by principals and supervisors to obtain extra services for the incoming students. Probably the most damning comment about the treatment received by the incoming pupils is the following account by a Bronx civic leader: 'A few years ago, about 30 to 35 kids were bussed into an elementary school here. They went on one bus and were deposited at a particular door, never in the school yard where the rest of the kids were. They went directly to their room and from 8.30 until 3.30 they stayed there. They ate their lunch in the room and did exercises there rather than recess. They left the room only to go to the bathroom and were taken directly to the bus and home at the end of the day.'[8]

The failure of these desegregation plans meant that the black children remained in segregated schools. But not only were they segregated in inferior schools with the highest percentages of substitute and temporary teachers and with the highest rate of daily teacher absenteeism. In the Ocean Hill-Brownsville schools, the daily absentee rate in the year before decentralisation was 25 per cent. Teachers who were found unacceptable to principals and supervisors in other, mainly white, areas were regularly transferred from school to school until they wound up in ghetto schools. This is not to say that all the teachers in these schools were like this, but enough of them were to do damage and to set the tone of the schools. The results were as could have been expected. Not only are black children behind whites in reading and arithmetic, but the longer they stay in the school system, the farther behind they fall. So children who were half a year behind at first grade level are two years behind by the sixth grade, and almost three years behind by the twelfth grade. Three times as many black teenagers as white are high-school drop-outs and even among those blacks who stay on to graduation, a majority do not receive either academic or commercial diplomas, but receive instead a general diploma which is largely useless in the job market.[9] The children in such a situation are largely alienated from the school system and one of the main tasks facing Rhody McCoy and the others running the decentralised districts is, in McCoy's words, to get 'these youngsters to understand that these are schools'.

This massive school system, involving over 1.1 million pupils, over 900 separate schools and over 56,000 teachers, is run by an enormous and largely unaccountable and inflexible bureaucracy. The educational bureaucracy has been unresponsive to the changing nature of the population of New York with 59 per cent of the schoolchildren now either black or Puerto Rican. The bureaucracy is still overwhelmingly white and Jewish — over 60 per cent of the teachers, and an even greater percentage of supervisors and headquarters bureaucrats, are Jewish. At the same time, only 9 per cent of the teachers are either black or Puerto Rican. This disparity is even more dramatic at the supervisory levels, where until 1967 there were only four black principals out of 865 — a little less than 0.5 per cent — and only 12 black assistant principals in the 1500 positions at that rank. This educational bureaucracy, which includes the faculty in the city colleges, as well as the bureaucrats and teachers, is phenomenally inbred. A recent study found only one top level headquarters bureaucrat who had been in the school system for less than ten years, and most had been in the system for twenty or thirty years. Certain ethnic groups are, as we have seen, over-represented. Both of these factors help to explain the crux of the problem of the school system, which is the system's unwillingness or inability to respond to the new demands being made on it. A United States Office of Education study of the school system concluded that it appeared 'paralysed' by its problems and that it had failed to stem a precipitous downhill trend. They also found that the system has not made any meaningful changes in curriculum, administrative structure, general organisation and teacher recruitment, appointment and training for at least three decades. This large, cumbersome school system has been hindered by a congested bureaucracy and has suffered from inertia and has responded dilatorily to new major demands being made on it.[10]

The bureaucracy, having used the claim of professionalism to defeat political interference by the big-city political machines many years ago, still clings to it as a shield against criticism. In this, they have been joined by the teachers, who use it as a defence against what they call interference from parents, especially lower class parents. This determination to cling to the facade of professionalism is probably more obstinate because there is really so little substance behind the façade. One astute observer of the school system has declared: 'While teachers and principals may know more about education than most laymen, ... they don't know very much. There is no codified body of knowledge that educators can learn and apply, as there is in medicine and law. There is little expertise to apply despite any myths to the contrary.'[11] Faced with the failure of the school system either to integrate the schools or to educate their children properly in ghetto schools, black parents have become increasingly more resistant to the bureaucracy's claims of professionalism and expertise. Indeed, they are basing their opposition to professional control not merely on the grounds of the failure of the professional but on broader theoretical considerations as well. Reverend C. Herbert Oliver, President of the Ocean Hill-Brownsville governing board, has said that the responsibility to educate the nation's young is the parents'. 'We have lost sight of this principle. It is not the duty and responsibility of the professional to educate children. Parents may employ professionals but it is their own function to see that their children are educated. The professionals have taken on the job and said to parents, particularly poor black parents, you get out. This must never be. Parents must educate children.'[12] In addition, their demands are based on the view that segregated schools are the given — that the real choice facing black parents is whether their children will go to good segregated schools or bad segregated schools — at least for the near future. Preston Wilcox, a Professor of Social Work at Columbia University, has said that 'most schools teach white nationalism; black children should be exposed to black nationalism. We have a dual system of education now but both are controlled by whites.'[13]

III

Given this situation the blacks turned from desegregation to questions of quality of education and of local control, which was seen as a necessary condition for quality education. They saw the necessity of limiting the powers of the school professionals if they were to accomplish their goals. This shift in emphasis in the black community coincided with Mayor Lindsay's attempt in 1967 to obtain more money from New York State for the city's school system by proposing the decentralisation of the system into five, borough-wide districts. The state legislature agreed to increase the State's contribution on the condition that a fully fledged decentralisation plan be worked out. Mayor Lindsay appointed a Panel on Decentralization under the Chairmanship of McGeorge Bundy, President of the Ford Foundation. In November 1967 the Panel reported in favour of decentralisation not into five very large units, but into between thirty and sixty smaller units of between 12,000 and 40,000 pupils. They recommended that local governing boards be established, chosen in part by parents in the district and in part by the Mayor. These local boards were to have control over expenditure, curriculum development, book and supply purchasing, and appointments. The main limitations on the latter power were that teachers already having tenure would be assured of its continuance and that all new teachers would have a New York State teaching certificate.[14] The Ford Foundation at the same time agreed to finance three experimental demonstration districts: one in East Harlem called the Intermediate School 201 Complex, Two Bridges in the Lower East Side of Manhattan, and one in Brooklyn, destined to become the centre of the fight over decentralisation, Ocean Hill-Brownsville. Each district was built around one or two intermediate schools with their feeder elementary schools.

These proposals were not universally welcomed and the fight over decentralisation began almost immediately. The central Board of Education, the United Federation of Teachers, and the Council of Supervisory Associations — the supervisors' trade union — all part of New York City's educational bureaucracy, responded to the attempt to decentralise the city's school system with determined and unscrupulous opposition. The stakes of this battle with the black community were very high-control of a billion dollar educational budget, control over many thousands of non-teaching jobs, the dominance of the teachers' union, lucrative construction contracts, and in the long run the continued dominance of the white power structure. These were all at risk if the decentralisation experiment was successful and if the entire system was decentralised. The tactics of these groups were based on the attempt to discredit decentralisation by proving that it led automatically to chaos, union-busting and racism, especially anti-Semitism. Each of these tactics was designed to mobilise particular groups: liberals and educationists by showing the chaos that would result; the city's powerful union movement by showing the union-busting; and the liberals and, most importantly, the city's large and influential Jewish community by showing widespread anti-Semitism inherent in decentralisation. This last has been the single most publicised aspect of the conflict, not only in New York and the United States but in Britain as well.

The central Board of Education and its mammoth bureaucracy, with all it had to lose from decentralisation and community control, played a crucial role in the battle. Their role as the all-powerful centre of the educational system would be destroyed if decentralisation succeeded, for they would be left as a rump organisation with limited powers and limited resources. Their role was crucial because the three demonstration districts, IS 201 in East Harlem, Two Bridges in the Lower East Side, and Ocean Hill-Brownsville in Brooklyn, had to establish the limits of their powers and their detailed terms of reference with the central Board. The Board, however, in the words of the New York Civil Liberties Union ' ... attempted to scuttle the experiment in Ocean Hill-Brownsville [the first of the districts to begin operations] by consistently refusing to define the authority of the local Governing Board'.[15] They refused to co-operate with the local board, utilising their bureaucratic expertise in delay and obfuscation. For example, when the steering committee in Ocean Hill-Brownsville, in accordance with a time-table laid down by the Ford Foundation, attempted to obtain the names and addresses of parents in their area so as to register them for an election for the Local Governing Board, the central Board refused. After further pressure and delay they agreed to allow two secretaries at the central headquarters to obtain this information. The local people were required to pay the secretaries for this operation. But, after agreeing, they were informed that the two secretaries were on holiday, and would not be back until after the election was due to be held. The local people did the best they could without this list: they sent notes home with the schoolchildren, and volunteer teachers canvassed the neighbourhood. After the election, in which 25 per cent of those eligible voted — a figure, incidentally, which was almost double the normal turnout in local elections in that district — the central Board refused to recognise the elected body, on the ground that they were not representative. By failing to define clearly the authority of the Local Governing Board and by refusing to co-operate with them, the central Board was ensuring that at some point the local people would overstep their authority and thus come into conflict with the central Board. This ploy worked, as we shall see, and it played a major part in the conflict over decentralisation.

The local Boards' main public protagonist has been the United Federation of Teachers under its President, Albert Shanker. While publicly declaring their support for the principle of decentralisation on a limited basis, they have consistently worked against any meaningful decentralisation programme. They lobbied extensively, expensively and effectively in the New York State Legislature in the Spring of 1968 against all strong decentralisation bills — bills that would have created between 30 and 60 local districts run by locally elected boards, with effective powers. Instead, they supported the bill, which finally passed, which postponed the decision for a year, and which kept the three demonstration districts under the jurisdiction of the central Board and of the State Commissioner of Education. They then proceeded to use that year to prove not only that decentralisation meant chaos, in which their prime ally was the central Board, but that it meant union-busting and anti-Semitism as well. Before discussing their tactics, let us look, for a moment, at their motivation.

The first, and most obvious, reason for their opposition to a far-reaching decentralisation scheme is a straightforward trade union one. They have established a productive relationship with the central Board of Education — productive in terms of improvements in pay and conditions — and do not want to lose the relationship. The alternative — having to negotiate with between 30 and 60 separate districts — is one which they obviously do not desire. This reason, however, is not sufficient to explain the virulence of their opposition, for if the will were there it should be possible to work out a mutually satisfactory structure — for example, something like the Burnham Committee — under which the union would negotiate a central contract for the entire system. One could also have an appeal procedure, chaired by an independent party to evaluate transfer policies and the like. But there was no such desire on the union's part. Shanker, believing in the domino theory, was determined to crush decentralisation in the bud rather than let it succeed in one place and spread to the rest of the system. It seems clear that his and the union's motivation was based on something much broader than that which we traditionally consider trade union self-interest. They have been determined to maintain the shield of professionalism against potential interference. At the heart of the black demands for decentralisation and community control, and indeed of the Bundy Committee's recommendations, was the idea that the parents had to be brought into the educational system in a significant way. This the UFT rejected, perhaps out of fear or perhaps because they saw how threadbare the cloak of professionalism really was and feared exposure. In their response to the Bundy recommendations the UFT declared that it was 'anti-professional' to allow a situation in which 'charges could be brought against a tenured faculty member by a community board of laymen with no professional expertise'. They also declared that 'the Bundy report ignores the new power and integrity of the professional teacher who will not continue to teach in any school or district where professional decisions are made by laymen'.[16] Why this fear of laymen and parents? Could it be that the teachers, having failed to reach these people's children, feared that they would then hold the teacher responsible? Could it be that deep down the teachers themselves felt a sense of failure that was not totally assuaged by their defence mechanisms and rationalisations? The evidence seems to indicate that this is the case and that this is a crucial part of the motivation for their fanatical opposition to decentralisation. Edmund Gordon placed the teachers' concern with what they call 'professionalism' into its proper context when he wrote:

> Professionalism is based on specialised competence, on independence of judgement concerning professional matters, on quality of services rendered, and on responsibility for that competence, that independence of judgement and that service. The concern with professionalism among educators has tended to favour the former two to the neglect of the latter two.[17]

Instead of consciously accepting responsibility for the failure of the system to educate black children, the teachers have erected, on very shaky foundations, a structure of rationalisations accounting for this failure. This shifts the full burden of blame on to the children, the parents and the neighbourhood. It is argued that these children are 'culturally deprived', that their parents are not only uninterested in education and therefore not supporters of the school but that they are often antagonistic, so that the teachers, doing the best they can, are faced with an all but impossible situation.

Despite the surface plausibility of these assertions there are major internal weaknesses in their case which threaten this entire defensive edifice and which, if linked to successful decentralisation, can only topple it. The assertions about parental indifference are supported neither by survey data (which show the very high expectations black parents have of education), nor by experience of parents in the decentralised districts. Outside observers as well as those running these districts have been struck by the response of these supposedly uninterested parents to real opportunities for participation. Even in districts which have not yet decentralised but which hope to be included in the wider plans for decentralisation there has been a tremendous response of parents. The United Bronx Parents Association has been holding a series of meetings in the Bronx and on a bitterly cold December evening over 800 parents attended one of their meetings in a low-income black and Puerto Rican area. They listened to detailed lectures on various aspects of decentralisation and broke up into work groups to discuss particular problems of curriculum development, teacher and pupil rights, and book and supply purchasing. This meeting lasted for well over three hours, and these supposedly are the parents who do not support the schools. Until now, no one has tried in any constructive way to enlist their support.

Another crack in the edifice has been occasioned by the growing evidence showing the importance of teacher expectations for pupil performance. One recent and major study found that the performance of a randomly selected group of children was significantly improved merely by changing teacher expectation of these children. The authors of this study have argued that

> the disadvantaged child is a Negro American, a Mexican American, a Puerto Rican or any other child who lives in conditions of poverty. He is a lower-class child who performs poorly in an educational system that is staffed almost entirely by middle-class teachers. The reason usually given for the poor performances of the disadvantaged child is simply that the child is a member of a disadvantaged group. There may well be another reason. It is that the child does poorly in school because that is what is expected of him. In other words, his shortcomings may originate not in his different ethnic, cultural and economic background, but in his teachers' response to that background.[18]

They found that the results obtained by changing teacher expectations were greater than were obtained by programmes using Title I money under the Elementary and Secondary Education Act of 1965 which was designed to provide special programmes directed toward disadvantaged children. The importance of teacher-expectation and self-fulfilling prophesies cannot be overstressed. Howard Kalodner, a New York University Law Professor and legal counsel to the Bundy Committee, has said that the first prerequisite for a chance at success for the decentralised districts is 'some way to destroy the professional educational bureaucracy. Seventy-five to eighty per cent of the educators do not believe that black and Puerto Rican children can learn. You can't have a professional educational system like that.'[19]

This, of course, is precisely what those in favour of community control wish to do. They want to bring into their schools teachers, regardless of race or religion, who will be sympathetic and understanding and not begin with low expectations of their children. And if they find teachers with these negative attitudes they want to be able to transfer them out of their district. The sum total of these threats to the teachers' defensive rationalisations is magnified by the fear that, if the schools in the decentralised districts succeed when they have failed, these rationalisations will be exposed. This has led to their unprincipled opposition to the experiment. As one UFT teacher with painful honesty put it: 'Either I buy a great big bag of guilt or I become a self-protective bigot ... and I am not prepared to buy the bag of guilt.'[20] This attitude and these fears can explain, but can never exonerate, the union's tactics, which, however successful they may have been in the short run, can only do major damage to race relations. In order to mobilise opposition from other unions against decentralisation, the union consistently, and very largely successfully, misrepresented the attempt by the Ocean Hill-Brownsville board to transfer 19 teachers out of the district. This is a common practice in the New York City school system, yet the central Board denied Rhody McCoy as demonstration district supervisor the powers normally given to district supervisors. The union claimed that these teachers had been unfairly dismissed in violation of their tenure rights and due process. They claimed this so often that soon the Mayor, the central Board and the press were all talking about the teachers who had been fired — despite the fact that none of the teachers had lost a single day's pay, that the letter informing the teachers of their transfer both offered an opportunity to appeal and instructed them to report to the central Board for reassignment. The New York Civil Liberties Union declared that 'there is no question that under present standards the United Federation of Teachers created the due process issue out of thin air'.[21] Another study of this controversy, under the chairmanship of the President of the Bank Street College of Education, found that under normal circumstances the Demonstration project might have been able to accomplish the transfer of 'unsatisfactory' personnel informally, but a larger struggle was being waged in the New York State Legislature over a general proposal to decentralise the entire school system.[22]

Thus it is clear that the UFT and the central Board were using this issue as a way of discrediting decentralisation in the eyes of the rest of the city and in the New York State Legislature. The UFT then tried to get an added bonus by escalating their demand for settlement of the ensuing series of teachers' strikes to include provisions which if the local board accepted would discredit the local board in the black community and if they did not accept them would provide justification for the continuation of the strikes and the suspension of the local board and of Rhody McCoy. All of the latter happened when the Ocean Hill-Brownsville people refused to abide by the terms of settlement of one of a series of city-wide teachers' strikes that closed the schools for 36 days from September 1968. They had had no part in drawing up this settlement, which would have had the local board welcome back, rather than merely allow the return of, the striking teachers. Another requirement was that the local board agree in advance to accept all orders and recommendations of the central Board. All of these were impossible if the local board was to retain any standing in the local community. Consequently the Ocean Hill-Brownsville Board is under suspension, although it is in fact still running the schools in the district.

The union strategy during the series of strikes was geared to the attempt to discredit and destroy the decentralisation experiment because Shanker saw it as part of a domino theory. If it succeeded in Ocean Hill-Brownsville it would spread to the rest of the city. Proof that this was his goal, rather than a settlement of the outstanding issues, can be seen in his firing of one of his vice-presidents, John T. O'Neill, who had attempted, and almost succeeded, in working out a settlement with McCoy.[23] The union's other main tactic was to convince the political leaders and the city's whites, and especially its Jewish population, that decentralisation was racist and anti-Semitic in origin and nature. The New York Civil Liberties Union has condemned this tactic in the following words:

> the UFT leadership, and in particular Albert Shanker, systematically accused the Ocean Hill-Brownsville Board and Rhody McCoy of anti-Semitism and extremism, and then 'proved' those accusations only with half truths, innuendoes and outright lies.[24]

An analysis of the material distributed by the hundred thousand by the union shows a large part of it to be fraudulent — either in terms of its having been concocted or in terms of two unrelated pieces of literature being put together on the same sheet in such a way as to imply that they belonged together. This approach has succeeded in mobilising the city's Jewish community against decentralisation and against Mayor Lindsay; he was prevented from completing a speech at a Jewish Community Centre by intense barracking by Jews convinced that he had sold out to the black anti-Semites. This inevitably exacerbated an already tense racial situation. It also succeeded in convincing the mass media that black anti-Semitism was a major problem worthy of magazine cover stories and leader-page articles deploring it. It even succeeded in becoming such a firm part of what is conceived to be common knowledge that the British Prime Minister, the Rt Hon Harold Wilson, in a speech on 10 March 1968 celebrating the twentieth anniversary of the *Jewish Vanguard*, declared, almost in passing:

> God help this country if anti-racialism were to breed a racialist
> backlash which could lead one section of the persecuted to strike out
> blindly, such as the manifestation, deplored and resisted, for example,
> by all decent Americans, under which black power becomes anti-
> Semitic.[25]

In fact, the truth about the Ocean Hill-Brownsville Board, and indeed about black anti-Semitism in general, is somewhat different from the UFT line which has been so widely accepted. Rhody McCoy and the local board issued a statement in which they declared that they have never tolerated nor will they ever tolerate anti-Semitism in any form. They further declared: 'Anti-Semitism has no place in our hearts or minds and indeed never in our schools'. Their actions as well have hardly been consistent with anti-Semitism and racism. Of the 350 new teachers they hired in the summer of 1968, 70 per cent were white and 50 per cent were Jewish. Over three-quarters of the district's teachers took a full-page advertisement in the *New York Times* supporting the local board and attacking the UFT and Mr Shanker for the unfounded charges of anti-Semitism and for the attempt to destroy decentralisation. The UFT succeeded in mobilising Jews as Jews to oppose decentralisation by playing on the growing Jewish fears of anti-Semitism in the black community. This blurred the essential fact that when Jewish teachers and Jewish administration opposed decentralisation they did so as teachers and administrators rather than as Jews. This mobilisation of Jews *qua* Jews can only exacerbate black anti-Semitism and make more credible the statements and charges of a relative handful of black extremists.

Despite talk of 'pogromist' and 'genocidal' tendencies and references to Hitler[26] it is important to keep the probable rise of black anti-Semitism and its causes in perspective. The most remarkable aspect of black anti-Semitism in the United States, a nation in which white anti-Semitism is still widespread, has been its very low level. Gary Marx, in his study *Protest and Prejudice*, found in 1964 that, on an index of anti-Semitism, 36 per cent of the black respondents were non-anti-Semitic and 40 per cent were 'low'.[27] Most blacks, 75 per cent, failed to make a distinction between Jewish and non-Jewish whites. By the 25 per cent that did make a distinction, Jews were seen in a more favourable light than other whites by a 4-1 ratio.[28] In another study, *What Americans Think About Jews*, by Gertrude Selznick and Stephen Sternberg, which was due to appear in the summer of 1969, it was found that, while blacks were more likely to accept negative stereotypes about Jews in the economic field than were whites, they were clearly less anti-Semitic in the action they would take with regard to discrimination against Jews; for example, almost all blacks, 91 per cent, stated that a private club has no right to exclude Jews — the comparable figure for whites was 69 per cent. Of the black population, 68 per cent would not be disturbed if their party nominated a Jew for President — the figure for whites was 51 per cent.[29] Selznick and Steinberg conclude that 'what seems to characterise anti-Semitism among Negroes is less an emotional than a *verbal* displacement of hostility'.[30] Their other major finding which reinforces the Marx data is that black anti-Semitism is part of a broader attitude toward whites. Gary Marx concluded that 'contrary to public opinion, much Negro anti-Semitism may be directed not at Jews as Jews, but at Jews as whites'.[31] In fact, he found that

> pure anti-Semitism, not accompanied by anti-white feelings, is to be found among only 4 per cent of the sample. Exactly the same proportion harboured anti-white sentiments unaccompanied by anti-Semitism. For the vast majority of Negroes, the two are relatively indistinguishable, and more than half of our respondents expressed very little hostility on either index.[32]

How can one account both for these 1964 findings and for the increase in anti-Semitism which seems now to be taking place? One important explanation appears to be related to the presence at the earlier period of an intervening variable which operated to minimise anti-Semitism. That variable was the fact that 'a sizeable percentage of the black population is aware of the support that Jews give to civil rights'.[33] In fact, Marx found that, among those blacks who had the highest degree of impersonal economic contact with Jews, with the latter in superior positions as shopkeepers, employers and landlords precisely the sort of contact which is most likely to produce high anti-Semitism — but who saw Jews as civil rights allies, only 21 per cent were high in anti-Semitism. On the other hand, 73 per cent of those with an equally high rate of contact but who did not see the Jews as allies were high in anti-Semitism.[34]

Given the situation, the declining relevance of this variable (that is, the growth of Northern Jewish, as indeed of Northern white, opposition to black demands in the fields of housing, education and employment) may account for a large part of the apparent increase in anti-Semitism. The resulting situation has involved conflict of interests between a large number of individuals who have a privileged position, and an increasingly active and vocal disadvantaged minority. The fact that among those whites with vested interests there are Jews must not blind us to the fact that the battle is not over their Jewishness — it is over their privileges. Thus in the fight over decentralisation the battle was fought in large part against Jewish teachers and Jewish administrators, not because they were

Jewish — despite the claims of the UFT on the one hand and some black militants on the other — but because of their position.

It is irrelevant and dangerous for these people who are fighting to retain their privileges to keep referring to the past when Jews were active in the civil rights movement and to then accuse the blacks of ingratitude. This is not to deny the presence of anti-Semitism, but it is to deny the centrality and extent which have been given to it by groups like the UFT. And it can only be increased by campaigns such as that run by the UFT which succeed in mobilising Jews as Jews to oppose institutional changes which are necessary if the blacks are to improve their position in American society.

The demonstration districts, even in the face of the chaos and disruption caused by the central Board of Education and the United Federation of Teachers, have made great strides towards improving the quality of education being provided as well as in improving the relationship between the schools and the community. I.F. Stone, after visiting Ocean Hill-Brownsville, commented: 'I found black and white teachers, Jewish and gentile, working together not just peacefully but with zest and comradeship .... The classes were orderly. There was none of that screaming, by teacher against pupil and among the children, which is common in most New York schools.'[35] Because of this commitment to improving education, the local board has encouraged experimentation and initiative, the sole test being how successful it is — not, as at present under the central Board, whether it fits into established programmes. One Ocean Hill-Brownsville teacher said, 'It's the first time in my eight years as a teacher that I have been allowed to use unconventional teaching methods.'[36] This factor has been responsible for the large number of New York teachers who have transferred into Ocean Hill-Brownsville and who are trying to do so: they want to teach and to use their initiative, and the present system does not allow this. For example, a major study of the city school system concluded that 'the greatest failing of the schools today is the failure to use the creative ability of teachers'.[37] The struggle over decentralisation has exacerbated racial and religious antagonism. It has brought the entire school system to a stop for the first three months of the 1968 school year and it has played a major role in the unification of the black community and in strengthening in them a sense of self-confidence and pride. As John O'Neill, who was fired by Shanker, said,

'Shanker has accomplished in five months what would have taken five years under normal conditions, in furthering the demands of community militants'.[38]

It is precisely this sense of unity and determination which will keep the fight for decentralisation going, despite the victory of the UFT and educational bureaucracy in the New York State Legislature. The State Legislature, after ten gruelling days, passed a decentralisation law on 1 May which gives the UFT virtually all that it asked for — one observer likened the law to a 'collective bargaining agreement' — and which will abolish the three demonstration districts. The law establishes thirty local districts under the supervision and judgement of a new Board of Education — one member to be elected by each of New York City's five boroughs and two to be appointed by the Mayor. Under the City's present political structure it is unlikely that a black or Puerto Rican will be elected. The Board and its Chancellor will have major powers of supervision as well as the final say on budgets; the Board of Examiners will be retained, as will the Civil Service list for appointments and promotions. The new decentralised districts are to be drawn up under an interim five-man Board, consisting of one member appointed by each Borough President. There are a few concessions given to supporters of decentralisation, but these do not compensate for the general pro-bureaucracy tenor of the law. Each district will be given $250,000 a year to spend on repairs, etc. and any district where children fall below 45 per cent on reading and arithmetic tests can appoint teachers from outside the Board of Examiners' list, provided that they have either a State or a National Teachers Certificate. This is fair but what happens if they succeed in raising the level of performance of the children? The district will then presumably go back under the Board of Examiners and be restricted in their choice of teachers and supervisors. The law has been bitterly attacked by the black community: Rhody McCoy called it a 'prelude to the destruction of public education'.[39] Charles Wilson, who is the Project Administrator of IS 201 in East Harlem, called the new law a 'disgrace' and declared:

> If you take away the hope of people who only have hope, you're on very dangerous ground .... After giving people a little taste of freedom and involvement, it is dangerous to put them back under the old order.[40]

The Rev. C.H. Oliver, Chairman of the Ocean Hill-Brownsville Board, indicated that one approach that they would take would be a law suit aimed at invalidating the part of the law calling for the election of one member from each borough, under the *Baker* v. *Carr* Supreme Court ruling. But beyond that, he indicated a quiet determination that the community's schools were not going to be put back under the control of the bureaucracy, regardless of what has to be done to prevent it.[41]

The blacks are determined to 'do their own thing' to control their own schools and, given the failure of the New York State Legislature to heed their legitimate demands, there is likely to be further disruption and violence because of this. Perhaps we can end with a quotation from a letter sent by David Spencer, Chairman of the IS 201 Complex Governing Board, in which he expresses the type of approach which may come to be seen in the black community as the only legitimate one, following their defeat in the legislature:

> We are convinced that the only language the city understands is disruption and turmoil. The Board of Education ignored our Governing Board until the UFT created a massive public crisis. Now we are discussing the necessary expansion of our powers with them. The city will continue to refuse to recognise local communities' rights to control their own schools until local uprisings *force* the Mayor to provide a voice in education for Black and Puerto Rican parents. It is still our firm belief that nobody is going to give us anything; the community is going to have to *take* it![42]

2 Race, Class and Civil Rights

The central thesis of this chapter is that, as far as the life conditions and chances of the mass of African-Americans were concerned, the attainments of the Civil Rights Movement (CRM) in the US were limited. For most blacks the removal of *de jure* segregation was a necessary, but insufficient, condition for fundamental changes.

In the US there is widespread structural inequality in the distribution of wealth, income and power. Institutional racism determines resource allocation: access to goods and services and opportunities including education, employment, health care and housing and assures that, compared with blacks, whites get privileged access to scarce resources. This version of equality in a *Herrenvolk* democracy maintains the class system by inculcating and reinforcing a race consciousness rather than a class consciousness among the white working class.[1] One has only to look at the history of 'race riots' — pogroms — against people of colour in times of economic and political crisis, for example, the race riots in Chicago and the current escalation of racial violence among unemployed and alienated whites.

White working-class racism represents an incorporation *of* the dominant ideology, as reproduced through the schools, the media and the political institutions of the society. This ideology serves the interests of the ruling class and is encouraged and reinforced both directly and indirectly.[2] While it is true that white working-class people are given psychic and, to a degree, material benefits from the racist system and, therefore, there is widespread acceptance of racism, it is important to note three points:

(a) racism is not a genetically determined, or human nature determined, set of beliefs and practices;

(b) the price white workers pay is very high indeed (as is the case for male workers and sexism); and

(c) working-class history contains many points at which the presence of an alternative ideology an alternative way of explaining the world and alternative conceptions about the ability to change reality lead to non- and anti-racist practice.

This threat fosters extensive political and ideological efforts on the part of the ruling classes (and their allies in the media and state institutions) to delegitimate these alternative ideologies. In the US, in the post-Second World War period, for example, massive, state-led anti-Communist hysteria and purges played a crucial role, not only in legitimating the Cold War but also in isolating alternative visions about how US society itself should be organised. Central to this was a determined effort to prevent any linking of race and class in the black community and in black politics. Black people and their white allies have to overcome this ideological assault, which aims at separating race from class, intellectually and politically.

Civil Rights and the Cold War in the United States

In analysing the development of black politics in the period since the Second World War, we must look at the following the interrelationship between political and economic spheres of life; the interrelationship between domestic and foreign policies; demographic, economic and political changes in the US; the class composition, ideology and hierarchies of the CRM; the incorporation of most industrial unions into the Cold War, anti-Communist consensus; and the repression of those individuals and organisations that resisted. This attempt to place the CRM in a framework of analysis is designed to enable us to understand its achievements as well as its limitations and to understand the position of black people in the US today. It is not intended in any way to deprecate the courage, determination and creativity of those who struggled, or the range of consequences which followed these struggles. It is clear, for example, that we cannot understand the politics of the 1960s and beyond — including the development of the New Left, the anti-war movement and, crucially, the second wave of feminism — without understanding the impact of the CRM.[3] But unless we situate the CRM in its appropriate framework, we are in danger of making a number of important and damaging mistakes. We would have to ignore (or fail to value) previous struggles of black people if we were unable to explain adequately why the CRM achieved what it did and why earlier struggles failed to achieve similar results. It is clear that African-Americans have struggled from the very beginning of their formation as a people — during slavery/resistance on the slave ships, through marronage and slave uprisings, and through their resistance to the re-establishment of the plantation economy, to Jim Crow (the system of *de jure* segregation) and to institutional racism. The outcome of the struggles of any people is determined not merely by their will and determination but also by the range and balance of forces against which they are struggling and the range and balance of forces on which they can call. A second and related danger in failing to place the CRM in its context, is that we may fall prey to the neo-conservative ideological campaign which purports to explain the position of the mass of black people at the bottom of the society in terms of their culture of poverty, or of the broken, pathological Negro family, or of other similar victim blaming explanations.

Bearing these caveats in mind, let us look at some of the fundamental shifts which were occurring in the US and which consequently altered the context within which black people struggled and achieved changes. The fight against Jim Crow's *de jure* segregation united all sections of the black community and reshaped social and political structures in the South. It also changed the nature of black leadership and of class relations. This legal form of racism denied fundamental rights to all blacks under its sway, irrespective of their class. It was a total system of racial humiliation designed not only to control blacks (then largely living in the former slave states), but also poor whites. By legislating in favour of racial supremacy the South's rulers gave poor whites a stake in a system which, in practice, kept them poor. Poor whites gave up their votes — when they had them — in return for this racial superiority and, consequently, their adherence to a highly unequal society was bought extremely cheaply. Whites in the South had lower wages, worse public services and fewer benefits than whites in the rest of the country. Any politician who dared to raise questions about this situation was defeated by demagogic appeals to racial superiority and unity.

It is important to see that, though *de jure* segregation was a powerful form of racial control, it was not the only one; Jim Crow did not embody all US racism and, therefore, its removal would not signal the end of racism. It was created to protect and reproduce the re-established plantation system of the South, in which 90 per cent of the nation's black people lived. The system depended on controlled (less than free) labour and terror and Jim Crow helped maintain the super-exploitation of a black rural proletariat for the benefit of Southern and northern capitalists. The system served the interests of all dominant financial and industrial capitalists — not merely the Southern white ones.[4]

The origins of the dismantling of Jim Crow can be traced back to the recruiting of black labour by Northern industry during the First World War. Despite the opposition of Southern political and economic elites, the imperatives of Northern capital proved too powerful to be resisted. This led to increased mechanisation of Southern agriculture, which was further encouraged by the New Deal, the Agricultural Adjustment Act (AAA) and other programmes which began the process of creating a capital — rather than a labour-intensive system of agriculture. This had the consequence of lessening the region's dependence on black labour and, therefore, its need to keep black people out of the national labour market and, thus, ultimately its need of Jim Crow itself. This is not to say, however, that there was not a strong determination on the part of large numbers of whites (or even of a majority of them) to maintain the system of petty apartheid. It is, however, to say that for the dominant section of large-scale Southern agriculture, Jim Crow was no longer necessary for its hegemony.

The South was also changing in terms of the mix of industry and agriculture. The Federal government played a crucial role during and after the Second World War in encouraging the industrialisation of the South and Southwest. This process increased the political and economic importance of industrialists (including Northern-based ones) in determining the future direction of the region. This dependence on outside capital provided a very important counter-pressure against Southern opponents of civil rights.

The experience of Northern industrialists throughout the twentieth century, but particularly since the First World War, proved to them that *de jure* segregation was unnecessary. When black labour was recruited for jobs in Chicago, Detroit, Pittsburgh and other industrial centres, it entered communities in which *de jure* segregation was not the norm and in which it was not created. Instead, the system of institutional racism was created through the efforts of local and federal government and the real-estate and financial institutions to contain and control black people, to facilitate their super-exploitation, to ration scarce resources so that the unequal system which had produced that scarcity in the first place could be maintained, and to separate white and black workers. It was, therefore, clear to industrialists that, however desirable, Jim Crow was unnecessary. Therefore, in a highly charged political atmosphere in which Jim Crow acted as the target, or lightening rod, of all black anger and political mobilisation, it was no longer clear that agribusiness and industrial leaders could, in the face of escalating disorder and instability, be counted on as steadfast allies of those determined to maintain Jim Crow.

As indicated earlier, black people were struggling in the years prior to the emergence of the CRM. In the post-First World War period, Marcus Garvey's UNIA (Universal Negro Improvement Association) became the largest mass movement of blacks in US history. The UNIA represented the nationalist strand of black struggle and its appeal is indicative of the massive anger against white racism felt by African-Americans.[5] During the late 1920s and 1930s, the Communist Party gave high priority to working with blacks and, though it never obtained great numbers of black members, it did put the concept of the links between race and class on the political agenda. It also was the most important white-led organisation to challenge white racism particularly in an era of unchallenged white supremacy. In 1945, Representative Adam Clayton Powell Jr said, 'There is no group in America, including the Christian Church, that practices racial brotherhood one-tenth as much as the Communist Party'.[6] The relationship between the CPUSA (Communist Party of the United States of America) and blacks, between race and class, was to be of growing importance and was a central target of the efforts of the US government and of white liberals and middle class black leaders.

Questions of who the leaders are and of who determines priorities are crucial to any discussion of black politics, as they are to the politics of any group. In his overview of black American politics,

Manning Marable[7] argues that:

> The central fact about black political culture from 1865 to 1985 is
> that only a small segment of the Afro-American social fraction, the
> petty bourgeoisie, has dominated the electoral machinery and
> patronage positions that regulate black life and perpetuate the
> exploitation of black labour. The buffer stratum has historically
> focused its energies on non economic issues, such as the abolition of
> legal segregation; and when it has developed explicitly economic
> agendas, more frequently than not it presumes the hegemony of
> capital over labour. Even during periods of black working-class
> insurgency within electoral politics, the Negro petty bourgeoisie tend
> to surface on the crest of such movements.

The system of white supremacy that had been created with the
defeat of the First Reconstruction involved the *shaping* of the black
community's leadership structures. As Bloom[8] has written:

> White power was able to reach into the black community itself and to
> shape it, to help determine the goals the black community sought, the
> means desired to seek these goals, the leadership the black community
> had, the kinds of personal options blacks often felt they had, and
> even the view that blacks had of themselves. As a result of the victory
> of white supremacy, blacks had few options. They were not in a
> position to confront the white-created social, political, and economic
> world in order to change its terms; rather, they had to find a way to
> survive in it, to adjust to it. Accommodation meant looking to
> powerful whites as benefactors, requesting favours, accepting
> paternalism and subordination. It meant that whites determined the
> black community's leaders by deciding with whom they would
> communicate and to whom they would grant their *largesse*.

Bloom[9] goes on to argue that, as a consequence,

> the dynamics of the old system had divided blacks along class lines.
> The divisions in the old system had a weak objective basis. Those
> considered of higher social rank often had a tenuous hold on their
> status. That was all the more reason for their subjective insistence
> upon an exaggerated social distance separating them from poorer and
> (in their view) less cultured blacks.

Emphasis on economic issues, especially for a socialist position,
represented a threat to the interests of this petit bourgeois stratum.
It challenged its class interests and the acceptability of its leaders

acceptable, that is, to the white power structure. It is interesting and important to note that W.E.B. DuBois represented just such a threat and thus was removed twice from leadership in the National Association for the Advancement of Coloured People (NAACP). His writings were apt and prescient. During the Depression he 'urged the NAACP to develop a meaningful economic programme to assist African Americans. In May 1932, the Crisis reported that the "first job" of the Association was "to fight colour discrimination" but it also stated that "our fight for economic equality" must include economic co-operation and "socialisation of wealth".'[10] He went on to declare[11] that the NAACP had to devise 'a positive program rather than mere negative attempts to avoid segregation and discrimination .... The interests of the masses are the interests of this Association, and the masses have got to voice themselves through it.'

This emphasis on economic issues and on the masses having power continued to be stressed by Dr Dubois and continued to be denied by the established leadership. Yet the Second World War brought to the forefront the reality of the mass of black people's anger and sense of alienation from US institutions. The Office of War Information carried out a survey in Harlem in the Spring of 1942 to determine black attitudes towards the war. It concluded[12] that, 'resentment at Negro discrimination [was] fairly widespread throughout the Negro population.' Only 11 per cent said they expected conditions to improve if America won the war. Lee Finkle quotes Ollie Stewart, a reporter who had visited many army camps, reporting that 'black soldiers were ready to start the fight at home before the European war ended. He said that with some encouragement and ammunition they would head for Washington to end discrimination.' He also quotes Joel A. Rogers[13] reporting a letter from a hostile reader complaining about 'so called intelligent race leaders ... yapping all out for victory. I ask what victory? The white man feeds his jive to the race leaders and they take up the yapping and feed it to the ignorant masses .... Each week when I read how the whites do the race it cements me against them and their war.' George Schuyler reported, 'the masses of Negroes are far more ready to fight and die than their leaders and spokesmen' (i.e. for their rights at home rather than for the US abroad). E. Washington Rhodes of the *Philadelphia Tribune* reported[14] 'the mass of Negroes is more radical than ... those of us who publish

Negro newspapers. The less vocal Negro ... is thinking more radical thoughts than we are thinking.'

These concerns were central to Gunnar Myrdal's *An American Dilemma* (1962), a classic liberal statement on race relations, in which he lays out the liberal agenda for the post-war period, including a clear statement on the underlying assumptions of that agenda. Themes running through this statement include the need for white Americans to re-evaluate race relations; the need to contain black militancy; and the international implications of American race relations. He makes clear that reforms are a necessary consequence of the growing black militancy. As he put it[15] 'America can never more regard its Negroes as a patient, submissive minority.' He was also at pains to stress that Negroes in America could count on the 'glorious American ideals of democracy, liberty, and equality' and the adherence to these ideals by white Americans. Therefore, 'the Negroes do not need any other allies'.[16] Presumably included among those allies they did not need was the Communist Party. Given that it was *An American Dilemma* and would be solved by white Americans being true to the *American Creed*, blacks would not need Pan-Africanism either.

Myrdal[17] then elaborates on the new mood among the black people:

> Reading the Negro press and hearing all the reports from observers who have been out among common Negroes in the South and the North convinces me that there is much sullen scepticism, and even cynicism, and vague, tired, angry dissatisfaction among American Negroes today. The general bitterness is reflected in the stories that are circulating in the Negro communities: A young Negro, about to [be] inducted into the Army, said 'Just carve on my tombstone, Here lies a black man killed fighting a yellow man for the protection of a white man'. Another Negro boy expressed the same feeling when he said he was going to get his eyes slanted so that the next time a white man shoved him around he could fight back .... There is more money in circulation and some trickles down to the Negroes. With a little money in his pocket even the poor Negro day labourer or domestic worker feels that he can afford to stiffen himself. Many white housewives notice strange thoughts and behaviour on the part of their Negro servants these days.

He quotes the 'troubled view' of a black clergyman, Dr J.S. Nathaniel Tross: 'I am afraid for my people. They have grown restless. They are not happy. They no longer laugh. There is a new policy among them — something strange, perhaps terrible.[18] The international implications are dearly stated by Myrdal, who is worth, quoting at length again: 'What has actually happened within the last few years is not only that the Negro problem has become national in scope after having been mainly a Southern worry'. The language is interesting: who has the problem and whose worry? It is also misleading in that it was always national in the obvious sense that blacks were American citizens denied their constitutional rights with the acquiescence of the national government and in the interests of the national economic system. Myrdal continues:

> It has also acquired tremendous international implications, and this is another and decisive reason why the white North is prevented from compromising with the white South regarding the Negro. The situation is actually such that any and all concessions to Negro rights in this phase of the history of the world will repay the nation many times, while any and all injustices inflicted upon him will be extremely costly.[19] The main international implication is ... that America, for its international prestige, power, and future security, needs to demonstrate to the world that American Negroes can be satisfactorily integrated into democracy .... The treatment of the Negro in America has not made good propaganda for America abroad and particularly not among coloured nations.[20]

And crucially in Myrdal's felicitous phrase:

> Particularly as Russia cannot be reckoned on to adhere to white supremacy, it is evident from the facts ... that within a short period the shrinking minority of white people in our Western lands will either have to succumb or to find ways of living on peaceful terms with coloured people.[21]

Thus, the stage was set. Fundamental economic and demographic forces had lessened the centrality of *de jure* segregation for the leaders of the New South. Blacks had become more urban and more Northern and, consequently, more important in terms of electoral politics and were, at the same time, being seen as potentially dangerous or possibly disloyal in future wars — particularly against coloured nations. The threat of renewed links between blacks and the CP red was worrying. Centrally for the politics of post-war America, Pax Americana was replacing Pax Britannica, with the US emerging from the war as the most powerful nation in the world, determined to organise the post-war world system for its benefit. This was to have implications for race relations within the US. Crucially, Southern blacks were increasingly prepared to resist racist intimidation and the domination of the white power structure and their own accommodationist leaders. The dynamics of a growing willingness to fight, the delegitimation of *de jure* segregation by the Supreme Court and other institutions, the rejection of leaders who refused to oppose segregation *per se* as opposed to negotiating marginal variations or concessions in its operation, the white Southern resistance to the 1954 Supreme Court decision, Brown v. the Board of Education of Topeka which declared the previous doctrine of 'separate but equal' which had legalised the system of *de jure* segregation, to be unconstitutional — all these led to what Jack Bloom has called, after the example of blacks in Harlem in the 1920s, the New Negro. This all took place in a world being reshaped by the development of television, ensuring regional, national, and world-wide coverage of the resistance, which in turn ensured that the uprisings of the post-Montgomery period unlike those of the earlier period became part of the public consciousness of blacks, North and South, of whites throughout the US and of people throughout the world.

The black-led coalition which reshaped Southern society included, in Bloom's analysis,[22] 'Southern business and middle classes, the Northern middle class, the national Democratic Party, and the federal government'. This coalition 'was the key to the victory of the civil rights movement'. The nature of this coalition was also the key to the limits of what the CRM could achieve. The essence of black politics was the understanding of the different goals of the various components of the coalition and of how to play one sector of the Southern elites off against the other and of how to put pressure on the various Northern components to act. The strategy was effective as long as the CRM's demands for freedom and equality were contained within the parameters of the dominant ideology, i.e. freedom from segregation and overt discrimination and equality of opportunity. These were the limits of the dominant ideology and the limits imposed by the structural interests of the white middle and business classes, North and South, of the national Democratic Party and of the federal government. These demands were also congruent with the class interests of the black middle class. When, as a result of the greater involve-ment of the black masses in the South in the mass actions of the CRM and in the North in the ghetto uprisings the meaning of free-dom and equality was expanded to include an economic dimension, a demand for structural change, the coalition broke apart.

The range of political forces supporting the status quo are very great. In the case of the status quo of *de jure* segregation these included: the dominant ideology and popular culture of the US which were racist; the effects on the legislative process of the com-bination of the Seniority system in Congress and the Solid South (the one-party system dominating post-reconstruction Southern politics — racist attitudes among decision-makers themselves; and, generally, the weakness of those wanting change in terms of polit-ical and economic resources.

Therefore, for the CRM to succeed in overturning a system of legalised segregation a range of pressures had to be brought to bear on decision-makers so that these forces could be overcome. Among these forces were, political pressure from Democratic politicians in the urban centres of the North and Mid West (who were becoming increasingly dependent upon the black vote); the moral delegiti-mation of overt racism as a result of the horrors of Nazism and the moral imperatives of the Second World War (which placed the defenders of Jim Crow and their allies on the defensive); threats to the order and stability of the wider society (particularly after the widening of support for the CRM in the non-South) through sym-pathetic boycotts and picketing; threats to order in the South, which increasingly came to be seen as putting at risk new invest-ment; and threats to the US position in the world from Soviet use of Jim Crow and later of Bull Connor, Jim Clark and George Wallace.

The removal of Jim Crow, therefore, had to be forced onto the agenda of an unwilling political system. There were forces which operated to limit the changes being made (under duress) to the removal of *de jure* segregation and overt discrimination. Equality of opportunity would require the removal of the latter so that blacks could compete like everyone else. It might represent a threat to particular whites or to particular institutions in terms of their current practices, but the wider imperatives of the system would work through these problems — as in the range of measures which had been taken and which involved limitations in the absolute rights of property for the greater good. Factory safety, social security and child labour laws had all been opposed as interferences with freedom, but, in the face of greater threats, threats of more fundamental demands and radicalisation, concessions had been made. It is important to note that these concessions, as the ones made in response to the demands of black people and their allies, were limited, did not involve fundamental shifts in the distribution of wealth or power and would be secure only to the extent that the forces which extracted the concessions remained strong.

If we now look in detail at how these forces and processes were played out we can see the salience of Myrdal's international agenda in forming the liberal agenda within which the CRM developed and was shaped. The final report of President Truman's Committee on Civil Rights defined 'moral' and 'economic' reasons for ending discrimination and then defined the 'international' reasons.[23]

> Our position in the post-war world is so vital to the future that our smallest actions have far-reaching effects .... We cannot escape the fact that our civil rights record has been an issue in world politics. The world's press and radios are full of it .... Those with competing philosophies have stressed — and are shamelessly distorting — our shortcomings .... They have tried to prove our democracy an empty fraud, and our nation a consistent oppressor of under-privileged people. This may seem ludicrous to Americans [which Americans? Presumably Afro-Americans, Native Americans, Asian-Americans, Latino-Americans do now count] but it is sufficiently important to worry our friends. The United States is not so strong, the final triumph of the democratic ideal is not so inevitable that we can ignore what the world thinks of us or our record.

The centrality of the Cold War and of anti-Communism is crucial to our understanding of post-war US society and institutions. The Cold War provided the framework for the creation of a 'permanent wartime economy' — as had been called for by Charles E. Wilson, President of General Electric in 1944 — and for the opening up of the markets and economies of the 'free world' for US exports and investment as Dean Acheson had declared was necessary if the US were not to return to depression after the war.[24] The use by the Soviets and by nationalists in Third World countries of US apartheid to challenge US claims to leadership of the democratic, free world had to be limited. The records of the Truman,

Eisenhower and Kennedy administrations, for example, are full of indications of how sensitive was the US government. These concerns worked their way through into the decisions of the executive branch of the federal government and were instrumental in the Supreme Court's landmark decision in the Brown case, as in many others.

The international benefits to the US of removing petty apartheid would be reinforced by anti-Communist benefits at home for the federal government. Since the Communists were supposedly concerned to exploit Jim Crow for their own purposes of destabilising US society, the removal of Jim Crow would presumably end that threat. Despite the limited membership of blacks in the CPUSA, it is clear that decision-makers were conscious of the danger, in their terms, of black-white unity around class issues which a black-red alliance represented and, therefore, were determined to combine repression of the left with their anti-Jim Crow policies.

The anti-Communist hegemony, which was established, shaped the debate on black rights as it did all other debates. The determination to prevent the linking of black and red was central so central that the FBI and other agencies used as *prima facie* evidence of probable disloyalty the fact that a white person had black friends or invited black people for a meal. The purges of the Communists, fellow travellers, 'comsymps' and others unable to prove their loyalty became the dominant feature of life in the US. Most individuals and organisations succumbed and often tried to use the terms of the anti-Communist hysteria for their own purposes. In his book on W.E.B. DuBois, Gerald Horne (1986), reports that, after the firing of Dr DuBois, the NAACP 'strongly implied that those Euro-Americans most opposed to Jim Crow and racism were Communists and should be carefully watched in the branches'.

Naturally this heavy-handed approach caused a wail of protest and was 'corrected' in a subsequent editorial. But this episode was indicative of how far anti-Communism had gone, for apparently there was sentiment for routing out white members of the Association (who often were influential and sizeable financial contributors) in a spurious anti-Communist crusade.[25]

So central was anti-Communism that people in every walk of life identified as Communists were purged from public life. In this context Paul Robeson's prominence as a fighter for black rights in the US and for the freedom of the colonised peoples, his openly leftist position on questions about the political economy and his opposition to the Cold War, marked him out as a prime target. The US government took away his passport so that he could not travel abroad. This was accompanied by a massive propaganda campaign to label him a subversive, a false prophet who was misleading his people. The House Un-American Activities Committee (HUAC) and other committees not only regularly called him to testify but also had a succession of prominent black people appear before them to attack him. It was said at the time that a condition for employment for black actors (for what little work was available for blacks in Hollywood) was that they had to attack Paul Robeson publicly. This campaign succeeded in denying Paul Robeson work in the US threats of economic and/or physical retaliation were sufficient to prevent venues being made available to him.

The intimidation increased and there was violence against him and those who came to hear him sing. Listening to and applauding his songs were considered proof of being a Communist, at least by Adolph Menjou's testimony before the HUAC. The pressure to turn Robeson into a non-person continued unabated. Gerald Horne recounts[26] what happened when Dr DuBois received a copy of Langston Hughes's book, *Famous Negro Music Makers*, and discovered that Paul Robeson had been totally excluded. DuBois wrote to the publisher and received a 'remarkably candid' reply from Edward H. Dodd Jr, president of Dodd, Mead & Company, 'Hughes was told by experts of his acquaintance and probably also told by our library advisers that the inclusion of Robeson would probably eliminate the book from acceptance by a good many school libraries, state adoption lists, etc.'[27]

Other examples of the creation of a non-person in a democracy are provided by his son, Paul Robeson Jr, who quotes contemporary experts rating his father as one of the greatest football players of all time. He goes on[28] to declare that:

> In spite of these credentials, my father is the only two-time Walter Camp All-American who is not in the College Football Hall of Fame. Not only that, the Hall of Fame is located at Rutgers, and Paul Robeson was the first Rutgers player to win All-American honours. It is also a fact that the book *College Football*, published in 1950 by Muray & Co. and labelled 'the most complete record compiled on

college football,' listed a ten-man All-America team for 1918, the only ten-man team in All-America history. The missing man was an end named Paul Robeson.

The NAACP supported US foreign policy and tried to use that support as a way of obtaining federal government backing for its anti-discrimination agenda. The following statement to rank and file members by Alfred Baker, an NAACP board member, is an example of this approach: 'If there is ... a group interested in the discussion of foreign policy, they might take a speaker on the bad effect of racial discrimination on our foreign relations ... [they] should be able to answer questions about ... our exclusion of Communists and our support of anti-Communist foreign policy measures'.[29] Horne's conclusion is that 'the NAACP was trying to run with the hares and hunt with the hounds; attempting to tweak Uncle Sam, they hammered on the hypocrisy of foreign policy when it came to race while eagerly supporting the glue that held the policy together anti-Communism'.[30]

This anti-Communist campaign involved political elites on the national and local scene (governmental and non-governmental officials alike) and had an anti-union, anti-welfare state, pro-Cold War, pro military-industrial complex agenda. Racism was always part of this campaign either up front or *sub rosa*. The consequences included the retarding and weakening of black struggles for structural change, as well as channelling struggles into an anti-Jim Crow, anti-*de jure* segregation mode — and thus retarding the wider struggle for black rights and, even, as we shall see, distorting and retarding the limited, legitimate campaign. Victor Bernstein, writing prophetically in 1943[31] argued that:

> Since the Wagner Act made open union-busting illegal, race-baiting has become almost the chief weapon of the anti-labour storm troops. Certainly this is true in the South where the union man, himself torn by prejudice, is inclined to fall easy prey to the antiNegro mouthings of demagogues like [Eugene] Talmadge and ['Pappy'] O'Daniel ... and professional hate promoters like Vance Muste, who once described the non-existent Eleanor Clubs as a 'Red Radical scheme to organise Negro maids, cooks, and nurses in order to have a Communist informer in every Southern home'.

This link between black rights and Bolshevism has a long history in the US. President Truman's secretary of state, James F. Byrnes, had an equally long history of mouthing such hysteria and hate. In a speech on the floor of the House of Representatives in 1919[32] he attacked the *Messenger*, the socialist newspaper published by A. Philip Randolph and Chandler Owen, in the following terms:

> The material in the magazine would indicate that the source from which the support comes is antagonistic to the Government of the United States. It appeals for the establishment in this country of a Soviet Government .... It urges the negro to join the IWW's [sic], pays tribute to Eugene Debs and every other convicted enemy of the Government, and prays for the establishment of a Bolshevik Government in this land. It is evident that the IWEW's [sic] are financing it in an effort to have the negro of America join them in their revolutionary plans.

This anti-red, anti-black rhetoric was used by capitalists in their attempts to divide black and white workers and to destroy industrial unionism. Victor Bernstein gives a number of examples of this in the campaign by Humble Oil, a Standard Oil subsidiary in Beaumont, Texas in 1943 against the Oil Workers International (CIO) organising drive. He[33] quotes from two issues of the company union's publication:[34]

> The CIO is openly committed to a policy of complete elevation of the Negro to absolute social and economic equality with the white .... They want political power, and to have this power, they must have votes ... and a coloured vote unrestricted and unrestrained represents the greatest single block of solid voting power in America .... That is why they promise [the Negroes] white men's jobs, white men's houses and complete social equality with the white race on and off the job.

The CIO has come into our Southern State of Texas brandishing the torch of racial hatred, seeking to tear down the hundreds of years of good feeling and understanding which has always existed here between white and coloured races. The place to check them is here and now. Tomorrow may be too late.

There is widespread agreement among those who have looked at these developments that, in the words of Wayne Clark[35] 'race relations in the 1950s and early 1960s were shaped to a great extent by the pronouncements of those individual members of the political elite who assumed responsibility not only for preserving white supremacy but also for awakening the nation to what they considered the inherent dangers of international communism'.

Don Carleton[36] writing about Houston, found a similar pattern:

> After World War II, Houston's establishment began to perceive a threat to its wealth and power from the growing labour movement in Texas and an ever expanding Federal government. Houston's leaders faced a federal government they believed to be controlled by Socialists and left-wingers. They saw Washington attempting to make further incursions into sacred areas such as the oil-depletion allowance, labour relations, corporate tax reform, medicine, education and race relations.

They used the red scare to achieve ideological, political and economic hegemony. On the national scale this process was being encouraged and orchestrated by the Chamber of Commerce. Leslie Adler[37] writes that:

> Recovering from a serious decline in status, wealth and power suffered during the depression decade, business leaders were clearly making an all-out effort at the war's end to regain control over the domestic sector of the economy and to reorient national priorities away from social reform and toward the business foundation they believed to be central to the American way of life. Efforts to curb newly established labour union power were high on their own list of priorities, and given the long-standing link in business thinking between unionism and communism, it would seem natural that the communists-in-unions theme would appeal to businessmen.

Adler[38] then discusses how they accomplished their goals:

> Seeing themselves in the position to bring a great deal of influence and pressure to bear on American thinking, members of the Committee on Socialism and Communism did not take their self-appointed task lightly, and set about to research those who could best shape public opinion. 'Authorities who have studied this type of problem carefully,' [Emerson P.] Schmidt wrote to Committee members in early 1946, 'are convinced that approximately 8,000 American people are the genuine creators of public opinion the rest merely follow. If we can reach a goodly portion of these 8,000 with such a brochure, its influence will automatically tend to spread into the lives and homes of most of the people.' Careful planning such as this and a thorough knowledge of how to appeal to the American public marked the entire Chamber of Commerce crusade.

Along with the related activities of HUAC[39] this campaign led the Senate Internal Affairs Committee; President Truman's Loyalty Security Program, the Attorney-General's List of Subversive Organizations and the activities of the FBI and state and local 'red squads' succeeded in purging those who disagreed with the dominant ideology.[40] Clark[41] concludes that:

> There is little doubt that resistance activities hindered the organising efforts of the labour movement and protracted the civil rights struggle in the Deep South. The white leadership understood that picket lines, boycotts, marches, and other forms of organised protest could be used to fight segregation before these methods were actively used by civil rights activists. They instinctively associated those tactics with communists, labour militants, and agitators for integration. As a result, public opinion was strongly united against protest methods, particularly those involving direct action. The Cold War consensus contributed to this climate of hostility towards groups and individuals who exerted pressure for social change. It facilitated the development by anti-union and segregationist forces of a resistance to racial integration that was based, in part, on the knowledge that segregation was as effective in maintaining class barriers as it was in sustaining the colour line between whites and blacks.

In the South this campaign had the effect of thwarting unionisation and struggles for the tenant farmers. In his study of Southern radicalism in the 1929-59 period, Anthony Dunbar[42] wrote that:

> Though Southern plantations were still inhabited by poorly paid, educated, and housed workers, there were few fresh attempts to rekindle the union spirit of the 1930s. One of the reasons, of course, was the history of failure. But another was that there was no longer a Socialist party or a coherent progressive community willing to underwrite the cost of pressing the one demand that had traditionally rallied Southern farm workers: land for the landless.

The purge of leftists from CIO unions and of leftist unions from the CIO had particularly deleterious consequences for blacks. Sumner Rosen[43] argues that, 'to the extent that the unions expelled had been the more militant and devoted advocates of racial justice, the cause itself lost much of its meaning and appeal'. Boyer and Morais[44] write that

> The expelled unions were the soul of the CIO .... It was those unions

that had fought the hardest for Negro representation in trade union office. It was they that had led the fight for equal pay for equal work for women and it was they that had fought for the rights of such minorities as Puerto Ricans and Mexican miners. And what organisation had been accomplished in the South hat been done mostly by them.

The consequences were starkly summarised by Charles W. Cheng:[45]

> the drive to organise the unorganised in the South never fully materialised. Certainly a concerted effort by either the CIO or AFL would have increased the number of blacks in the labour movement. Instead, black workers in particular and large numbers of white workers, in general, continued to be economically exploited. The wall of white supremacy gained a new lease on life, and this wall would not be massively confronted until the 1960s. In any case, it seems probable that the expulsions, and thus the fragmentation of labour, were in part responsible for the failure of labour to organise in the South.

These purges, including those in Hollywood and in academic institutions at every level and in every area of the United States, reinforced the ideological hegemony of corporate America. In an interesting discussion of the issues dealt with (or avoided) by Hollywood in this period, Leslie Adler[46] has written:

> Though the changing composition of Hollywood films after 1947 cannot be attributed entirely to the impact of HUAC, a basic change did occur which oriented the industry further away from dealing with serious social themes and which seems clearly related to the investigations. The 1945-7 period had seen an increase in the film treatment of such themes, and as calculated by Dorothy B. Jones, approximately 28 per cent of the films in 1947 were of a serious social bent. From 1947-9, however, the trend was reversed, with only approximately 18 per cent of the films in 1949 qualifying. An even sharper break occurred from 1950-2 with an upswing in war films, pure entertainment films, escapist films, and a larger number of anti-Communist films. In 1950 only 11 per cent dealt with social questions and by 1953 that figure was further reduced to 9 per cent.

J. Fred MacDonald,[47] discussing similar developments in the newly emerging medium of television, reports:

The broadcast industry readily fell in with the government purgists. Entertainers adversely touched by the [HUAC] hearings found themselves blacklisted from radio and, more important, the burgeoning new medium, television. It made little difference to broadcasters if, in the jargon of the day, these political deviates were 'card carrying members' (actual dues-paying members of the CPUSA), 'dupes' (those fooled into supporting Red goals without realising the error of their ways), 'Pinkos' (those who were leftists, but not Red enough), or 'comsymps' or 'fellow travellers' (those who sympathised with Communist ends without joining the party). The CPUSA was considered to be an arm of the Soviet Union, not a legitimate political party springing from the fabric of American society. Those said to be associated with Communism, then, were considered anti-American conspirators. They were unwelcome in broadcasting. In this way the entertainment business became a political arena in which Cold War fears and ignorance became the basis for exclusionary professional policy. This was to be expected in a business that had been heavily politicised during the war .... In news and entertainment programmes television presented Americans a picture of world affairs in which the honest, selfless United States was forced to defend the Free World against the barbarous onslaught of Communism — with its godless ideologues and automaton commissars intent upon conquering the planet. Those not wholeheartedly in favour of the national crusade were often suspected of being at least tolerant of the evil empire. It was an over-simplified picture. But in the context of the United States at mid-century, it was widely perceived as genuine.

The Truman administration fully supported the development of this ideological strait-jacket and gave its highest priority to the pursuance of the Cold War and the creation of the national security state. Its tactical support for civil rights was always a lower priority, despite the periodic rhetorical emphasis on equal rights. Symbolic appointments and policy statements, combined with a limited number of executive actions (forced by pressure from blacks and from the foreign policy pressures of the Cold War) were the major aspects of the administration's practices. The red-baiting and purges, as has been discussed, actually adversely affected the struggle for black rights.

That struggle escalated in the 1950s, particularly after the Brown decision. The *Brown* v. *Board of Topeka* decision of 1954 overturned the 1896 *Plessy* v. *Ferguson* decision which had declared 'separate but equal' to be constitutional and held that *de jure* segregation was unconstitutional. *Brown II* was the 1955 enforcement decision which ordered implementation of the 1954 decision on the basis of 'all deliberate speed'. What should have been the crowning glory of the NAACP's elite dominated strategy of litigation and lobbying, in practice turned out to be the beginning of a new phase of black struggle. The reason for this apparent contradiction is that the Court in Brown II — its implementation decision — developed the unique concept of black children being granted their constitutional rights 'with all deliberate speed' and with the onus on black parents throughout the South having to go to court to obtain desegregation. Not surprisingly, this provided valuable breathing space for Southern racists determined to resist integration — especially as the president, Dwight D. Eisenhower, never supported the moral imperative of the decision and did not throw the weight of his tremendous popularity into the fray on behalf of the constitutional rights of black people.

Following the massive resistance to the Brown decision there was a growing disillusionment among blacks with the NAACP strategy and a receptivity to new forms of struggle. This disillusionment must be seen as being directed primarily at the NAACP on the national level. Local chapters and leaders were often in the vanguard of struggle, were subjected to local government and State repression, and often co-operated with other more activist groups. The most famous example of this new strategy developed in Montgomery, Alabama in 1955 when the black community carried out a year-long boycott of the bus company. This strategy of non-violent direct action became associated with the teachings of Dr Martin Luther King Jr and the Southern Christian Leadership Conference (SCLC), which emerged out of the Montgomery struggle and related struggles throughout the South. Dr King and non-violent direct action held centre stage for more than a decade. Following student sit-ins in 1960 and the formation of the Student Non-Violent Co-ordinating Committee (SNCC), there was mass mobilisation of Southern blacks and mobilisation of Northern support, among blacks and whites.[48]

These struggles received the attention of the print and visual media of the world, as they were intended to do. The strategy required the intervention of the federal government in all its forms, but to overcome the power of the Southern Committee Chairs in Congress, the lack of interest on the part of the FBI and other governmental agencies, and the electoral interests of Kennedy, countervailing pressures had to be brought. For example, the pressures on President Kennedy as a result of the Birmingham, Alabama campaign were dramatic. Carl Brauer[49] writes that:

> The Birmingham crisis touched another sensitive Kennedy nerve when it attracted a great deal of publicity abroad .... In several countries, particularly in Ghana and Nigeria, the media poured out caustic denunciation of the racial outrage. Radio Moscow, after a hesitant beginning, was currently diverting a quarter of its output to Birmingham, much of it beamed to African audiences. Given Kennedy's expansionist view of his country's role in the world, the damage Birmingham had done to America's image undoubtedly concerned him.

This strategy clearly worked in terms of forcing President Kennedy to introduce civil rights legislation. He told civil rights leaders that, 'the demonstrations in the streets had brought results, they had made the executive branch act faster and were now forcing Congress to entertain legislation which a few weeks before would have had no chance'.[50] The problem black people and others would face in the years following these victories, was what would happen when the protesters' demands touched on structural racism and the bases of inequality in the US political economy?

There were, however, important differences within the black community about both strategies and goals. The major (moderate) establishment groups defined the problem as that of blacks being excluded from an otherwise fair, just and democratic system much like the later bourgeois, mainstream feminists. The solution was to allow blacks (or women) into that system on the same bases of competition and individualism as was presumed to be the norm in the US meritocratic system. These groups either supported US foreign policy or did not comment on it an implicit recognition that the limits of assimilation, integration for blacks, meant that blacks could speak on race questions but not on foreign policy or other fundamental questions of the political economy. The radical black groups challenged these positions across the board. They did not accept the view that, apart from the exclusion of black people (or women in the case of the socialist feminists), the US was a fair, just and democratic society. Instead, they argued that the political economy was a highly unequal, unjust system, not just for blacks but for all. The solution, therefore, involved not the integration of individual blacks into that competitive system, but more collective responses designed to change the system as a whole. Increasingly these tendencies came to oppose US foreign policy, particularly in Africa and Vietnam. The established groups bitterly attacked these interventions on the grounds that they would put at risk the gains that had been made.

The political repression of Paul Robeson and W.E.B. DuBois — and the collaboration of the NAACP and other moderate groups in the repression focused very directly on their opposition to US foreign policy. As indicated above, Paul Robeson's passport had been taken away by the State Department. The government's reasoning is apparent in the following extract of the US State Department's deposition:[51]

> Furthermore even if the complaint had alleged ... that the passport was cancelled solely because of applicant's recognised status as spokesman for large sections of Negro Americans, we submit that this would not amount to an abuse of discretion in view of the applicant's frank admission that he has been for years extremely active politically on behalf of the colonial people of Africa.

If it appears surprising that the government of the US, which prides itself on being the leader of the free world and an anti-colonial nation, used as the basis of denying a passport to an American citizen the fact that he had frankly admitted to having worked on behalf of the colonial people of Africa, it is because of the widespread acceptance of US *bona fides*. It is important, therefore, to look behind the façade of US beneficence and anticolonialism. The *New York Times*, as much an establishment newspaper as one could wish for, wrote in its editorial on 22 November 1949 that, 'Africa is the continent of the future. We learned its strategic value in the Second World War. Its economic potentialities are the hope of Western Europe ... as well as the rest of the world .... The United States need not be afraid of the label of reactionary if [we] oppose too hasty independence.'[52]

Given the economic importance of Africa and the US government's acceptance of the advice of *New York Times* leader writers, it is not surprising to find the US expanding its economic and political role in Africa and acting as a leading anti-revolutionary power in conjunction with South Africa and Israel propping up an array of corrupt and brutal client regimes and destabilising nationalist and socialist governments. It is also not surprising to find W.E.B. DuBois a target of the US government alongside Paul Robeson. Dr DuBois had a long history of support for the 'colonial people of Africa' and for Pan-Africanism. Manning Marable and Gerald Horne have written about this aspect of DuBois's politics, which linked Pan-Africanism, the struggle for black rights and freedom inside the US to a critique of the reactionary role played by the petit bourgeois leaders of establishment-oriented moderate groups. Horne[53] writes:

> DuBois and the Council [on African Affairs] were rooting on a hasty independence for the continent and the fact that he was both black and influential was guaranteed to cause tensions. It was important that those of African ancestry in the United States be brought into line in support of US foreign policy, but DuBois and the Council were not cooperative .... The Council was not only sharply critical of the State Department and the United States-based transnational corporations but they also turned their microscope on potential friends and allies. They commended the NAACP for their resolution on colonialism in 1953 but criticised the use of the term 'natives' and the equating of the 'persecution' of Britons in South Africa with blacks; they questioned their lack of forthright support for specific organisations like the ANC and United States votes in the United Nations on Africa. A specific reference to East Africa by the Association — 'We view with alarm the terrorist methods of the Mau Mau in Kenya' — was strenuously attacked.

Marable[54] quotes DuBois saying that 'American Negroes freed of their baseless fear of Communism will again begin to turn their attention and aim their activity toward Africa.' They would soon recognise the role of American capitalism in the exploitation of African people. 'When once the blacks of the United States, the West Indies, and Africa work and think together,' DuBois concluded hopefully[55] 'the future of the black man in the modern world is safe.' DuBois's foreign policy activities were sufficiently threatening to US government and business interests that not only was his passport taken away but he was 'indicted for allegedly serving as an "agent of a foreign principal" in his work with the Peace Information Center in New York'.

The 82-year-old black man was handcuffed, fingerprinted and portrayed in the national media as a common criminal. Before his trial, the *New York Herald Tribune* convicted him in a prominent editorial: 'The DuBois outfit was set up to promote a tricky appeal of Soviet origin, poisonous in its surface innocence which made it appear that a signature against the use of atomic weapons would forthwith insure world peace. It was, in short, an attempt to disarm America and yet ignore every form of Communist aggression.'[56] The charges were dismissed but the government's determination to silence Dr DuBois was clear for all to see.

When Dr King came out in opposition to the war in Vietnam he was subjected to the same vitriol. Henry Darby and Margaret Rowley[57] studied these responses and have written:

> Well-known civil rights leaders and other prominent blacks such as James Farmer, director of the Congress of Racial Equality; Roy Wilkins of the National Association for the Advancement of Coloured People; Ralph Bunche, former United Nations under-secretary; Edward Brooke, senator from Massachusetts; Carl T. Rowan, newspaper columnist; Jackie Robinson, then special assistant on Community Affairs to Governor Rockefeller of New York; and some members of SCLC were fearful that King's opposition would result in a loss of support for the civil rights movement.

Charles Cheng[58] argues that, 'the NAACP's Roy Wilkins adopted the stance that the Vietnam War was not "a proper sphere for public analysis or criticism" at least not by a civil rights organisation.'

One of the most fundamental conflicts between the moderate and the radical black organisations was over anti-Communism. As the former had accepted the Cold War so had they accepted anti-Communism both were the price of admission into liberal America. The SNCC from the beginning had refused to accept the hegemony of Cold War liberalism, had refused to use the standard anti-Communist disclaimer as a condition for membership and had refused to follow the anti-Communist dictates about which organisations they could work with. This was particularly contentious in the run-up to Mississippi Freedom Summer in 1964. The SNCC had been working with the left-wing lawyers' association, the National Lawyers Guild (NLG). NLG lawyers had been providing desperately needed legal assistance and representation for the SNCC field workers in the face of massive Southern legal repression. There were few other lawyers available or willing to provide this assistance. The NAACP and other mainstream civil rights groups tried to put pressure on the co-ordinating committee to break with the Guild and when they failed the Justice Department joined the fray.

James Forman of the SNCC describes how he and two colleagues from the SNCC were called to a meeting with Burke Marshall of the Justice Department 'ostensibly to discuss the situation in the Third Congressional District [in delta Mississippi] .... But when it finally took place, the Lawyers Guild seemed to be the main subject on the minds of our hosts.' Describing the contribution of Cold War liberal historian and Presidential aide and hagiographer, Arthur Schlesinger Jr, Forman[59] goes on:

> Suddenly he spoke and when he did, we knew he spoke with the consent of the government officials present and the elder Bingham [Member of the House of Representatives]. 'There are many of us who have spent years fighting the communists,' he said as if he had made this speech many times. 'We worked hard during the thirties and the forties fighting forces such as the National Lawyers Guild. We find it unpardonable that you would work with them,' he concluded .... What blindness and arrogance, I thought. He knew nothing about the reality of our struggle in the South.

Forman[60] describes the fundamental re-evaluations that were taking place within the SNCC which were to lead to increasingly open challenges to the dominant ideology.

> By the end of the summer, it was firmly established in the minds of the sisters and brothers that SNCC was like an underdeveloped nation, struggling for its own self-determination. We would take help from anyone, always insisting that no one who gave us help had the right to dictate our policies. We knew only too well that there were people who wanted us to 'fight Communism', to engage in their factional struggles. Whitney Young [of the NAACP] was not the first nor would Arthur Schlesinger be the last. These forces would continue to attack us, claiming that by allowing the guild to participate in the Summer Protest, SNCC was destroying years of hard work years of Red baiting, they should have said, and years of character assassination .... Therefore what SNCC had done was crucial. In effect, SNCC was breaking through the circle of fear that had been imposed on people by McCarthyism and which still lingered on. It deserves infinite praise, I believe, for its attitude on freedom of association, because SNCC fought not only for its own

friends, but for the civil liberties of all.

This process of challenging the anti-Communist hegemony continued with the SNCC challenging Dr King's decision to fire Jack O'Dell from the SCLC because of pressure from the FBI and Kennedy administration over O'Dell's communist associations. Stokely Carmichael demanded that King and other established civil rights leaders 'stop taking a defensive stand on communism'.[61]

The challenge the SNCC presented to the status quo was reflected in the pressures Forman described above and in the conflicts between it and the other components of the CRM.[62] These were apparent over which priorities the movement should establish, over the seating of the Mississippi Freedom Democratic Party at the Democratic National Convention in Atlantic City in 1964 and in terms of the relationship between black organisations and liberal and labour organisations and in terms of whether civil rights organisations should be all-black, which then would form alliances with anti-racist whites. These divisions were heightened by the nature of the 1963 March of Washington (see discussion below), by the urban uprisings which raged through the US from the Summer of 1964 through 1968, and by differences over foreign policy (as discussed above). In these disputes over the direction and priorities of black struggle, access to and control of resources was an important variable affecting the outcomes of the conflicts. Herbert Haines made a detailed study of the funding of the CRM from 1957 to 1970 and found that the total amounts contributed to the seven groups he studied increased during the late 1950s and 1960s, and peaked in the late 1960s. He found that these increases primarily reflected increased funding for the moderate groups and an injection of new money. His conclusions are worth quoting at length.[63]

These findings suggest that positive radical flank effects contributed significantly to increases in the outside funding of moderate civil rights organisations in the 1960s. The increasing importance of corporations, foundations, and the federal government, moreover, suggests that a portion of the nation's corporate elite recognised that it had a crucial interest in pacifying the black population, particularly in the volatile cities, and in accommodating certain manageable black demands. It also suggests that many previously uninvolved groups were 'enlightened' by the glow of burning cities, after years of indifference to non-violent cajoling by the National Urban League and the NAACP. Some whites came to realise that the integration of blacks into the US mainstream was not such a bad idea after all, that it was in their own best interests given the more radical alternatives, and that it was something they ought to be encouraging with their resources. The prime beneficiaries of such changes of heart were the big moderate groups.

The conflict over the nature of the 1963 March on Washington was indicative of these growing splits. Malcolm X called it the 'Farce on Washington'. His description was rejected by liberals in all sections of US society as extremist though, as we shall see, it has been validated since then by the writings of those involved. Malcolm X speaking in Detroit two months after the March said[64]

The Negroes were out there in the streets. They were talking about how they were going to march on Washington .... That they were going to march on Washington, march on the Senate, march on the White House, march on the Congress, and tie it up, bring it to a halt, not let the government proceed. They even said they were going out to the airport and lay down on the runway and not let any airplanes land. I'm telling you what they said. That was revolution. That was revolution. That was the black revolution. It was the grass roots out there in the street. It scared the white man to death, scared the white power structure in Washington DC to death; X was there. When they found out that this black steam-roller was going to come down on the capital, they called in ... these national Negro leaders that you respect and told them, 'Call it off,' Kennedy said. 'Look you all are letting this thing go too far.' And Old Tom said, 'Boss, I can't stop it because I didn't start it.' I'm telling you what they said. They said, 'I'm not even in it, much less at the head of it.' They said, 'These Negroes are doing things on their own. They're running ahead of us.' And that old shrewd fox, he said, 'If you all aren't in it, I'll put you in it. I'll put you at head of it. I'll endorse it. I'll welcome it. I'll help it. I'll join it.' This is what they did with the march on Washington. They pined it ... became part of it, took it over. And as they took it over, it lost its militancy. It ceased to be angry, it ceased to be hot, it ceased to be uncompromising. Why, it even ceased to be a march. It became a picnic, a circus. Nothing but a circus, with clowns and all .... No, it was a sell out. It was a takeover .... They controlled it so tight, they told those Negroes what time to hit town, where to stop, what signs to carry, what song to sing, what speech they could make, and what speech they couldn't make, and then told them to get out of town by sundown.

In his glorified history of Kennedy's thousand days, Arthur Schlesinger Jr wrote:[65]

> The conference with the President did persuade the civil rights leaders that they should not lay siege to Capital Hill .... So in 1963 Kennedy moved to incorporate the Negro revolution into the democratic coalition.

Manning Marable's analysis[66] of the politics of the 1963 march also supports Malcolm X's contemporary analysis:

> Months before Kennedy announced his decision to obtain a new civil rights act, however, [A. Philip] Randolph proposed organising a second March on Washington DC, both as a means of dramatising the campaign for desegregation and as a method by which to place 'additional pressure on the Kennedy administration to support equal employment legislation.'... The response within the civil rights front was at best mixed. The CORE's [Congress of Racial Equality'] national steering committee 'eagerly agreed to act as a co-sponsor.' SNCC leaders, particularly chairman John Lewis, and theoretician James Forman, viewed the March as an opportunity to stage demonstrations at the US Justice Department against its abysmal failure to protect civil rights workers' lives. SCLC leaders Clarence Jones and Reverend George Latency projected 'massive, militant, monumental sit-ins on Congress .... We will tie up public transportation by laying our bodies prostrate on runways of airports, across railroad tracks, and in bus depots.' Such rhetoric threw a chill into the NAACP and Urban League bureaucrats. After learning that Kennedy objected to the march, [Roy] Wilkins [of the NAACP] contemptuously dismissed the mobilisation before reporters, stating, 'That little baby does not belong to me.' By late June, however, the call for a second march had acquired a life of its own, and it was too late for Randolph, Wilkins or anyone else to cancel.

Marable describes how the moderate leaders worked in conjunction with the Kennedy administration — as Schlesinger has written and Malcolm X stated — and hijacked the march and insured that it would not be confrontational. Randolph, playing the traditional role of the petit bourgeois leader, told Kennedy that blacks were now on the streets and it was 'very likely impossible to get them off. If they are bound to be in the streets in any case, is it not better that they be led by organisations dedicated to civil rights and disciplined by struggle than to leave them to other leaders who care neither about civil rights nor about non-violence?'[67]

Many radicals stayed away from the March — for example, Stokely Carmichael declared that the 'struggle for voting rights in Mississippi was more important than a showy display in Washington'.[68] John Lewis attended and prepared a speech which was so threatening in terms of the issues raised that the Catholic archbishop of Washington let it be known that he would boycott the March if it were delivered. After massive pressure, Lewis and Forman redrafted the speech which was still of a different order from the other speeches of the day:[69]

> We came here today with a great sense of misgiving ... It is true that we support the administration's Civil Rights Bill in the Congress. We support it with great reservations, however .... In its present form this Bill will not protect the citizens of Danville, Virginia who must live in constant fear of a police state. It will not protect the hundreds and thousands of people who have been arrested upon trumped charges .... It will not help the citizens of Mississippi, of Alabama and Georgia who are qualified to vote but lack a sixth grade education .... We must have legislation that will protect the Mississippi share-cropper who is put off his farm because he dares to register to vote. We need a bill that will provide for the homeless and starving people of this nation .... My friends, let us not forget that we are involved in a serious social revolution .... Where is our party? Where is the political party that will make it unnecessary to march on Washington? Where is the political party that will make it unnecessary to march in the streets of Birmingham?

The Civil Rights Act of 1964 and the Voting Rights Act of 1965 passed after the assassination of President Kennedy marked the apex of the achievements of the CRM. *De jure* segregation had been swept away and blacks could now enjoy the fruits of their class position middle class enjoying and the mass going hungry and could use the ballot box to achieve whatever was possible to achieve. The problems raised by Lewis in his speech, however, remained. The problems faced by blacks in the urban ghettos, for example, had not been created and were not being maintained by *de jure* segregation. The structures of the political economy have created the ghetto, have determined resource allocations which determine housing, education, health, employment and policing. None of these issues were addressed, or could be addressed, by the civil rights legislation. It was not surprising, therefore, that

Northern blacks whose pride had been raised by the CRM's bravery and dignity and whose interests were not being addressed were increasingly angry. The uprising in Harlem in the summer of 1964 began a chain of over 200 uprisings which raged through urban America for the next four years. The consequences of those uprisings were less clear-cut than the legislative victories of the CRM. There were a range of symbolic responses, an increase in welfare rolls, co-optation of activists, and an increase in training, equipping, and intelligence gathering by police forces at every level. What there wasn't was any fundamental change in the social, economic and political conditions which had produced the uprisings.[70]

The achievements of the CRM were real but limited. Spin-off from the movement led to increased and new types of political mobilisation in cities such as Chicago. The burden of Jim Crow was removed from the backs of black people in the South. But the class differences in the black community and the commitment to the capitalist economy of the black leadership, and the incorporation of large sections of the black middle class into various levels of the state bureaucracy, continued and increased the isolation of the mass of black people and their needs from the political agenda.

W.E.B. DuBois continued to raise such issues through the 1950s up to his death on the day of the march on Washington in 1963. In 1958 he received an honourary degree at Prague's Charles University and declared that:[71]

> [During the 1930s] I repudiated the idea that Negroes were in danger of inner-class division based on income and exploitation. Here again, I was wrong. Twenty years later, by 1950, it was clear that the great machine of big business was sweeping not only the mass of white Americans ... it had also and quite naturally swept Negroes in the same maelstrom.

In 1953 he had explored 'the economics of racism, he elaborated on the fight involving those fearless enough to go against the prevailing consensus, simultaneously, there was the potential Shangri-La facing those who wished to go along. He predicted the fall of segregation in public accommodation and schools, which would mean blacks 'will be divided into classes even more sharply than now'.[72] Marable[73] argues that:

> In early 1960, Dr DuBois argued that 'class divisions' within Negro

communities had so divided blacks 'that they are no longer [one] single body. They are different sets of people with different sets of interests.' At the University of Wisconsin, DuBois indicated that the civil rights movement's strategy of non-violent demonstrations and sit-ins 'does not reach the centre of the problem' confronting blacks. Nearly alone among major civil rights leaders, DuBois urged the proponents of desegregation to chart 'the next step' of their collective struggle. The abolition of Jim Crow meant little if Negroes were unemployed. Blacks must 'insist upon the legal rights which are already theirs, and add to that increasingly a Socialistic form of government, an insistence upon the welfare state'. The demand for civil rights must ultimately check the power 'of those corporations which monopolise wealth'. DuBois now recognised that full equality for Negroes was not possible beneath the capitalist system.

Dr Martin Luther King Jr made a similar progression in his politics. By the time of his murder he had moved not only to open opposition to the war in Vietnam but to a race/class politics. He was organising a Poor People's March at the time of his death. Fortunately for the US status quo, Dr King, like Malcolm X in 1965, was murdered and, as Paul Robeson, had been turned into a non-person in the Cold War period. David Garrow[74] has traced Dr King's trajectory in the following terms:

By 1967 King was telling the SCLC staff, 'We must recognise that we can't solve our problems now until there is a radical redistribution of economic and political power', and by early 1968 he had taken the final step to the admission that issues of economic class were more crucial and troublesome and less susceptible to change, than issues of race. 'America,' he remarked to one interviewer, 'is deeply racist and its democracy is flawed both economically and socially.' He added that 'the black revolution is much more than a struggle for the rights of Negroes. It is forcing America to face all its interrelated flaws racism, poverty, militarism, and materialism. It is exposing evils that are rooted deeply in the whole structure of our society. It reveals systemic rather than superficial flaws and suggests that radical reconstruction of society itself is the real issue to be faced.'... by early 1968 he publicly was stating, 'We are engaged in the class struggle'. While his emphasis was not purely materialistic, redistribution of economic power was the central requirement. To one audience King stated, 'We're dealing in a sense with class issues, we're dealing with the problem of the gulf between the haves and the have nots'.

The position of the mass of black Americans at this time illustrates the validity of these perceptions of Drs DuBois and King. The deteriorating position of the large body of white Americans as capitalism is being restructured at the expense of the working class is further proof of the centrality of class in the US. The failure of the white working class to confront successfully the systemic causes of its predicament is largely a consequence of its failure to confront racism. The challenge facing progressive whites is to engage in a serious campaign to confront that failure. The challenge facing progressive blacks is to fight for control of black struggle against the traditional petit bourgeois leaders and to create space for the black masses to emerge into establishing their own agenda.

3 British Anti-discrimination Legislation

The Government and Race Issues

The British government has twice legislated against racial discrimination, in 1965 and in 1968. These Acts have been the most dramatic indications of Britain's new position as a multi-racial state. The path towards the acceptance of the implications of this new situation has not been smooth. There has been a marked reluctance on the part of many political leaders, as well as large portions of the population, to come to terms with the requirements imposed by this situation. These attitudes and expectations, as well as the political situation, have shaped the legislation, as they have shaped the nature of other governmental actions designed to deal with the problems related to the influx of large numbers of Afro-Caribbean and Asian people.

The initial response of most public officials to the large-scale immigration, which began in the mid-1950s, was basically, as Sheila Patterson has described, *laissez-faire.* They assumed that whatever problems emerged from this entry would largely solve themselves and, therefore, that no special government activity was needed. This approach continued until the early 1960s when it was partially eroded. It was replaced by a Conservative Party commitment to immigration control, culminating in the Commonwealth Immigrants Act of 1962. But this element of governmental interference was not accompanied by any comparable commitment to positive government action to deal with the social or racial problems associated with immigration. There has been more emphasis in recent years — mainly from the Labour Party, but also from some Conservatives — on more positive governmental activity, including the passage of anti-discrimination legislation. It is important to note, however, that the basic assumptions underlying the Labour government's commitment have led to the view that the level of activity needed was not very great.

The government has assumed that the problem was a small and easily manageable one, because of the size of the Black and Asian population, the relative recency of their arrival, and the fact that British people are basically law-abiding. There is an element of truth in each of these assumptions, but they are not completely accurate and the real advantages they bring are temporary. The fact that the Afro-Caribbean and Asian population of about one million is roughly only 2 per cent of the total population, is less significant than the fact that they are concentrated in certain areas. These areas are characterised by high job opportunities, but are also, unfortunately, noted for overcrowded housing and inadequate social services. Patterns of discrimination have formed despite the recency of the problem, as outlined in Chapters 4 to 7, and the extent to which British people are naturally law-abiding, can be overplayed. It is important to note that to a significant extent people obey the law because their value of so doing is not outweighed by a countervailing value. When it is, they will obey the law to the extent that the consequences of not doing so are both unattractive and likely. It is, therefore, important not only that legislation be passed to act as a guide-line for the population, but that such legislation be enforceable and enforced, if it is to be effective.

In a strange way, the relative newness of the problem made possible the passage of anti-discrimination legislation while militating against the passage of effective legislation. The newness meant that the opposition to any legislation at all was less intense than has been found, for example, in a country like the United States with its long history of racial conflict and its centuries of white vested interest in black suppression. This was reinforced by the nature of the British political system which limits the opportunities available to those who want to block completely government legislation.

Both factors, however, worked the other way as well when it came to ensuring effective legislation. The newness of the problem and its seemingly small size made it possible for political leaders to cling to their assumptions about the ease with which it could be dealt.

They saw the role of the government as largely declamatory. James Callaghan, who had responsibility for shepherding the 1968 Race Relations Bill through Parliament, expressed this point of view in his first interview as Home Secretary on 28 January 1968. The following statement is interesting not only because it was the basis on which he acted with regard to the 1968 Bill, but also because it had been made after the failure of previous government declarations to stem the tide of discrimination, and after both the PEP and Street reports, and was, therefore, seemingly immune to the large body of evidence about the nature of the problem and the required solutions. Mr Callaghan said in that interview:

> The race problem is as much a question of education as of legislation. I think the law can give comfort and protection to a lot of people who do not wish to discriminate but who might otherwise be forced by the intolerant opinions of their neighbours to discriminate. *Any legislation introduced, I think, will have less emphasis on the enforcement side than on the declaratory nature of the Act itself, which must show where we stand as a nation this issue of principle.*[1]

These assumptions, as we shall see, were largely responsible for the weaknesses in the 1968 Bill, as they were for those in the Race Relations Act 1965. Another factor which influenced the outcome of these legislative battles, and which affected the nature and extent of other governmental activity, was the political situation facing the Labour government. Although Labour won the 1964 general election its candidates lost a number of previously solid Labour seats. The most shocking of their outcomes was the defeat of Patrick Gordon-Walker, the shadow Foreign Secretary, in the West Midlands constituency of Smethwick. The general election was the culmination of an anti-immigration (that is, anti-Afro-Caribbean and Asian immigration) campaign which included the vicious slogan 'If you want "a nigger" for a neighbour, vote Liberal or Labour'. On 20 April 1968 Enoch Powell delivered his famous 'rivers of blood' race speech in Birmingham in which he warned of bloodshed and the destruction of the English way of life because of the influx of aliens. This speech was greeted with outrage by many and with enthusiasm by many, including a larger group of London dockers who marched on the House of Commons on 23 April, during the Second Reading of the Race Relations bill.

In 1968 there were few, if any, votes to be won by Labour

taking a clearly liberal line on this issue. In 1964, the government, with a majority of only three, had to be especially conscious of this fact and in 1968, despite their large majority, they felt it necessary to avoid Conservative opposition at Third Reading. These factors strengthened their reluctance to get far in advance of public opinion, which was based on their basic assumptions about the nature of the problem. It resulted in limiting positive government action and governmental leadership, and in weakening the enforcement side of the 1968 Bill.

This combination of forces has militated against a broad programme of positive governmental measures against prejudice and discrimination. To be effective, anti-discrimination legislation cannot operate in a vacuum. It must be accompanied by positive governmental programmes designed to eliminate the social problems which cause and exacerbate racial prejudice, which, in turn, justifies discrimination. This prejudice must also be countered by vigorous leadership from the political leaders of the land. Without these activities, the Black and Asian population will continue to be a ready scapegoat for whatever social and economic pressures, inadequacies, and frustrations are felt by the host population. If this happens, or is allowed to continue, then the assumed willingness to obey anti-discrimination laws upon which the government has been counting, will not be present; and the law will not be able to control and eliminate discrimination effectively. Despite this, and despite the availability of information about the nature of the social problems and prejudices of the white population, little in the way of positive programmes has been forthcoming until very recently. There has been a marked reluctance to provide special assistance to areas with special problems — assistance which would have benefited not only the Afro-Caribbean and Asian inhabitants but also the white residents who have suffered for decades because of the low priority successive governments have given to social programmes. It would have been politically risky to be seen giving special help to these people when 'our people' were in need. If political leaders were to risk this and educate the population about the truth of the situation, that is, that the Afro-Caribbean and Asian immigrants did not cause the social problems of overcrowded and inadequate housing, schools, and hospitals, they would have had to admit their responsibility for these shortcomings.

The Local government Act of 1966 made a tentative start in the direction of helping local authorities with special problems by authorising, in Section II, the Home Secretary to pay a proportion of the extra expenditure incurred by those local authorities who are required to make special provisions because of substantial numbers of Commonwealth immigrants but only in respect of the employment of staff. During his Second Reading speech on the 1968 Race Relations Bill, the Home Secretary said that £3 million had been spent in the 57 local authorities which had especially large concentrations of immigrants. This was hardly a magnificent sum and was hardly likely to make a significant impact on the problem. On 22 July 1968, the Home Secretary announced that subject to legislation in the forthcoming session of Parliament, the government would provide a further £20 to £25 million over the next four years. He indicated that priority would be given to nursery education and child care. While this is to be welcomed as an important step in the right direction, one may query whether the sum will be sufficient to make a major impact and whether housing might not have been a more important place to start. The government has hitherto been reluctant to use its powers to force local housing authorities to stop discriminating in the allocation of council housing. The consequence of this failure has been the development, and hardening, of inner-city incipient ghettos. This is a problem which should receive the highest priority, if the worst consequences of the American racial conflict are to be avoided.

There similarly needs to be a high degree of public education led by the political leaders of the country to counter prejudice and discrimination. The government has been content by and large to leave this to the National Committee for Commonwealth Immigrants a body which, incidentally, has received more money for its activities than has the Race Relations Board to enforce the anti-discrimination legislation. One would have expected, if the problem had the priority it deserved, that the political leaders of the country would have acted more expeditiously and courageously than they did to oppose Enoch Powell's race speech on 20 April 1968. Much of the public reaction to it was so frighteningly favourable that Britain can no longer go back to believing that racialism is not a major factor in British life. Despite this, government leaders were remarkably slow in mounting a counterattack, and their leadership was very restrained, often accepting the legitimacy of some of Powell's points, for example, the relevance of voluntary repatriation. It took the Prime Minister two weeks to speak out and he did not follow it up with any further speeches. In a major television appearance, the Home Secretary talked in terms of 'our people' and 'them', and argued that it was unfair to accuse the government of not having a programme of voluntary repatriation by pointing to such a programme administered by the Ministry of Social Security. He did not, interestingly enough, challenge the relevance of such a programme for most immigrants and did not point out the dangers inherent in making repatriation a legitimate alternative to solving the problems of prejudice and discrimination in Britain.

In this situation, it is perhaps understandable that the political leaders did not give this problem the priority that is deserved, essential if their overall programme in this area were to be fully effective. For reasons of both attitudes and politics, they were reluctant to admit that the problem needed a major commitment of government time, energy, and money that it needed solutions that would seem to be almost revolutionary, entirely new and far in advance of anything that had been done before. They were reluctant to admit the relevance of much of the North American experience in this area. Here lies one of the most important aspects of the British experience in the fight against discrimination. If the political leaders are unwilling to be responsive information other countries' experiences, merely the availability of this information will not be sufficient to ensure that the same mistakes will not be made again.

The British government has dealt with this problem, as indeed, to be fair, they deal with most problems, in a piecemeal fashion. Each additional piece of government action is an important increment in the fight against discrimination. But each increment is not as effective as anticipated, for at each stage the problem becomes more difficult to deal with. Therefore, action which might have had a dramatic impact if taken in 1965 will tend to have a more marginal impact when taken in 1968 because patterns of behaviour have hardened in the intervening period.

The following discussion of the passage of the Race Relations Acts of 1965 and 1968 will highlight many of these points.

The Race Relations Act 1965

A History of the Act

The origins of the Race Relations Act 1965 can be found, in part, both in an ideological commitment to the principal of brotherhood and in political considerations. There always has been a strong ideological section of the Labour Party who felt that discrimination was morally wrong and that it should be outlawed by the government. There were a number of attempts to implement this view in the 1950s, starting with a Bill introduced by Reginald (now Lord) Sorenson in 1950 to make discrimination in public places a criminal offence. This attempt failed to obtain the support of the Labour government of the day, but was continued throughout the rest of the decade by Sorenson's long-time colleague Fenner (now Lord) Brockway, who introduced the first of his nine Private Member's Bills on the subject in 1956. The Brockway Bills kept the criminal aspect and provided that anyone found guilty of discriminating on the grounds of 'colour, race or religion' would be liable to a maximum fine of £25 and withdrawal of his licenses and registration, if any. The legislation was to apply to keepers of inns, lodging-houses, restaurants, public houses, and dance halls, as well as to employers of more than fifty people as regards hiring and firing. This exemption of employers of fewer than fifty employees was withdrawn from the 1958 Bill, and the whole field of employment was dropped in 1960, at the behest of trade-union-sponsored MPs. This was one of the first indications of trade-union attitudes towards legislation in this field, and the emphasis of the 1968 Bill on voluntary machinery was in part the price that had to be paid for Trades Union Congress (TUC) support or at least neutrality.

The Brockway Bills never achieved a Second Reading despite the fact that each successive Bill was supported by a wider spectrum of opinion, not only within the Labour Party, but from the other parties as well. The National Executive Committee of the Labour Party pledged in 1958 to 'introduce legislation to stop discrimination in public places', and Harold Wilson promised both in the Commons debate on the Expiring Laws Continuance Bill (on 27 November 1963) and at a Trafalgar Square meeting (on 17 March 1963), that if Parliament persisted in rejecting Fenner

Brockway's private member's Bill, 'when we have a Labour majority we will enact it as a government measure'.

This commitment to enact anti-discrimination legislation became even more important in terms of maintaining party unity when Labour came to power in 1964. Having experienced the Smethwick, Eton and Slough, and Leyton defeats on the race issue, the government decided to diffuse the race issue by strengthening the 1962 Commonwealth Immigrants Act despite their intense opposition to that measure when it was debated in Parliament in 1962. This strengthening, formalised in the White Paper of 1965 in *Immigration from the Commonwealth*, eliminated the 'C' vouchers, limited the number of Commonwealth immigrants to be admitted each year to 8,500 (with 1,000 reserved for Malta), limited the classes of dependants to be allowed free entry, and tightened controls on Commonwealth immigrants. It was bound to create a storm of opposition within the Labour Party. Given its tiny majority of three in the House of Commons, the government had to ensure party unity and this made the introduction of anti-discrimination bill even more important.

This commitment did not, however, involve the details of legislation, which were built around the Brockway formula of making discrimination a criminal offence. There was little consideration of the problem of discrimination outside public places or of the actual details of enforcement. The Labour Party appointed two committees to look into the question of detail in early 1964. One, chaired by Sir Frank Soskice, was made up of three members of the Shadow Cabinet (Soskice, Douglas Houghton, and Gilbert Mitchison). The other, set up by the Society of Labour Lawyers, was chaired by Andrew Martin. The Soskice Committee was much more restrictive in its approach, as was the government; and while basically accepting the Brockway approach, limited it by excluding discriminatory leases, the right of the complainant to bring civil suit, and Brockway's proposal that the discriminator should also be liable to the loss of license or registration, if any. They emphasised the difficulties of enforcement as justification for these omissions an argument which runs throughout the history of legislation in this area, The Martin Committee, which accepted the applicability of criminal penalties for discrimination in public places, went further than the Soskice Committee in wanting to include all places of public resort run by local authorities and by indicating that discrimination in other areas was more important and that, with reference to them, other methods might be more applicable — such as the American administrative machinery, based on conciliation.

Another group of outsiders who saw the importance of widening the scope of anti-discrimination legislation and of creating an administrative agency based on the conciliation process, was one led by Anthony Lester, a barrister familiar with the American experience. His group argued that the areas of employment, housing, credit and insurance, and government departments were of more importance than the restricted list of places of public resort which the government were considering and that a statutory commission, which had full powers of investigations and subpoena and authority to enforce its decisions through the courts, should be created. This commission could attempt to settle the complaint by conciliation in the first instance, but if that failed they would then use their statutory powers. The Lester group won over the Campaign Against Racial Discrimination (CARD), and other interested groups, and lobbied extensively on behalf of their proposals. They won over most of the interested Labour MPs who, unfortunately for the success of their attempt to get effective legislation, were all back-benchers and, therefore, not in a position to make the crucial decisions about the shape of the legislation.

Before moving on to a discussion of the legislation introduced by the government, it might be of interest to note that the Lester group talked of conciliation as merely one method of obtaining compliance. If it failed, the commission would use other methods. Unfortunately, in the debate both within Parliament and outside that followed Soskice's criminally based Bill, conciliation came to be seen as an end in itself, as the counterpoise to criminal sanctions, and almost, indeed, as the alternative to sanctions themselves. This misconception of the meaning of conciliation unfortunately continued and, as we shall see, was partly responsible for the weaknesses in the enforcement machinery of the 1968 Bill.

Unfortunately, the Lester group and their allies were not able to convince the government, and on 7 April 1965 Soskice introduced the Race Relations Bill 1965 which was restrictive in its scope, based on criminal penalties, and required the authorisation of the

Director of Public Prosecutions for legal action. In two other sections, it made illegal the incitement to race hatred in speech or writing and extended the scope of the Public Order Act. These later provisions are extraneous to the real purpose of the Bill, but were urged very strongly by such groups as the Jewish community who feared the revival of fascism and were part of the background to the Bill. This fear was related to the formation of Colin Jordan's National Socialist Movement and its slogan, 'Free Britain from Jewish Control'. The Jewish Defence Committees of the Board of Deputies of British Jews began its 1962 report with this revealing sentence: '1962 was without doubt one of the busiest years for the Jewish Defence Committee since its formation, and the events of the latter months of the years were in many respects, reminiscent of the situation provoked by the fascist activities of the late 1930s'. The Board, in co-operation with the Association of Jewish Ex-Servicemen and Women, the National Council for Civil Liberties, and the newly formed Yellow Star Movement, collected over 430,000 signatures on a national petition calling for legislation against racial incitement. In addition, a deputation led by the Chief Rabbi and the President of the Board met the Home Secretary, Henry Brooke, to ask for such legislation. While these efforts were unsuccessful in obtaining such legislation from the Conservative government, they did strengthen the Labour Party's resolve to link legislation against racial incitement with legislation against racial discrimination.

The Bill was attacked both by those who wanted no legislation and by those who wanted effective legislation. As happened again in 1968, this tended to lead the government to assume that since its policies were being attacked from both 'extremes', they must be correct. The Bill's criminal penalties drew most of the fire of those opposed to legislation and enabled them to appear to be in favour of more moderate legislation based on conciliation. *The Times* attacked the Bill's criminal provisions in the following terms:

> The trouble with the law making a criminal offence out of discrimination in place of public resort is that there is a risk of hardening attitudes and exacerbating prejudice in the few places where race relations are explosive, in return for some acceleration of full integration where things are proceeding in that direction anyway. Surely it would be better to try the effect of local machinery for conciliation and adjustment before dragging in the law.[2]

But those who were against legislation in this field were not the only ones to criticise the criminal penalties. It was argued that the North American experience clearly showed that few, if any, prosecutions would be brought and that it would be very difficult to prove beyond a reasonable doubt before a jury that discrimination had taken place. Also, as leading lawyer Louis Blom-Cooper argued: 'The criminal law is aimed at punishing the wrongdoer, it does nothing to correct the harm done to the victim'.[3] (This, incidentally, is a criticism which has been validly levelled against the 1968 Bill, i.e. that the Bill does not correct the harm done to the victim.)

Those opposed to legislation also centred their fire on the idea of a specially protected class, an attack which has continued throughout the years in which this problem has been discussed. This theme appeared in most of the leaders which opposed the Bill.[4] It also provided a large part of the Conservative opposition's arguments against the Bill in the Second Reading debate. Henry Brooke stated:

> I said in the House two years ago that I had no desire to be the Home Secretary who first introduced into our law the concept that some of my fellow citizens are to be singled out for special protection or distinction from others because of the race to which they belong. My successor appears to have committed this act of unwisdom.[5]

C.M. Woodhouse went even further, seeing such legislation as the beginning of the descent down the slippery slope of *apartheid*:

> However benevolent the original intention, once a dominant race starts deciding that it knows best what is needed for the well-being of other races living in the same geographical boundaries, it is only a matter of time before a still more paternalistic attitude creeps in, and then a big-brotherly attitude, and, finally, *apartheid*. The lesson of this is, to my mind, simple, namely, that racial discrimination is just as bad when it is discrimination against minority and other races.[6]

Those who wanted effective legislation criticised not only the Bill's reliance on criminal penalties but also its narrow scope. They argued that the principles underlying this legislation were equally and more importantly applicable to those central areas of life excluded from the purview of the proposed law. David Ennals spoke for the critics when he argued this case:

I believe that the Bill is too limited. The net is not thrown wide enough. Clause 1 tackles the problem of theatres, cinemas, dance halls, and other places of public resort, but it does not deal with the problem of employment which is the most serious one. It does not deal with the problem of local authority and private housing. It does not deal with insurance ... with the granting of credit facilities. Admittedly, humiliation from exclusion in respect of restaurants and other public places is wounding and provocative, but in the long run, if we want to achieve equality, the right to fair employment practices is the most important right of all. It is a matter in which conciliation is more suitable than prosecution. Successful conciliation needs the force of law behind it. This is why I believe that we need the Bill, and a statutory commission.[7]

Aware of their lonely position supporting criminal penalties the government changed their mind in the month that elapsed between the publication of the Bill and its Second Reading. Indeed, Soskice began his speech with the significant phrase: 'We shall take note of what is proposed in that regard [about conciliation procedures] in argument in this debate'.[8] This was a sure indication of the government's intention to withdraw, especially when taken with the following statement:

> We will listen most closely to the arguments advanced in favour of the introduction of a conciliation process. If we feel that it is practicable and in the public interest, we will, either before or during the Committee stage, amend the Bill to give such effect as we feel able to the general wish of the House.[9]

The narrowness of the government's legislative majority played a part in this decision.

The government's intentions vis-à-vis the Bill were very narrow, as can be seen in this quote from Soskice's speech: 'Basically, the Bill is concerned with public order'. This was true despite the wider problems of employment, housing, and education:

> The Bill had, designedly, the more limited objectives which I have described. It is intended to implement the specific statement in the Labour manifesto of our intention to legislate with regard to discrimination in public places and to incitement.[10]

The Conservatives, led by Peter Thorneycroft, exploited the government's confusion to the hilt. They were able to play a number of different lines at the same time. They could criticise the criminal penalties, emphasise conciliation, and challenge the government for the narrowness of the Bill's scope, while at the same time questioning whether there really was as much discrimination as the government assumed and, thereby, question the necessity of such legislation. In 1965, they were not averse to using the North American experience in support of their arguments in favour of the conciliation process, something they shied away from later at the Committee stage and in 1968. Thorneycroft argued that:

> We have rather a good test case there, because some of the States have applied the criminal solution and others have adopted the conciliation method. Where they have adopted conciliation, it has, on the whole, worked not too badly; where they have tried the criminal approach, it has not worked at all, or practically not at all.

Taking a position from which the Conservatives backed away in practice, he then went on to state:

> He [Soskice] must choose between the two; either conciliation — supplied, if he thinks it necessary, with teeth through the civil proceedings, as has been attempted in a number of States in the United States of America — or the criminal law.[11]

The government won the day at Second Reading, with Liberal support, and Soskice introduced, as an amendment, a rewritten enforcement section, substituting conciliation machinery for criminal penalties. This machinery was based on a Race Relations Board in London which would create local conciliation committees around the country; these committees would receive and investigate complaints of discrimination on the grounds of race, colour, or ethnic or national origins, and if the complaints were found to be justified, the committees would attempt to conciliate. If they failed, the cases were to be sent to the Board who could merely decide whether conciliation had, in fact, failed and whether a course of conduct was likely to continue. If they decided both in the affirmative, they would then send the cases to the Attorney-General. Only the Attorney-General would be allowed to authorise court action. The local committees were not given any powers of subpoena and the Board was to be merely a post box once it had created the local committees.

And so the Bill remained limited in scope. The critics who wanted a stronger Bill were thus faced with the worst of both worlds: a Bill based on criminal penalties necessitated tight and narrow definition of its scope; and a Bill based on conciliation machinery did nothing to widen its scope.

This confusion was the basis of the first of the four main attempts to strengthen the Bill made by the seven Labour back-bench critics Donald Chapman, Ivor Richard, Paul Rose, David Ennals, Reginald Freeson, Shirley Williams, and Dr Maurice Miller supported by Norman St John Stevas and John Hunt from the Conservative side. This was an attempt to make the definition of places of public resort inclusive and, thus, to widen the scope of the Bill. However, the seven Labour back-benchers, including Chapman, who had moved the amendment, abstained on the vote. Presumably, they did so out of a desire not to embarrass the government and in the hope of finding the Home Secretary amenable to some of their proposed amendments. They were to be disappointed in this hope and were themselves embarrassed by the spectacle of only the two Conservatives, St John Stevas and Hunt, voting for an amendment proposed by a Labour critic. After this debacle and after they realised that Soskice was not going to accept their amendments, the Labour critics joined St John Stevas and Hunt in voting against the government. The government was able to beat off such attacks because of the consistent support provided by the rest of the Conservatives, who were similarly opposed to strengthening the Bill in any way. This alliance defeated attempts to include shops as places of public resort; to allow the Board to use the local conciliation committees for work on problems not actually outlined in the Bill; and to allow the complainant to bring civil actions in those cases in which the Attorney-General refused to act.

The Committee stage was marked by the government's unwillingness to go beyond the Bill in any meaningful way. It was also marked by the unwillingness of the Conservative front benches to see to it that the conciliation machinery was backed up by the terms Thorneycroft had suggested at Second Reading. The level of argument used by the government to justify their unwillingness to move beyond the Bill can only be explained by their basic assumption that the Bill was intended more to provide a lead than to be enforced and that one could not go too far, as this was new legislation. This alone could account for the argument used by Soskice against Chapman's amendment to include shops within the terms of the Act. Soskice argued that shops were different from places of public resort because the latter are places where; 'broadly speaking, a person goes to stay for a time and enjoy all the amenities which are provided in that place' and at, that therefore, discrimination in those places is more 'injurious and wounding to the feelings' than discrimination in shops. Secondly, he argued that the amendment would greatly enlarge the scope of the Bill. In opposing the amendment, he incorrectly assumed that it would include employment in shops and very revealingly used the sort of argument that many Conservatives were later to use against the 1968 Bill:

> There is also an enormous variety of offices. Many of them have almost the private quality which a club has. It is not quite the same but nevertheless an office is a place where people work closely together in the performance of a common task and in the carrying out of an enterprise whether of a business or other nature.[12]

He then went on to raise the spectre of the adverse consequences following from a Bill that could not be enforced, using as his example the proposed wording of the amendment which included the phrase 'Neglects to afford him access ... or facilities', and suggesting that a person who had been kept waiting in a crowded store could conceivably make a complaint. This, incidentally, was a technique used by the government in 1968 in defending their refusal to budge from their previously announced position.

The Labour critics were so disillusioned and angry as a result of the government's intransigence at Committee stage that the government made a concession in the form of a sentence in Soskice's concluding speech at the Third Reading to ensure their support. Soskice promised that 'the government will most certainly consider carefully what emerges in the coming months and years and will take such steps as may be dictated to suit the needs of the developing situation'.[13]

The shape of the Race Relations Act 1965 with its limited and very inadequate scope and its weak enforcement procedures, was a consequence of the government's minimalist expectations about the role of such legislation and of their very limited knowledge about the requirements of effective anti-discrimination legislation.

There was a marked reluctance on the part of the government to take any cognisance of the relevant North American experience. Such use as was made of this experience by most Conservatives, and certainly by the Conservative leadership, was only of a temporary tactical nature. Only those critics — both within and, mainly, outside Parliament — who wanted effective legislation understood and made use of this experience. But information by itself is not the most important variable in political decision-making. Without the will to act effectively, governments will not be receptive to the information, or they will use only that part of it which supports their limited measures.

The Race Relations Act 1965

Contents of the Act

The Act, passed on 8 November 1965, makes it unlawful for the proprietor or manager of a specified 'place of public resort' to practise discrimination on the grounds of colours race, or ethnic or national origins against persons seeking access to facilities or services at that place. The Act does not cover discrimination on religious grounds. It gives an exclusive and, therefore, restrictive definition of places of public resort. The Act covers public hotels, restaurants, cafés, public houses, theatres, cinemas, dance halls, and scheduled transportation services; but it does *not* cover private hotels, shops, offices, night-clubs, holiday camps, chartered transportation facilities, and, most importantly, the Crown. This leads to many anomalies: such as, discrimination by a hairdresser may be unlawful if his premises are inside a hotel, but not if they are outside it; discrimination in an off-licence is not against the law, but discrimination in a pub is unlawful. The Act establishes the Race Relations Board to obtain compliance with the law. The Board is required to create local conciliation committees which must receive and consider complaints of discrimination, make any necessary inquiries about the facts alleged in such complaints, and use their best endeavours to settle any differences between the parties and to obtain satisfactory assurances against further unlawful discrimination. One weakness in the law is that neither the Board nor the local conciliation committees are granted powers of subpoena and, thus, respondents can refuse to talk to members or staff of the Board's machinery. If a local committee is unable to secure such a settlement and assurance or if it appears to the committee that any such assurance is not being complied with, the committee must report to the Board to that effect. If the Board agrees that, on the basis of that report, a 'course of conduct' has taken place and is likely to continue, it must refer the matter to the Attorney-General. The Act empowers the Attorney-General, and only the Attorney-General, to bring civil proceedings in the county court to enjoin the defendant from practising unlawful discrimination. No other proceedings, whether civil or criminal, may be brought in respect of unlawful discrimination under the Act.

The Race Relations Act 1968

A History of the Act

The fight for wide and effective anti-discrimination legislation did not end with the passage of the token Act of 1965. In fact, soon after the enactment of that inadequate measure, it began anew with the replacement of Soskice (who was elevated to the House of Lords as Lord Stowhill) as Labour Home Secretary by Roy Jenkins. Seeing himself as a reformist Home Secretary, Jenkins had fewer compunctions about State action in the sphere than had his predecessor, and appointed Mark Bonham-Carter as Chairman of the Race Relations Board. Bonham-Carter, a long-time personal friend and intellectual colleague of Jenkins, was determined to get a better law, seeing the present Act as considerably inadequate; and there was a mutual understanding that this was a desirable goal. The Board, including Sir Learie Constantine and Alderman Bernard Langton, established this goal as its highest priority and devoted much of its time to building up the case for extended legislation.

Following the 1966 General Election, Jenkins began the process of public education necessary to make extension a legitimate exercise of government power and to ensure it a place in the government's legislation time-table. On 23 May 1966, in a speech before the National Co-ordinating Conference of Voluntary Liaison Committees, he defined integration 'not as a flattening process of assimilation but as equal opportunity accompanied by cultural diversity, in an atmosphere of mutual tolerance'. About the 1965 Act and the need for new legislation, he said:

> Some of you, I know, will think we have a better Race Relations
> Board than we have a Race Relations Act. I would say two things on
> this. First, I think a lot can be done under the present Act, and
> secondly, *as I have told the Board*, my mind is far from being closed
> about future changes to the Act .... By far the best way to get a wider
> Act is to work this one effectively and to show that this is a field in
> which legislation can help.

Many, I know, take the view that discrimination in employment and, indeed, in housing, should be covered by legislation. For the moment, I reserve judgement on the legislation point but I am in no doubt that the employment aspect of the matter in particular is rapidly becoming central to the whole future success of our integration policy. The problem is now developing with almost every month which goes by, because we are beginning to move from the era of the first generation immigrant to those [*sic*] of the second generation immigrant.[14]

In a major speech before the Institute of Race Relations on 10 October 1966, he went even further and indicated one of the main strategies of those in favour of extending the legislation to the important areas of employment, housing, and credit and insurance, i.e. making the case that discrimination was widespread. This involved the sponsoring of an objective study to show the extent of discrimination (the PEP report), alongside the Board's building up of a record of complaints outside the scope of the 1965 Act. Jenkins stated:

> It is not surprising that one should find what might be called
> mechanical faults in a wholly new type of legislation. I understand
> that the Board and the local committee are finding some. They find,
> for example, that the very process of conciliation which is central to
> the whole idea — is hindered by the lack of power to compel alleged
> discriminators even to talk to the local committees. It then becomes
> very difficult in certain circumstances to investigate complaints, much
> less to settle them by conciliation. The Board is finding other
> mechanical difficulties too, and I certainly do not exclude the
> possibility of the government amending the Act in due course to take
> account of experience.[15]

Before moving on to the Home Secretary's discussion of the possibility of widening the scope of the Act, it is interesting to note that this very essential power of compelling alleged discriminators to talk to the local committees was central in the Board's own recommendation in its first annual report, published in April 1967. The Board declared that:

> In some cases, persons against whom discrimination has been alleged have refused to meet representatives of the conciliation committee. This hampers their investigation and could, in certain circumstances, render them impossible. It should be considered whether, with appropriate safeguards, there should be power to compel attendance before the committee, or the disclosure of information to it.[16]

Despite the virtual unanimity of those experienced in administering the 1965 Act and those outside the government with knowledge of the North American experience, including the Street Committee, this provision was not included in the 1968 Bill through Parliament; James Callaghan, as we shall see, steadfastly refused to accept any such power for the Board, largely because of his assumptions about the nature of such legislation, which differed dramatically from those of his predecessor, and because of his misconception of the Board's role as 'conciliatory'. As indicated above, there has been a misconception of the meaning of the word conciliation, which sees it as an end in itself rather than as merely one method among many designed to achieve compliance with the law, which, to succeed, has to be supported by the force of law. In Mr Callaghan's eyes, giving the Board powers of subpoena would conflict with its role as a conciliator. One may hypothesise that had Mr Jenkins not changed positions with Mr Callaghan during the crucial phase of drafting the 1968 Bill, its enforcement provisions would have been very different.

In his speech to the Institute of Race Relations, Mr Jenkins went on to declare:

> When it came to amendment, the government will of course also consider matters of substance. We welcome the fact that, jointly with the National Committee for Commonwealth Immigrants, the Board is sponsoring an enquiry into the extent of racial discrimination in the fields of housing, employment, financial facilities and places of public resort not already covered by the Act [the PEP study]. This enquiry will report early next year. Along with this, the Board and the

National Committee are sponsoring a study of legal restraints on discrimination in other countries and their relevance to our own situation [the Street Committee study]. I look forward to reading these reports and needless to say, the government will not ignore them in considering any amendments to the Act.[17]

During this period, outside groups were equally active in their attempts to keep the issue before the public and to build up an overwhelming case in favour of extending the 1965 Act. The Race Relations Committee of the Society of Labour Lawyers published its third report in November 1966, which criticised the 1965 Act and made a case for new legislation, including detailed recommendations about the new Act. The Fabian Society held a conference on Policies for Racial Equality in November 1966, which was attended by Maurice Foley, then the member of the government with special responsibility for Commonwealth immigrants. This conference published papers in July 1967 in the Fabian Research Series (No. 262); edited by Anthony Lester and Nicholas Deakin, these papers made a very strong case for new legislation. During the period, CARD was active in encouraging victims of discrimination to send complaints to the Race Relations Board even, perhaps especially, if the cases were outside the Board's present jurisdiction. To keep up the pressure, Maurice Orbach, MP, introduced, as a Private Member's Bill in December 1966, a Bill to amend the 1965 Act and to extend its scope and strengthen its enforcement machinery. Drafted by CARD lawyers, led by Anthony Lester and Roger Warren Evans, and, with the assistance of Nicholas Deakin, this Bill had no chance of obtaining a Second Reading, but was designed to keep the pressure on the government and to continue making the case for such legislation. Mr Foley gave a lukewarm indication of the possible government attitude towards the findings of the PEP report, but added: 'Clearly, the extent of the comprehensiveness of the survey and the extent to which it can clearly demonstrate fields in which much needs to be done will have a decisive effect on the government in terms of their future attitude.'[18]

This build-up reached its peak in April 1967 when the PEP report on *Racial Discrimination* in England was published.[18] While its findings and conclusions were not a surprise either to the Black and Asian community or to those activists who had been working for better legislation, they did have a dramatic impact on the mass media and on public opinion. There was enormous coverage the report and newspaper leaders gave an overwhelming degree of support for new legislation. *The Times* shifted its position on the role of law as a result of the report, and *The Sunday Times* cogently declared:

> The first and indispensable step towards the provision of equal opportunities for all men is the enshrinement of equality in the statute book .... The message implicit in every line of the report was this: if the law does not guarantee a coloured immigrant's right to a job for which he is qualified and a home for which he can pay, no one else will. The gradualist myth was exploded by the facts. Left to the insidious guidance of their own fears and suspicions, too many employers, union leaders, landlords, estate agents and credit merchants do not and will not regard a coloured man as the equal of a white. As promoters of spontaneous integration they are simply not to be trusted.[20]

This report was followed by the publication of the Board's first annual report which reported that 238 of the 327 complaints received by the Board were outside the scope of the Act, with the largest single group of complaints (101) involving employment and with housing accounting for another 37 complaints. The Board recommended that the Act be amended to cover housing, employment, financial facilities, and places of public resort. It also recommended that certain mechanical deficiencies in the Act be improved: for example, a single act of discrimination should be sufficient to justify action, rather than the required 'course of conduct'; the Committee should have some form of subpoena power; the Act should bind the Crown; only communications made during the conciliation process should be exempted from admission in later proceedings; and, finally, the Attorney-General should be removed from the operation of the Act. It is interesting to note that except for the last of these enforcement recommendations, only those regarding scope were adopted by the government. Within a week of the publication of the PEP report, 106 Labour MPs signed a motion calling on the government to extend the Act to cover housing and employment.

The latter was to prove the major stumbling-block. Despite the Conference on Equality in Employment sponsored by the National Committee for Commonwealth Immigrants in February 1967, the Trades Union Congress (TUC) and the Confederation of British Industry (CBI) remained adamantly opposed to legislation in this area. They argued that there was at most only a minor problem and that it could best be dealt with by the traditional industrial machinery. The battle was fought with the government as well, with Ray Gunter and the Ministry of Labour taking a similar line. In order to carry the TUC and CBI along, the legislation was drafted to include voluntary machinery to be established by the unions and the employees, who would have first crack at complaints of discrimination in the employment field. This procedure has been criticised on the grounds that it is too cumbersome and time-consuming and that it is not directly under the Board. There is, as well, the danger of cosy arrangements to the detriment of the complainant. As *The Times* pointed out in an excellent leader:

> What is wrong here is not that the voluntary machinery is given the first opportunity but that a government department is to become involved at all. In principle it would be better to keep the government right out of the whole conciliation procedure ... it would be more reassuring for coloured people to feel that one independent body was in charge, even if it delegated its powers in certain fields to other bodies. It would be better for this new Department of Employment and Productivity which will have quite enough to do as it is, to be spared involvement in an area where discussions are very delicate and where it has little or no specialised experience. Above all, it would be advisable for industry's own arrangements to come under the scrutiny of a body that is dealing full-time with race relations — otherwise there is the very real danger that voluntary machinery could conceal a cosy agreement between management and workers to keep on discriminating.[21]

On 26 July 1967, the Home Secretary announced in the House of Commons that the government was going to extend the coverage of the Race Relations Act to include employment and housing. While many newspapers welcomed this announcement,[22] as did those groups outside Parliament that had been working so long and continuously for this announcement, there were many groups that continued their opposition unabated. The *Yorkshire Post* typified this latter group when it declared its opposition to the Home Secretary's announcement:

> The latest dose of well meaning foolishness from the Home Office would extend the Act to deal with discrimination on grounds of colour, race or ethnic or national origins in employment, housing,

insurance and credit facilities. Discrimination on those grounds alone in any of these fields is wicked and uncivilised but we doubt whether it happens as much as people are being led to imagine it does. The trouble is that immigrants are being encouraged to believe that the factors which discriminate against sections of the native population (such as lack of qualifications for the job, the absence of guarantees for credit facilities or housing, and the high fire risk in overcrowded houses) do not apply to them. They are being encouraged to believe that if they are asked to leave a first-class railway seat when they have only a second-class ticket it is because of their colour. Some immigrants may even take advantage of anti-racialism laws to get through subtle intimidation what they would not get through merit, or would not get, everything else being equal, if they were white.[23]

The details of the legislation had yet to be worked out, and the last part of the *scenario* in building up the case for legislation, and most particularly effective legislation, was yet to come: this was the Street report, published on 2 November 1967.[24] The report not only recommended the extension of legislation to include those important areas of life excluded from the 1965 Act, but also made detailed recommendation about the nature of the enforcement machinery required for effective legislation. Unfortunately, most of the Street Committee's valid proposals based on a perceptive analysis of the successes and failures of the North American agencies and made relevant for the British situation were ignored. The Board's recommendations and those of Equal Rights, the lobby group set up by those persons who in previous years had actively worked for new legislation, were similarly ignored.

The Bill introduced by the Home Secretary on 23 April 1968 was a courageous step forward in terms of its scope. The Bill included all the areas previously mentioned plus the field of education and closed the loop-holes in the 1965 Act. Yet its enforcement provisions seemed far too weak to ensure effective implementation of the legislation and apparently included a number of thoroughly obnoxious and dangerous loop-holes. One loop-hole exempted the merchant navy in instances where shared sleeping accommodation would be required. Another loop-hole would have exempted 'anything which is done in good faith for the benefit of a particular section of the public and which has the effect of promoting the integration of members of that section of the public into the community'. There was no definition of 'good faith', and this exemption could presumably have allowed separate but equal treatment, justifying the maintenance of segregated facilities on the grounds that it was being done in good faith for long-term integration.

The most important and controversial exemption is that for acts which are done 'in good faith' and designed to secure or preserve a 'racial balance' which is 'reasonable in all circumstances'. This allows discrimination against individuals if it is in the interests of 'racial balance'. Besides the obvious weaknesses of this exemption it neither defines 'good faith' nor does it state what constitutes a 'reasonable' racial balance there is an overwhelming objection in principle. This exemption violates the basic principles underlying the legislation, in that it authorises unequal treatment of individuals based on racial characteristics. In addition, there is the danger that once a pattern of discriminatory treatment of Afro-Caribbean and Asian people has become legitimised, it will be that much more difficult to combat later when the second generation of black British youngsters who are to be treated as white British youngsters as long as they were educated 'wholly or mainly' in Great Britain — is applying for jobs. There is also the danger of a disproportionate concentration of black and Asian employees in low-level, dead-end jobs, without adequate opportunities for promotion or training for new skills. This will establish a vested interest on the part of white employees in the maintenance of such a situation and will be infinitely more difficult to deal with at a later date. This provision was presumably put in to satisfy the TUC and CBI, to prevent the development of firms or departments with all-coloured work forces and to protect employers who wish to take action to prevent this happening.

The Bill's weaknesses in the enforcement sections spring from the two basic misconceptions outlined above: namely, the declaratory nature of the Bill, which is assigned greater importance than its enforcement procedure, and the meaning of conciliation. The government elevated conciliation to an end in itself and, consequently, opposed giving to the conciliating body the powers of either enforcement or subpoena. This ignored the Street report, the Board's own recommendations, and the lessons of the North American experience, all of which warned of the dangers of powerless enforcement agencies. Consequently, the Board was not given the power to subpoena witnesses or documents; there would conceivably be those occasions when the Board would have to face the choice of sending inadequately investigated cases to the courts and risking their dismissal, or not sending those cases that had not been fully investigated, which is likely to be most of the cases.

The operation of the legislation also embodied a basic misconception of the role of the complainant. He has been denied the right to go to court if he is dissatisfied with the Board's handling of the complaint; he has also been denied any meaningful appeal procedure within the terms of the Bill. He has been denied any satisfactory remedy because the courts, and, therefore, the Board, are not empowered to make positive orders requiring the provision of the job or accommodation in question or the next available ones. The only remedy provided is the payment of damages — of provable loss and of loss of opportunity, the latter being an entirely new concept which is likely to lead to a great deal of litigation and unlikely to be very relevant to the complainant. As the Home Secretary indicated in his speech at Second Reading: 'I do not expect that the amount of damages involved would normally be very large but there may be cases in which a claimant can demonstrate substantial loss as a result of discrimination, and I think that this should be payable in full if the case can be proved'.[25] The first part of the statement is likely to be the most relevant.

These weaknesses went against the Street Committee's conclusion that the aims of the implementing machinery were 'to secure a satisfactory settlement when there appears to be discrimination and to provide adequate enforcement against discriminators when conciliation has not been achieved'. The machinery certainly did not satisfy their three criteria of 'fairness, speed and effectiveness'.[26] These weaknesses did, however, bring the Bill closer to the Conservative leadership and, most particularly, Quintin Hogg's view of the role of such legislation. Under Hogg, their front-bench Home Affairs spokesman, the Conservatives had moved away from the outright opposition to legislation that had been their position under Peter Thorneycroft. But despite the general support for the principle of legislation, the detailed positions taken by Mr Hogg were to weaken the Bill's enforcement provision and widen the exemptions, including the total exemption of financial facilities which would have the effect of largely negating the inclusion of housing, for most people would be unable to purchase a house without a mortgage or a loan. Hogg's position was based on the view that such legislation was intended for the public good, not for the benefit of any particular individual; and he was, therefore, unsympathetic to arguments urging more satisfactory individual remedies.

For internal party reasons, the Conservative leadership decided to table a reasoned amendment at the Second Reading. This decision was opposed by a group of liberal Conservatives led by Sir Edward Boyle who ostentatiously abstained on the division. The Conservative leaders were hard put to justify this decision intellectually, but the fear of a three-way split in the party, especially in the light of Enoch Powell's race speech on 20 April, won the day.

But following on from that vote, at Committee stage and at Third Reading, there was a determination on the part of both the government and the Conservative leadership to avoid Conservative opposition at Third Reading. This determination helped, in part, to define the nature of the Committee stage and shape the outcome of most of the divisions in the Committee. Of importance, too, was the tendency of the Home Secretary to see himself as the representative of common sense and the average 'Britisher', and to assume that because he was being attacked by 'extremists' on both sides, his middle course was of necessity the correct one. And, as the representative of the middle course, the Home Secretary was determined not to go too far ahead of public opinion. There was, in addition, the government's great reluctance to back down from a position to which they had publicly committed themselves a factor that was also found in the government's reaction to amendments to the 1965 Bill offered by Labour back-benchers. Both times there was an impatience with criticism, an almost contemptuous dismissal of detailed points about the enforcement machinery as 'lawyer's points', and, therefore, either irrelevant or damaging.

This was a marked characteristic of the entire legislative history of this Bill. The critics were predominantly lawyers, organised in Equal Rights; and they prepared briefing material and draft amendments for sympathetic Labour back-benchers and their Liberal and Conservative allies. Their campaign was hindered by their isolation both from the Afro-Caribbean and Asian communities, which were either unorganised or involved in militant organisation not particularly concerned with anti-discrimination legislation, and from a largely uninterested white community. This is not to say that they did not have any support in these communities, but such support as they did have, was not immediately or easily transferable to political action and, therefore, was not an important variable in the decision-making process. The critics were labelled as extremists by the government, who had successfully occupied the middle ground, arguing that they had introduced courageous and advanced legislation and yet some groups were still not satisfied and wanted even more. Additionally, there was an almost total lack of both trade-union or business support for the critics' amendments or pressure from sympathetic community and civic groups a very different situation from that found in the various American communities which have adopted such legislation. The legislative battles there were marked by a great deal of trade union activity and leadership on behalf of such legislation and political support provided by religious and civic groups.

The campaign, finally, was weakened by the decision of the Race Relations Board not to engage in public lobbying for a stronger Bill, despite the fact that virtually all its recommendations about the enforcement machinery needed for effective legislation, had been ignored. This decision seemed to follow from a number of factors, including the Board's fear that public lobbying would endanger its public position as a neutral, umpire-like, conciliation body. In addition, the split in the Conservative ranks complicated the issue from the Board's point of view, for it was essential not to be seen to be interfering in internal Conservative Party affairs and the Board felt, as did the government, great concern lest the government go too far out ahead of public opinion. It relied on contact and communication within the government, but was not as successful as it, perhaps, hoped to be. This was very largely due to the fact that the Board and its Chairman did not have the same, unusually close, ties that it had with Jenkins. In addition, the other factors mentioned above were obviously too strongly felt by the Home Secretary and the government to be challenged by the representations of the Board.

These factors led to an alliance of sorts between the two front benches, supported by most of the Conservative back-benchers on Standing Committee B and a handful of largely silent Labour back-benchers. Arrayed against them were most of the Labour back-benchers (ten out of fifteen), two Tories — Sir George Sinclair and Nicholas Scott — who showed extraordinary political courage in consistently voting against the rest of their colleagues, and the Liberal MP for Cheadle, Dr Michael Winstanley. The latter group wanted to strengthen the Bill's enforcement procedures, to close the loop-holes, and to limit the exemptions. The Conservatives, except for Sinclair and Scott, wanted to restrict the scope of the Bill to the larger employers and landlords, to provide greater exemptions in the fields of private housing and employment; and to exclude financial facilities altogether. The government was willing to make concessions on questions of scope, though it would not go as far as the Conservatives wanted. They were joined with their Conservative allies in a determination to resist attempts to strengthen the Bill's enforcement procedures.

This alliance was strong enough to dominate the Committee's voting on the enforcement provisions of the Bill, and the last weeks of the Committee's deliberations were marked by an increasing sense of frustration and despondency on the part of the Bill's critics, as amendment after amendment was voted down. This was despite the fact that, objectively, the critics had the better of the argument because they were following the logic of the reasoning behind such legislation in attempting to ensure that it was effective and inclusive. The government were forced to fall back on very naive and low-level arguments, knowing all the while that they had the votes to win the divisions. One such argument was used by the government against Nicholas Scott's motion that the courts be empowered to make positive orders so as to provide meaningful remedies for those who had been aggrieved. Speaking for the government, David Ennals declared that such remedies would not be desirable because it would be wrong to fire the innocent man who was hired in place of the complainant. This, surely, is not the point, for in a large operation men are being hired continuously and a suitable remedy would be to promise to offer the complainant the next attainable job for which he was qualified. The shocking aspect of this situation is that such a low-level argument could have been used at that late a date and after the government had had so much evidence about the North American experience.

The government's unwillingness to make concessions did not apply to Conservative attempts to limit the scope of the Bill and to increase the range of exemptions. In the early stages of the discussions, the government made a number of such concessions to the Conservatives: e.g. to increase the exemptions for small boardinghouses, lodging-houses, and hotels; to stagger the application of the Bill's housing provisions; to increase the size of firms to be granted exemptions for the first two years from those with 10 employees to those with 25, and in the second two years from 5 to 10; and to accept the so-called 'Colorado clause', which provided for the exemption of owner-occupiers who sell their houses privately and who do not use either an estate agent or public advertising. When the Conservatives wanted to go further, however, to exempt credit and insurance facilities from the Bill altogether, or to re-establish the 1965 Act's strict requirement of a course of conduct rather than the 1968 Bill's more liberal provision authorising action in the event of a single act of discrimination, or to remove damages from the Bill — which would have left the complainant with virtually no redress at all — the government, joined by the critics who wanted a stronger Bill, defeated the Conservatives. The concessions that were made, however, were sufficient to ensure Conservative abstention at Third Reading, especially when linked to the coalition's success in defeating attempts to strengthen the Bill.

After the critics' one major victory, the deletion of Clause 2, Subsection 3 — the 'separate but equal' clause — the government and Conservatives voted together to defeat all other attempts to strengthen the Bill: the government not only refused to remove the exemptions involving shared sleeping accommodations in the merchant navy — which represented defeat for the critics — but widened these exemptions to apply to discrimination on passenger ships and the shared mess and other common-room facilities on merchant ships. The critics' major defeat came over the racial balance clause when they failed, by a vote of 14-10, in their attempt to have it deleted. The critics who feared that in the absence of any criteria as to what constitutes a reasonable racial balance, employers who wanted to say 'no more coloureds' would be given the cover to legitimacy, seemed to have these fears confirmed when Eldon Griffiths, speaking for the CBI, said that it should be up to the employers and shop stewards to decide what constitutes a proper balance in their plants and departments.

When the Committee began its discussion of Part II of the Bill, dealing with the enforcement procedures, the differences in approach between the government and their critics became most apparent. The Home Secretary's position on the declaratory effect of the law and on the Board's role as a conciliator, linked with his need to avoid antagonising the Conservatives lest they vote against the Bill at Third Reading, meant that he and the government were not receptive to arguments pointing out the need for a law with teeth and for an administrative agency with adequate powers to carry out its function. He, therefore, responded negatively to an amendment moved by Nicholas Scott that would have empowered the Board to go to the county court to obtain the right to summon witnesses and order the production of documents. This was an attempt to get around the government's opposition to giving the Board that power directly — in spite of the Street report and the Board's own recommendations. It was widely assumed that the government would accept this compromise formula. But both Hogg and Callaghan felt that even this indirect power would interfere with the Board's performance of its conciliation function, and that, in any case, it was unnecessary; and both feared that such powers might violate the respondent's constitutional rights. This was a hard blow to the critics, which was only slightly softened by the government's concession empowering the Board to take a case to court on the basis of having 'formed an opinion' rather than having to 'determine' that discrimination had taken place.

The amendment designed to give the courts the power to make positive orders, which would provide satisfaction for the complainant and bring about changes in patterns of behaviour, was opposed and defeated by the government — Conservative coalition. As the 1968 legislation stands, therefore, the courts can only make a negative order or a restraining injunction, or order the payment of damages. The courts cannot order the affirmative action which has been found essential in North America.

These defeats helped to ensure Conservative abstention at Third Reading — despite the last minute revolt of a small group of right-wing Tories. From that point of view, one may characterise the government's strategy as a success.

The Bill completed its Parliamentary passage on 24 October and carne into effect on 27 November.

The Contents of the 1968 Act

The Act extends the areas in which discrimination on the grounds of colour, race, or ethnic or national origins is made unlawful, to include employment, housing, credit and insurance facilities, education and all places of public resort including shops and offices. The Crown is specifically included in the Act. The Act exempts discrimination in employment where such discrimination is done in good faith to maintain a racial balance that is reasonable in all the circumstances, but non-whites born in this country are not so exempted. It also exempts employment in private households and on merchant ships where the sharing of sleeping or mess facilities would follow from the ending of discrimination. It exempts for the first two years employers of 25 or fewer employees; in the second two years, employers of 10 or fewer employees will be exempted, after which time the Act will cover all employers except for those exempted by the provisions mentioned above.

In the housing field, there is an exemption for the private sale of property by the owner-occupier without the use of either estate agents or public advertising. In addition, there will be a phased implementation of the housing provisions, with shared accommodation involving fewer than 12 persons in addition to the landlord and his family being exempt for the first two years, and with a permanent exemption for shared accommodation involving six or fewer persons thereafter.

The size of the Race Relations Board is to be expanded to 12 persons and it will be empowered to initiate investigations where it has reason to suspect that discrimination has occurred. This is an improvement over the limited powers of the Board under the 1965 Act, but it is not matched by the granting of subpoena powers to the Board these have still been denied to the Board and its committees. There is a special procedure for the handling of employment cases involving the referral of all complaints to the Department of Employment and Productivity which will decide whether suitable voluntary machinery exists in the industry concerned. If it does, the Department will refer the case to that machinery for an initial period of four weeks, which is extendable. If the voluntary machinery is unable to settle the case satisfactorily, or if the settlement reached is unacceptable to the Department, advised by the Board, the case will go to the Board for investigation, but only if one of the parties informs the Board that he is aggrieved by the settlement. If the Board finds that discrimination has occurred they will attempt to obtain a settlement by means of conciliation. If they fail, they may take the case to one of the specially designated county courts to obtain injunctive relief (the Attorney-General has, thus, been removed from the proceedings completely). The courts can only issue negative orders — i.e. an injunction restraining the defendant from engaging in such conduct in the future but cannot order the hiring of the complainant or the provision of the next available accommodation, or the filing of compliance reports with the Board. It can order the payment of special damages, i.e. out-of-pocket expenses and damages for loss of opportunity.

Conclusion

Britain has legislated against discrimination much more quickly than most people in Britain could have predicted and more quickly than did any American community at a comparable period of the development of its racial problems. Britain's political leaders deserve credit for this. But when one looks at how they legislated and at the nature of the laws passed, it is hard to avoid the conclusion that they have not benefited from the availability of a great deal of information about the experience of various North American government bodies in enacting and enforcing similar laws. This meant that they had available information which, at the least, should have warned them about certain pitfalls. One of the most dramatic of these pitfalls has been the passage of unenforceable legislation, which not only fails to improve the situation but actually worsens it because both the discriminator and the victim come to have little or no confidence in the law and in the agency administering it. Another pitfall is that of overemphasising 'conciliation' as an end in itself rather than seeing it as part of compliance machinery, whose objective is 'compliance' not 'conciliation'. Kenneth MacDonald, Chairman of the Washington State Board Against Discrimination, addressed himself to this subject in a speech to the 1967 Conference of Commissions for Human Rights, a conference, incidentally, which was attended by the Minister with Special Responsibility for Commonwealth Immigrants, the

Chairman of the Race Relations Board, and a number of senior staff officials. MacDonald said:

> Statements by politicians, commissioners and staff members, and by enthusiasts for the legislation extolled the conciliative, educational and persuasive aspects of the law. For a long time the new agencies struggled to change attitudes, not regulate behaviour, and so not much was said then or now by public officers about the need to use 'law enforcement' or the 'coercive power' of the state to exert pressure for improving race relations. Thus words such as 'voluntarism', 'education', 'persuasion', 'conciliation', 'the necessity to change the hearts and minds of men' remained for years part of the jargon and litany under these new laws.

The North American experience also warns against weak enforcement agencies, with minimalist views of their role. As George Schwerner, a noted American practitioner, put it: 'A position of neutral, umpire-like disinterest by a commission has been demonstrated as only slightly more effective than no commission at all. A commission must make itself felt.'

Yet when we look at the legislation passed, so quickly in terms of the development of the problem, we find little or no awareness of these lessons. The 1965 Act seemed almost to be a result of an ignorance of the evidence. While unsatisfactory, it is somewhat understandable given the newness of the problem and of the assumptions with which government officials and political leaders approached it. That the 1968 Bill should have similarly evidenced a failure to take cognisance of the relevant experience of other societies, can only be deplored as wrong-headed. There is no immutable law which requires every country to make the same mistakes as others. Given the ease of communications and, especially in this case, the availability of information, one could have expected a greater awareness of the problems that have to be solved and the methods for their solution. This highlights the difficulties faced by those individuals and groups who are concerned about a problem and who are aware of relevant experience elsewhere. The political leaders must be receptive to the stimuli of this information. If they are not, then they may make the same mistakes as the pioneers who did not have this relevant experience to guide them.

It is, therefore, of great importance to see how Britain's anti-discrimination law will work in practice. The 1965 Act, with its restricted and largely irrelevant jurisdiction, does not provide a meaningful guide as to how this new law, dealing with important areas of life, is likely to be greeted by potential discriminators and their victims, and how effective it will be. In their first two years of operation, the Board, and its local conciliation committees, received a very small number of complaints, as was to be expected given its limited jurisdiction. In its first year of operation, the Board received 327 complaints, of which 89 were within the scope of the Act; and the corresponding figures for the second year were 690 and 108.

The actual case-handling of the small number of complaints falling within the Board's terms of reference again may not prove a very useful guide for the future. First of all, the new Act by-passes the local committee in the all-important area of employment and the voluntary machinery is likely to prove to be a delaying factor. This is something to be closely watched, given the absolute centrality of speed in handling complaints. Secondly, the Board's handling of many of the complaints was not as expeditious as it should have been, nor was the level of expertise and efficiency totally satisfactory. A number of obvious factors account for much of this, e.g. the inexperience of everyone concerned, inadequate staffing arrangements, and office procedure. There were also the Board's own priorities which placed working for new legislation as the top priority, followed by staffing the local committees and then actual case-handling. In terms of long-term improvement of race relations in Britain, this was in all probability the correct evaluation of priorities. We, therefore, cannot predict very accurately how well the Board will handle the increased and more complicated case-load that will follow from the 1968 Act, although the Board has built up a body of good staff, committees, and Board members. This is of absolutely crucial importance, for the attitudes and experience of the agency personnel have accounted for a great deal of the success (or failure) of the North American laws. This will be even more important in Britain, given the inadequate enforcement aspects of the 1968 law. These shortcomings will make the Board's inescapably taxing job that much more difficult because it lacks powers of subpoena; because it is necessary to use voluntary machinery; because it is impossible to issue positive orders; and, perhaps, because of the racial balance clause. Much will depend on the determination, skill, and ingenuity of the Board's personnel. They cannot operate in a vacuum, however, and much will also depend on other government programmes, such as major expenditures to remove the social problems in the twilight areas of the central cities which cause and exacerbate prejudice. Much will depend on the willingness of political leaders to provide leadership on this issue and on their willingness to use government resources to combat discrimination. Since 1966, the government have been giving urgent consideration to the question of including a non-discrimination clause in all government contracts. Such a clause, if properly enforced would strengthen the hand of the Board and would also foster the development of meaningful affir-mative action programmes, for as the Street Committee concluded:

> The government are such huge customers of industry that they have a unique opportunity through the medium of their contracts to control racial discrimination .... We believe that through the medium of government contracts the opportunity should be taken of controlling discrimination by methods which would not at present be feasible in other areas of employment.[27]

Whether these programmes will be forthcoming, and whether such weaknesses as emerge in the operation of the 1968 law will be removed, only time will tell. On 22 October 1969 the government announced the introduction of a non-discrimination clause in all government contracts. The enforcement provisions, however, looked so weak that it is doubtful whether it will have much impact. One would have been more optimistic about the outcome and effectiveness of anti-discrimination legislation had there been a greater willingness to learn from the North American experience. Perhaps the British experience will demonstrate to the political leaders of other nations, the importance of receptivity to such information.

4 Parameters of British and North American Racism

The urban uprisings that have erupted in Britain's inner cities have raised fundamental questions about racism and the state in advanced capitalist societies. The urban ghetto uprisings in the United States in the 1960s and the responses engendered provide an important body of data which can illuminate the range of choices open to the British state and help predict which it will choose.

The US responses involved developments in police technology, tactics, training and command and control to pre-empt or put down future insurrections more expeditiously; efforts to relegitimise the system in the eyes of the black community; co-optation of sections of black leadership and repression of other sections, and an overall attempt to defuse the situation by de-emphasising the importance of race in American politics. But before we can analyse these responses, we need to look at the basic differences between Britain in the 1980s and the United States in the 1960s and the specific racial situation out of which the rebellions arose.

The US in the 1960s was in the midst of one of its longest unbroken periods of economic growth. The military-engendered boom was strengthened in the short run by the war in Vietnam. The economy functioned as it did on the basis of state intervention in two forms — massive military expenditure and huge investment in the creation and construction of the suburbs and the related infrastructure — generating growth in the construction, automobile and petroleum sectors of the economy. These provided the framework for the necessary political stability — based on the depoliticisation of large parts of the white, particularly male, unionised working class in the primary sector of the economy. In return for job security and wages in line with, and perhaps a bit ahead of, inflation, the unions provided a disciplined and reliable labour force. This facilitated the long-term planning that the monopoly corporations had to engage in. Blacks, as well as other racially oppressed groups, and most women and the white male poor, were left out of this cosy arrangement.

The key point was that, to maintain its profitability, monopoly capital, with and through its political allies, was willing to make material concessions to its labour force to ensure stability and growth. This meant that if the need arose there was already an economic and political framework within which concessions could be made to blacks to cool them out and reintegrate them into the system. As we shall see, however, this framework did not last out the decade of the 1960s and state strategies changed. The concessions were functional and when they were no longer necessary or could not be afforded, they were withdrawn.

In Britain in the 1980s, we find an economy under attack from competitors abroad and from the government at home. The government's monetarist strategy is predicated on cutting non-repressive state expenditure, relying on market forces to facilitate profitable economic activity — in Britain and outside — and cheapening labour within Britain by cutting the social wage and weakening or destroying working-class organisations. The ideological and material framework is thus very different from that of the New Frontier America of the 1960s, and the range and type of responses available to Britain are limited.

There are fundamental differences, besides, between Britain and the US in terms of their racial histories. Although racism emerged out of the creation and extension of capitalism as a world system, in which Britain played a leading part, and for whom the slave trade, the plantation economies and the conquest of India provided the major part of the surplus needed to fuel the creation of the industrial capitalist economy, Britain did not rely on black labour within its national boundaries for a major part of its work force. It used Irish labour and labour displaced from its own countryside. That is, until, starved of an adequate work force, it turned to its colonies for labour in the boom period of post-war reconstruction.[1]

The United States, on the other hand, virtually from its

inception as Britain's North American colony, has depended on black labour — and later, on that of the Hispanic peoples incorporated into the territory in the course of imperial expansion. Ideologically, therefore, the choices before white America have not included the repatriation of its black population.

A third and more striking point of difference follows from these distinctions. Because of its particular history of black employment and settlement, in Britain, unlike in the US, poor whites and poor blacks live cheek by jowl in many of the inner city areas and are subjected to the same deprivation, giving rise to the joint rebellion of blacks and whites against the system. These rebellions are not 'race riots' as such.

Background to the Uprisings

But there are common denominators between the uprisings in Britain and the ghetto riots of the US. Here I have concentrated on three key issues — the nature of policing, employment and education — which highlight the state practices that led to the rebellions.

Police

One central factor common to both Britain and the US has been the nature of policing in the inner cities. Not only have the police failed to protect the black communities of those areas, they have indulged in deliberate and sustained harassment of them, particularly of black youth. In the most run-down areas of Britain, this type of policing has also spilled over on to white working-class youth. There is a striking similarity in the nature of the 'special units' deployed in Britain and the US, and their use of deliberately aggressive tactics. In Britain, the Special Patrol Group and similar units are special squads deployed in large numbers, often without any preliminary warning, in the 'high crime' areas of the inner cities. Their concern is not, however, with major larceny, fraud or 'white-collar' crimes, but with 'policing' the inner city on the streets.

The Kerner Commission's[2] assessment of such practices in the ghettos of the US could equally well serve as a description of what takes place in Britain:

These practices, sometimes known as 'aggressive preventive patrol', take a number of forms, but invariably they involve a large number of police-citizen contacts initiated by police rather than in response to a call for help or service. One such practice utilises a roving task force which moves into high-crime districts without prior notice and conducts intensive, often indiscriminate, street stops and searches.[3]

The immediate trigger of the uprising in Brixton in the London borough of Lambeth in April 1981 was a police operation, felicitously named 'Swamp 81'. Margaret Thatcher had played the race card in the 1979 General Election by asserting that the British people had a legitimate fear of being swamped by an alien culture. Without warning, Brixton was flooded with plainclothes officers; in four days over 1,000 people were stopped and around one hundred arrested. This operation, which was pronounced a success by the officer in charge despite its consequences, was mounted even though only 4 per cent of black youth in Lambeth commit street crimes.[4]

This common pattern of harassment and invasion is reinforced in both societies by the criminalisation of large sections of the black communities — particularly the youth. In Britain, this has taken the specific form of what the Institute of Race Relations has called 'Sus 1' and 'Sus 2'. Sus 1, or the Sus law, is in fact a section of the 1824 Vagrancy Act,[5] under which an accused person can be brought to trial on no other evidence than that of acting suspiciously in the eyes of two police officers. The evidence of independent witnesses is hardly ever called. It is used primarily against Afro-Caribbean males — making parts of London, such as the West End, virtual 'no-go' areas for them. In 1977, for example, young Afro-Caribbean males, who made up only 2.8 per cent of the total population of London, accounted for 44 per cent of all Sus arrests.[6]

Sus 2, used mainly against the Asian population, is embodied in the 1971 Immigration Act, under which the police have 'the power to arrest anyone whom they suspect of being an illegal entrant'. And for suspected illegal entrants there is no right to a trial in open court — instead they are held indefinitely in detention until either removed or reprieved. 'Since all blacks are considered "immigrants" and some of them are illegal, the only way to tell an illegal black from a legal one is to suspect the lot.'[7] It is significant that this process of criminalisation and control has been accomplished by a combination of executive actions and judicial decisions, which have widened the scope of what is culpable under the Immigration Act — even including the failure to answer questions that were not asked in the first place. At the same time, basic common law protections have been eroded — habeas corpus is not available for people detained as suspected illegal entrants.

Sus 1, while specific to Britain in its details, is similar to police tactics used against young blacks in the US. It has been operated to increase fear and insecurity among the white public and to identify the source of that fear as young blacks. The creation of a scare about the new crime of 'mugging' in Britain is a case in point. There is, in fact, no such crime on the statute book, and if it means handbag-snatching or robbery with violence, it did not arrive with the coming to puberty of young Afro-Caribbean males. But mugging already had a meaning in Britain thanks to the media misreporting of events in the US and to the popularity of TV police series. Given this sensitivity, it did not take the British media, police and courts long to fasten the label mugger on young Afro-Caribbeans in general and create an atmosphere in which police invasions of black communities seemed reasonable and necessary for the common good. Sus 2 is similar to the experience of the Hispanic population in the US and, as the scapegoating of the so-called 'undocumented workers' increases, we will see an ever-increasing use of state power against them.

Police practices are further reinforced by the 'normal' racist functioning of the criminal justice systems in both societies — through the definition of crime itself, through selective, discretionary and discriminatory law enforcement, through differential access to bail and adequate legal representation, differential rates of plea bargaining and guilty pleas, differential conviction and sentencing rates — all adding up to a process which channels an increasingly significant portion of the black community into criminalisation and imprisonment. Blacks are grossly over-represented in America's prisons, and the same pattern is increasingly evident in Britain. Plea bargaining, with the threat of harsh sentencing if the accused exercise their legal rights and plead not guilty, thus 'wasting' the judge's time and the taxpayers' money, is widespread in both countries.[8] Legal representation and legal rights are commodities to be purchased — if you have the money. The Kerner Commission was forced to recognise this reality:

Some of our courts, moreover, have lost the confidence of the poor ....
The belief is pervasive among ghetto residents that lower courts in
our urban communities dispense 'assembly-line' justice; that from
arrest to sentencing, the poor and uneducated are denied equal justice
with the affluent, that procedures such as bail and fines have been
perverted to perpetuate class inequities.[9]

If those are the characteristics of criminal 'justice' in normal times,
what happens in times of insurrection? The Kerner Commission
concluded that 'the massive influx of arrested persons resulted in
serious deprivation of legal rights' and that 'judicial procedures
became oriented to mass rather than individualised justice'.[10]

The Legal Action Group (LAG) in Britain, commenting on the
operation of magistrates' courts after the 'riots' during the summer
of 1981, described them as 'taking dangerous short cuts', in some
cases simply assisting the police in 'street-clearing operations', and
concluded that 'in many cases normal judicial principles and standards are being disregarded'. LAG sees calls by government
ministers for quick justice, riot courts, new riot laws, heavy deter-
rent sentences and prison camps as 'inimical to the cool and
orderly dispensation of justice'. It is afraid that sentencing will
become 'punitive and arbitrary — as happened in many of the
cases involving Southall defendants following the disturbances
there in 1979'.[11]

The system has not only created the conditions for the oppression of black communities, but has also fuelled their anger and
created the framework for a high degree of radicalisation of black
prisoners. George Jackson and his colleagues were African-
American prisoners in Soledad who were accused of killing a
prison guard in retaliation for the death of a black prisoner.
Jackson became a member of the Black Panther Party and published two books before being killed at St Quentin penitentiary.
Jackson and the other Soledad Brothers were not alone in becoming politicised while in prison, and there is evidence that this
process is taking place in Britain and feeding back into the communities and their struggles.[12]

There is another disturbing similarity in the police response to
black rebellion. Tom Hayden, who observed the Newark, New
Jersey, rebellion of 1967, wrote:

Thus it seems to many that the military, especially the Newark police, not only triggered the riot by beating a cab-driver but created a climate of opinion that supported the use of all necessary force to suppress the riot. The force used by the police was not in response to snipers, looting, and burning, but in retaliation against the successful uprising of Wednesday [12 July] and Thursday [13 July] nights.[13]

A similar pattern of violence and revenge by the police and/or the National Guard in other US cities, such as Watts, Los Angeles, and Detroit, has been reported.[14] In Britain, after the hit-and-run killing of David Moore, a crippled 22-year-old man, by a police Land Rover, in Toxeth, Liverpool, one journalist reported:

> It is no exaggeration to say that Toxeth believes Moore was deliberately run down and that his assailant will never be brought to book. It is also widely believed that, beginning last Sunday, Liverpool police set out on a deliberate vendetta, using the fresh riots as an opportunity to settle old scores.[15]

And in Brixton, some days after the latest street violence, there was a massive police raid on homes and businesses on the 'front line', Railton Road. Even toilets and televisions were smashed in what police claimed was a search for petrol bombs, but which was in fact consistent with their less publicised attempts — since the 'riots' of April 1981 — to reassert their control, teach the people of Brixton a lesson and get their revenge.

But of immediate and central importance as the police are, they are not the only racist institution that we need to look at for the background to the current wave of rebellion.

Employment

In both Britain and the US, blacks have been, and are, channelled into the dirtiest, lowest paid, lowest status and most insecure jobs, or into the reserve army of unemployed — or, today, into the never-to-be employed category. Changes in technology and investment have created the situation in which large parts of the black community, particularly the youth, are surplus to requirements.

In the US in the 1960s, even in the war-induced boom, black unemployment was double that of whites. In 1967, 26.5 per cent of non-white teenagers were unemployed, while the figure for white teenagers was 10.6 per cent — and these statistics understate the reality, based as they are on an extremely narrow definition of unemployment, which excludes all those not registered and those who can only take part-time work. A US Department of Labour analysis in 1966 found a sub-employment rate in the ghettos of 32.7 per cent — nearly nine times the national official unemployment rate.

The position of black people in Britain, particularly in Britain's cities, is shaped by a number of factors which make their current position similar to that of the urban blacks of the US. When the US southern blacks migrated to the older cities in the north and west, they became part of an urbanised, and often unionised, working class. But even as they did so, industry was moving out of the city centres — to non-city, non-union sites, indeed increasingly to Third World countries. The blacks were left stranded. In Britain, where black migrant labourers became a settler labour force, the massive process of deindustrialisation that occurred in the 1980s, to a significant extent as the result of government policies, is rebounding on the black communities. While there has been widespread discussion in the media — particularly since the uprisings — of black youth unemployment, it is important to note the growing level of unemployment among black men and women generally. The industries that they have been concentrated in (for example, textiles) have been hard hit in the current economic climate, and black workers are likely to get laid off first. Cuts in social and welfare services many of which have been major recruiters of Afro-Caribbean and Asian women — have also meant job losses.

Black teenagers attempting to enter a massively declining job market find it many times more difficult to find such work as exists — or even obtain places in government stop-gap schemes — than their white counterparts. In some areas there are black teenage unemployment levels of 50-60 per cent — comparable to the current situation in America's ghettos. In addition, young black people are vigorously resisting attempts to channel them into the jobs that their parents have done. The latter put up with the shit work of society on the understanding in the hope — that things would be better for their children. This clearly has not been so — indeed, as one black mother put it after the second round of battles in Brixton: 'These children are British, but they don't stand a chance. The police get after them, the employers won't give them a job and the teachers downgrade them.'[16]

Education

The educational system has been an important arena of struggle in both countries, central as it is not only to the reproduction of class relations but also to 'the web of urban racism', in which the various institutions of society interconnect to create, maintain and re-create racism.[17] Annie Stein, a courageous veteran campaigner and researcher, has analysed the functioning of the educational system in the US and has identified the 'strategies for failure' that have been developed and implemented by the state.

> The average child in eighty-five percent of the Black and Puerto Rican schools is functionally illiterate after eight years of schooling in the richest city in the world [New York].

This is a massive accomplishment.

> It took the effort of 63,000 teachers, thousands more administrators, scholars, and social scientists, and the expenditure of billions of dollars to achieve. Alone, however, the 'Professional' educators could not have done it. They needed the active support of all the forces of business, real estate interests, trade unions, willing politicians, city officials, the police and the courts.[18]

These schools have not 'failed' to educate black youngsters, they have succeeded in channelling them into failure, in blaming them and their parents for that failure and in channelling and training white youngsters, in class terms, to fill their appropriate places in the system. The whole range of processes, including low teacher expectations, which become self-fulfilling prophecies, racist or irrelevant curriculum materials, tracking/streaming, the use of IQ tests and segregation — *de jure* and *de facto* — have all worked to produce such an outcome. Malcolm X gives a painful — and by no means atypical — example of what happened when he told his favourite teacher that he wanted to be a lawyer.

> Mr Sostrowski looked surprised, I remember, and leaned back in his chair and clasped his hands behind his head. He kind of half-smiled and said, 'Malcolm, one of life's first needs is for us to be realistic.

Don't misunderstand me, now. We all here like you, you know that. But you've got to be realistic about being a nigger. A lawyer — that's no realistic goal for a nigger. You need to think about something you can be.'[19]

In the 1960s the language changed — from 'nigger' to 'cultural deprivation' and then back to genetic inferiority — but the processing of black children into failure, into shit work or unemployment continued. It was not accidental, therefore, that one of the most highly contested issues in the black struggles of the 1960s in the US was that of the miseducation of their children. These battles moved from demands for integration, through compensatory education programmes to struggles for community control of education.[20] There is not the space here to detail the outcome of these struggles — suffice it to say that, on the whole, they failed to gain control or to make the schools accountable to the black community.

In Britain in the 1980s we find a similar pattern of educational practice and black sense of betrayal and anger. The processing of black children into failure was noted as early as the late 1960s when black parents campaigned against the London borough of Haringey education authority for sending a disproportionate number of their children to schools for the educationally subnormal.[21] And throughout the 1970s black parents continued to campaign against the miseducation of their children, pushing for positive, non-racist teaching materials to counter the negative stereotypes and low teacher expectations and setting up nurseries, play groups and supplementary schools to counter the effects of state schools. Black children in Britain were being incorporated into a class-based educational system at the very lowest level. A recent committee set up by the government to investigate black 'under-achievement' concluded: 'we are convinced from the evidence that we have obtained that racism, both intentional and unintentional, has a direct and important bearing on the performance of West Indian children in our schools'.[22] It is perhaps not entirely coincidental that the chairman of that committee was subsequently persuaded to resign.

The range of processes, of acts of commission and omission, which the committee identified as contributing to the failure of West Indian children is directly comparable to those found in the US, ranging from low teacher expectations and racist curricula to the possibility that West Indian children were still being unfairly assessed and were over-represented among those suspended or excluded from school or sent to disruptive units. The similarity with ghetto miseducation in the US indicates that British schools are succeeding all too well in separating and channelling black youngsters into second-class status, clearly making education part of the contested terrain.

State Responses to Urban Rebellion

Public Order and Community Policing

What have been the US responses to urban rebellion? If we are to draw lessons from them as to possible courses of action for the British state, we must bear in mind the differences in the British and American political economies. It is also necessary to keep in mind the way in which some of the US state responses have changed in accord with changes in the political economy.

The first set of responses, which have continued to obtain since the 1960s, had to do with increasing the size and improving the efficiency of the state's repressive apparatus. One indication of the seriousness of purpose in this area is that the rate of increase in US government spending on criminal justice between 1966 and 1971 was five times as great as it was in the previous decade. In 1971 over $10.5 billion was spent in this area, and by 1974 the figure reached over $14 billion, with over $8 billion of that for the police alone.[23] Another indication of the seriousness of the state's determination to reassert control was that during the 1960s and early 1970s there were four separate federal commissions studying these questions, and several more set up by corporations and foundations.[24]

Of these, the Kerner Commission was of major importance for its recommendations, which can best be summed up in the old cliché of the iron fist in the velvet glove.[25] Its prime concern was to develop a more effective policy for the restoration of public order. Its apparently liberal, and more widely publicised, concern over the causes of the riots indeed its very composition and approach — can be seen as an attempt to re-legitimise and restore confidence in the system. But the heart and substance lay in making police methods more effective. What the Commission diagnosed was police 'over-reaction', bad or non-existent command and control and an inadequate range of weapons. What it recommended was improved control capabilities, improved discipline and command within police departments, improved tactics and sufficient personnel to implement these, and the development of a wide range of non-lethal weapons, including a specific recommendation in favour of the use of CS gas. The Commission specifically recommended federal funding of certain programmes — 'community service officers, development of portable communications equipment, a national clearing house for training, information and non-lethal weapons development', as well as increased support to 'pay for the large capital investment necessary for experimental programs or development of new equipment'.[26]

It was in this area that the Commission's recommendations were most enthusiastically and expeditiously implemented, in response not only to the urban insurrections, but also to the development of the New Left, the civil rights movement and the emerging anti-war movement. The Center for Research on Criminal Justice saw the initial government response as one whose 'overall thrust was toward reorganising the police as an effective combat organisation'.[27] Criminal justice information systems — police files — underwent a major computerisation programme, largely funded by the federal government's Law Enforcement Assistance Administration (LEAA). In addition, LEAA supplied money to police departments for the purchase of new guns, automobiles, riot control equipment, helicopters, computers and sophisticated intelligence-gathering systems.

It is here that we can see the clearest similarity with both existing and probable future British government policies. Indeed, since the Metropolitan Police first established the Special Patrol Group in London, most major cities have created their own special squads. This development, combined with the creation of Police Support Units (PSUs), involving an even wider group of police obtaining riot control training, clearly indicates the British state's approach. The Thatcher government's pledge — and its enthusiastic honouring of it — to increase police spending in real terms and to increase police pay (even, or especially, at a time of pay restraint for most of the rest of the public sector workers) is further indication of this approach.

The immediate reaction of Home Secretary William Whitelaw, police chiefs, police union officials and Tory backbenchers to the urban insurrections has been to call for new weaponry and training. Armoured cars, protective clothing, rubber bullets, CS gas and water cannons are all to be made available as police chiefs determine. The primary objective is to restore law and order and reassert police hegemony in black neighbourhoods.

But the adoption of harsher and more sophisticated measures of containment was not the only response of the US state. A necessary adjunct to them was a greater emphasis on community involvement. This not only served the function of acting as a sop to the black community, an attempt to deflect black resistance and legitimate the police in the eyes of blacks, it was also useful as a means of gathering information on the black community. As the Kerner Commission put it: 'Negro officers also can increase departmental insight into ghetto problems, and provide information necessary for early anticipation of the tensions and grievances that can lead to disorders'.[28] On the reasons for police involvement in community service, it was even franker:

> First, police, because of their 'front line position' in dealing with ghetto problems, will be better able to identify problems in the community that may lead to disorder. Second, they will be better able to handle incidents requiring police intervention .... Third, willing performance of such work can gain police the respect and support of the community. *Finally, development of non adversary contacts can provide the police with a vital source of information and intelligence concerning the communities they serve* .[emphasis added][29]

This approach has become an important part of federal government activities in the race field over the past decade. The Community Relations Service, originally established as an ally of the civil rights movement, has functioned since the late 1960s as an intelligence-gathering body for the state and has placed undercover operatives in ghettos throughout the US to provide early warning of tensions which might lead to disorder. The operatives cultivate local black elites and intervene to defuse struggles and isolate militants and activists.[30] The Kerner Commission has indeed borne fruit, and it is interesting that two Community Relations Service officials were brought to Toxteth for a Granada TV programme on 27 July 1981 to talk about the importance of having operatives in such communities. Community policing is important to the state in that:

it [is] useful to decentralise police functions without decentralising police *authority*, that is, the police should have close contact with the community, but the community should not be allowed to have any real influence on the police. The aim of this kind of decentralisation is to enable the police to integrate some citizens into the lower levels of the police system itself, on police terms, thus blurring the distinction between the police and the people they control.[31]

Repression and Concession

It is no coincidence that even as the community policing strategy was being developed, the US state was mounting a massive counter-insurgency programme (COINTELPRO) against black militants, the anti-war movement and other left groups. Patterned on previous campaigns against internal 'enemies', it involved the infiltration, destabilisation and disruption of organisations. Activists were arrested on trumped up charges and inordinately high bail prices were set, which, together with long pre-trial delays, ensured that the accused would be kept off the streets for up to two years. Frequent acquittals proved only that 'justice' still worked after all. There were, in addition, shoot-outs and the killings of activists, as in the murders of Mark Clark and Fred Hampton of the Black Panther Party in Chicago.

But this mix of outright repression and 'community policing' was still not considered sufficient. For by now, it was recognised that blacks could not be counted on to be quiescent. Their willingness to fight for 'freedom and democracy' in the future could no longer be assumed and the concessions of the early 1960s — civil and voting rights — were no longer enough. When Harlem exploded in 1964, soon after the passage of the Civil Rights Bill, it became clear that additional concessions — material concessions — would have to be made to cool out the ghettos, restore stability and provide the framework for a process of co-optation. Given the expanded economy of the time, such an argument had an appeal. New programmes needed personnel, and potential personnel were on the streets making trouble. Their incorporation into the system would help both to legitimate it and to defuse opposition to it. This was encouraged by foundations such as Ford, which provided large sums of money in the attempt to penetrate and buy off militant organisations (the internal struggles in CORE [Congress of

Racial Equality] exemplify the conflicts that such a strategy engendered).[32]

Before looking at the fate of these programmes and concessions and their implications for the political struggle of the black community it is important to reiterate that such an approach cannot automatically be reproduced in Britain in the 1980s. The level of US state expenditure, though totally inadequate, was on a scale that is extremely unlikely to be entered into by the monetarist Thatcher government. The US's expanding economy made the Keynesian approach appear as a reasonable way of ensuring social peace. Such an approach was also predicated upon the existence of a significantly large group of people who, if not co-opted, might become dangerous enemies. While it is clear, as Sivanandan cogently argued in *Race, Class and the State*,[33] that British policy towards the Asian population has, in part, been predicated on the possibility of utilising the existing class and age structures within that community to control the Asian working class and youth, such a strategy with regard to the Afro-Caribbeans, an overwhelmingly working-class community, has not been possible. Instead, part of the British state's strategy has been geared to creating a functionary stratum within that community through the race relations industry, for example, the Community Relations Commission, the Race Relations Board, the Commission for Racial Equality and the local community relations committees. But this stratum just does not appear large enough, nor does the pool of potential recruits, given the functioning of the racist British educational system. There is massive evidence that the entire strategy of dividing the Asian and the Afro-Caribbean communities, and using the divisions within each to maintain control, has come unstuck.

The crucial point to bear in mind is that the liberal, concessionary approach — allied, of course, to the repression — was not the only possible response of the American state and was dependent upon a particular set of political and economic circumstances. As these circumstances changed so did the ideological argument. And even in the mid-1960s we can see the forerunners of the rightist arguments that would come to dominate thinking and reflect government policy in the 1970s and 1980s. In 1965, for example, New York senator Daniel Moynihan, then working for the Johnson administration, prepared a report which blamed the structure of black families for their own situation.[34] The 'culture of poverty' approach was already widely used by social scientists and being popularised by people such as Edward Banfield, a professor at Harvard and major proponent of the cultural of poverty approach,[35] who saw crime and delinquency as stemming directly from the culture of the lower class. The poor lived in slums because they preferred it that way, having made the areas slums in the first place. It therefore made little sense to talk about slums, unemployment and poverty as causes of riots. The emphasis on moral decay and lack of parental discipline being offered by Whitelaw and others following the recent British uprisings is strikingly similar. In a recent issue of the *Daily Telegraph*, John O'Sullivan, editor of *Policy Review* (the journal of the far right-wing Heritage Foundation, a crucial organisational link between the neo-conservatives and the moral majority in the US), had this to say: 'all the youth employment schemes and social workers in the world will not reduce or eliminate rioting. That will only be done by enforcing the law and holding people responsible for their lawless actions.'[36] Or, put more succinctly by Mrs Thatcher recently: 'You can't buy your way out of the riots'.

Another strand of intellectual racism that re-emerged in the 1960s was that of scientific racism and its emphasis on the genetic inferiority of blacks.[37] Where Banfield and Moynihan and their ilk emphasised the blacks' pathological culture, the major proponents of the idea that intelligence was genetically determined, Shockley, Jensen, Herrnstein and their British ally Eysenck, emphasised the hereditarian basis of black inferiority.[38] Both positions postulated that the victim's position was due to his or her basic characteristics — a useful approach for a political system under attack for its racism.

Market Forces and Black Capitalism

By the end of the 1960s, the US political economy had moved and with it state strategies and ideological currents. The weakening competitive position of the economy, the inflationary pressure following the war in Indochina, the worsening profit position of capital, the growing indebtedness of American business and the development of what capitalist economists could label but not understand or cure, 'stagflation', all necessitated a counter-attack on the working class as a whole, and particularly against the material concessions which had increased the social wage and set some limits on the operations of the corporations and their ability to generate and realise profit. All such impediments would have to go, and go most of them did.[39]

This had disastrous consequences for the mass of blacks, and the new strategy also went hand-in-hand with the development of a neo-conservative movement that argued vigorously against the liberal interpretations of the 1960s, that attacked the gains won then and that claimed that the poor should be left to market forces, and to their own devices. Government strategy abandoned such reform efforts as had been attempted in the Johnson years; henceforth the market was to provide the basis for-individual black advance. Black capitalism became the rhetoric of the time. None of the reforms accomplished in the 1960s tackled the fundamental structures of the political economy. Consequently, the patterns of black un- and under-employment did not change; for even in the boom period new investment was capital- not labour-intensive, and was not made in the inner-city ghettos. The ratio of black/white incomes, the relative proportions of black and white poverty and the relative rates of infant mortality, for example, did not fundamentally change. And under the policies of benign neglect, the extent of deterioration is undeniable. As US economist William Tabb states:

> Even before the economic downturn in 1974-75 Black economic gains of the 1960s had vanished. Between 1970 and 1973 Black family income fell behind as inflation eroded monetary gains (White family income rose by over six per cent). The number of Black families living in poverty rose while the number of white poverty level families continued to decline.[40]

And these patterns continued for the remainder of the decade.

What has had a more lasting effect has been the co-optation strategy — resulting in the growth, small and insecure as it is, of a black middle class, in the state bureaucracy and in the major corporations.

> Growth of Black college enrolment, white-collar employment and entrepreneurship has gone hand in hand with continued high

unemployment. The rising Black bourgeoisie urges self-reliance on the Black poor and working classes, while it as a class has gradually abandoned the relative independence of self-employment for jobs as hired hands of government and big business.[41]

The goal of creating black capitalism has, however, not been achieved. All that is left from earlier initiatives is a residue of small, mostly family-owned shops and businesses, extremely vulnerable to the recession. Berkely G. Burrell, head of the black National Business League, put his finger on it: 'A banker is a banker is a banker and if the S.O.B. isn't going to make me a loan, he isn't going to make it with government money behind him either'.[42] The government backing did not last long in any event. Black capitalism as a slogan in Nixon's 1968 presidential campaign soon gave way to 'minority business enterprise' and to benign neglect and calls for corporate involvement, thus making it even less likely that the 'S.O.B.s' would make the loan. At the height of the appeals for corporate investment in the ghetto, a survey of 700 major corporations revealed that only 112 of them 'indicated a willingness to build new plants in or near slum areas'. In addition, not one of them would make the move unless certain conditions were met, including:

· A large and non-aggressive labour pool.
· Programs to train local workers with new and useful skills.
· Ample land at reasonable prices, roads and utilities, and new zoning codes.
· Pleasant environmental conditions, including quality housing in the immediate area and assurances that ghetto 'blight' would be removed.
· Lower real estate taxes.
· Adequate security and fire protection.
· Relations only with 'responsible community groups' not with militants.[43]

The British state and British finance capital are unlikely to be any more successful in the creation of black capitalism — particularly Afro-Caribbean capitalism. And no matter how many inner-city coach-tours Environment Minister Michael Heseltine organised for businessmen in 1982, it will be interesting to see how many of the conditions demanded by US corporations he will be able to deliver in monetarist Britain — even if there are any firms willing to take advantage of them. The free-enterprise zones mooted by government may be able to supply some of these requirements — but in their present watered-down form they are unlikely to attract significant investment.

Conclusion

The black uprisings of spring and summer of 1981 were increasingly joined by alienated, unemployed white youth who feel anger against the police and the system. Their experiences with the police, though not as severe or total as those of the blacks, have nonetheless given them cause for rage. In a racist and highly class stratified society, the struggle of the black community, essentially against the racism which permeates society, is also a struggle against the class system. For the white youth — and the white left — struggle against the class hierarchy cannot by itself lead to fundamental change — they need to confront and overcome the racism which has historically retarded and distorted white working-class consciousness.[44] It is also important that when looking at the British uprisings that began in St Paul's, Bristol, in 1980, blew up in Brixton in April 1981 and in city after city in July 1981, they are not isolated from the continuing struggles of black youth and the black community in general against escalating fascist/racist attacks.

The British state has begun the attempt to contain the uprisings as well as the more problematic task of preventing future ones. The media and the ideologues have entered the fray as well. The New Right from the US has been peddling its noxious doctrines of selfishness, black inferiority and repression alongside its British allies. The more sophisticated and liberal elements have raised the question of concessions of one sort or another — but not material ones, for after all, as Heseltine has said, there is 'no crock of gold'. More co-ordination of government activities has been proposed, as has an attempt to overcome racial disadvantage in housing and employment. As *The Times* put it: 'The more these disabilities can be removed, the easier it will be for black and Asian people to find satisfactory places for themselves in accordance with their individual abilities'.[45] A strategy to find 'satisfactory places' — at least for some — is made even more necessary because, as Sivanandan shows, changes in production related to micro-technology, and the investment decisions associated with those changes, are such as to make unemployment a permanent condition for a significant portion of the working class.[46] And we can be sure that blacks will be round in that group in large numbers. So central is this reality that even *The Times* had to acknowledge — albeit in muted fashion — that 'we have moved into a different economic climate in which jobs will be in short supply for years to come'.[47]

Meanwhile, the Labour Party and the trade unions have belatedly had to confront the consequences of their own racist policies and have proved unable to deal with them. The Labour Party, committed by both policy and practice to managing a capitalist economy (with some state ownership), will also have to give priority to capitalist requirements and capitalist economic activity — rather than to maintaining, let alone improving, social and welfare benefits. Given the massive and sustained erosion of Britain's economic and industrial base, and the lack of any Labour policies to deal with that, there is no way that it will be in any position to make the sort of material concessions made in the US in the mid-1960s by the Democrats. It is unlikely, therefore, that even with a change of government the conditions which give rise to the uprisings will be significantly altered. In the short run, there will be more repression, various symbolic gestures and increased attempts at co-optation.

This article began by looking at the US black insurrections of the 1960s, and the various state responses. We have seen that as the economy retrenched, capitalist imperatives required the clawing back of many of the material and procedural concessions made to the black community, in favour of repression allied to co-optation. It appeared throughout the 1970s that the strategy had worked. There were, however, a number of indicators that the ghetto blacks were not as quiescent as had been assumed. During a power failure in New York City in 1977 and during a blizzard in Baltimore — both of which put the police temporarily out of action — blacks engaged in widespread looting. In 1979 a black uprising in Miami followed the acquittal by an all-white jury of four white policemen who had beaten a black man to death.

The ideological disarray among liberals in the US, and the lack of concern about race — it is no longer an 'in' subject — has given the New Right allies of capital a dominant position. Their anti-black, anti-woman, anti-gay ideology provides the cover for a massive reallocation of state funds from the working class as a whole — with blacks and other racially oppressed groups bearing a disproportionate burden — in favour of capital.[48] On the whole, the co-opted black functionaries, at least those not being laid off as a result of cuts, can be counted upon to defend their new class position. But the danger from the state's perspective is that the mass of poor blacks will take matters into their own hands. US Attorney General William French Smith has stated that the possibility of racial violence erupting as a result of cuts in social programme budgets will be monitored by an 'early warning system' (he is referring to the Community Relations Service). But so far, 'we haven't had any great alarms that have gone off anywhere .... It's quite possible that the effect of these so-called budget cuts won't materialise at all in terms of causing temperatures to rise.'[49]

What this indicates — apart from the obvious propaganda element is a state on the attack, relying both on its domestic intelligence network and its agencies of force to contain trouble. At the same time, the ideological offensive against blacks and the poor is heightening, as evidenced in two recent major articles in the *Los Angeles Times*.[50] They are worth discussing in some detail because they exemplify current thinking, and give an alarming foretaste of future trends.

The articles argue that while twice as many whites as blacks are part of a new permanent underclass, the black underclass is more worrying because it is concentrated in America's major cities rather than being scattered in the Appalachias and other semi-rural areas. Structural factors in maintaining and creating this underclass are mentioned, but the overriding theme is that of its own responsibility for its position. And if statistics will not do to bring the message home to the reader, there is a case study of a day in the life of a South Side Chicago black welfare mother, with ten illegitimate children, five of whom are on welfare with her, and one of whom has just had an illegitimate child — under the invidious title 'The underclass, how one family copes'. These blacks are not only living off the rest of us because they cannot or will not work, but they also engage, we are told, in widespread criminal activity which also costs the rest of us. The experts quoted agree that not a great deal can be done, the economy is shrinking, and it's all the fault of the poor anyhow.

But more dangerous than the familiar 'blame the victim' structure of the debate is the way we are encouraged to fear and loathe the victim. The second article, appearing one week later, drops all pretence at social concern. Luridly titled 'Marauders from inner city prey on LA's suburbs', it begins as follows: 'One by one and in small bands, young men desperate for money are marauding out of the heart of Los Angeles in a growing wave to prey upon the suburban middle and upper classes sometimes with senseless savagery'.[51] Robbery (with bloodcurdling violence) and the rape of two white women is the stuff, we are informed, of one such 'raid'. We are then returned to the ghetto with these savage marauders to watch them showing off and spending their ill-gotten gains. We are repeatedly told that the police do not have enough powers or manpower and that the courts are too lenient.

The President of the Los Angeles Urban League, John Mack, sees the solution lying with placing 'the major focus on the ones who are still salvageable .... We are a race of people who are equal to anyone else, but within that framework we have some winners, and we have some losers. We have to go with the winners.' Mayor Tom Bradley has a solution for the 'losers'.

> I think that there is a concept where you have a controlled environment, where you keep the child not just while he or she is in school but in the hours outside school, you have that child in a controlled environment. The kibbutz in Israel is one such concept .... It, of course, would not be a kibbutz, but it would be that kind of concept.[52]

Bradley's 'concept' — the twenty-four-hour a day controlled environment for the unco-opted members of the underclass — is the frightening logic of the current US situation. Is that where Whitelaw's army camps turned prisons for the rebellious youth of Britain's inner cities will also lead?

5 The United States: The Revocation of Civil Rights

In the US today we are witnessing a reversal of many of the legal and political reforms stimulated by the civil rights movement of the 1950s and 1960s. This repeal of what may be termed the Second Reconstruction is proceeding in much the same manner as the reversal, a hundred years ago, of the First Reconstruction reforms that followed the American Civil War. In both cases, the executive and judicial branches of the federal government worked together in an increasingly racist, popular and intellectual culture to turn the clock back. In the last decades of the nineteenth and the twentieth centuries, black rights to equality in the economy were abrogated — as were their rights to be considered as 'real Americans'. In both cases, the 'counter-revolution' followed an incompletely conceptualised and implemented 'revolution' in which the economic basis of freedom was neglected by the political leadership of the African-American community and denied by the corporate political and economic elites.

First Reconstruction

In the case of the First Reconstruction, it was the denial of land to the freewomen and freemen which undermined their ability to protect their limited political rights. Radical Republican Congressman Thaddeus Stephens posed the challenge facing the victorious Union following the Civil War in stark and prophetic terms, when he stated that political democracy was impossible in a situation in which the majority were landless and most of the land was owned by a tiny group of 'nabobs'. So powerful was his insight that northern industrialists and their political representatives, the Republican Party, refused to confiscate the land and distribute it — '40 acres and a mule' — to the former slaves or to make it available at low prices with low rates of interest to poor whites. For, if political democracy in the South required a Jeffersonian economic democracy, would not political democracy in the industrialising North require a form of economic democracy as well?

What the industrialists and their allies wanted from the South was cheap cotton and that would be best produced by a re-established plantation economy. They also needed to keep control of the federal government to further their own economic and political interests. And, since only the enfranchisement of the former slaves would ensure the political dominance of the industrialists' party, the Republicans, in the immediate future, that also was key to the Reconstruction reforms.

Of these two aims, the re-established plantation system producing cheap cotton for export and for domestic mills remained inviolate until the First World War. The second goal was a more temporary one, for, as time went on, the black vote became less and less necessary to maintaining the new national political economy and the cost of protecting it became too high. Consequently, the political rights that had been extended to black men were swiftly eroded — by terrorism; lack of military protection for blacks in the South; the withdrawal of federal commitment to black rights as the price for Hayes's victory in the 1876 presidential election, and by a series of Supreme Court decisions. The latter overturned Reconstruction laws designed to protect the rights of the former slaves and overwhelmingly interpreted the Fourteenth Amendment, which guaranteed equal protection before the law, in such a way as, in fact, to deny it to black Americans — while at the same time providing protection for corporations against state regulation.[1]

The Supreme Court began the process of neutralising the gains blacks had made with the *Slaughterhouse Cases* of 1873. The Court argued that the adoption of the Thirteenth, Fourteenth and Fifteenth Amendments to the constitution — which formed the legal basis of Reconstruction — was not intended 'to destroy the main features of the general system' which gave the individual states primacy over their own affairs, including civil rights, 'and over the definition of the basic terms of citizenship within its boundaries'.[2] In 1876 the Court limited the rights of African-Americans further in the case of *United States* v. *Cruikshank* which

> established the principle that the Fourteenth Amendment guarantees the rights of citizens only against encroachments by the states, and not against ... private individuals. In addition, it held that the violation by a private person of the civil rights of another could only be a crime when it interfered with an act connected with national citizenship.[3]

In the *Civil Rights Cases*, decided in 1883, the Court overturned the Civil Rights Act of 1875, which had implemented the Thirteenth and Fourteenth Amendments by outlawing discrimination in places of public resort and transport facilities. This decision is crucial, not only because of the practical consequences following the repeal of the Act, but also because of the Court's rejection of the notion of 'special treatment':

> When a man has emerged from slavery ... there must be some stage in the progress of his elevation when he takes the rank of a mere citizen, and ceases to be the special favourite of the laws, and when his rights ... are to be protected in the ordinary modes by which other men's rights are protected. There were thousands of free coloured people in this country before the abolition of slavery ... yet no one, at that time, thought it was any invasion of his personal status as a freeman because he was not admitted to all their privileges enjoyed by white citizens, or because he was subjected to discriminations ...[4]

The Court had effectively equated the protection of equal rights for black Americans with 'special treatment' — thus placing them outside the category of American in the same way in which race-based chattel slavery served to exclude black from the Declaration of Independence's definition of men in its assertion that 'all men are created equal'.

The final stage in the legal process of creating an apartheid society in the South was reached in 1896 in the *Plessy* v. *Ferguson* decision. In this case the Court upheld a Louisiana statute establishing segregation of whites and blacks on railroad trains and held that the Fourteenth Amendment, 'in the nature of things could not have been intended to abolish distinctions based upon colour, or to enforce social, as distinguished from political, equality'.[5] Justice Harlan challenged the Court's majority decision in a vigorous and famous dissent, arguing that:

> The present decision ... will not only stimulate aggressions ... upon the admitted rights of coloured citizens, but will encourage the belief that it is possible, by means of state enactments, to defeat the beneficent purposes [of] the recent amendments of the Constitution, by one of which the blacks of this country were made citizens ... whose privileges and immunities, as citizens, the States are forbidden to abridge.[6]

This undermining of the First Reconstruction, with its consequent denial to African Americans of their political and economic rights, and the locking of most into debt peonage as tenant farmers in the South, followed on from the actions of the leaders of the former slaves as well as those of the white power structure. The black petit bourgeois leaders were committed to the capitalist political economy and thus failed to challenge its logic or to articulate the social class interests of the black majority. Frederick Douglass, an escaped slave who became a major figure in the abolitionist movement before the Civil War and key leader of African America in the post-Civil War period, said in 1880:

> Could the nation have been induced to listen to those stalwart Republicans, Thaddeus Stephens and Charles Sumner [who had favoured the confiscation of Confederate estates], some of the evils we now suffer would have been averted. The negro would not today be on his knees ... supplicating the master class to give him leave to toil .... He would not now be swindled out of his hard earnings ... because left by our emancipation measures at the mercy of the men who had robbed him all his life and his people for centuries.[7]

Indeed, this failure had even more deleterious consequences: it helped legitimate the repeal itself. Demands for justice and material compensation for blacks were transmuted into demands for 'special treatment' — clearly unacceptable in a society in which every individual was in competition with every other individual. Failing to challenge this stereotype, black leaders could not make the entirely valid case for group rights for those who had been enslaved for two centuries and then freed without compensation.

Second Reconstruction

Some hundred years later, a parallel process could be seen working to overturn the gains of the so-called 'Second Reconstruction' — brought about by the civil rights movement of the 1950s and 1960s. These gains were limited but real. The burden of Jim Crow — that is the system of *de jure* segregation which affected every aspect of a black person's daily life — was removed from the backs of black people in the South, and spin-off from the movement led to new types of political mobilisation in the cities of the North. But the class differences in the black community, the commitment to the capitalist economy by the black leadership and the incorporation of large sections of the black middle class into various levels of the state bureaucracy continued the isolation of the mass of black people and their needs from the political agenda.

Nonetheless, a liberal national agenda, combined with the changing economic and political situation in the South, facilitated a series of concessions which, fundamentally, overturned petty apartheid, *de jure* segregation, and provided for the incorporation of blacks into an existing, structurally unequal, political system on a (more or less) colour blind basis. The civil rights movement also acted as a catalyst for women, young people and other racially identified groups whose movements in the 1960s challenged a whole gamut of assumptions about what had been accepted as 'natural' in American society — for example, definitions of sexuality, the nature of the family, the truthfulness and significance of media representations, as well as institutional discrimination against blacks.

The Supreme Court, under Chief Justice Earl Warren, responded with a range of decisions which extended rights to groups in addition to blacks and in areas beyond the removal of de jure segregation. For example, establishing the right to counsel in *Gideon* v. *Wainwright* (1963); the right to remain silent in the face of police custodial interrogation in *Miranda* v. *Arizona* (1966); the right to be free from unreasonable searches and seizures in *Terry* v. *Ohio* (1968); the right to exclude illegally obtained evidence from trial in *Mapp* v. *Ohio* (1961). The liberal majority on the bench remained even after President Nixon appointed Warren Burger as Chief Justice, and the extension of rights continued in *Roe* v. *Wade* (1973), which legalised abortion, and in cases involving blacks, such as *Riggs* v. *Duke Power Co.* (1971) in which the Court unanimously placed the burden of proof in 'disparate impact' cases on the employer.[8]

The *Duke Power* case upheld affirmative action, which was one of the major concessions wrested from the system by the spreading of black struggle to the urban ghettos and by the urban uprisings of the 1960s. Another set of concessions involved the relaxation of some of the procedural barriers which had prevented many of those eligible for social benefits from obtaining them and the establishment of job training and creation programmes. These programmes did not, of course, address the fundamental inequalities of the society. Nor did they guarantee jobs. But they did provide an increased range of benefits to poor people.

Severely limited in terms of the continued structural inequalities though such reforms were, they were, nonetheless, vigorously opposed by those individuals and groups that came to be known as the New Right. Even symbolic measures of limited substance, designed to relegitimate the system, triggered visceral rage as the overthrow of the established order. This was seen, for example, in the New Right's defence of the patriarchal, nuclear family as the 'norm' and in its attempts to blame poverty, welfare dependency and other social problems on the supposed 'breakdown' of family values under the influence of the change-oriented movements.

Most importantly, whites were seen as threatened by black demands for equality in the labour market, in education and in other public spheres. The New Right built on Nixon's 'Southern Strategy', which set out to recruit white votes from the Democrats on the basis that they had become the party of blacks, 'women's libbers' and homosexuals, whereas the Republicans were a 'white man's party'. Nixon used the code-words 'law and order' to appeal to the white South and to white working-class voters in the rest of the country. And, once elected, he appointed as a special advisor Daniel Moynihan, author of the infamous Moynihan Report of 1965 and later a Demoratic senator to New York, which argued that the 'pathological' black family was responsible for the poverty of blacks. Moynihan justified Nixon's confidence when he advocated a policy of 'benign neglect' towards the issue of race and argued, in effect, for the political isolation of the black underclass:

The Negro lower class must be dissolved .... It is the existence of this lower class, with its high rates of crime, dependency and general disorderliness, that causes nearby whites ... to fear Negroes and to seek by various ways to avoid and constrain them. It is this group that black extremists use to threaten white society with the prospect of mass arson and pillage. It is also this group that terrorises and plunders the stable elements of the Negro community ... forced to live cheek and jowl with a murderous slum population.[9]

The Repeal of the Second Reconstruction

Nixon set in train a process of changing the composition of the Supreme Court and other federal benches in order to get judicial repeal of large parts of the Second Reconstruction, a process that was continued under Presidents Reagan and Bush. All three Presidents used racism — and antagonism towards the gains made by women and gays — as central planks in their social agenda, which, in turn, has diverted attention from their economic goals.

These had basically to do with the necessity, given the decline in America's economic dominance, of rolling back a variety of concessions granted in the post-war period to a stratum of the working class — largely white, male, unionised and employed in the primary labour market. These concessions included relative job security, recognition of collective bargaining rights, pay levels linked to increases in inflation and company contributions to pensions and health care insurance. This augmented social wage bought for capital a disciplined work force, co-operative trade unions and political support for the Cold War and the permanent war-time economy. But loss of markets to the Japanese and Germans and higher labour costs than its international competitors eventually pushed American capital to seek a reconstruction of this Keynesian accommodation with labour. Capital required repeal of the high social wage and an increase in workers' output through speed-up, increasing the intensity of work and lessening, if not removing altogether, health and safety protection.

This economic strategy required a political framework, in which the attack on affirmative action was to play a central part. It scapegoated blacks and women as responsible for the deteriorating position of the white, male working class. One measure of the price now being paid by the working class is that the average

American family income, in real terms, is lower than it was in 1973, and it takes the paid labour of more family members to earn that income. The reorganisation of the economy has meant the replacement of higher paid working-class jobs with low-paid, non-unionised, temporary or part-time jobs. Two million Americans were poor in 1986 even though they worked full-time and year-round, and there were another 6.9 million people working part-time or part of the year and earning less than the poverty level. At the same time, job-training and job-subsidisation programmes, among the benefits of the governmental response to black militancy in the 1960s, were cut by nearly 70 per cent. Spending on welfare also dropped and the real income of welfare recipients has fallen nationally by approximately one-third.[10]

The Reagan administration mounted a consistent attack on the enforcement of civil rights legislation, staffed enforcement agencies with opponents of the legislation and consistently encouraged legal challenges to past civil rights gains. Reagan's appointees to the Supreme Court were uniformly opponents of the rights of blacks, women and the working class. Reagan also appointed half of the lower federal judiciary in his eight years in office. Frank Deale, legal director of the Center for Constitutional Rights, sees this combination as particularly dangerous because lower court judges are now free to innovate in pursuit of their ideological goals with little fear that the Supreme Court will overturn their decisions.[11]

The Supreme Court's Assault on Black Rights

The Supreme Court, with its Reagan appointees giving it a reactionary majority, made a series of decisions in 1989 which set back significantly, if not repealed, the previous Court's decisions and legislative measures of the Second Reconstruction. In January 1989, in the case of *Richmond* v. *Croson*, the Court overturned the 1980 *Fullilove* v. *Klutznick* case when it declared unconstitutional a requirement in Richmond, Virginia, that construction firms must subcontract at least 30 per cent of their city contracts to minority-owned businesses. Despite the fact that prior to this requirement less than one per cent of contracts were awarded to minority-owned businesses in a city which is half black, the Court's decision, written by Justice Sandra Day O'Connor, held that: 'The 30 per cent quota cannot in any realistic sense be tied to any injury suffered by anyone .... Racial classifications are suspect, and that means that simple legislative assurances of good intention cannot suffice.' Justice Thurgood Marshall, in a strongly worded dissent (echoing Justice Harlan in 1896), said the decision marked a full-scale retreat from the commitment to equality of economic opportunity. He argued that:

> In concluding that remedial classifications warrant no different standard of review ... than the most brute and repugnant forms of state-sponsored racism, a majority of this Court signals that it regards racial discrimination as largely a phenomenon of the past, and that government bodies need no longer preoccupy themselves with rectifying racial injustice.[12]

In *Wards Cove Packing Co.* v. *Atonio*, the Court overturned the 1971 *Duke Power* decision, in which the Court unanimously placed the burden of proving that an employment practice is 'related to job performance' on the employer whose practice was being challenged. This decision had created the category of 'disparate-impact' cases that relied on statistical evidence to force employers to defend practices that had the effect of discriminating against blacks or women. In *Wards Cove*, the Court shifted that burden to employees, who must now prove that the challenged practices are not, in fact, necessary and employers need only show that what they did was a 'reasonable employment practice'. Justice Harry Blackmun, in a dissenting opinion, wrote: 'One wonders whether the majority still believes that race discrimination — or, more accurately, race discrimination against non-whites — is a problem in our society, or even remembers that it ever was'.[13]

In *Martin* v. *Wilks*, the Court overturned the 1979 *United Steelworkers* v. *Weber* decision in which the Court held that an affirmative action plan agreed in labour negotiations did not violate whites' civil rights. In *Martin*, the Court ruled that white fire-fighters in Birmingham, Alabama, could sue to reopen an affirmative-action settlement, approved eight years earlier to remedy discrimination that had kept blacks out of all senior positions in the department. The Court held that a voluntary settlement in the form of a consent decree between one group of employees and their employer cannot possibly 'settle' the conflicting claims of employees who do not join in the agreement. It was felt by critics of the decision that this would lead to the reopening of many cases long closed.

In *Patterson* v. *McLean Credit Union*, the Court ruled that the Civil Rights Act of 1866 applied only to discrimination in hiring but not to discriminatory treatment on the job. A week later, on 22 June 1989, the Court, after suggesting this line of argument to the plaintiff, ruled again by a 5-4 majority in *Jett* v. *Dallas Independent School District* that the Civil Rights Act of 1866 cannot be used to bring damage suits against state or local governments for acts of racial discrimination. Under the ruling, plaintiffs can succeed only if they can show that the discrimination was not the random act of an individual public employee but resulted from an official 'policy or custom'. Justice Brennan, speaking for the minority, termed the ruling 'astonishing', adding that, 'Before today, no one had questioned that a person could sue a governmental official for damages due to a violation' of the 1866 law. By deciding as it did, the Court removed the benefits following use of that law, the obtaining of damages, and will force victims of discrimination in the future to use other legislation which does not provide for damages.[14] In the period between 15 June 1989 — when the Patterson decision was handed down — and 1 November 1989, there were ninety-six bias claims dismissed in federal courts without any substantive rulings on the claims themselves.[15]

In another decision, which, while ostensibly having nothing to do with race relations, will have disproportionate consequences racially because of a justice system which criminalises blacks and Latinos, the Court ruled in 1989 in *Murray* v. *Giarrantano* that indigent inmates on death row do not have a constitutional right to a lawyer to assist them in a second round of state court appeals. This has major implications because in capital cases these proceedings result in the death sentences being set aside in as many as two-thirds of all cases. In states which do not provide lawyers for such appeals, the supply of volunteer lawyers is drying up because of the costs in time and money involved.[16] This decision capped a series of decisions of the Reagan Court which overturned earlier decisions of the Warren Court equalising, to some degree, the rights of defendants in the criminal justice system with the powers of the police and prosecution.

Another crucial limitation on the right of blacks and other

victims of discrimination to use the courts to obtain redress is the recent application of Rule 11 of the judicial code. Under this rule, designed to prevent frivolous cases, a losing litigant who was deemed not to have a good faith argument for the 'extension, modification or reversal of existing law' could previously be penalised by having to pay his or her opponent's court fees. More recently, in an attempt to stop business-sponsored cases clogging up the courts, this penalty was extended to cover the other side's legal expenses as well. This rule is now being applied, by courts dominated by Reagan-appointees, to civil rights cases. Thus, lawyers and organisations defending black rights now run the risk of heavy financial penalties if they lose cases. The NAACP Legal and Defence Fund was hit by a $90,000 penalty.

The cumulative effect of these Supreme Court decisions was summed up by Justice Thurgood Marshall in an address to federal judges on 8 September 1989. They 'put at risk', he declared, 'not only the civil rights of minorities but the civil rights of all citizens .... It is difficult to characterise last term's decisions as the product of anything other than a deliberate retrenchment of the civil rights agenda .... Thirty-five years after the Supreme Court ended the era of legal segregation with the decision in *Brown* v. *Board of Education*, we have come full circle. We are back where we started.'[17]

6 Racism, the National Health Service, and the Health of Black People

Racism has been and is central to an understanding of the health of black people in Britain. Black people have played and are playing a central role in the National Health Service (NHS). Their role is, however, shaped by racism. Their experiences as consumers of the NHS are also shaped by racism — in terms of their treatment for both physical and mental health problems. In addition, their specific health problems such as sickle cell anaemia have not received the attention they deserve. The NHS has become part of the internal control system of the British racist immigration system. The cuts in the NHS, and in other areas of the welfare state, since 1979 have created the conditions for increasing racial conflict on the one hand and for interracial class-based resistance on the other.

> Good health is not merely the absence of illness and disease; it is a
> state of complete physical, mental and social well-being. Whether we
> are healthy, therefore, is determined almost exclusively by our
> working conditions, the standard of our housing, our access to health
> and welfare services and the treatment we receive from them.[1]

Black people have been involved with the National Health Service (NHS) from its inception. As in other areas of British life, their contribution has been great, but structured within the framework of racial stratification. Their role as consumers within the health service has also had the characteristics we have seen elsewhere and has to be seen in the wider context of racism, which creates special or augmented health problems as well as limiting or distorting the responses to those needs. Racism has structured the ways in which black people's experiences have been interpreted — or ignored. For example, *The Black Report*, which is regarded as the most detailed study of health in Britain, devotes less than three pages to the discussion of the health of Britain's black population, which it describes in terms of immigration. There is little or no discussion of racial inequalities in health care.[2] Much of the research that has looked at the health of black people has been based on ethnocentric assumptions, and has identified ethnicity and the cultures of black people as the key questions and as problems whose solution lies in the changing of those cultures. The training based on such assumptions has, not surprisingly, been misleading, often dangerous, and has diverted attention away from institutional racism.[3]

By 1948 when the NHS was established, local selection committees were established in 16 British colonies, including Nigeria, Sierra Leone, British Guyana, Mauritius, and Trinidad and Tobago, to recruit nurses and midwives; 63 hospitals agreed to accept colonial recruits. This process, like the associated recruitment of overseas-born doctors and ancillary workers, represented a solution to labour shortages similar to that adopted by other sectors of the British economy and by other Western European and North Atlantic countries. In these cases, labour from former colonies or from poorer, underdeveloped regions was channelled into the richer, developed countries thus continuing the historical processes accompanying development in the first instance and represented a form of foreign aid, i.e., the transfer of human capital from the poorer to the richer regions and countries.[4]

In the case of the British health service, the structure of employment of black people, at all levels, paralleled the often more obvious patterns found in other sectors. The lower the status, the less desirable the position, and the dirtier the job, the greater the proportion of black workers. Although the presence of large numbers of professionals may have given a misleading impression of equity, the reality of racial stratification within the medical and nursing professions was similar to that found in the divisions between the clerical and non-clerical ancillary sectors in the health service. In the case of both doctors and nurses, overseas-born professionals are disproportionately recruited to lower status and lower prestige hospitals and specialities. For example, one recent study found that although overseas-born doctors account for 30 per cent of all hospital doctors, only 19 per cent are in the prestigious teaching districts, and those in general practice are concentrated in areas of high Asian settlement. In 1983 a Commission for Racial Equality (CRE) study documented the failure of the NHS to promote Asian and other overseas-born doctors. The study identified the maldistribution of overseas-born doctors not only in terms of status but also in terms of specialities. The CRE found that while overseas doctors accounted for 8.6 per cent of consultants in general surgery, they constituted 24.3 per cent of consultants in mental illness and 43.4 per cent of those in geriatrics.[5]

The CRE, in a study of two of the 14 Regional Health Authorities in England (the North-Western and the Merseyside Authorities) published in January 1987, found this pattern continuing. The study found that 'one in three of the overseas doctors who were not in their first choice of speciality had to change because they could not get a job in the speciality they had hoped for. This was true of only 12 per cent of the white British trained doctors.'[6] It also found that 'overseas doctors were over-represented in locum posts and that they held these posts for longer periods with fewer prospects of promotion' and that they were 'under-represented in the Teaching Authorities';[7] and 'four out of ten white doctors and five out of ten ethnic minority doctors felt that there was discrimination in the Health Service'.[8]

Sir Raymond Hoffenberg,[9] President of the Royal College of Physicians, delivered the Centre for Contemporary Studies 1985 Winter Lecture, 'The Health Service and Race', in which he noted this evidence. He argued that these patterns were more the result of 'a not-unexpected tendency to favour graduates of one's own medical schools' than of racial discrimination. He interpreted the meaning of an anecdote about the fate of a graduate of his own medical school who was of Indian descent and had great difficulty in obtaining admission into a training scheme for general practitioners (GPs) until Sir Raymond wrote indicating that although the doctor was of Indian origin he had been educated in Britain. Sir Raymond states that this example 'might be construed to support my feeling that ethnicity is a less important factor than the stable in which the young doctor was trained'.[10]

Other experts, however, locate the cause of these patterns firmly in racism within the medical profession and the NHS. Steve Watkins,[11] Senior Registrar in Community Medicine in Manchester, quotes the Medical Practitioners Union evidence to the parliamentary Social Services Committee in which the Union declared that 'overseas doctors have been shunted by the processes of medical racialism into the least attractive and least educational posts where they have been systematically exploited by employing authorities and ignored by their professional colleagues'. Dr Watkins concludes that:[12]

> Health workers at all grades suffer from both overt and covert racialism. The medical profession clearly uses black doctors as pairs of hands to do the work which white doctors do not want to do. It measures the status of a hospital by the proportion of its staff who are white, the status of a speciality by the extent to which it can fill its posts without resorting to the use of black doctors, and the status of a job by the number of white applicants it receives. It barely conceals its use of these criteria for judgement.

A similar pattern has been found in the types of hospitals and specialities in which black nurses are employed and in their under-representation in the posts of senior nursing officer (sister) or principal nursing officer (matron). New entrants into the nursing profession are finding a similar pattern of racial discrimination. Young black British people have been channelled into becoming pupil nurses, leading to the less prestigious SEN (State Enroled Nurse) qualification, rather than student nurses, leading to the SRN (State Registered Nurse) qualification. Recent evidence shows that as separate categories of nurse training are being phased out, black youngsters are being denied entry altogether on the grounds of unsuitability, even after meeting the objective requirements.

Sir Raymond Hoffenberg sees this pattern as 'more complex' for nurses than for doctors since relatively few nurses have been trained overseas.[13] Other commentators, including black health workers and patients, are quite clear about the nature of the racism that produces these outcomes. A black nurse working in 1981 at St Ann's Hospital in London described her treatment and the treatment of other black health workers in the health service as a whole and in St Ann's Hospital thus:

> In the last 30 years, black people, mainly women, have been cleaning up the mess in NHS hospitals as nurses, cleaners, laundry assistants, kitchen maids, etc. in some places working in the most archaic environments. In many hospitals, for example, the laundry area, where some of the least desirable work is done, has not improved

since the period when it was a work house. Apart from bad working environment, many of the jobs which black workers are channelled into are extremely low paid and they are the most degrading jobs in the hospitals. So what you have is an apartheid system of job division between black and white workers in NHS hospitals — you find black women cleaning up the shit and the whites telling them how to do it .... What actually occurs is that ward domestic and black staff nurse both find themselves in the same position for ten or 15 years, neither even being considered for promotion and if they do leave, they'll only get a similar position in another hospital.[14]

The ambulance service is known as a virtual 'no-go' area for black people. As in the emerging situation for those who want to become nurses, potential ambulance service employees have to satisfy white personnel officers of their suitability and respectability, and are obviously failing. A number of detailed studies of particular hospitals[15] or of a health authority[16] have validated the general observation that black people are concentrated in the ancillary services, catering and portering and cleaning rather than clerical, and, as McNaught[17] has found, 'in those units providing geriatric, psychiatric and community health services'. The Greater London Council (GLC) Health Panel found 'the concentration of black people in the most unpopular jobs and the least favourable working conditions'. These patterns have been noted for a number of years and little or nothing has been done.[18]

Before discussing the amount and nature of health care that black people receive as users of the NHS, and consequently, analysing the character of that service, we will look at the forces shaping the health status of Britain's black population. As *The Black Report* and other studies have demonstrated, social and economic factors are major determinants of health.[19]

In March 1987 the Health Education Council published *The Health Divide: Inequalities in Health in the 1980s*, which updated *The Black Report*. They concluded that:

Serious social inequalities in health have persisted into the 1980s. Whether social position is measured by occupational class, or by assets such as house and car-ownership, or by employment status, a similar picture emerges. Those at the bottom of the social scale have much higher death rates than those at the top. This applies at every stage of life from birth, through to adulthood and well into old age. Neither is it just a few specific conditions which account for these higher death rates. All the major killer diseases now affect the poor more than the rich (and so do most of the less common ones too). The less favoured occupational classes also experience higher rates of chronic sickness and their children tend to have lower birthweight, shorter stature and other indicators suggesting poorer health status.[20]

In a racist society, racism that shapes the life conditions of black people therefore crucially affects their health — either directly or indirectly. The general picture, as summarised by Allan McNaught, is that:

> While there are a handful of health conditions with a strong racial link, the bulk of mortality and morbidity of black and ethnic minority groups are from diseases and conditions which affect the whole population. However, black and ethnic minority group members seem to experience worse levels of mortality and morbidity, with some exceptions.[21]

The unemployment rates, low pay, and poverty rates of Britain's black population are clearly worse than those for white Britons. When in work, black workers are concentrated in unskilled or semi-skilled occupations, in jobs with awkward or unsocial hours, with an unpleasant or dangerous working environment, and with relatively low earnings. Some or all of these characteristics are the norm for black workers. Among the health consequences that follow from these characteristics are inadequate diet because of low income, which leads in extreme cases to deficiency diseases or in the case of pregnant women to low birth-weight children, and to debilitation and lower resistance to illness. Unemployment, as a number of recent studies have shown, leads to a variety of stress-related illnesses and medical consequences including increases in mental illness, suicides and attempted suicides, and increased use of the health service. A recent study carried out by Dr Norman Beale and Ms Susan Nethercott for the Royal College of General Practitioners has shown a 20 per cent increase in consultations with family doctors and a 60 per cent increase in visits to hospital outpatient departments connected with unemployment.[22] The Health Education Council concluded that 'It is now also beyond question that unemployment causes a deterioration in mental health and there is increasing evidence that the same is true of physical health'.[23] Poverty and low income in contemporary society similarly create stress and stress-related illnesses. The dirty, dangerous jobs in which blacks are concentrated have health consequences; for example, brick works, textile mills, and foundries are industries associated with long-term industrial diseases as well as with industrial accidents. There have been a number of recent studies showing the health consequences of shift work, and one of the characteristics of black employment is a high degree of shift work.

Black people are disproportionately found in worse housing, in the least desirable accommodation, with more overcrowding and lack of amenities, and with a larger proportion of the population lacking sole use of amenities. Among the illnesses associated with such housing are respiratory and rheumatic complaints, stress-related illnesses, and tuberculosis. As the GLC Health Panel concluded: 'Asians are at particularly high risk from tuberculosis and while there is little doubt that some of the disease experienced here results from infection originating overseas, there can equally be little doubt that its spread and re-emergence is helped by unsatisfactory housing conditions and overcrowding experienced in this country'.[24] The comparable tuberculosis rates per 100,000 are 9.4 for whites, 354 for Indians, and 353 for Pakistanis and Bangladeshis.

The concentration of black people in run-down inner city areas has consequences for the primary health care received by black people. Studies in Liverpool and London have documented 'the broad correlation between the areas where ethnic minority communities have settled and the areas where primary health care problems are at their most intense: single-handed GPs working from inadequate premises, often without the support of a primary health care team'.[25] Ntombenhle Protasia Khotie Torkington[26] in her study, *The Racial Politics of Health — A Liverpool Profile*, extends the discussion by pointing to the right of individual GPs as independent contractors to refuse to accept individuals or groups of people onto their lists, so that black people can and are denied service because of the prejudices of GPs.[27]

The health consequences of the high level of racial violence experienced by black people are marked. In 1981 the Home Office calculated roughly and in a manner likely to underestimate the reality of racial violence — that West Indians were 36 times more likely to be the victims of an interracial attack than were whites and that Asians were 50 times more likely to be victims. The lack of police protection has been so marked that the Policy Studies

Institute has calculated that to get the true figure, these rates would have to be multiplied by a factor of 10.[28] Under such conditions, where, for example, sections of the black community are living under siege conditions (as is the case for Bangladeshis in London's East End) and the rest of the black community never knows when it will be attacked, the stress caused by this terrorism is enormous. The implications for the mental as well as the physical health of black people are severe and reinforce the related strains of coping with life in a racist society.

In the case of mental health and mental illness we come up against not only the illness-causing forces of a racist society but the racism within the particular institutions of that society under consideration, in this case the health service itself. In a study of Mental Health Services in London, the GLC Health Panel has identified a number of trends that are indicative of this problem. Among them are the following:[29]

- Black people are more likely to be mental patients than whites.
- Black patients are four times more likely than white patients to reach a mental hospital through the involvement of the police; twice as likely to have been sent to hospital from prison; and twice as likely to be detained in hospital under the mental health legislation.
- Black mental patients are more likely to be diagnosed as schizophrenic — and twice as likely as white British patients to have their diagnosis changed during treatment. At the same time depression is more likely to be missed in black than in white patients.
- There is a greater reliance on physical treatment — major tranquillisers and electro-convulsive treatment (ECT) for black patients; while scarce psychotherapy resources are more likely to go to white patients.

These patterns are the result of the operations of a racist system. Black patients are diagnosed, or misdiagnosed, by professionals who may not speak their language, who may not understand or value their culture, who may not understand the reality of racism and its consequences, and who are overwhelmingly white males from middle- and upper-class backgrounds. The recent increase in the proportion of women in medical schools has not redressed the class and racial stratification characteristic of the student body, which is still being trained within a scientific and ethnocentric framework. An example of the consequences of such an array of forces was the committal of a Rastafarian prisoner, Steven

Thompson, to Rampton Mental Hospital under Section 72 of the Mental Health Act days before he was due to be released from prison, on the grounds that his belief in the tenets of his religion constituted evidence of mental illness. He was only released three months later after a campaign and a review by an independent group of psychiatrists, one of whom was a West Indian, challenged the original diagnosis.

This ignorance of, and disrespect for, black culture has been present throughout the health service. For example, the campaign against rickets established by the Department of Health and Social Security (DHSS), the Stop Rickets Campaign, has placed its primary emphasis on health education. Rickets, a vitamin D deficiency disease, now affecting primarily Asian children, had previously been so widespread in working-class areas of British cities that in the rest of Europe it was known as the English disease. It is a disease of poverty and was eliminated, not by changing the culture of the working class but by fortifying basic foods such as margarine with vitamin D. Sir Raymond Hoffenberg, after analysing the various explanations for the outbreak of rickets in the Asian community, is clear about the solution: 'the disease may be prevented and cured by supplementing the diet with vitamin D'.[30] The government has refused to follow such advice and to do for the Asian community what it had done for the white working class. Instead, emphasis has been placed on changing the Asian diet, thus transferring responsibility on to the culture of Asians. This approach also has the danger of exposing Asians to the health dangers of changing from a pulse-based, high-fibre diet to a Western high-fat, meat-based diet and thus to a range of diseases such as cancers of the stomach, colon, and rectum.

Distortion of black culture, blaming the culture for medical problems, and placing priority on changing that culture rather than changing the practices of existing institutions have become important characteristics of the operations of medical institutions. The Brent Community Health Council in 1981 published a report entitled *Black People and the Health Service* in which this process is discussed. The authors quote the statement of a group of GPs in Brent that 'the pain threshold for Asians is half that of Caucasians they complain twice as much for half the reasons they come with minor symptoms'.[31] A related 'truth' that medical professionals are being taught about Asian culture is that to justify sympathy and support an Asian who is ill 'should go to bed and stay there until he gets better. It is considered natural for the sick to express anxiety and suffering. Asian patients may cry and moan in a way that upsets the other patients in a British hospital. They are unlikely to realise that they are disturbing other people.' This version of Asian culture is from Alix Henley's Asian Patients in Hospital and at Home,[32] which is widely used in training medical professionals. The Brent Community Health Council rejects this interpretation of Asian culture on the grounds that 'there is absolutely no truth in any of this'.[33] (The author was told by a nurse of a situation she witnessed that illustrates the implications of such views. When she was in hospital having a child, an Asian woman in the next bed was having a very prolonged and obviously very painful labour. Understanding professional etiquette the nurse/patient did not interfere, but after a time she felt that she had to intervene. When she suggested to the ward sister that the doctor should be called she was informed that it was not necessary, because 'these people' have a low pain threshold and cry out disproportionately. The finale of the story was that the Asian woman's baby was born dead. The point is not that there is evidence that earlier medical intervention would necessarily have saved the child, but that such 'truths' about black people's cultural characteristics have profound professional behavioural implications.)

Black people — patients and health workers — have identified a similar disrespect for black culture by white professionals in the areas of family relationships, child-rearing, and birth control. The Brent group found that Asian women who desired the presence of female relatives at the birth of their children and their participation in the rearing of the children came up against disapproval from professionals who presumed that such desires were unhealthy because they differed from current theories about the role of husbands and about mother-child bonding. Health education material addressed to black people has been primarily about diet, antenatal care, and birth control. We have already discussed this professional concern with diet in the context of the Stop Rickets Campaign. The concentration by professionals on educating black women about the necessity of using antenatal provisions assumes that it is the ignorance of these women about such facilities that leads to under-utilisation and that the solution lies in health education.

There are, however, important questions to be raised about the nature of the existing antenatal provisions before we accept such assumptions. It is necessary to note, for example, that white working-class women also have a low utilisation rate of such services. If services are not used or are under-used by both working-class white women and by black women and are most used by white middle-class women, perhaps it is necessary to examine the organisation of the services rather than to assume that the under-users are ignorant. If, for example, Muslim women wish to be examined by a female doctor but the antenatal service provided fails to respect that desire, then we should not be surprised if the take-up level by those women is lower. The question to be asked is why that option is not made available as a right rather than how to change the Muslim women's culture. If interpreters are not routinely made available in antenatal clinics in areas inhabited by women whose first language is not English, then we must question the suitability of the service not the intelligence of the women. If the clinic is located not in the neighbourhood with easy access but in a central hospital some distance from the homes of the women and requires expensive and time-consuming travel, then we should expect lower take-up levels.

Torkington challenges the mainstream professional view and argues that 'In a racist patriarchal society black women are at the bottom of the hierarchical ladder and in consequence among their children there are higher than average rates of mortality and morbidity'.[34] She quotes the study of Oakley and MacFarlane,[35] which shows the limitations of antenatal care in dealing with the problems of low birth-weight children (who in 1977 accounted for two-thirds of perinatal deaths) through dietary advice during pregnancy. The key to reducing perinatal mortality lies in improving the environmental conditions of the mother and the woman's nutrition throughout the whole of her life rather than in a compensatory diet during pregnancy. (The perinatal mortality rate in manual worker families is five times higher than that in professional families.) There is the slight problem, in addition, of how poor women are to afford such a compensatory diet, and black women are disproportionately located in that category. Oakley and MacFarlane also point out that traditional antenatal care is stress producing and may actually be counterproductive for some women since it gives rise to 'precisely those problems it is designed to avoid',[36] and therefore, in this area as in many others, the experience of black women exposes the class as well as the racial and sex biases of the system.

Given the centrality of the numbers game in all discussions of race, the centrality of racism in the government's immigration policies, and constant legitimisation of racism by the actions of the government and the effusions of the media, it is not surprising that more leaflets about birth control are translated into Asian languages than about any other topic. Birth control has been a central theme of health education directed toward both the Afro-Caribbean community and the Asian community. The widespread assumption that the number of black people in the society is a determinant of good race relations and, in Margaret Thatcher's felicitous phrasing, that there is a danger of black people 'swamping' British people (note the exclusion of black people from the category of British), it is not surprising to find this emphasis. The numbers game and the ignorance of black people and their cultures have combined in the use of Depo-Provera (DP), an injectable progesterone-based contraceptive with many unpleasant side effects, in black women. There are great doubts that informed consent has been obtained from the women, and the GLC Health Panel concluded that racism is a fundamental factor in its use:[37]

> There are indications that DP is given primarily to black and working-class women in this country. The panel of experts appointed to hear the evidence for and against the use of DP in this country has admitted that it will be difficult for many women to give informed consent to receiving the drug because of the lack of time available for explanation and counselling by medical and nursing staff, and the lack of training and skills in such counselling among doctors not specialising in family planning. This is particularly worrying for women whose first language is not English and who will be in an extremely disadvantaged position in terms of being fully informed of the side effects of the drug and the lack of data on its long-term safety.

Black women testifying before the GLC Women's Committee clearly stated that there should be 'less attention and pressure on birth control and more attention on services for mothers and babies, on mental health, and on services and policies which support women caring for others in the community'.[38]

The Brent Community Health Council identified the central

themes underlying the white health professional approach to black people:

> What is perhaps most interesting is the similarity between the stereotypes being generated within the health service and those in other parts of the state. In the NHS the mythology is that Afro-Caribbean women are feckless and irresponsible, while Asian women are compliant but stupid. West Indian women are dubbed as having no culture, the problem for Asians is their culture. Either way black people's diets, child rearing practices, family relationships, highly established medical systems are seen as either inadequate or downright harmful. Meanwhile the SUS law has helped create the stereotype of Afro-Caribbeans as reckless, irresponsible and criminal,[39] while the immigration law has encouraged white people to see Asians as law abiding perhaps, but only because they have no legitimate reason for being in Britain in the first place. The similarity between the two sets of stereotypes is not remarkable, but it reminds us just how much what goes on in the health service reflects, is reinforced by and itself reinforces values which serve the interests of the state.[40]

Just as damning and damaging has been the NHS's refusal to respond to the specific health problems of Britain's black population. Sickle cell disease is a common inherited disorder that affects mainly people of African descent. It is estimated that at least 50 babies are born in London every year with the disease and that there are at least 4000 sufferers in Britain yet until recently there were no central guidelines or resources provided by the NHS. In contrast, phenylketonuria with an estimated incidence of about 10-12 cases in London every year is covered by a central new-born screening and follow-up program, and haemophilia with about four to five thousand sufferers in Britain is well provided for by the NHS. The GLC Health Panel concluded about this disparity in NHS response (or lack of response): 'the signal failure by the NHS so far to produce an effective response to the problem which deeply concerns large numbers of black people, can only be attributed to racism'.[41]

Faced by this lack of concern, black communities, assisted by dedicated medical and nursing staff, organised and demanded the establishment of sickle cell screening and counselling services. A number of centres have been created in response to these pressures, five in London and one each in Liverpool and Manchester. Most of these, however, are on short-term funding and have not succeeded in obtaining long-term funds. This creates major difficulties in terms of future planning, long-term development work, and training. The authors of the most comprehensive survey of sickle cell disease and the NHS reported that the only course for sickle cell counsellors (when they published their study in July 1985) was that offered by the Brent Sickle Cell Centre. The Centre had repeatedly failed to obtain recognition, validation, or funding.[42]

Racism has also functioned to use black people as scapegoats for shortcomings in services and provisions available to the white working class. Such shortcomings, whether in housing, education, social benefits, or employment as well as in health, have little to do with black people, who receive even less of the provisions. But the centrality of a racist ideology constantly being legitimated and reinforced by state action makes such claims newsworthy and believable. These claims also lay the groundwork for additional state racism and controls imposed on black people and for continued deterioration of services for the working class as a whole; it is interesting, therefore, to note the use of such tactics in the field of health. The demands for immigration control in the late 1950s and in the early 1960s, i.e., control of black immigrants, used scare tactics concentrating on the supposed dangers of leprosy, tuberculosis, and various 'tropical' diseases being brought in by black people. Black women already in Britain were accused of overloading the NHS maternity services and preventing 'our' women from obtaining maternity beds. The numbers game was thus combined with using black people as scapegoats for shortages in NHS provisions.

Examples of such scapegoating include the declaration by rightwing Labour MP, Harry Hynd, on 3 April 1958, in support of a special motion on immigration, that 'The immigrants [from the Commonwealth] are undoubtedly adding difficulties to our health authorities. When these people arrive in our country, they immediately become eligible for National Assistance. We know the financial difficulties which the Government have had in that connection and it is something which cannot be ignored'.[43] On 29 October 1958, the extreme right-wing Conservative MP, Cyril Osborne, who had been pushing for immigration control of black people since 1950, declared in Parliament that he would deny access on the grounds of ill health, and using what he assumed to be a clinching argument asked, 'What would happen if a shipload of lepers came here from West Africa? Would there be any power to refuse them admission?'[44]

Such stereotypes and antagonism to black people not only contributed to the passage of racist immigration legislation but has also continued to be a determinant of its enforcement. Dr Peter Cooper, head of the health control unit at Terminal Three at Heathrow Airport, expressed similar views in an interview with the medical magazine *Pulse*. The interviewer indicated that Dr Cooper evidenced 'strong feeling beside the calm reasonableness of his views'. Cooper declared: 'The health system is too open to abuse .... A Moslem immigrant might bring in four tubercular wives, eight spastic children and an aged grandmother. Now you tell me' — he goes on aggressively — 'is that right?' One might assume that the possession of such views may have had some effect on his role in the administration of virginity tests on Asians' fiancées. When asked about this barbarous practice he said, it 'makes you think' and 'no comment .... In any case I don't remember anything about it. I've got a shocking memory.'[45]

In the Thatcher years the deterioration of the NHS, despite promises that it would be safe in her hands, has been accompanied by scares of foreigners swamping the service and leaving less for those of us who were entitled to its use. Despite the absence of any evidence of misuse, the DHSS in 1979 issued a circular entitled 'Gatecrashers' to all health authorities in the London area, instructing staff to ensure that only eligible people received service. Within a month there were reports of black people being challenged to prove their eligibility, including a black member of the Commission for Racial Equality. The *Guardian* quoted an administrator at St Stephen's Hospital as saying: 'It is just a matter of common sense, whether we go on their being foreign, or their colour or whatever. All we can do is ask someone politely if they can show their passport and if they do, then this immediately clarifies the matter. It is a practice that is well established, a lot of London hospitals do it'.[46] In 1981, citing 'fairly widespread abuse' but no evidence, the government announced the introduction of charges for certain people from overseas using the NHS, and although it was forced to modify certain features of the scheme, the measure came into operation in October 1982. Organisations ranging from the Commission for Racial Equality (which said that the proposals were 'damaging to race relations and ... inevitably discriminatory') to the Confederation of Health Service Unions, the Trades Union Congress, and the Joint Council for the Welfare of Immigrants condemned the measure as divisive and racist. The measure was clearly going to be directed against black people, would reinforce the view of black people as somehow having less right to be here and use services than the rest of us, and would be another step toward a 'pass law society' for black people.[47]

This state racism legitimated racialist ideas on the streets and in the hospitals. In 1981 when lawyers acting for Ibrahim Khan, who had been thrown out of a window by three youths, wrote to St Mary's Hospital in London to request a letter from the hospital so that a claim for criminal compensation could be made on his behalf, they received the following reply:[48]

> No one here is prepared to write a report for you about this patient ... Mr Khan has been extremely fortunate to receive treatment that exceeds the cost of a heart transplant. There is absolutely no reason why this patient should receive preferential treatment or become a burden on the tax-payers here. I find it immoral to use public money allowing Mr Khan to become a burden on their dwindling resources. Signed: Orthopaedic secretary and over-burdened taxpayer.

The increasingly widespread demand that black people produce their passports to prove eligibility for health care, for the education of their children, for social security benefits, and for housing illustrates the development of the system of internal controls of black people. The hospitals, schools, housing offices, and welfare offices become outposts of the Home Office and adjuncts of the immigration service. These controls are directed at black people, black people as immigrants, black people as suspected illegal immigrants, black people as abusers of Britain's welfare state all views legitimated by racist immigration laws and by the media and politicians. Therefore, if the immigration laws are themselves racist (and the state makes no attempt to deny that fact), then it is logical that black people would be the targets of the extension of immigration controls into the community. Given the need to explain away inadequate services available to the white working class worse housing, worse medical care, lower levels of unemployment benefits and lower pensions than are available in other industrialised countries, and lower wages and higher levels of unemployment the attack on black people as illegal immigrants and abusers of the various services diverts attention from those responsible and from those who benefit from the present system of resource allocation. These attacks and controls make black people less likely to claim benefits to which they are entitled. They may be fearful that if they claim benefits they will get into trouble and be deported, a not imaginary fear given the links between DHSS and the Home Office and the large number of highly publicised cases of deportation proceedings being taken by the Home Office against black people who had gone to DHSS offices to claim benefits. This fear and consequent reluctance to claim in the face of government's implementing racist immigration laws and consciously keeping black families apart is but one part of a process that makes black people second-class claimants in a system that already stigmatises claimants as 'scroungers, spongers and lead swingers'. The social security system denies claimants information and stacks the deck against them by purposely creating excessively complicated claims forms, using different criteria for different benefits and maintaining secrecy and discretion as key characteristics of implementation. It is not surprising, therefore, to find massive underclaiming as the norm in the British welfare system.

In conclusion, to quote again from *The Heart of the Race*:

> The combined effects of racism, discrimination against women workers and the steady loss of health services for working-class people generally have been more apparent to us than to any other group of hospital workers because we have experienced them simultaneously, on all three levels, for some time.[49]

These experiences, described so painfully by the authors and the other black women who contributed to this book, have located black people at the centre of resistance to both the destruction of large parts of the welfare state and the dehumanising practices that have been such a major characteristic of that system. The racist disrespect for black people was built on a system that disrespected women and the working class generally. The hierarchical structures that oppressed lower status workers and distorted the services delivered to all clients disproportionately but not exclusively oppressed black people. The cuts that have already affected the ability of these institutions even to offer the services they had hitherto offered have most affected black people both as workers and clients.

The greater burden borne by black people has had the effect of masking the full scale of what has been happening from the white community. If black people were not really part of 'us' anyway and if they were 'gatecrashing' and 'abusing' the services provided for us, then their exclusion from benefits or services was only right and proper and did not have anything to do with us. If jobs had to be lost, surely 'our people' had the right to the remaining jobs. If the old, decrepit hospitals that got older and more decrepit, and subsequently had to be closed, were in inner city areas largely populated by black people and by the white poor, who would notice or care? Privatisation would save money and was therefore necessary, and anyway, who were disproportionately working in the hospital laundries and kitchens? If costs had to be cut in the provision of nursing services and by the worsening of career prospects and job satisfaction, the worst consequences could be hidden by the use of agency nurses, and who were disproportionately on the agency books?

In each case the working class as a whole, and women in particular, as workers and clients have suffered, are suffering, and unless these policies are reversed, will suffer the consequences of these so-called radical reforms in the welfare state. In each case black workers and black women in particular have paid an even higher price. In each case black people as a whole have been the most aware and the most militant in their resistance, as consumers and as workers. Their resistance in the 1972 ancillary workers' strikes and in the long and bitter health workers' struggles of 1982-3 has been central in the development of a new consciousness among health workers, including nurses. The organisation of the health service, the nature of services provided, and the need to take militant action to resist cuts and to improve services have been placed firmly on the agenda.

Black people as clients in the welfare system have struggled against the racist ideology and practices that have taken their children into care and into white foster homes. It was their resistance that forced adoption agencies and social service departments to recognise the need for black children to have an authentic and appropriate environment in which to grow and mature. It is their resistance that is forcing many social workers to reconsider their assumptions about the black family. Perhaps those professionals who are forced to question their previous 'common sense' and professionally legitimated assumptions about black people and their culture might understand the necessity to re-evaluate their class- and sex-biased assumptions. It is clear that without such black struggles, such revaluation is highly unlikely.

7 The Political Economy of White Racism in Great Britain

The plight of the white working class throughout the world today is directly traceable to Negro slavery in America, on which modern commerce and industry was founded, and which persisted to threaten free labour until it was partially overthrown in 1863. The resulting colour caste founded and retained by capitalism was adopted, forwarded and approved by white labour, and resulted in subordination of coloured labour to white profits the world over. Thus the majority of the world's labourers, by the insistence of white labour, became the basis of a system of industry which ruined democracy and showed its perfect fruit in World War and Depression.[1]

Racism has blighted the lives of millions of people of colour all over the world and has functioned to maintain class-stratified societies. Racism has been contested for its entire history. Whites and people of colour, as both individuals and groups, have resisted the imposition of racist ideology and the racialised organisation of society. Given the continued influence of racism, it is important to understand the conditions within which some whites have opted for a more inclusive definition of 'us'.

In this chapter I shall trace the development of white racism accompanying, and engendered by, the development of the British capitalist system during the eighteenth and nineteenth centuries. I will analyse the institutionalisation of racism in British society, particularly against people of colour, and the implications of that institutionalisation — for the distortion and limitation of working-class consciousness and organisation. I will also review the contemporary position of the British working class, the crisis in the capitalist system, and British workers' abilities to challenge the destruction of much of the social wage and welfare state protections they had previously extracted from the state and capital. The paper concludes with a discussion on the resistance to such racism and the need to construct alternative visions and practices.

Slavery, Early Capitalism and the Origins of Racism

Plantation economies based on slavery in the New World underwrote the development of manufacturing in Britain in the eighteenth and nineteenth centuries. Triangular trade between Africa, the West Indies and Britain's North American colonies, and Great Britain was a stimulus for British manufacturers and for economic development in the British settler colonies of North America. Africans were bought in exchange for British manufactured goods. Those slaves who survived the middle passage in British ships had to be clothed and fed by British firms. The crops that Africans produced on the plantations provided both the raw materials for industry and capital for investment in new plant and equipment in other words, providing crucial funding for the industrial revolution.[2]

The importance of the slave trade can be gauged by the following quote from a Liverpudlian authority writing in 1797:

> This great annual return of wealth may be said to pervade the whole town, increasing the fortunes of the principal adventurers, and contributing to the support of the majority of the inhabitants; almost every man in Liverpool is a merchant, and he who cannot send a bale will send a bandbox. It will therefore create little astonishment that the attractive African meteor has from time to time so dazzled their ideas that almost every order of people is interested in a Guinea cargo.[3]

Professor H. Merrivale delivered a series of lectures in 1840 at Oxford on the theme 'Colonisation and Colonies' and asked:

> What raised Liverpool and Manchester from provincial towns to gigantic cities? What maintains now heir ever active industry and their rapid accumulation of wealth? .... Their present opulence is as really wing to the toil and suffering of the Negro as if his hands had excavated their docks and fabricated heir steam engines.[4]

These material acts were reflected in the ideological sphere and produced the ideological contradictions inherent in an economic system based on human slavery. In the first instance, this dependence on slavery posed a moral question. Equiano, an ex-slave and one of the leaders of the anti-slavery movement in eighteenth-century Britain, posed the problem as follows: 'Can any man be a Christian who asserts that one part of the human race were ordained to be in perpetual bondage to another?'[5] Interestingly enough, on the other side of the English Channel the French philosopher Montesquieu articulated the problem in similar terms when he wrote: 'It is impossible for us to suppose these creatures to be men because, allowing them to be men, a suspicion would follow that we ourselves are not Christians'.[6] Thus, British society was being faced with a moral and political challenge. To continue on the path of economic development based upon the enslavement and dehumanisation of people of African descent and become progressively dehumanised and desensitised in the process, or build an alternative society based on an inclusive definition of humanity. The choice, of course, would have fundamental consequences not only for Africa and Africans, but for the indigenous population of Britain itself in terms of the reproduction of class inequality and the development of associated ideologies justifying such inequalities in terms similar to the permanent inferiority's of the poor.

The triumph of capitalism as the dominant economic system was accompanied, and validated, by the triumph of classical liberalism as the dominant political ideology. Both systems of thought emphasised the individual as the key actor with the fundamental value of private property being seen as central to the political and economic systems. Individual transactions in the free market were seen as the basis of economic activity and social progress; each individual was 'free' to sell her or his labour to any would-be purchaser. People were to be 'freed' from feudal ties to the land and, of course, landowners would be 'free' to displace labour no longer required to maximise profitable use of the land as a commodity.

Individual freedom and equality, however, had to be constrained in terms of political power and responsibility because of the need to protect private property as the core value of liberalism. Therefore, the political system constructed to provide representation and to hold the executive accountable had to be based upon property — that is, only those with property could be trusted to participate in their own governance. Thus, there were fundamental class contradictions in this new political economic system. There were even greater racialised contradictions in building a new social system theoretically dedicated to individual equality and freedom on the backs of slaves. One crucial solution to the latter contradiction, which also functioned to mask the former, was the adoption of a racist ideology of white supremacy.

This rationalisation was very similar to that adopted earlier by the British *vis-à-vis* the Irish Catholics. Irish land and freedom had been stolen by England, and justified by defining the victims of these processes as apelike, less than human, and savage.[7] Moreover, there was also an ideological congruity between stereotypes of the British white working class who were exploited in the mills, mines and factories, and the slaves. For example, it was argued that the white poor were lazy, lived from hand to mouth, and seldom thought of the future, and that poverty was the necessary goad to their participation in the labour market. Therefore, the argument went, increasing their pay and removing the threat of hunger would only make things worse for them and for society as a whole.

The fact that there was this congruity in the ideology was, however, not the whole story. There was also the racist ideology which posited the particular inferiority of the Irish and of the peoples of the conquered periphery. The white and English poor were encouraged to adopt racism in order to have a feeling of superiority over another group of people in a hierarchical society. But, the property-owning minority in a liberal democracy no matter how limited the democracy cannot rely solely upon assertions of class superiority and authority to rule the propertyless majority. Because the latter are seen as a potential threat to order and property and, in fact, periodically rise up in riots or other disturbances; the ruling forces must find ways of dividing the majority. Indeed this was the tactic employed by Great Britain as a means of ruling the Empire. But it was no less necessary or effective in ruling the metropole.

It is important at this juncture to point out that the construction of a racialised identity as an essential part of the divide and conquer strategy did not reflect a natural racism of the white, British working class. Indeed, the history of class struggle in Britain is the history of attempts by major sections of the working class to develop its own consciousness and development of class consciousness among nineteenth-century workers, John Foster found that militants in Oldham Lancashire, were very conscious of the need for solidarity with the Irish working class:

> In 1834, a mass meeting demanded the elimination of wage differentials and the levelling up of labourers' pay. The year before there had been a call for an end to coercion in Ireland and throughout the period a predominantly English population was willing to accept Irishmen among its leaders. The very fact of class formation meant that the controlling spell of the ruling-class had been broken, and with it the subgroup system by which people accommodated 'unfairness'.[8]

The defeat of Chartists and other reform movements weakened the ability of working-class individuals to construct their own, more inclusive identities and weakened their confidence in alternatives to the 'subgroup system.' As Foster noted,

> ... In the 1850s ... there was a rapid expansion of Orange Lodges; in 1861 serious Anglo-Irish riots; and from then on mass politics in Oldham largely hinged on the existence of two racial communities.[9]

But, within a decade, it became clear that many state policies underpinned a racist ideology which was being constructed to limit the consequences of the dislocations, tensions and conflicts which accompanied the rise of the new order. For instance, the state implemented policies in Britain physically to separate the Irish and the English working class, and ideologically to separate the white European working class from the people of colour in the periphery. As we shall see in the next section the development of racialised identities was actively pursued by state officials, particularly, but not exclusively, in the educational arena.

Racism in the Post-Slavery Period

> ... I wonder the working people are to quiet under taunts and insults offered to them. Have they no Spartacus among them to lead a revolt of the slave class against their political tormentors?[10]

> ... it was 'our ignorance of society and of government our prejudices, our disunion and distrust' which was one of the biggest obstacles to the dissolution of the 'unholy compact of despotism'.[11]

Prejudices, disunion, and distrust were all characteristics of the response of the majority of the working class in Britain to the triumph of capitalism. This response involved the acceptance of the hierarchy, and the placement of oneself and one's group into hierarchies based on skill, job status, ethnicity, gender, and race. These divisions were further reinforced by the distribution of material resources. State action directly and indirectly maintained this social order which made possible the continued functioning of the system to control the production and distribution of the material resources. Politics based on an inclusive class consciousness had to confront these ideological and material forces. It is not surprising, therefore, that alternative political projects typically failed.

Prior to World War I, Britain was the world's leading manufacturing, trading and investing nation.[12] While Britain led the world in colonisation, foreign trade, manufacturing, railroads and shipbuilding, many scholars have identified several problems inherent in British imperialist policies due to the burden of the costs of maintaining the Empire, the falling rates of profit abroad, and the fact that 'The British as a whole ... did not benefit economically from the Empire ... [while] individual investors did.'[13]

Moreover, in late nineteenth-century Britain, 40 per cent of the population were living in poverty. Two-thirds of those in poverty were likely to be reduced to abject pauperism at some point in their lives.[14] Less than 11 per cent of the manual labour class led what could be called comfortable lives. At the other end of the spectrum, only six per cent of the population left any property worth mention, with only four per cent leaving more than 300 pounds. The social consequences were grave. Eleven- to twelve-year-old boys from private schools were, on average, five inches taller than boys from industrial schools. Teenage boys from private schools averaged a three-inch height advantage over the sons of artisans. During the Boer War, three out of every five Manchester volunteers were turned down as medically unfit. Of all the young men called up for military service in Britain in 1917, 10 per cent were rejected as unfit, 41.5 per cent had 'marked disabilities', and 22 per cent had 'partial disabilities'.[15]

While organisations such as the International Working Man's Association, founded by British, French and German workers in London in 1864, attempted to offer an alternative vision of the nature of the working class and of society, the British working class did not want to accept these social conditions. However, there was occasional support for colonised peoples in some part of Great Britain. For example, Lancashire textile workers supported the anti-slavery struggle in the United States and the Union in the US Civil War.[16] Irish employees of Scotland Yard helped Indian nationalists smuggle their political literature into England. But the British working class remained oblivious to the plight of the workers in the periphery.[17]

This indifference, or ignorance, was not only found among the working class of Britain. This racism served not only to reinforce the *class hierarchy* at home, but also the *racial hierarchy* at home and abroad. It became an element of the dominant culture of Britain in part through conscious efforts by the state to keep the have-nots in a constant state of repression. Horn has noted that, 'As early as 1878, Her Majesty's Inspectors of Schools were directed by the Education Department to encourage the study of "the Colonial and Foreign Possessions of the British Crown" ... '[18] Furthermore, in the Code of 1890, the 'acquisition and growth of the colonies and foreign possessions of Great Britain' was to be part of the history syllabus. The purpose of such an educational system was clearly articulated by Edmund Holmes in 1899. Holmes, later to be chief inspector for elementary schools, stressed that even the village school had an imperial role to play. 'Its business is to turn out youthful citizens rather than hedgers and ditchers; ... preparing children for the battle of life ... which will be fought in all parts of the British Empire.'[19] Historian J.A. Mangan has observed that,

> A major purpose of this education was to inculcate in the children of the British Empire appropriate attitudes of dominance and deference. There was an education in imperial schools to shape the ruled into patterns of proper subservience and 'legitimate' inferiority, and one ... to develop in the rulers convictions about the certain benevolence and 'legitimate' superiority of their rule.[20]

In 1911, one pioneer of the 'Empire Day'[21] movement, the Twelfth Earl of Meath wrote:

> In former ages the burdens of Empire or of the State fell on the shoulders of a few; now the humblest child to be found on the benches of a primary school will in a few years be called on to

influence the destinies not only of fifty-four millions of white, but of three hundred and fifty millions of coloured men and women, his fellow subjects, scattered throughout the five continents of the worlds.[22]

Another example of how imperialist ideology became accepted as common sense is Roberts' recollection of the educational system in early twentieth-century Salford. He noted that pupils gazed

> with pride as they were told that 'This, and this, and this' belonged to Britain. It was difficult to see what the 'underclass' gained from the Empire, but once instructed they remained staunchly patriotic. 'They didn't know,' it was said, 'whether trade was good for the Empire, or the Empire was good for trade, but they knew the Empire was theirs and they were going to support it.'[23]

Imperialist culture was reproduced in newspapers, music halls, juvenile fiction, and melodrama. MacKenzie identified the move from class to racial tensions in melodrama during the nineteenth-century as follows:

> Some plays from the early nineteenth century did display class tensions. By the end of the century such class antagonism had disappeared from melodrama. By then imperial subjects offered a perfect opportunity to externalise the villain, who increasingly became the corrupt rajah, the ludicrous Chinese or Japanese nobleman, the barbarous 'fuzzy-wuzzy' or black, facing a cross-class brotherhood of heroism, British officer and ranker together. Thus imperialism was depicted as a great struggle with dark and evil forces, in which white heroes and heroines could triumph over black barbarism, and the moral stereotyping of melodrama was given a powerful racial twist.[24]

> Thus, the acceptance of the inevitability of hierarchy by most of the working class weakened their ability to resist the ideological and cultural hegemony of the ruling class. The inability of the British working class and its allies to create alternatives was a major factor in the continued domination of the working class. As Karl Marx indicated in his letter to Engels about anti-Irish racism,

The antagonism is artificially kept alive and intensified by the press, the pulpit, the comic papers, in short by all the means at the disposal of the ruling classes. This antagonism is the secret of the impotence of the English working class despite their organisation.

It is the secret by which the capitalist class maintains its power. And that class is fully aware of it.[25]

Racism in Modern Britain

Britain acquired a black population not out of spirit of highmindedness nor in a fit of absence of mind as some liberals have argued, but because of the need for cheap labour.[26] Black workers were first brought to Britain during World War I. In 1919, several riots were reported in centres of black population, such as Liverpool and Cardiff. Faced with demobilisation and job insecurity, white seamen responded with vicious attacks against non-whites.[27] In South Shields, attacks on Arab workers were encouraged by the leadership of the National Union of Seamen.[28] Overall, there was a rise of support for fascism and racism. For instance, MP David Logan asked in the House of Commons:

> Is it a nice sight, as I walked through the south end of the city of Liverpool to find a black settlement, a black body of men I am not saying a word about their colour all doing well, and a white body of men who face the horrors of war walking the streets unemployed? .... To see Chinamen ... in the affluence that men of sea are able to get by constant employment while Britishers are going to public assistance committee?[29]

The British Government responded to these events by institutionalising racism. The major instrument of British policy aimed at the black population was the Alien's Restriction Order (Coloured Seamen) of 1925. As Neil Evans has put it:

> This was a solution very much in the imperial tradition of legislation which was racist in intent but not in the letter .... There was no formal challenge to the right of imperial subjects to enter the motherland. That would have been too embarrassing in the wider world and fired a thousand empire nationalists. Instead, coloured sailors were required to have an identity card with a thumb print (because they all looked the same!) in order to go about their business.[30]

The turning point for Britain's becoming a multiracial society, however, occurred in the 1950s. Between the end of World War II and 1957, there was a high demand for cheap labour to rebuild the economy, to staff the public service, and to cheapen indigenous labour. The British state responded to these demands by allowing over 350,000 Europeans into Britain under a variety of programmes. Since this move was insufficient to meet labour requirements, Britain then turned to the colonies which had a surplus of labour, and blacks were recruited into British industries as cheap labour.

Immigrants typically did the jobs that indigenous workers were unwilling to take. For example, the textile industry in Lancashire introduced new technology which required the continuous operation of a night shift. Even the weak unions in this industry would not accept capital's demand that there be no night-shift differential for white male workers. Women were 'protected' by law from working the night shift. The union leaders and rank and file, however, were ready to agree to a solution which satisfied almost everyone. Asian male workers were hired to work a permanent night shift at single rates of pay. Other jobs performed by blacks had similar wage differentials. Immigrant workers from India were recruited into the foundries of the West Midlands. These cases exemplify the role that immigrant workers were expected to play namely, occupying the dirtiest, lowest paid, lowest status and most dangerous jobs — a pattern found still to be prevalent in the 1990s by the Policy Studies Institute.[31]

During this period, Afro-Caribbean and Asian migrants entered a racist political culture where the white working class had largely accepted the dominant racist ideology. It was this acceptance which helped maintain the context within which these people were treated as cheap labour. There was, obviously, nothing inherent in them which made them cheap. It was the unwillingness of white-dominated institutions, even those supposedly serving the interests of the working class, (e.g., the Labour Party), to challenge structural and ideological racism which channelled Afro-Caribbean and Asian migrants into these disadvantageous positions. However, this acceptance was not irrevocable. While British political leaders found the British public insufficiently racist,[32] it was the leadership of the Labour Government after 1945 which acted on the basis of their own racist attitudes to create the post-war racist ideological and structural context.[33] There were other voices in the Labour Party and the wider labour movement. For example, Fenner

Brockway, MP, combined opposition to colonialism with opposition to racism within Britain and introduced a number of private member's bills throughout the 1950s to outlaw racial discrimination.[34] Tom Driberg, MP, who had opposed the colour bar associated with US forces in Britain during World War II raised, as Chairman of the Labour Party in 1961, a crucial question in a speech to the Trades Union Congress:

> People talk about a colour problem arising in Britain. How can there be a colour problem here? Even after all the immigration of the past few years, there are only 190,000 coloured people in our population of over 50 million that is, only four out of every 1,000. The real problem is not black skins, but white prejudice.[35]

Although the system of welfare capitalism constructed after World War II was a major reform of capitalism, it did not mark the shift of all power to the working class. Despite overall improvements in the health and education of the working class, class inequality remained.[36] But, as social conditions deteriorated, the racial scapegoating took on a turn for the worst. Many racist politicians used immigrants as scapegoats for the social problems facing the country. Blacks were blamed for housing shortages, for the failure of the educational system to provide high quality education for white working-class children, and for shortages in health care provision.[37] This racial scapegoating legitimised, and was legitimised by, a series of racist immigration laws that emerged in the 1960s and 1970s. One such law was the 1962 Conservative Government's Commonwealth Immigration Act which marked the institutionalisation of racism and the transition in labour recruitment from those with no citizenship rights to contract workers to those who did hold such rights.

Following the 1964 general election won by the Labour Party, the Labour Government's 1965 Immigration White Paper established a quota of 7,500 for the New Commonwealth and 1,000 for Malta, and abolished the 'C' entry voucher for unskilled workers without a specific job. The 1968 Kenya Asians Act abolished the right of entry for non-white holders of British passports. The Conservative Government's 1971 Immigration Act ended the right of entry for non-white Commonwealth citizens as primary immigrants. As a result, many families were kept apart, and attempts at reuniting family members were portrayed as an invasion into

Britain by a flood of illegal immigrants. Women and children were subjected to indignities, humiliations and doses of radiation.[38] These laws exemplify how institutional racism underpinned and legitimated popular racism by strengthening the racist belief that immigrants were the sole cause of existing social problems in the country.

Racist scapegoating has always served to reinforce the operation of a system based on the reproduction of class inequality. Since racism can be utilised to provide the means for business together with conservative politicians to bring about the restructuring of the relationship between capital, labour, and the state, the race card was introduced to ensure sufficient support for destroying the old social contract from sections of society whose interests would be harmed by the restructuring. This political manipulation was facilitated and maintained by the vigorous and vicious racism of the British press.[39]

The Race Card and the Triumph of Thatcherism: Racism, Politics and the Media

Margaret Thatcher first played the race card in 1978 during her infamous 'swamping' speech in which she declared that the British people had a legitimate fear of being swamped by people of an 'alien culture'.[40] Playing the race card was an effective strategy primarily because year in and year out there was a constant reiteration of an appeal to Britain's identity as a white, civilised European country with a history of bringing civilisation to the backward peoples of the world, whose identity was being threatened by floods of violent, criminal and culturally inassimilable *immigrants, refugees, bogus asylum-seekers*, and *alien wedges*.[41]

The *Daily Mail* published a three-part series in October 1991 on 'The Invasion of Europe' with headlines such as: 'Out of Africa onto our Doorstep', 'Swamped ... by the New Underclass', and 'Dark Shadows over the New Germany'.[42] The author of the articles wrote that the invaders represented a 'tidal wave' of immigrants who came armed not with weapons of war, but with passports and tourist visas, and sought to remain by 'utterly fraudulent' claims for asylum.[43] The *Daily Star*, a tabloid, ran a campaign in 1991 to 'halt the influx of foreigners who end up living off the state'.[44] The writers claimed to have uncovered illegal immigration rackets and falsely charged that a family of nine arriving from Bangladesh only knew one word in English, 'House', which they repeated 'parrot-style' until they were given a 'rent-free council flat'.[45]

Having produced what writer and educator Chris Searle calls, 'Your Daily Dose of Racism',[46] the media was then able to tie these doses directly to support for the Conservative Party during elections. In 1992, for example, the *Daily Express* produced nine articles during a three-week campaign, warning of the threat of Britain being swamped by undesirables, i.e., nonwhites.[47] A taste of these stories can be obtained from the following sample: 'Let Bogus Migrants Stay' (election day, 9 April 1992); 'Baker's Migrant Flood Warning' (7 April 1992, front page); 'Open Door to Chaos' (2 April 1992); 'Fake Immigrants: An Explosive Problem' (2 April 1992).

Among the five stories published in the *Daily Mail* during the campaign dealing with immigration was the only story targeting the Liberal Democrats for failing to protect (white) Britain from mass immigration of nonwhites — 'Paddy Puts Out the Welcome Mat for 4m from Hong Kong'.[48] Additionally, the *Daily Mail* used the image of black criminality and violence to delegitimate Labour: 'Race and the Rapist: Cultural Differences are Behind Some Sex Attacks, says Expert'.[49] On 7 April a story was published entitled, 'Rapist "Boasted of Taking Revenge on White People"'.[50]

The ending of primary black immigration did not, as its proponents asserted, lead to the end of the immigration issue in British politics and the production of good race relations. In fact, immigrants were continuously portrayed as outsiders who did not belong in Britain. Right-wing politicians continued to raise the spectre of 'swamping' and the replacement of church bells with calls to worship at the mosque. In 1993, right-wing Tory MP Winston Churchill asserted,

> We must call a halt to the relentless flow of immigrants to this country, especially from the Indian subcontinent .... The population of many of our northern cities is now well over 50 per cent immigrant, and Moslems claim there are now more than two million of their co-religionists in Britain .... With this government continuing to bring in immigrants each year at a scale, in Mrs Thatcher's immortal phrase of 15 years ago 'equivalent to a town the size of Grantham' a halt must

be called — and urgently — if the British way of life is to be preserved.[51]

Right-wing newspapers, columnists, and politicians played the 'race card' to its fullest. Writing in the newspaper of 'Little England', *Daily Mail*, right-wing columnist, Paul Johnson described what he perceived to be the problem as follows:

> The smouldering anger among the British people reflects the fact that they believe they have been lied to twice. The first time was when a flood of Commonwealth immigrants arrived without anyone asking the British electorate if they were welcome. Within a generation, fundamental changes had taken place in the composition of the nation and we had become a multi-cultural, multi-racial society without any of us being given the smallest choice in the matter.[52]

The 'Triumph of Thatcherism' — greatly influenced by the race card played by British politicians as well as the media — has had some significant impact on the social and economic climate of the country. It has meant a fall in real wages, massive cuts in the social wage, and increasing insecurity for workers. These depressed social and economic conditions have created a situation ripe for racial violence.[53] In 1981, the Home Office calculated that West Indians and Asians were 36 and 50 times more likely to be the victims of a racial attack than were whites, respectively.[54] The Policy Studies Institute has calculated that the incidence of racial harassment was probably ten times that estimated in the 1981 Home Office survey.[55] The Institute study also found that of those who had experienced racial harassment, 60 per cent had not reported these cases to the police.

In 1984, the Greater London Council concluded that 'racial harassment in London is an increasingly serious problem'.[56] A poll commissioned by London Weekend Television's London Programme in 1985 found that one in four Asians in the Boroughs of Redbridge, Waltham Forest, Tower Hamlets and Newham had been attacked due to their ethnicity.[57] A report commissioned jointly by the Sheffield City Council and the Commission for Racial Equality concluded that, 'No black person, male or female, young or old, from any ethnic group, is safe from harassment and violence'.[58] A survey by the Leeds Community Relations Council found 305 cases of harassment over an 18-month period in a population of about 4,000 which suggested a level ten times that estimated by the 1981 Home Office survey.[59] A 1986 survey found that one in four of Newham's black and ethnic minority residents were victims of racial harassment in the 12 months prior to the survey, and that two out of every three victims had been victimised on more than one occasion. Interestingly enough, only one in 20 of the 1,550 incidents recorded by the survey had been reported to the police. Eight per cent of the black and ethnic minority victims reported being dissatisfied with the way in which the police handled their case. Indeed, the Scottish Ethnic Minorities Research Unit of Glasgow has found that in 1987, 44 per cent of racial incidents were not reported to the police.[60]

The European Parliament's Committee of Inquiry into Racism and Xenophobia indicted Britain for its 'intolerably high level of racial harassment and violence', and estimated that there was a racist attack every 26 minutes in Britain.[61] A special report in the *Guardian* documented the massive rise in racial attacks in Britain, which the *Guardian* saw as more widespread than in Germany. In 1992, eight people were killed as a result of racist attacks and Home Office figures indicated that there were nearly 9,000 racial attacks in 1993 alone.[62]

The Government has been faced with the reality that the situation may be even worse than is estimated. Peter Lloyd, Minister of State in the Home Office, told the Home Affairs Select Committee of the House of Commons in July that racial attacks could be as much as 20 times the reported level.[63] Although the British Crime Survey reported 7,793 attacks a year, nearly double the 1988 figure, the true figure has been estimated to be as high as 140,000.[64] The level of racial violence in Britain during the last decade has been the worst in the European community. The reported deaths of at least 17 people in racist attacks in 1993 and 1994, and the high rates of racial violence and harassment in Britain are indications of the effects of popular racism fostered by the activities of the state and the media.

Unfortunately, the Conservative Government, suffering the worst public opinion standing in decades, has begun once again to play the race card. Michael Howard, the Home Secretary, announced in 1995 that the government was considering legislation to 'crack down on illegal immigrants'.[65] The proposed measures would further restrict the rights of asylum-seekers following the passage and implementation of restrictive legislation in 1993.[66] A report in the *Guardian* reported the Home Secretary's decision in the following terms:

> Mr Howard's decision to prepare legislation to be published this summer and introduced this autumn indicates that the government sees a need to placate the demands from the Tory right for further tough action. Immigration welfare groups have voiced concern that Ministers were prepared to play the 'race card' in an attempt to reverse the spiralling decline in party fortunes.[67]

According to the *Financial Times,*

> A vision of a UK swamped by immigrants was revived by a Department of the Environment report on Monday. It forecasts a net inflow of 50,000 people a year for the next two decades, whereas a 1991 report had predicted no net immigration. Indeed, for the year to June 1993, the last period for which figures were available, there was an outflow of 11,000 people and tougher checks and the unreliability of figures may mean that the projected flood of migrants few of them the 'benefit tourists' or low-skilled workers of Mr Wardle's vision could never materialise. If they do not, the forecast of 4.4m new households in England over the next 20 years an increase of nearly a quarter begins to sound dubious too.[68]

> The Home Secretary's proposals of further restrictions on the rights of asylum-seekers and those of Peter Lilley, the Secretary of State for Social Security, to deny social security benefits to those who have applied for political asylum after entering Britain or who are waiting for their appeals to be heard, have been seen as blatantly playing the race card in anticipation of the next general election. This tactic has been so obvious that *The Times* has condemned the proposals by stating that,

> The covert racism in these proposals must be apparent to Conservative Central Office; otherwise it could surely not have felt the need to prepare the defensive guidance notes to Tory MPs which were leaked this week. These are ugly cards for ministers to be playing and will be seen as such by a majority of the British public.[69]

The combination of racist state policies legitimating popular racism and the destruction of working class jobs have created a collapse of hope and a sense of community in Britain's cities. This process has been exacerbated by the failure of the Labour Party and trade unions to defend these communities. The racism of the white working class has left the immigrant community susceptible to the appeals of the far-right racist and fascist movements.[70] The Labour Party had not only passed two of the four key restrictive, racist immigration laws of the 1960s, but had failed to challenge the increasing stereotyping of blacks and other ethnic groups as criminals and illegal immigrants whose sole purpose is to live off the welfare system.

The playing of the race card by politicians and the press continues to encourage popular racist attitudes. An ICM poll conducted for the *Guardian* in March 1995 found that 79 per cent of white Britons polled think there is prejudice towards black people, defined as those whose families originally came from the West Indies or Africa.[71]

Conclusion

In sum, this paper has traced the development of the dominant racist ideology and of current state policy which have defined blacks and other migrants as outsiders. These factors have been of central importance historically in preventing the development of an inclusive working-class consciousness and of an inclusive working-class politics. Thus, although the British working class had been able to obtain concessions from the state and capital, particularly following the shift in the moral imperative resulting from the coalition politics of fighting the good war — World War II — its ability to gain power or to defend those concessions was weakened by its acceptance of the dominant racist ideology. This weakness has both facilitated the electoral victory of Margaret Thatcher and maintained social order as Thatcherism fundamentally restructured the British social and economic systems. The triumph of Thatcherism has meant the cheapening of labour, massive cuts in the social wage and increasing labour flexibility namely, increasing insecurity, stress and dislocation. The challenge that the capital and its political allies face in liberal democracies such as Britain is how to obtain the acquiescence of the majority of the population whose interests are being sacrificed as the price of this restructuring. Racism has played a central role in ensuring the necessary divisions and hatreds and fears among the majority to ensure the support on racial grounds of a significant enough portion of the white working class.[72] Thus, despite massively increased economic insecurity, large sections of the white working class voted for Thatcher and continued to buy into the racist scapegoating which she and her colleagues had provided. There was no massive increase in class mobilisation during this period.

The increasing inequality in income and wealth, which characterised the years of Conservative rule from 1979 to 1997, was accompanied by cuts in the welfare-support systems leading to greater insecurity for the majority of society dependent upon collective provision for health, education and support for the elderly or for periods of unemployment. The inability of the political and economic systems to meet the needs of the bottom 30 per cent of the population and the increasing insecurity of the next 30 per cent of the population create a real challenge for progressive antiracist forces. The willingness of the state and capital to buy acquiescence from the white working class by material concessions has clearly diminished. In the absence of such concessions, those in power are relying ever more centrally upon scapegoating and division. Such is the crisis facing large parts of the displaced and insecure populations that an opportunity is present to challenge the fundamental myths of the system and to expose its class nature and create an alternative, more humane democratic system. But, such an outcome depends largely upon the willingness of the white working class to reject that identity and the limited, illusory privileges based on racism. Failure to develop an inclusive and democratic politics will lead to acceptance of an increasingly polarised, impoverished and imprisoned society with the politics of racism and division establishing the limits of democratic involvement and participation.

8 Racism and Anti-Racism in Western Europe

There is mounting fear for the safety and future of Europe's estimated 15 million people of black, Third World, and peripheral country origin. This fear is based on an increasing level of racial violence and murders in Western Europe and the increasing share of votes received by far-right political parties such as France's Front National and Germany's Republikaner Partei. Fears have also increased due to the increasingly unaccountable and undemocratic nature of decision making with regard to 'racial' populations within what has been called 'Fortress Europe'.

Races do not exist biologically or genetically, but are defined by physical categories and from geographic locations.[1] At different points in European history, groups have been defined in racial terms without having different skin colour. For example, the Irish were defined as a race by the English in the seventeenth century during the conquest of Ireland and displacement of the Irish Catholic peasants from their land.[2] Although skin colour has been used to determine racial hierarchy in white settler societies such as the United States, Australia, and South Africa, racial dominance does not depend on different skin colour. The potential for 'racial' conflict exists among people with few physical distinctions, but who differ in culture, religion, and national origin.

In most European countries, a variety of identifiable groups are defined racially and treated differentially: Polish miners in France and Belgium; recently settled migrant workers from the colonial empires, such as Surinamese and Indonesians in the Netherlands; Afro-Caribbeans and Asians in Great Britain; North Africans and

Africans from sub-Saharan Africa in France; and recently settled migrant workers from peripheral countries, such as Turks in Germany. Then there are settled minority populations like the Roma people in various European countries, as well as various refugees and asylum-seekers.[3] How these groups are defined, what subordinate roles they play in Great Britain, France, Germany, and other Western European countries, and how they are controlled come out of historic racial practices. This process, now under way in Western Europe, is the subject of this chapter.

Race and the European Community

Europe, particularly the countries of the European Community (EC), has been constructing a new European identity while it has been constructing the barriers of Fortress Europe. This new identity is a racialised identity. Europe is being defined in terms of its imperialist past, with its civilising mission in opposition to the Third World and the countries of the periphery, and in terms of Christianity in opposition to Islam. In doing so, Western Europe has excluded what has been called the EC's thirteenth nation, the 15 million or so descendants of other nations.[4] This racist ideological construction has been paralleled by racial discrimination in terms of immigration policy, policing and criminal justice policies, education, and health and housing policies state racism. This is a common, European racism with a common view, which defines all Third World people as immigrants and refugees, and all immigrants and refugees as terrorists and drug-runners, [which] will not be able to tell a citizen from an immigrant or an immigrant from a refugee, let alone one black from another. They all carry their passports on their faces.[5]

It is important to analyse the root causes of these developments and to attempt to identify their ramifications for Europe and its people. It is essential to challenge the media and politicians, who place the responsibility for the rise of racism on the victims of it — migrants, settler workers, asylum-seekers, and refugees. For example, the Conservative government in Britain and most of the British media have blamed the rise of neo-Nazi violence in Germany and the rise of neo-Nazi groups in continental Europe on the invasion of bogus asylum-seekers. In March 1992, Douglas Hurd, the

British Foreign Secretary, linked 'feeble immigration laws' with the rise of Europe's neo-Nazi right and asserted 'There is no sign that the Labour Party understands it [the tenfold increase in asylum applications in the past three years] or can be trusted to deal with it. On past form they will handle it with slogans and ambiguities.'[6]

The debate in Germany over racist violence has been structured by the government as a debate over Germany's constitutional obligation to receive asylum-seekers. There has been an attempt to 'explain' German violence as a result of the economic and social dislocations associated with reunification, particularly unemployment in the former East Germany. The newly unemployed, especially the young, facing the collapse of the old order and lacking the skills, psychological orientation, and competitive values necessary to survive in the new capitalist environment, have turned on guest workers and asylum-seekers as scapegoats. It is their view that these 'foreigners' are getting everything, whereas they, good Germans, are getting nothing. This explanation is not adequate and does not explain the rise of neo-Nazi violence and political activity in the former West Germany, as well as in France, which has not gone through unification.

Roots of the New European Racism

European racism was an integral part of the historical processes of nation- building and economic development, which involved the conquest of large parts of the rest of the world and the construction of a world system based on slavery, plantation production, and superexploitation. Instead of being isolated in the colonies, racism and superexploitation continued after World War II as Europe sought to meet its need for cheap labour.[7] Subsequent changes in European economies decreased the demand for labour-intensive industries. As a result, the demand for cheaper labour increased; this demand could be filled only by marginal, illegal employment in the service sector.[8] Massive deindustrialisation, deskilling, and underemployment of the citizen workforce reduced the demand for higher-priced domestic labour as a whole.[9] As transnational corporations penetrate the Third World, they have taken European jobs with them.[10] Furthermore, social and economic dislocation in the Third World, due to European domination, has generated refugees and asylum-seekers eager to enter the European mother economy.

Racial differences between the European mother country and the external colonies are now used to control and exploit the majority of the population in Western Europe.[11] These differences are internal. The Western European 'common person' is now faced with a decline in the standard of living and more competition for fewer jobs. As in the days when Western Europe held external colonies, those responsible for exploitation are not held accountable. Instead, the crisis is due to the 'racialised' immigrants, refugees, and asylum-seekers.

Popular racism emerges out of and is validated by state racism. In this case, increasing class division and insecurity have led to racist stereotypes and fears. Therefore, 'in our time, the seed-bed of fascism is racism'.[12] This analysis has been supported by the findings of a number of other scholars.[13] Political and media manipulation has fostered and legitimated racialist and xenophobic ideas. The experience of those at the cutting edge, migrants and refugees, provides further validation of this crucial analysis. The Refugee Forum and Migrants Rights Action Network found that,

> it is no coincidence that countries such as Italy which did not experience racial attacks on its North African workers, began to see vicious attacks at the time when its government began imposing immigration restrictions. Unlike wealth, racism does 'trickle down' from the top, and when governments define people as unwelcome and undesirable, their populations follow.[14]

This understanding is central to the development of a strategy to challenge this racism.

The Development of Post-war State Racism

Working-class militancy after World War II created the political environment for welfare capitalism the social wage expanding the state role in providing a safety net. Working-class institutions and social democratic parties failed to build upon that militancy, and the increasing tendency of trade unionists to see themselves as an 'established' middle class led to a weakening of the working class ability to defend its gains. Imperialism and unequal international development provided populations available for recruitment to the metropolis as cheap labour. This labour was cheap not because of anything inherent, but because of the racial and national hierarchies into which it was slotted. Outsiders were brought in to do the menial work of Western society, in the hospitals, hotels, the kitchens, the foundries, on the buses, at building sites, and outside the trade unions. They arrived fully grown, fully educated, ready to work at little cost to the receiving country thus, they represented a form of foreign aid from the periphery to the metropolis.

Immigrants work for less because the historic racist view, reinforced by political parties and trade unions, excludes rather than includes them. As in the United States, European trade unionists assumed that by keeping the 'coloured' out, they were defending higher-income jobs. They were convinced that, because they were white and European, they would never have to step down to the lower-paying, dirty service jobs the class of work beneath them. This was reflected in a variety of ways, including a refusal by the post-World War II British Labour government to confront the racist culture and take measures to incorporate Afro-Caribbeans and Asians into the polity and society. The leaders of the Labour Party acted as if the white working class was naturally racist.[15] Post-war French governments, including Socialist and Communist parties, fought brutal and fundamentally racist colonial wars in Indochina and Algeria to maintain France's position in the world and to continue to validate its civilising mission. These wars reinforced racist assumptions and the presumed link between race and nationality. Other ex-colonial countries such as Belgium and the Netherlands have had similar histories and cultures, which also reinforced nationalist and racist political culture and identity.

Germany's defeat in World War II was not followed by root and branch de-Nazification primarily because of Western Europe's preoccupation with anti-Communism. The determination to leave affairs of state in 'safe' hands was accompanied by a reluctance of those safe hands to confront the ideological bases of Nazism, including its definition of what constitutes Germanness. The consequences of this failure are still playing out in Germany today. German-born children of Turkish settlers are not German citizens, yet so-called ethnic Germans from the former Soviet Union who have never lived in Germany and do not speak German are allowed entry and automatic citizenship on the basis of blood, as institutionalised in Article 116 of the German Constitution.

In the words of Oskar Lafontaine, deputy Social Democrat leader, Germany should, like France and the United Slates, adopt a 'Truly Republican understanding of nationhood', because history has shown that nationalist radicalism flourished where the 'law of blood' ruled. Cornelia Schmalz-Jacobsen, the government-appointed commissioner for foreigners, has declared, 'Nowhere has blood dripped so thickly into law. Many of the problems we have with immigrants today would not have arisen if we had allowed people who have long formed a ... part of our population to become Germans.'

Naturalisation is not granted as a rule. At the moment, only about 1,000 Turks a year manage to get through the immensely complicated process of naturalisation. If automatic citizenship were granted to children of the fourth and fifth generations, 1.5 million foreigners would be living in Germany as citizens with restricted rights. Figures show that 25 per cent of immigrants' children are under 18 years old, and that two-thirds of them were born in Germany, making up what is called 'youth without a German passport'.[16]

Migrants are at the Low End of the Totem Pole

The concentration of migrants/settlers in the worst jobs with the worst working conditions at the lowest pay and status has reinforced the view that immigrants do the jobs that host country workers no longer have to do. The 'native' race is raised in status validating the race/nation hierarchy. Racial ideological stratification is thus reinforced by material stratification. Migrants lack political rights because they are not citizens and thus their social wage is lower than the social wage of indigenous workers. They occupy the worst and most overcrowded housing, pay social security/national insurance taxes, and do not receive commensurate benefits. These workers subsidise the higher social wage of the indigenous workers. They are also more exploitable, lacking citizenship and the protection of working-class organisations. Even where migrants are skilled, or professional, a pecking order exists, with the migrant professionals occupying the lower-status sectors of the professions.

Criminalisation of Migrants

The exclusion of migrants/settlers from the political process has reinforced the processes of marginalisation and criminalisation of these communities by the media and the state. In Britain, Afro-Caribbeans, particularly young Afro-Caribbean males, are criminalised as muggers by the press.[17] An important parallel to these developments can be found in the Netherlands, where in early 1993 the chief police officer in Amsterdam, Eric Nordholt, claimed on a radio program that 'black youth from Surinam, the Antilles and Morocco committed 80 per cent of street crime' and warned of Los Angeles-style riots. However, a city police spokesman admitted that the figure referred only to suspects not those arrested and convicted and that figures for all crimes were not available as 'the police only analysed street crime on the basis of a suspect's racial origin'.[18]

Similar attempts to criminalise migrants have been made by police and politicians in France, Germany, and other EC countries and have served as the basis for legitimating increasingly repressive violations of the legal rights of migrants. In 1986, the senator for internal affairs in West Berlin called refugees 'drug containers'.[19] Linking migrants, refugees, and asylum-seekers with drugs and crime has been central to the rightward march of national politics and to EC-wide controls and restrictions. The TREVI group of interior ministers has as its mission the interdiction of terrorism, radicalism, extremism, violence and immigration.

Responding to the equation of migrants and criminality, Bashy Qureishy of Third World Voice in Denmark said at the Communities of Resistance Conference on 11 November 1989,

> In May 1980 Mrs Thatcher said, 'I did not join Europe to have free movement of terrorists, drug traffickers, animal diseases, rabies, and illegal immigrants.' I for one object to being put in the same class as a disease. At Heathrow, on my way to this conference I was treated as a suspect by racist immigration officers.[20]

The combination of criminalisation; bad housing; the worst jobs; high levels of unemployment; differential, racist education; and a racist criminal justice system has led to a black male imprisonment rate in Britain twice that of white males and a black female imprisonment rate three times that of white women. France, Germany, and other Western European countries have seen similar patterns of criminalisation and stereotyping.

The channelling of young settlers into unemployment or marginal employment has become a feature of Western European life. Although the ghettos that have been created are not so racially monolithic as those in the United States, there has been a pattern of racial concentration in areas of deprivation, poor housing, and lack of amenities. This racial concentration is then turned into a blaming-the-victim syndrome, whereby the residents of these areas, who are confined to them, are blamed for their existence and identified as the outsiders who produce such alien environments.

The European Move to the Right

In France, by the early 1990s, mainstream right-wing politicians had moved so deep into the terrain of the far-right that Jacques Chirac, mayor of Paris and now president elect, spoke of 'a family with a father, three or four wives, 20 children and 50,000 francs in welfare benefits without working'. With these neighbours 'and their noise and smell', French workers 'would go crazy' as a result of 'an overdose of immigration'.[21] In September 1991, former president Valéry Giscard d'Estaing described immigration as an 'invasion' and demanded the end of the automatic right of nationality by birth on French soil.[22] (This would bring France in line with Germany and Britain, which abolished that right in the Thatcher government's 1981 Nationality Act. One of the first acts of the right-wing French government elected in 1993 was to implement d'Estaing's recommendation.) Following these comments, Jean-Marie Le Pen declared that he now considered himself to be the leader of the centre.

This move to the right was in response to the extreme right's use of racist appeals, particularly in the area of immigration control.[23] The need for the centre to move to the right was articulated by Giscard ally and former Interior Minister Michel Poniatowski, who said that unless the right allied with Le Pen, 'France would become an African and socialist boulevard given over to anarchy'.[24] Le Pen welcomed the promise by Prime Minister Edith Cresson to fight illegal immigration with mass expulsion, including the use of charter planes — a position from which she was forced to retreat, after reviving memories of the deportation of 101 Malians on a charter plane in 1986, ordered by Charles Pasqua, right-wing Minister of the Interior.

Efforts to Force Migrants Out

There was a spectacular increase in deportation orders in France under the 1989 Joxe law, which succeeded the 1986 Pasqua laws. In 1989, 9,647 people were issued deportation orders; by 1991, the figure had jumped to 32,673 and the figures for the first quarter of 1992 maintained this increase.[25] The National Association for the Assistance of Foreigners at Frontiers (ANAFE) issued a report criticising the conditions in which refugees and immigration prisoners are kept in detention zones. In July 1992, the French government passed the Quiles law, whereby ports and airports were authorised to set up detention zones. The judicial process for detainees and the violent methods by which people are deported was described as a 'farce'.[26]

The construction of the migrant worker/settler as the outsider both limits migrants' rights during the period in which their labour is required and has laid the groundwork for attacks on them in this period of deindustrialisation, deskilling, and resurgent mass unemployment. The European governments have tried to pressure migrants to 'return' to their homelands without great success. They have even pressured migrants born in Western European countries. Attempts to buy migrants out have failed for three reasons. First, the continuing pattern of uneven economic development means that conditions for returnees in sending countries are still much worse than those in the host countries. Second, the amount of money offered was insufficient to make a fundamental change upon return to the native country. Finally, migrants have formed new social ties in their adopted countries.

All of these measures, including forced repatriation, have been insufficient to remove more than 2 million people. But state racism has been successful in labelling them as people who do not belong and reinforcing their role as lightening rods for fear and hatred, as social and economic problems have increased through no fault of the migrants'.

Ideological Justification of Repression

The ideological justifications for attempts to rid European nations of their now unwanted settlers laid the groundwork for increased racialist feeling and racist violence racism 'trickling down.' As researchers Simpson and Read conclude, there is a 'momentum which seeks to describe Europe's future in terms which are increasingly white, continental and Christian. It is, in essence, the re-creation of Christendom'.[27] In December 1982, an editorial in the *Frankfurter Allgemeine* declared:

> the interchange between Slav, Romanic, Germanic, and other Celtic peoples has become a habit. A tacit 'we-feeling' has arisen in one and the same European culture. But excluded from this are the Turk-peoples, the Palestinians, North Africans and others from totally alien cultures. They, and only they, are the 'foreigner problem' in the Federal Republic.[28]

Rathzel argues that an 'unintended "co-operation"' between left and right has constructed 'a negative image of the migrant'.[29] The liberal and highly respected newspaper *Die Zeit* published an article by the general secretary of the German Red Cross, arguing that non-Central European people should be repatriated to avoid a break in German history. About the same time, the 'Heidelberger Manifesto' was published. The work of a number of professors from different universities, it argues that the 'mixture' of different cultures would be damaging to everybody; all people should live in their own' place. And whereas the public version of their manifesto wrote of different cultures, the private version (leaked to the press) discussed people as biological and cybernetic systems with different traits passed on to subsequent generations through genes and tradition.[30]

On the European Community level, member states have constructed a range of institutions to control immigration refugee/asylum policies in a fashion that denies accountability to the European Parliament and facilitates the construction of Fortress Europe. Among these intergovernmental bodies are the TREVI group of ministers, the Ad Hoc Group on Immigration, and the Schengen Accord, in which participating nations set the agenda for a community-wide system of control. These structures are not subject to democratic controls or accountability by the European parliaments. Tony Bunyan, editor of *Statewatch* in

Britain and keen student of policing in Europe, sees lurking behind these institutions 'the beginnings of another state apparatus, made up of ad hoc and secretive bodies and separate inter-governmental arrangements, which reflects the repressive side of European political development and is largely unaccountable and undemocratic in its workings'. He makes the point that,

> Crucially, [all of these intergovernment arrangements] focus on immigration in terms of a 'law and order' issue and the development of international co-operation on policing. The equation of blacks with crime and drugs and terrorism and all of that with illegal immigration, has spread across Europe so that it now forms a basis for the new European state.[31]

Measures taken by EC countries throughout the 1980s and into the 1990s were designed to stigmatise asylum-seekers as bogus and as economic rather than political refugees. The real goal is to limit the numbers who successfully gain citizenship. In fact, there is little basis in the contemporary world for a differentiation between economic and political refugees.

The Effects of Transnational Economics

A factor that blurs the apparently clear-cut differences between political and economic refugees is also a consequence of the relationship between transnational corporations (TNCs), governments, and local elites. Local elites argue that they must offer attractive conditions for transnational capital to obtain investment, especially because they are in competition with elites from other countries of the periphery for that investment. They therefore offer cheap labour and little regulation or interference with TNC activities. This ultimately places the elites in conflict with their own populations, the majority of whom pay the price of attracting and retaining the TNC investment. Governments in such circumstances have tended to become repressive to maintain order and retain power, and often create or exacerbate ethnic, tribal, or racial differences to divide and rule. People fleeing from massacres and pogroms that have been encouraged or tolerated by governments are fleeing from the consequences of economic penetration, as are unemployed migrants displaced from rural farmland.

Refusal by governments to recognise their involvement in the situation of migrants, refugees, and asylum-seekers is purposeful and designed to limit responsibility and the rights of such people to enter their countries.[32]

Government Policies

An Amnesty International report[33] concludes that Europe's increasingly restrictive approach to asylum-seekers is threatening to undermine universal standards meant to protect people who are fleeing from serious human rights violations and that, too often, would-be asylum-seekers are treated as illegal immigrants. A 1992 study by the Organisation for Economic Co-operation and Development (OECD) concludes that,

> The relatively high refusal rate revealed by a study of claims for asylum in several OECD countries suggests that in 1990 and 1991 claims continued to be motivated by reasons that had nothing to do with the original objectives of the asylum seeking procedure. By and large, in the European OECD countries, applications are scrutinised more briefly and treated more harshly than in the past.[34]

In Germany, a controversial law aimed at speeding up asylum procedures and allowing refugees to be housed in collection camps came into force on 1 July 1992, to deal with the estimated 400,000 asylum-seekers that year. The law concentrates power over asylum-seekers and deportations in the central government and stipulates that applications that are 'obviously unfounded' must be dealt with within six weeks, after which time unsuccessful applicants will be sent back to their homeland. The head of Germany's central office for the recognition of refugees, Norbert Von Niedig, resigned in protest of the new law. He argued that existing legislation could have dealt with the backlog of 300,000 applicants if the central government had provided funding and staff. He said the new law gave the 'false impression' that all future applications would be handled in record time and would create mistaken expectations and fuel anti-foreign sentiment. Governments have committed themselves to a regime of permanent deflation, and consequently mass unemployment. The ideological remnants of the supposed triumph of free market monetarism in countries such as Britain have added to the problem because of low inflation. These economic conditions have political consequences:

> The poor, discontented and marginalised, who are in increasing numbers paying for this, will note the apparent failure of democracy. At best they will become alienated and cynical. But more and more of them are clearly turning to authoritarian and xenophobic ideologies.[35]

Gerald Holtham, then chief economist for Lehman Brothers International, discussed in similar terms the consequences of the Thatcher-Reagan agenda, which,

> cut back access to social security and unemployment benefit, reduce[d] the latter in real terms, bust the unions, [encouraged] private state enterprises to subject their workers to 'market forces,' ma[d]e the workers more insecure and the labour market more competitive. That agenda, or part of it, was followed in most OECD countries.[36]

If immigration had not been racialised and blamed for Europe's declining standard of living, the state and private sector policies responsible for the decline would be apparent. Current levels of unemployment and job flight would not be tolerated.

Trades Unions

Faced with attacks on their living standards and future opportunities, working-class Europeans have searched for support and leadership. Unfortunately, their trade unions and social democratic parties have been unable and/or unwilling to provide that leadership. A loss of militancy and awareness of interest are the outcomes of labour s participation in the welfare capitalism of the post-war period. Higher status for national labour was partly due to widespread acceptance of immigrants as non-union cheap labour. In time, European labour institutions became willing participants in their own demise. The racist compromise also led to the exclusion of the most militant and most class-conscious portions of the working class from positions of leadership within the post-war union organisations.

Migrant workers and settlers could have been valuable members of the union movement. Due to their repression and exclusion from the social benefits of compromise, they were potentially more aware of economic trends and practices that would ultimately lead to the demise of labour in Europe. Instead of being part of labour, participating in its leadership and bringing their perspective to bear, they had to fight against the racist practices of European trade unions as well as state racism.

Use of Race in Politics

Faced with the failure of their union organisations, white European working-class people had to find explanations of and solutions to their dilemma. It is not surprising that right-wing politicians and parties, whether within the mainstream or on the fringe of the political system, have used the race card to divert attention from the capitalist agenda.[37] If blacks, Turks, Algerians, and the like are 'the other', and if they 'the civilised' are being swamped by alien cultures, then it is clear that the others are the cause of problems. Hordes of aliens are trying to take over their living standards and pose a threat.

The growing appeal of far-right racist and fascist parties in Western Europe must be seen in this context. In the French regional elections of March 1992, exit polls indicated that the Front National made strong inroads into the industrial working class. The far-right continued the pattern of winning more votes than either the Socialists or the Communists in the so-called 'red belt' around Paris. The Front's 19 per cent support among workers nationally equalled that of the Socialist Party and the conservative union. The working-class vote amounted to around 28 per cent of the FN's total 13.9 per cent vote, and the FN was able to gain increased support from the people in the 18-25 age range, among whom unemployment stood at 28 per cent.[38] Although the Front National did not win any seats in the 1993 National Assembly elections, and indeed lost the only seat it had held, it gained over 12 per cent of the vote, compared to 9 per cent in 1988, emerging as the third party in many key urban areas.

In the 1992 elections in Berlin, the fascist Republikaner Partei (REP) gained its biggest support in those working-class districts of west Berlin said to be Social Democratic Party strongholds. In elections in April 1992, 13 per cent of the REP votes in Baden Wurttemberg and 7.4 per cent of the neo-Nazi Deutsche

Volksunion (DVU) vote in Schleswig-Holstein were garnered in urban areas. This support was particularly heavy among voters under 30 years of age and industrial workers in the bigger cities, where the fascists exploited resentment against foreigners with claims that 'they are taking jobs from Germans'.[39] The REP, which campaigned on law and order issues, the expulsion of 'foreign criminals', and a reduction in the number of asylum-seekers, increased its share of the vote in local elections in Hesse in March 1993. In Frankfurt, the REP won 10 seats on a 93-seat city council. An opinion poll carried out after these elections and published in *Der Spiegel* found support for the REP running nationwide at 6 per cent — up from 4 per cent before the Hesse elections and 80 per cent of Germans believing that it is 'probable', even 'certain', that the REP would gain seats in the Bundestag in the 1994 national elections.[40] However, the REP vote plummeted to less than 2 per cent.[41]

The French and German political elite have pointed to these outcomes as justifications for 'necessary' and 'pragmatic' responses to public support for increasingly restrictive immigration controls. In May 1993, the German government, with the support of the SPD opposition, pushed through the Bundestag legislation that ended the guaranteed right of all foreigners to seek asylum. The justification, accepted by the leaders of mainstream parties, was that the legislation was needed to preserve social peace in Germany. According to Wolfgang Schauble, parliamentary leader of Chancellor Helmut Kohl's Christian Democratic Union, 'Our citizens are frightened by the unchecked refugee influx .... We owe them a social order that allows Germans and foreigners to live peacefully side by side'.[42]

Restrictions against racialised foreigners were seen as another crucial step toward the construction of Fortress Europe, administered by increasingly unaccountable institutions and defined by increasing control of settlers, migrants, and blacks. The reality of the development of a common European identity an identity based on racism is that such measures leading to a new social order will not allow white Europeans and foreigners to live peacefully side by side. In Britain, the level of racist violence and harassment is much greater in the 1990s than it was in 1962, 1965, 1968, or 1971, when the state made attempts to enable whites and blacks to live peacefully side by side.

Ford[43] estimates that there was a racial attack in Britain every

26 minutes in the early 1990s. Home Office[44] figures for England and Wales for 1992 indicate that there were nearly 9,000 reported racial attacks that year double the number reported five years earlier.[45]

Anti-racist Strategies

Given the specific nature of contemporary European racism, it is clear that an anti-racist policy in Europe must fight for the rights of refugees and asylum-seekers at the same time it is fighting for full democratic rights for settlers. Such a policy must challenge the historical definitions of 'us versus them' rooted in the identities of Western Europeans. European identities are integrally connected with the history of imperialism, the slave trade, colonialism, the ideology of bringing civilisation to other countries. The racist construction of European national identities has accompanied and legitimated the widening class inequalities of the capitalist nations of Western Europe. This racism has also been effective in distorting the class consciousness constructed by the European working class.[46]

But these racist national identities have not been internalised at all times and under all circumstances. Racism is not normal, natural, or biological. It is the product of distortion, and can be overcome by principled struggle. The very fate of Western democracy may rest on the outcome. For just as unauthentic socialist democracies in the East did not last, unauthentic capitalist democracies may fall under the weight of racism.

A principled anti-racist strategy is necessary to challenge the acceptance of the new international order at home and abroad that impoverishes people in and outside metropolitan Western Europe. The domestic policies of corporate capitalists and their political agents are racist, nationalist, and fascist. Settlers, migrants, refugees, and asylum-seekers have been scapegoated by popular racism. Meanwhile, a new and more effective system of profit seeking is being put in place that is producing high unemployment and high insecurity for labour both in and outside Europe. Britain's Campaign Against Racism and Fascism (CARF) argues:

> Unity needs to be worked at. And experience shows that racism can best be challenged by working within the working class on a long-

term basis, over issues of housing, education, employment, low pay, [and] policing football. It is around these issues that, in some areas at least, black and white unity has become a reality. But if we are to enlarge and extend that unity, we must discard old orthodoxy s and see anti-fascism not as a dogma or anti-racism as a cause, but both as being part of a creative socialist process.[47]

From a more comprehensive perspective, it is crucial to challenge the idea that racist violence can be stopped by focusing only on skinheads, neo-Nazis, and other extremists. Europe cannot rely on organising primarily against fascists, because the popular culture of racism, deriving its sustenance and sanction from state racism, provides the seed-bed of fascism. State racism is incorporated into the German Constitution in Article 116; in the increasingly restrictive and undemocratic institutions of Fortress Europe; and in the racialised educational, health, employment, housing, and criminal justice systems of European countries. These institutions shape the lives of the settlers, migrants, and refugees in Western Europe as well as the political awareness and understanding of white working people. Thus,

> the fight against fascism must begin in the fight against racism, in the community, and involve the whole community. Fighting fascism per se will not eliminate racism; but eliminating racism would cut the ground from under fascist feet.[48]

The new struggle must be organised from the bottom up rather than the top down. Organisations that have attempted top-down change, such as the Socialist Party in France, claim to lead the anti-racist struggle, but they have proved unable to organise and represent the settlers and migrants. Top-down organisations have proved unable or unwilling to challenge state racism. As a result, they are unable to stem the tide of popular racism and the rightward shift of European political institutions.

For example, although the FN lost its only seat in the French Parliament in the 1993 elections, the new right-wing government of Edouard Balladur began implementing many of the FN's proposals. On his first day as prime minister, Balladur promised to crack down on 'illegal immigrants' and to change the nationality law to oblige children of migrants to apply for French citizenship, long demanded by the extreme right.

Large and well-attended protest marches may represent for

many an expression of revulsion against neo-Nazi offences, but they are reactive. The agenda has been set by the fascists, and the presence of governmental and political leaders diverts attention from the state racism that underpins popular racism. Micha Brumlik, professor of education in Frankfurt and Heidelberg, has argued that the tens of thousands of Germans who took part in the *Lichterketten*, the recent processions of candle-carrying protesters through the streets of Germany's cities,

> overlooked ... that the heightened risk of other people being persecuted does not stem solely from torches of young arsonists, but from what took place under cold neon light the discussions and suggestions made to change Germany's asylum laws [and] in the searchlights of the border police on the River Oder.[49]

Bottom-up Organising

Examples of organising from the bottom up call be found throughout Europe. In 1991, a group of Leeds United fans decided that they could no longer allow racist and fascist recruiting activities, which had been dominant at Elland Road throughout the 1980s, to continue. They formed Leeds Fans United Against Racism and Fascism and began distributing leaflets discussing their concern about the unacceptable nature of racist behaviour. They feel they have succeeded,

> where other groups like the Anti-Nazi League failed because our campaign is based around football — for fans, by fans .... What we have succeeded in doing is to show ordinary fans of other clubs that racist behaviour can be successfully combated by fans themselves.[50]

In 1992, fans of St Pauli, a German second-division club based in a multiracial area of Hamburg, organised a strong anti-racist, anti-fascist campaign against racism in German football. The symbol of the campaign has been the St Pauli Fans Gegen Rechts (St Pauli Fans Against the Right) stickers, which have appeared all over Europe The campaign made contact with local black communities and paraded massive anti-racist banners on match days.[51]

Anti-racists have participated in campaigns against the deportation of refugees throughout Europe. In Denmark, a group of Palestinians from Lebanon sought sanctuary in a church in

Copenhagen after being served with deportation orders. They were supported by a wide range of Danish people. As a result, the Danish government was forced to allow the Palestinians to stay. Others have supported campaigns initiated by settlers and migrants, such as those in Germany calling for repeal of Article 116, so that people born in Germany can become citizens and long-term residents can have access to citizenship. Gaining citizenship would enable migrants and settlers to struggle more effectively for their democratic rights and to challenge their continuing definition as outsiders. A similar campaign is being waged in Belgium. The key to the participation of anti-racists is that they are prepared to accept the leadership of settlers and migrants rather than continuing the historic pattern of Eurocentric expectations of leadership.

A number of organisations monitor and work against racism in Europe. The Early Years Trainers Anti-Racist Network, Save the Children Fund in Scotland, and the Working Group Against Racism in Children's Resources produce anti-racist resource materials. Among the other organisations that have been monitoring and organising against both racism and fascism are the Campaign Against Racism and Fascism, with its bi-monthly publication *CARF;* the Institute of Race Relations, with its European Race Audit project and journal *Race and Class*; the Runnymede Trust, with *Runnymede Bulletin;* Statewatch, which monitors European developments in its eponymous publication; *Sage Race Relations Abstracts*; *Searchlight*; Refugee Forum and Migrants Action Network; the Anti-Racist Initiative in Berlin; the Churches Committee for Migrants in Europe in Brussels; and the Dutch Federation of Anti-Discrimination Centres.

Conclusion

The economic and political crises facing Western European societies are fundamental and interconnected. The creation and maintenance of mass unemployment and the cuts in the social wage are not only producing despair and hopelessness, they are also producing conditions suitable for the spread of authoritarianism and fascism. They enable mainstream right-wing governments to play the race card for electoral benefit and to divert systematic decisions away from the cause of social misery. The more racial stereotyping and scapegoating are used, the more historically rooted popular racism is validated.

The greater the appeal of fascists and the far-right, the greater the danger that mainstream politicians will move farther to the right to keep up with public support. Right-wing politicians will continue to play the race card, and we may very well see the re-emergence of right-wing, fascist governments in Western Europe such as those that led up to World War II. The other potential is the decreasing ability of the state to provide material benefits to enough sections of the white working class to buy their acquiescence and loyalty.

Increasing inequality and deskilling much of the white working class are necessary to advance transnational capitalism. Politics as usual is proving incapable of maintaining standards of living and has reduced the likelihood of transmitting high standards to the next generation. Conditions for Europe's black and migrant/settler communities continue to worsen. The stage is set for a repeat of Europe's worst hour.

Anti-racist and anti-fascist political education and mobilisation of both European whites and people of colour are desperately needed. A successful struggle depends upon its being inclusive. British miners and their families during the 1984-5 strike learned whose interest the state serves not theirs. A disproportionate share of the support they received came from Britain's black communities. As a result, miners were able to see common interests with blacks. Clearly, there is the potential for other white people to learn from these conditions and reject racism and fascism as part of the common best interest.

The choice facing the people of Western Europe is not one of white, indigenous democracies on one side and racism and authoritarianism for blacks, migrants, and settlers on the other. An inclusive nonracist democracy must be forged that can provide a decent standard of living for all. The alternative is an authoritarian European state. Which outcome will come to pass depends on the ability of the anti-racist movements in Europe to mobilise successfully; to organise from the bottom up; to create a vision of a humane alternative; and to unify black and white, settler, migrant, asylum-seeker, and the native-born.

9 *The Political Economy of White Racism in the United States*

In the fourteen years since the first edition of *Impacts of Racism on White Americans*, there has been a massive increase in racial polarisation in the United States, Britain, and the rest of Europe, both East and West. There has been an increase in racial violence in these areas and increasing scholarly recognition of the centrality of racism in the organisation of modern Western societies.[1] The successful playing of the race card in election after election has been accompanied by a rightward shift of mainstream political parties and a narrowing of the parameters of legitimate political discourse in the United States and Western Europe.[2] This rightward shift in political and governmental action led to an increase in popular racism the racism of common sense. Politicians then used this increase as a justification for further racist state actions, which in turn exacerbated popular racism .... This growth of racism has accompanied, and made politically possible, greater class inequality and a restructuring of the political economies of the advanced capitalist countries at the expense of the working classes. All these events were anticipated in the first edition chapter,[3] and developments in the decade and a half that have passed since 1981 have validated that analysis.

Another tendency that has appeared in the intervening years is an intellectual/ideological distancing of mainstream policy commentators from the analysis that sees the class implications and functions of racism in a global capitalist system. It is the argument of this chapter that the events of the 1980s and 1990s in the United States, Britain, and Europe have validated the analysis of the first edition and made it more necessary than ever for the relationship between racism and capitalism to be put on the political agenda.

The fundamental argument is not only that racism has blighted the lives of tens and hundreds of millions of people of colour all over the world. It has also functioned world-wide to maintain class-stratified societies.[4] However, this racist system has been contested terrain for its entire history. Whites and people of colour as both individuals and groups have resisted the imposition of the racist ideology and the racialised organisation of society.[5] It is important to study that resistance and to understand the conditions within which whites opted for a more inclusive definition of 'us' as opposed to the racially exclusive basis of identification that has been the dominant mode for most of the period under review.

In this chapter I will look at the development of racism during the development of capitalism, paying particular attention to the roles of slavery and imperialism. I will outline the institutionalisation of racism in the early twentieth century and its implications for different races in the metropole, and I will develop this theme in the context of the growth of working-class consciousness and organisation. Finally, I will look at the contemporary position of the working class, the crisis in the capitalist system and its impact on workers in the metropole, and the resistance to that racism and the construction of alternative visions and practices.

Slavery, Early Capitalism and the Origins of Racism

Plantation economies based on slavery in the New World provided for the development of manufacturing in the centre of the world system. The triangular trade was a stimulus for British manufacturers and for economic development in the British settler colonies in North America. It provided both the raw materials for industry and the capital for investment in new plant and equipment in the South and in New England. It was thus crucial politically and economically[6] for the United States as a whole, not merely the Southern slave states. The development of a racialised system of chattel slavery within Britain's North American colonies was a crucial development in the construction of a hegemonic racist ideology. Britain initially used both indentured white labour and black labour, either indentured or semi-enslaved. The need for a system that would meet both the demands for a controllable labour system and the continuing political domination of the large landowners was made apparent by Bacon's Rebellion in Virginia in the mid-seventeenth century. Bacon's Rebellion fundamentally threatened the status quo because it was a joint action by both racial groups. A way had to be found to maintain stability and order, to increase the supply of cheap, controllable plantation labour, and to avoid adding to the future numbers of yeoman farmers contesting for political power with the planter elite. The solution involved the enslavement of black labour and the non-enslavement of white labour. This strategy was bolstered by a series of concessions to white labour, which worked to divide the two groups further. Clearly, if no white could be a slave, and if all slaves were black, the objective conditions for racial separation were well established. This constructed a racial identity for both whites and blacks — an identity of racial superiority for the former, who could never be slaves, and of racial inferiority for the latter, who were racially suited for slavery. Furthermore, laws were passed further providing for white supremacy. For example, it was against the law for a slave not only to raise her/his hand to a master but to any Christian white. Thus, we see yet again the crucial role of state racism constructing and underpinning popular racism by providing material and psychic rewards for accepting a white identity, that is, a racialised identity in opposition to a more inclusive identity.

The political structure created by the Constitutional Convention of 1787 reflected that importance. Slavery was incorporated into the basic structure of the new political system in a number of ways: the slave trade was protected until 1807, slaves were counted as three-fifths of a human being for both taxation and representation, and a fugitive slave provision was incorporated.

The ideology of racism was incredibly effective, even given the costs to the vast majority of the Southern population. So important was this separation of whites from blacks that George Fitzhugh, the slaveholding sociologist, could declare,

> The poor (whites) constitute our militia and our police. They protect men in the possession of property, as in other countries; and they do much more, they secure men in the possession of a kind of property which they could not hold a day but for the supervision and protection of the poor.[7]

Thus, in the United States white supremacy was constructed and reinforced by race-based chattel slavery and a racialised definition of us as opposed to *them*, which was an integral part of racist ideology.[8] This white supremacy was found not only in the slave South but throughout the society. W.E.B. Du Bois argued that even when white workers received a low wage '[they were] compensated in part by a ... public and psychological wage.'[9] It is the argument of this chapter that this compensation has played a central role in the creation of a *white* identity, even among workers, farmers and the poor throughout American history. That identity has retarded the development of an inclusive class identity and has, thus, facilitated the reproduction of class inequality in the United States. David Roediger, who has written perceptively on the construction of *whiteness* has argued that:

> whiteness was a way in which white workers responded to a fear of dependency on wage labor and to the necessities of capitalist work discipline. As the US working class matured, principally in the North, within a slaveholding republic, the heritage of the Revolution made independence a powerful masculine personal ideal. But slave labor and 'hireling' wage labor proliferated in the new nation. One way to make peace with the latter was to differentiate it sharply from the former.

The effective way this was done was through

> the rallying cry of 'free labor'.... At the same time, the white working class, disciplined and made anxious by fear of dependency, began during its formation to construct an image of the black population as 'other' — as embodying the preindustrial, erotic, careless style of life the white worker hated and longed for.[10]

This was underscored by the Naturalization Act of 1790, which established the requirements for citizenship, one of which was the necessity of being white. It was not merely that one had to be white to be an American, but obviously to be white was to be superior. The construction of a white identity provided the basis for incorporation of European immigrants into the society. So the Irish driven out of their own country by the consequences of Anglo-Saxon imperialism arrive in another country largely controlled by Anglo-Saxon elites but are able to avoid permanent suppression and inferiority by virtue of being able to become white rather than remaining Irish and Celtic. Thus, angry Irish miners in Pennsylvania denounced Daniel O'Connell, the Irish Republican leader, for his call for Irish American opposition to slavery. Despite their own exploitation and the attacks on them from nativist forces, they declared that they would never accept blacks as 'brethren', for it was only as whites that they could gain acceptance and opportunity in the United States.

Furthermore, acceptance and opportunity are of crucial importance in the construction of 'whiteness'. Although the Irish suffered discrimination at the hands of the 'white, Anglo-Saxon Protestant' (WASP) elites, they had the basis of gaining acceptance in US society as whites rather than as Catholic Celts.[11] It is also conceptually important in challenging the 'ethno-racial umbrella' thesis advanced by scholars such as Nathan Glazer,[12] with the argument that ethnicity was 'an umbrella term subsuming all racial, religious and nationality groupings' to form a part of a single family of social identities.[13] Cornacchia and Nelson test the validity of this ethno-racial umbrella thesis in contrast with the 'black exceptionalism' thesis and conclude that it is the latter that has greater validity: 'The findings on the black political experience demonstrate that it would be inappropriate to treat racial minorities as merely ethnic groups competing in the interest group arena for entitlements and preferments. The political system was nearly sealed shut to blacks.'[14]

The extension of democracy in the United States, particularly during the Jacksonian era, was an extension of democracy or at least of formal incorporation into the Republic as citizens to white males. The outcome was the creation of a 'Herrenvolk democracy' or, in Roediger's terms, 'Herrenvolk Republicanism.' This incorporation of whites regardless of class played a crucial role in ensuring the triumph of racism throughout the United States, in the free states and in the slave states. Before the Civil War, poor whites and the non-slaveholding yeomanry in the South, free soil farmers in the West, and artisans and the emerging working class immigrant and native in the North were all made citizens in the great white Republic and given an identity that was oppositional to people of colour, slave or free. Not only were whites given a *psychological wage* state racism provided fundamental objective racialised rewards:

They [whites] were given public deference ... because they were white.
They were admitted freely, with all classes of white people, to public
functions [and] public parks .... The police were drawn from their
ranks and the courts, dependent on their votes, treated them with
leniency .... Their votes selected public officials and while this had
small effect upon their economic situation, it had great effect upon
their personal treatment .... White schoolhouses were the best in the
community, and conspicuously placed, and cost anywhere from twice
to ten times colored schools.[15]

To be white was to be a citizen of the Great Republic. To be white
was to be a voter — unheard of for most of the immigrants. The
immigrants could become American by successfully asserting their
whiteness. Their whiteness and their Americanness was validated
when they marched in triumphal parades to vote and then to pic-
nics. Not only were the black slaves excluded from these public
events but in most states of the ante-bellum United States, so were
free blacks. Free blacks could not protect their employment, political or civil rights nor could they protect the rights of their children
to a decent education and to a secure and profitable future in the
American Dream. Nor could they take part in the great frontier
experience, for in most territories on the frontier, free soil meant
free soil for free white men. Not surprisingly, wave after wave of
European immigrants opted for whiteness and free blacks were
impoverished, undereducated and disproportionately imprisoned.

Because 'Herrenvolk Democracy' was not and could not be a
reality in terms of 'Democracy' despite its state constructed and
supported 'Herrenvolk' character, there remained a class tension
within American society. This class tension became central at various points and remained more marginal at others in societal
terms; for some working people it was more central to their identity than for others. The point is that it was part of an ongoing set
of struggles and that the racially defined identity as whites was not
always hegemonic. As Herbert Aptheker, one of the leading anti-
racist scholars in the US since the 1930s, has argued, the rank and
file of the anti-slavery and abolitionist movements among whites
were made up largely of poor people:

The hundreds of thousands of people who signed anti-slavery
petitions were common people, the poor and the working class. The
subscribers to the abolitionist newspapers had to struggle to assemble

their pennies .... It was also common white people who took risks during this period. Those who saved Garrison from lynching were plain and ordinary people.[16]

There were, therefore, white people who acted on the basis of values that were alternative to those based on an identity as whites. The triumph of the white identity, therefore, was not an inevitable consequence of natural or genetic forces but the outcome of unequal struggles. In text we find that opposition to racism could and did go hand in hand in anti-slavery movements in Britain and the United States with attitudes and politics that opposed slavery without rejecting racism. Thus, the outcomes of the struggle against slavery, including the Civil War in the United States did not lead to systems of racial justice or of class equality. For example, the ending of slavery in the British West Indies followed the rise of alternative centres of political/economic power. Fears of successful slave uprisings such as Haiti's, the increasing cost of suppressing such uprisings, and diminishing levels of profit overshadowed the moral crusade that had been waged against the evils of the slave trade and of slavery.

In the United States the Civil War was fought by the leaders of the Union less to free the slaves than to extend the sway of the emergent industrial capitalists and serve the interests of their free soil allies. Emancipation in neither the Caribbean nor the United States required the overthrow of racialist attitudes or of racist structures, despite the commitment of anti-racist whites and free people of colour and slaves struggling for freedom. Thus, slavery died so that capitalism could continue to flourish, and with it racism.

Racism in the Post-slavery Period

Prejudices, disunion, and distrust were all characteristics of the response of the major part of the working class to the triumph of capitalism. This response involved the acceptance of hierarchy itself and the situating of oneself and one's group into hierarchies based on skill, job status, ethnicity, gender, and race. One owed and was owed respect in relation to one's position along these scales. These divisions were reinforced by the distribution of material resources. State action directly and indirectly maintained this invidious social order and made possible the continued functioning of the system to control the production and distribution of the material resources. Politics based on an inclusive class consciousness had to confront and overcome these ideological and material reinforcements, including state repression, and it was not entirely surprising that such politics had an up-hill battle and were successful less frequently than they failed.

The United States

The development of class consciousness among the rapidly growing working class in the post-Civil War United States, was, as in Britain, fundamentally shaped and distorted by racism.[17] There was the presence of freed slaves and of other racially distinct colonised peoples within the metropole itself in large numbers. There was a massive immigration of European workers into the United States. Racism provided the ideological and material framework within which the millions of European immigrants who joined the labour force in the half century between 1865 and 1914 became 'American'. Then they and the indigenous white working class were given a racialised identity (or a racialised working-class identity) as an alternative to a working-class identity and this shaped their responses to being made wage-labourers.

The choice that presented itself throughout this period in US history was between a politics based on an inclusive definition of 'us' and one based on an exclusive racial definition. An inclusive definition and political strategy would have necessitated challenging the racialist ideology that had become a dominant characteristic of American identity in the ante-bellum period.[18] It would have required that workers recognise a common interest and need to cooperate to achieve common objectives. Although this was not the path chosen by most of the white working class and its organisations, there is evidence that there was consideration of such an option and evidence of attempts to develop such a politics. The Address of the National Labor Congress to the Workingmen of the United States in 1867, for example, declared that 'unpalatable as the truth may be to many', Negroes were now in a new position in the United States, and the actions of white working men could 'determine whether the freedman becomes an element of strength or an element of weakness' in the labour movement.

The solidarity option was not chosen. The exclusive racial definition of 'us' was the dominant response. This divisive definition was based both on possession of craft skills and on racial prejudice. As Du Bois put it,

> [the National Labor Union] began to fight for capital and interest and the right of the upper class of labour to share in the exploitation of common labour. The Negro as a common labourer belonged, therefore, not in but beneath the white American labour movement. Craft and race unions spread. The better-paid skilled and intelligent American labour formed itself into closed guilds and, in combination with capitalist guild-masters, extorted fair wages which could be raised by negotiation.[19]

The craft- and race-based unionisation operated to retard the development of mass unionism until the Great Depression. It culminated in the formation of the CIO (Congress of Industrial Organisations) industrial unions of the late 1930s. Exclusiveness ensured the availability of large pools of workers willing to, or having no choice but to strike-break and thus weaken the effectiveness of the craft unions. These factors were reinforced by racial and ethnic divisions in the workplace and in housing, education, and social and political activities. This situation goes a long way toward explaining the present political weakness and lack of class consciousness of the American working class.[20]

Matters were further complicated by white labour being encouraged to feel superior to non-whites and thus become 'white'. Central Pacific Superintendent Charles Crocker, for example, pointed out the benefits to white labour from Chinese immigration:

> I believe that the effect of Chinese labour upon white labour has an elevating instead of degrading tendency. I think that every white man who is intelligent and able to work, who is more than a digger in a ditch ... who has the capacity of being something else, can get to be something else by the presence of Chinese labour more than he could without it .... There is proof of that in the fact that after we got Chinamen to work, we took the more intelligent of the white labourers and made foremen of them. I know of several of them now who never expected, never had a dream that they were going to be anything but shovellers of dirt, hewers of wood and drawers of water, and they are now respectable farmers, owning farms. They got a start by controlling Chinese labour on our railroad.[21]

Not only could white male workers be elevated by the use of Chinese labour, and become 'white' men, so could white women become 'white' women. Takaki quotes an article by Abby Richardson in *Scribner's Monthly* titled 'A Plea for Chinese Labour', in which she argued: 'This is the age when much is expected of woman. She must be the ornament of society as well as the mistress of a well-ordered household.' Thus, 'Chinese labour could become a feature of both the factory and the home'. Tensions of class conflict in white society could be resolved if Chinese migrant labourers became the 'mudsills' of society, white men became 'capitalists', and their wives 'ornaments of society'.[22]

These privileges, or more correctly for many white working-class men and women, these promises of privileges were only part of the process through which racism remained a dominant characteristic of the American ideology. Repression of those who challenged that response of the working class to their designated position in society also existed. There is a long history in the United States of legal and extralegal repression, ranging from the terrorism directed against blacks and their white allies during reconstruction in the post-Civil War South, to the suppression of the Molly McGuires, a militant nineteenth-century working-class organisation, the Industrial Workers of the World (IWW) (the major class-consciousness working-class in the pre-first world war period which was suppressed by the government during the war) to the judicial murders of Sacco and Vanzetti (anarchists convicted and executed for the murder of a payroll guard in what many still regard as a political trial) then the Rosenbergs (the only Americans ever to be executed in peacetime for supposedly supplying atomic secrets to the Soviets) in the twentieth century.

Clearly, the threat posed by class-conscious interracial co-operation was perceived by the ruling class and its agents in control of the state. Repression was accompanied by propaganda campaigns against populist efforts in the last two decades of the nineteenth century. There was a massive campaign appealing to white supremacist attitudes. The spectre of black equality was used to divert the poor whites away from any incipient class consciousness, toward a renewed racial consciousness. For example, the power of racial identity was tested in Lawrence County, Alabama, which represented Alabama's 'strongest and most persistent opposition to the Democratic party' and in which 'Free labour ideology and biracial class politics survived ... because of the efforts of local black and white radical Republicans, who during congressional Reconstruction refused to be intimidated by Ku Klux Klan terror'.[23]

Horton identifies the campaign waged by the local, Democrat newspaper, the *Advertiser*:

> Because the Democratic party was threatened by the possible emergence of a biracial brotherhood of working men ... the *Advertiser* resorted to a campaign of racial hatred that resembled its earlier pronouncements in support of the Klan .... To stir up racial discontent, the *Advertiser* on election day fell back on its tried and tested formula — race-baiting. The front page of the *Advertiser* was filled with reports of assaults by blacks on white women. 'The Negroes ... were getting very troublesome' in Mississippi. 'Several Negro women of Tuscumbia' were reported to 'have addressed a very insulting letter to several respectable white ladies.' Jourd White (the editor) stated that they would 'hug a barrel or look up a rope' as a just reward for the insult. The 'white men of Lawrence County' were urged by white to 'do' their 'duty' to 'protect the white race from this animalism.[24]

Horton concludes that, 'A strong tradition of free labour-oriented biracial politics coupled with worsening agricultural depression during the post-Reconstruction period could not overcome the dominance of racial politics even in a county where a legitimate space had been created for class politics'.[25]

The Southern state governments legitimated the process by establishing the Jim Crow system of *de jure* segregation, that is, of apartheid. The federal government accepted and legitimated the process through a number of Supreme Court decisions culminating in the 1896 *Plessy* v. *Ferguson* decision, which established the 'separate but equal' principle: This decision justified segregation in all aspects of life in the South. The federal government's acceptance of the disenfranchisement of the Southern black population, of the lynch terror that took hundreds of black lives a year, and of the total denial of blacks' citizenship rights were crucial developments. So was Northern capitalist support. This took the form of not recruiting Southern black labour into the growing industrial proletariat and by largely excluding the Northern black population as well. Capitalist reinforcement of racial hatred also meant recruiting blacks solely as strike-breakers. This ensured the maintenance of the controlled labour force necessary for the Southern share crop system that produced the cotton that was still so crucial to the economy of the United States. This also ensured the exclusion of black labour from the national industrial proletariat just like it had been excluded from the previous fundamental determinant of American life, the frontier. Now when blacks entered the labour force, they would be entering turf considered by whites as white.

In addition to the psychological privileges that poor whites obtained from the Jim Crow system (being told that they were superior to all African Americans regardless of their own class position), they received some material privileges. These privileges were unequally distributed within the white working class and were tenuously held. There was the ever-present threat of cheap substitute black labour if whites stepped out of line. The price white labour paid in the South for its superior position included wages significantly lower than those in other regions, lower levels of public services than in other regions, and the contempt of their ruling class 'white allies' who looked upon them in much the same way as they did the blacks. A politics characterised by the absence of issues and the absence of opportunities for poor whites to obtain benefits, even by the standards of the rest of the country, became normal. Poor whites, in effect, gave up their own suffrage through the denial of suffrage to African Americans as part of the price paid to become 'white'.

Faced with the political culture of racism, the white working class failed to create its own culture to challenge the class-based ethos or to defend and maintain the attempts to do so that were made during this period. Thus, the white working class was unable to meet the growing attacks on its interests that the rise of monopoly capital represented. The growing concentration of capital and centralisation of control brought with it increased exploitation of the population by suppressing wages and benefits. It made possible the process of 'de-skilling' and the degradation of labour associated with 'Scientific Management'.[26] The skilled/unskilled hierarchy was reinforced in ethnic and racial terms, and the craft-based unions were unable to defeat the power of the monopoly capitalists and their political allies. Rather than reconsider its basic assumptions, the American Federation of Labor (AFL) became more and more exclusionist as it faced the competition of cheaper labour. This pattern was similar to that which characterised British trade unions in the same period. In 1898 an article in the AFL's official organ, the American *Federationist*, declared that blacks were unfit for union membership because they were 'of abandoned and reckless disposition', lacking 'those peculiarities of temperament such as patriotism, sympathy, sacrifice, etc., which are peculiar to most of the Caucasian race'. The AFL therefore recommended deportation of blacks to Liberia or Cuba. Samuel Gompers, First President of the American Federation of Labor, went further in a speech in 1905 when he declared that 'the Caucasians are not going to let their standard of living be destroyed by negroes, Chinamen, Laps, or any others'.[27]

White opposition to such attitudes came from movements that posited a class, rather than a sectional or racial, analysis of society. The IWW, for example, took a principled inclusive position and was consequently the target of repressive action by state and capital. The threat that such a position would challenge the common-sense popular racism that was being pushed by capital and the state and would offer an alternative identity for the new immigrants to that of 'White American' was a serious one. This elicited a mixture of propaganda and repression, with the additional weight of science thrown in for good measure. As science and technology became more central to the economy, scientists and engineers became more important as authority figures.[28]

For example, the expanding field of psychology became an especially important ally of the capitalists, who in their role as philanthropists provided resources for scientists. Edward Thorndike received $325,000 from the Carnegie Foundation from 1918 to 1934 and was the author of one of the basic textbooks used until the 1950s in major American universities. He and his colleagues, Terman and Goddard, adapted Binet's intelligence test for American use, propagandised the theories of genetically inherited intelligence, and offered scientific 'proof' of the superiority of some races (the Nordic and Teutonic) and the inferiority of others. Coincidentally, the 'inferiors' were not only the victims of the 'white man's burden' overseas, and were the non-white superexploited races within the United States itself; they were also the recent immigrant employees of the philanthropists, such as the Italians, the Poles, the Slavs, and others. Science simply documented that the class hierarchy was as it should be. If the United States were the land of opportunity, those at the top got there because of their intelligence and hard work. Those at the bottom deserved to be there.

The scientifically objective data produced by such experts as Thorndike were used to justify the racist 1921 and 1924 Immigration Acts that kept out further immigrants from Southern and Eastern Europe. The demands for such control on immigration from the AFL and from nativist groups such as the Immigration Restriction League had all failed until after World War I. Why? Although sections of the working class supported such restriction, it was not in response to their wishes that restriction was adopted. World War I had stopped the flow of immigrant workers from Europe. There was a continuing, and indeed increasing, need for workers in the United States, first to supply the British and French war efforts and then its own. This need was met by recruiting black workers from the South. Racialist attitudes and — crucially — the construction of institutional racism by the local state, ensured that there would be antagonism between white workers and their new African-American colleagues. Racist practices ensured that the latter would be concentrated in particular low-level jobs and in particular ghetto residential areas that were then systematically denied the level of public services to which they were entitled. Thus, the labour force would continue to be divided and controllable.[29]

After the war, fear of the spread of Bolshevism made the prospect of recruiting labour from areas contaminated by its virus particularly unsatisfactory. Segregated reserves of black labour in the South made it unnecessary for capitalists and the state to take that risk. The racist culture provided the guarantee that lower levels of white immigrants and the new black industrial proletariat would be divided. The consequences for the white working class of adherence of most of its members to a system in which they were exploited as workers and were recipients of privileges, or the promise of privileges, as whites can be seen in their political weakness, low level of unionisation, high level of economic insecurity, and low level of state benefits. This situation was challenged by large sections of the working class during the Great Depression. How successful that challenge was to be and to what extent white workers would develop a class, rather than a racial, consciousness is the subject of the next section.

Racism, Welfare Capitalism, and the Authoritarian State

The development of welfare capitalism in the aftermath of the Great Depression and World War II has been one of the major developments of the contemporary period. It has been argued that capitalism has thus changed its nature. The state was now the protector of the weak and defenceless, the provider of a safety net to catch those who fell, for whatever reason, and the provider of services on the basis of need rather than the ability to pay. The corporations themselves were seen to have become 'soulful', in Harvard economist Carl Kaysen's felicitous phrase. Power was seen to have become dispersed because of widespread stock ownership, the separation of ownership and control, and the responsiveness of the new managers in the post-industrial society to interests wider than the hitherto exclusive concern for profit maximisation. There were no longer to be struggles over the distribution of scarce sources in an age of plenty and affluence. Class had become an irrelevant concept and, consequently, there was an end to ideology.

During this same period, there had been major changes in race relations. Civil rights legislation, executive action, judicial decisions, and political leadership had all been responsive to liberal ideology and political pressure from the civil rights movement. The state no longer endorsed racism, *de jure* segregation was overturned, and racial minorities could now compete and rise on the basis of their own worth. Although prejudice might still remain as a residual problem, racism was not — and could not be seen as — a structural characteristic of society in the United States.

Given the reality of capital's most recent counterattacks and revocations of most of these concessions over the past decades, it is, perhaps, hard to remember how taken-for-granted such fairy tales were in the dominant ideologies of American society from the end of the Great Depression to the present. The soulful corporation has turned out to be a transnational corporation moving production and jobs around the globe in search of ever-greater profits and using its ability to do so to force its remaining workforce in the metropole to accept an escalating series of 'take-backs' as a condition of being allowed to continue to work. The state has turned out to be more committed to capitalism than to welfare, which is being eroded as a condition of keeping and attracting jobs. The ending of *de jure* segregation did not mean the end of racial polarisation. But these challenges to the dominant ideology have not led to a reconsideration of the ideological assumptions of mainstream commentators. Far from it. It is either the genetic or cultural inferiority of the victims that accounts for continuing and increasing inequality. Indeed, it is the very welfare system itself that created a dependency culture in unemployment, homelessness, drug abuse, and so on.[30] Racism, in both its material and ideological forms, continues to be a central characteristic of American society and has played a crucial role in capital's ability, along with the state's, to overturn what were supposed to have been fundamental changes in the nature of capitalism and in the nature and operations of the liberal democratic state.

The Modern Period

The Great Depression, the New Deal, World War II, and the working-class response to these events played a major role in extracting concessions from capital and in shaping the forms of the state. The federal government came to play the central role in subsidising capital, in ensuring that a favourable investment climate existed within the United States and abroad, and in ensuring order and stability within the United States. Performing these tasks often brought the federal government into conflict with the states and with local authorities and into conflict with the belief in free enterprise, minimal government, and the inferiority of blacks. For example, in order to ensure that black struggles in the post-war period did not continue the link with the Communist Party and with issues of class, it was necessary to combine repression of those wishing to continue that link, W.E. B. Du Bois and Paul Robeson, political activist, actor and singer, for example, with sufficient concessions to ensure the triumph of Americanism, despite racism.

Such concessions required changes in the Jim Crow system of the South. *De jure* segregation was no longer necessary to maintain the Southern system of agriculture, which was being rapidly mechanised, in part supported by the policies of the New Deal. These policies served as a lightning rod for black demands and were a force of instability that the newer power centres in the South associated with industry and commerce and wished to defuse. Racial segregation was a contradiction for the United States in its efforts to shape the world order after World War II, a world in which two-thirds of the people were not white and in which US apartheid was available for the Soviets and other nationalist critics to challenge US claims to moral leadership. Plus, incorporation of African Americans into the formal democracy would channel the African American middle class into the system rather than run the danger of it becoming a counter-elite. This reasoning did not mean that the white leaders of the old order in the South would give up their power and privileges without a struggle. Also, poor whites in the South were not going to give up power either, especially after being assured by word and deed by those with power in the South and in the nation as a whole that they too were superior to blacks because they were white.

The federal government was, therefore, going to be in conflict with rural Southern elites as it attempted to overturn *de jure* segregation, with African Americans taking the lead and being beaten and killed as a necessary part of the campaign. The national administration had, at the same time, to deal with overt racial discrimination in the rest of the country where racial segregation was not legally required. Here, the federal government came into conflict with the principles of private property, which held that individuals could do whatever they wished to with their property, and could hire whom they wished, and rent to whom they wished. The level of struggle by African Americans and the imperatives of running the world required that overt racial discrimination be outlawed.[31]

The desegregation efforts of the federal government did not mean the end of institutional racism or the end of the role of the state in legitimating popular racism. Racism continued to be part of the normal operations of the state at every level. For example, one of the key engines of state intervention in support of the economy in the post-war years was support for suburbanisation, which by 1965 had led to the construction of more than $120 billion worth of owner-occupied housing — 98 per cent of which was owned and occupied by whites. This was the result of official government policies administered through the lending decisions of the Veterans Administration and the Federal Housing Agency. State and local governments made similar decisions that led to the construction of what Arnold Hirsch has called Chicago's Second

Ghetto.[32] The racialised economic consequences of encouraging and financially subsidising white flight to the suburbs included the loss of jobs, tax revenues, and affordable housing in the inner cities — which were becoming more black as African Americans were displaced from Southern sharecropping and came North looking for work. The decisions of the state at every level constructed the increasingly racialised ghettos with their underresourced education and health systems, appalling housing, and high levels of un- and underemployment. The construction of racialised criminal justice systems ensured the lack of police protection and a massively racialised disparity in imprisonment. These realities of state policy have to be set against statements in favour of tolerance and brotherhood and even against assertions of the decline of racism and the presumption that past civil rights legislation have fundamentally eliminated systematic racism in the United States.

Just as there is this contradiction between the ostensible purposes of the state in the field of race, so there is a similar contradiction in the state's relations with the white working class. An essential part of the construction of 'Pax Americana', the period of American economic, military and political hegemony following World War II, was the great or Keynesian accommodation that augmented the new era of welfare capitalism discussed above. Workers in the primary sector of the economy were allowed to enjoy high pay, job security, and a social wage. But the price they had to pay actually undermined their ability to protect these gains. The purge of the Left from the unions associated with the anti-Communist purges and the requirements of the Taft-Hartley Act (the first post-war limitation of the rights of organised labour) was accompanied by the acceptance of the ideology and practice of the Cold War, of anti-Communism, of Military Keynesianism, and by the cessation of serious attempts to unionise the non-union majority of the working class.[33]

The consequences of these concessions have proven devastating over the medium term for those workers who were to be the beneficiaries of this accommodation and devastating for those excluded. The purges of the unions had driven out those militants and activists who had wanted to challenge the structural racism within the workplace and within the unions themselves. It was these workers who wanted to create objective conditions of racial equality. The failure to continue unionising drives, particularly in the South, created a potential region where capital could locate future investment and employ labour with a lower social wage. The lack of unionisation created the basis upon which capital, the state, and the media could scapegoat organised labour as the cause of inflation and other ills of the society. The ensuing weakness of the working class made it even more difficult for members of that class to resist the transmission of the dominant racist ideology of white supremacy. The acceptance of Pax Americana helped capital and the state to define the national interest in terms most favourable to themselves.

This defining of interest included seeing any foreign government on the periphery that attempts to improve the living conditions of its people by taking control of its economy as an enemy of the United States and as part of the 'International Communist Conspiracy' of the 'Evil Empire'. The consequence of such a hegemonic definition of the national interest has been political, military, covert, and economic interventions to overthrow such governments and to put and keep in power regimes that would allow transnational capital a free run in their countries, that would sell their people more cheaply than their neighbours and thus provide opportunities for the export of jobs from the metropole to the periphery.[34] The limitation of private sector unionisation primarily to the major industrial sectors had another consequence the expanding sectors of the economy (service, sales, and clerical) were not unionised and consequently were based on cheap labour. The weakening influence of organised labour, a political system that was coming to be more and more under the control of capital, and no meaningful alternatives offered by the Democratic Party has left large parts of the white working class alienated from the system and from the Democratic Party.

The essence of the Republican strategy since 1964 has been an appeal to the white South and to whites in the rest of the country on the basis that the Democratic Party had been captured by blacks and was no longer the white Man's Party. Race has become the best single predictor of voting behaviour: For example, two thirds of all white voters voted for Reagan in 1984 and 60 per cent voted for Bush in 1988. Manning Marable, the director for the Institute of Research in African-American Studies at Columbia University, has calculated that overall white support in the South for Republican presidential candidates has been 70 per cent and among white evangelical Christians, 80 per cent. 'Since the election of Ronald Reagan in 1980, in presidential contests the Republican Party operates almost like a white united front, dominated by the most racist, reactionary sectors of corporate and finance capital, and the most backward cultural and religious movements.'[35]

Racialised politics has made it possible for capital to use the electoral system to restructure the political economy, as done in Britain under Thatcher and Major, with large portions of those who will pay, and have paid, the highest price. For example, the median family income in the United States in 1993 in real terms was lower than it was in 1973, and it takes more family members working to earn that lower income. De-skilling, deindustrialisation, decertification of trade unions, take-backs by capital from unionised workers, and cuts in the social wage have all been imposed during the decade since the first edition of this volume was published. During this period there has been an ideological assault on state and collective provision; on the supposed 'dependency culture'; and on large sections of the reserve labour force, now called the 'underclass'. The level of state attacks on African American and Latino communities has increased massively during this period, and the level of imprisonment has escalated exponentially with the United States now the most imprisoned nation in the world. The United States is racialised to the extent that an African American male is more likely to be imprisoned than to be in higher education and is five times more likely to be imprisoned than is a black African in South Africa.[36]

The racial and gender divisions of the working class have weakened its ability to resist the dominant racialised and gendered ideology. This lack of working-class consciousness and autonomous culture severely weakens its ability to respond to these attacks on its living standards and hopes for the future. The increasing level of scapegoating of African Americans and women is an indication of the determination of those in power to stay in power and to use the system to their maximum advantage. Their ability to buy acquiescence through material concessions to white working-class men is becoming more and more limited and therefore they are relying more and more on scapegoating and division.

Until the working class creates its own identity and a racially inclusive consciousness and culture, it will continue to be unable to advance its own interests. The European American working class will have to reject the white part of that identity and the illusory privileges based on racism and sexism. The damage done is not only to people of colour: European Americans are damaged as well. The dominant ideology of white racial supremacy has served, and continues to serve, the interests of capital and its political allies. Opposition has come from individuals and groups of whites, African Americans, Latinos, and others. This opposition to a racialised identity illustrates that it is possible to choose an alternative identity to that constructed and transmitted by agents of capital. Thus, it is possible for the individual effort and talent used in everyday struggles to survive and to resist class oppression, to be used to create a just and truly democratic society.

Reference Notes

Introduction

1. W.E.B. Du Bois, *Black Reconstruction in America*, London, Frank Cass, 1966, p.30.
2. J.L. Graves, Jr., 'Evolutionary Biology and Human Variation: Biological Determinism and the Mythology of Race', *Sage Race Relations Abstracts*, vol.18, no.3, 1993, pp.4-34; S. J. Gould, *The Mismeasure of Man*, New York, W.W. Norton, 1981; D. Roediger, *The Wages of Whiteness: Race and the Making of the American Working Class*, London, Verso, 1991; J.H. Stanfield, 'Racism in America and Other Race-Centered Nation-States: Synchronic Considerations', *International Journal of Comparative Sociology*, vol.32, nos3–4, 1991, pp.243–61.
3. M. Hechter, *Internal Colonialism: The Celtic Fringe in Britain's National Development*, London, Routledge & Kegan Paul, 1975.
4. B. Rolston, 'The Training Ground: Ireland, Conquest and Colonisation', *Race and Class*, vol.34, no.3, 1993, p.16.
5. Ibid., pp.16-17.
6. Ibid., p.17; See also M. Rai, 'Columbus in Ireland', *Race and Class*, vol.34, no.3, 1993, pp.25-34.
7. S.J. Smith, 'Race and Racism: Health, Welfare and the Quality of Life', *Urban Geography*, vol.11, no.6, 1990, p.607.
8. R. Bailey, 'The Slavery Trade and the Development of Capitalism in the United States: The Textile Industry in New England', *Social Science History*, vol.14, no.3, 1990, pp.373–414. See also E. Williams, *Capitalism and Slavery*, London, André Deutsch, 1967.
9. Institute of Race Relations, *Patterns of Racism*, London, Institute of Race Relations, 1982, p.26.
10. J. Pope-Hennessy, *Sins of the Fathers: The Atlantic Slave Traders, 1441-1807*, London, Sphere, 1970, p.155.
11. Leo Huberman, *Man's Worldly Goods*, New York and London, Monthly Review Press, 1968, p.167.
12. R. Bailey, 'The Other Side of Slavery: Black Labor, Cotton, and Textile Industrialization in Great Britain and the United States', *Agricultural History*, vol.68, Spring 1994, p.38.
13. J. Walvin, *The Black Presence: A Documentary History of the Negro in England*,

1555-1860, 1971, p.10.

14. P. Fryer, *Staying Power*, London, Pluto Press, 1984, p.109.
15. R. Drinnon, *Facing West*, New York, Schocken, 1980, p.138.
16. M. Marable, *Black American Politics*, London, Verso, 1985, p.141.
17. A. Briggs, 'The Language of "Class" in Early Nineteenth-Century England', in M.W. Flinn and T.C. Smout, eds, *Essays in Social History*, Oxford, Clarendon Press, 1974, p.177
18. Ibid.
19. A. Smedley, *Race in North America: Origin and Evolution of a World View*, Boulder, Westview, 1993.
20. J.H. Stanfield, op.cit., pp.246, 247.
21. M. Davis, *City of Quartz*, New York, Vintage, 1992; K.B. Hadjor, *Another America: The Politics of Race and Blame*, Boston, South End Press, 1995; A. Hirsch, *The Making of the Second Ghetto: Race and Housing in Chicago*, Cambridge and New York, Cambridge University Press, 1983; D. Massey and N. Denton, *American Apartheid: Segregation and the Making of the Underclass*, Cambridge, MA, Harvard University Press, 1993.
22. Hadjor, op.cit., p.38.
23. Ibid., p.39.
24. Ibid.
25. Massey and Denton, op.cit., p.57.
26. Hirsch, op.cit. pp.252–4.
27. Hadjor, 1995, op.cit., p.44.
28. See Lucy A. Williams, 'The Right's Attack on Aid to Families with Dependent Children', *The Public Eye*, vol.10, nos 3–4, Fall/Winter 1996, pp.1-18.
29. J. Krieger, *Reagan, Thatcher and the Politics of Decline*, Cambridge, Polity Press, 1986.
30. See *Race and Class*, "Europe: Variations on a Theme of Racism", vol.32, no.3, January-March 1991 (Special Issue).
31. P. Horton, 'Testing the Limits of Class Politics in Postbellum Alabama: Agrarian Radicalism in Lawrence County', *The Journal of Southern History*, vol.57, no.1, 1991, p.77.
32. A. Lansley, 'Accentuate the Negative to Win Again' *Observer Review*, 3 September 1995, p.4.
33. K. Eichenwald, 'Texaco Executives on Tape, Discussed Impeding a Bias Suit', *New York Times*, 4 November 1996, pp. A1, C4.
34. D. Kairys, 'Unexplainable on Grounds Other Than Race', *The American University Law Review*, vol.45, no.3, February 1996, p.737.
35. Ibid., p.748.
36. A. Sivanandan, Editorial, *Race and Class*, 'Europe: Variations on a Theme of Racism', vol.32, no.3, January-March 1991, p.v [Special Issue].
37. S. Allen and M. Macey, 'Race and Ethnicity in the European Context', *British Journal of Sociology*, vol.41, no.3, September 1990, p.378.
38. Refugee Forum and Migrant Rights Action Network, *The Walls of the Fortress: European Agreement Against Immigrants, Migrants and Refugees*, London, Refugee Forum, 1991, p.16; see also A. Simpson and M. Read, *Against a Rising Tide: Racism, Europe and 1992*, Nottingham, Spokesman for Nottingham Racial Equality Council and European Labour Forum, 1991.
39. A.D. Smith, 'Racist Party Wins Over the Workers', the *Observer*, 3 November 1996, p.21.
40. Du Bois, op.cit., p.30.
41. H. Aptheker, 'Anti-Racism in the US: An Introduction', *Sage Race Relations Abstracts*, vol.12, no.4, November 1987, pp.3*f*32.
42. James Jennings, 'Puerto Ricans and the Community Control Movement in New

York City's Lower East Side: An Interview with Luis Fuentes', *Sage Race Relations Abstracts*, vol.21, no.1, February 1996, p.28.

43. Quoted in A. Duval-Smith, 'Race Bias Back in US Schools', *Guardian*, 9 April 1997, p.7.
44. J. Kozol, *Savage Inequalities*, New York, Crown Publishers, 1991.
45. R. Herrnstein and C. Murray, *The Bell Curve: Intelligence and Class Structure in American Life*, New York, Free Press, 1994.
46. J.L. Graves, Jr. and T. Place, 'Race and IQ Revisited: Figures Never Lie, but Often Liars Figure', *Sage Race Relations Abstracts*, vol.20, no.2, May 1995, p.43.
47. See V. Polakow, 'The Shredded Net: The End of Welfare as We Knew It' *Sage Race Relations Abstracts*, vol.22, no.3, August 1997.
48. This article has been cited in the following publications: H.H. Fairchild and M.B. Tucker, 'Black Residential Mobility: Trends and Characteristics', *Journal of Social Issues*, vol.38, no.3, 1982, pp.51–74; J. Williams, 'Redefining Institutional Racism', *Ethnic and Racial Studies*, vol.8, no.3, 1985, pp.323–48; J. Gabe, 'Explaining Race: Education', *British Journal of Sociology of Education*, vol.12, no.3, 1991, pp.347–80.
49. K.B. Hadjor, 'Race, Riots and Clouds of Ideological Smoke', *Race and Class*, vol.38, no.4, April-June 1997, p.30.
50. This article has been cited by M. Ellison, 'David Duke and the Race for the Governor's Mansion', *Race and Class*, vol.33, no. 2, 1991, pp.71–9.
51. This article has been cited in the following publications: S.J. Smith, op.cit., pp.606–16; W.I.U. Ahmad, 'Reflections on the Consanguinity and Birth Outcome Debate', *Journal of Public Health Medicine*, vol.16, no.4, 1994, pp.423–8; C. Smaje, 'The Ethnic Patterning of Health: New Directions for Theory and Research', *Sociology of Health and Illness*, vol.18, no.2, 1996, pp.139–57.
52. Commission for Racial Equality, *Appointing NHS Consultants and Senior Registrars: Report of a Formal Investigation*, London, CRE, 1996, p.13.
53. S. Beishon, S. Virdee and A. Hagell, *Nursing in a Multi-Ethnic NHS*, London, Policy Studies Institute, 1995.
54. MSF, *The Ethnic Status of NHS Staff: Damning New Statistics*, London, MSF, 1997, p.1.
55. Ibid, p.2.
56. E.J. Cornacchia, D.C. Nelson, 'Historical Differences in the Political Experiences of American Blacks and White Ethnics: Revisiting an Unresolved Controversy', *Ethnic and Racial Studies*, vol.15, no.1, 1992, pp.102–24. See also P. Horton op.cit., pp.63–84; J.H. Stanfield, op.cit., pp.243–61.
57. M. Marable, 'Race and Class in the US Presidential Election', *Race and Class*, vol.34, no.3, 1993, pp.75–85.

1 Race, Class and Power
The New York Decentralisation Controversy

This chapter first appeared in the *Journal of American Studies*, 32 (2), 191–219, 1969, published by Cambridge University Press. I wish to thank the University of Manchester for the travel grant which made this research possible.

1. David Rogers, *110 Livingston Street: Politics and Bureaucracy in the New York School System*, New York, Random House, 1968, p.83.
2. Wallace Roberts quoted in 'The Battle for Urban Schools', *Saturday Review*, no.16, 1968, p.97.
3. Quoted in Mario Fantini and Richard Magat, 'Decentralizing Urban School Systems' in *The Schoolhouse in the City*, ed. Alvin Toffler, New York, Frederick A. Praeger, 1968, pp.134-5.
4. Rogers, op.cit., p.473.

5. 'For example, 39 of the 106 projects in the board's 1964-1965 building program were for local school areas where it was estimated that 90% or more of the pupils would be Negro and Puerto Rican', ibid., p.18. See also p.70.
6. Ibid., pp.63–4.
7. Ibid., p.306.
8. Ibid., p.309.
9. Cf. Kenneth Clark, *Dark Ghetto*, New York, Harper and Row, ch.6, pp.120–5.
10. *New York Times*, 13 August 1967, about release of Co-operative Research Project no.3237 of the US Office of Education's series entitled *Investigations of Fiscally Independent and Dependent School Districts*.
11. Rogers, op.cit., p.269.
12. Interview with the Rev. C.H. Oliver, 21 May 1968, in London. Cf. also Lillian S. Calhoun, 'New York: Schools and Power — Whose?', *Integrated Education*, 8, no.1, January-February 1969, p.18.
13. Ibid., p.23.
14. *Reconnection for Learning — A Community School System for New York City*, New York, Panel on Decentralization, 9 November 1967.
15. NY Civil Liberties Union, 'The Burden of Blame: A Report on the Ocean Hill-Brownsville School Controversy', New York, 9 October 1968, mimeo., p.1.
16. 'UFT Statement on Decentralization', New York, United Federation of Teachers, 10 January 1968, mimeo.
17. Edmund W. Gordon, 'Decentralization and Educational Reform', *IRCD Bulletin*, vol.4, no.5; vol.5, no.1, November 1968–January 1969, p.3.
18. Robert Rosenthal and Lenore F. Jacobson, 'Teacher Expectations for the Disadvantaged', *Scientific American*, 218, no.4, April 1968, p.19. Cf. also their book *Pygmalion in the Classroom*, New York, Holt Rinehart and Winston, 1968. Cf. also Clark, op.cit., pp.125–53, and Estelle Fuchs, 'How Teachers Learn to Help Children Fail', *Transaction*, 5, no.9, September 1968, pp.45–53.
19. Calhoun, loc.cit., p.17.
20. Private communication, November 1968.
21. 'Burden of Blame' op.cit., p.6.
22. *An Evaluative Study of the Process of School Decentralization in New York City*, New York, Bank Street College of Education, 30 July, 1968, p.95.
23. Cf. interview with John O'Neill in Fred Ferretti, 'Who's to Blame in the School Strikes', *New York Magazine*, 18 November 1968, pp.34–5.
24. New York Civil Liberties Union, Memorandum to Special Committee on Religious and Racial Prejudice, 26 November 1968, mimeo., pp.2–3.
25. *Daily Telegraph*, 11 March 1969, p.36.
26. Cf. for example, Abraham G. Duker, 'Negroes versus Jews I. Anti-Semitism is Asserted', *Patterns of Prejudice*, 3, no.2 (March-April 1969), pp.9–13. Much of the following discussion is based on the author's 'Negroes versus Jews II. Anti-Semitism is Denied', ibid., pp.13–15.
27. Gary T. Marx, *Protest and Prejudice*, New York, Harper and Row, 1967, p.131.
27. See Lucy A. Williams, 'The Right's Attack on Aid to Families with Dependent Children', *The Public Eye*, vol.10, nos 3–4, Fall/Winter 1996, pp.1–18.
28. Marx, op.cit., pp.138-9.
29. Quoted in Memorandum from Oscar Cohen on 'Negro anti-Semitism and Negro anti-Semites', 23 January 1969, mimeo., p.2.
30. Ibid.
31. Marx, op.cit., p.179.
32. Ibid., p.182.
33. Ibid., p.153 (italics in the original).
34. Ibid., pp.158-9.
35. I.F. Stone, 'The Mason-Dixon Line Moves to New York', *I.F. Stone's Weekly*,

vol.16, no.22, 4 November 1968, p.2.

36. Ibid.

37. George D. Strayer and Louis Yavner, quoted in Rogers, op.cit., p.283. Rogers also quotes Dr Mortimer Kreuter of the Center for Urban Education saying that teachers have become 'infantilised' by a system whose functionaries grade and inspect them much like children. Ibid. He also quotes a school official who said, 'It is known by everyone that headquarters doesn't know what's going on. Information does not get back from the field and people don't even know what policy actually is. They get no help from headquarters, only a mass of paper directives. It is set up like a machine, and the basic set throughout the system is not in any way toward experimenting or even pushing at a rule. A coherent plan has to aim at loosening up the central bureaucracy to begin with, and you have to build in rewards to innovate.' Ibid., pp.279–80.

38. Ferretti, op.cit. pp.34–5.

39. 'Lindsay Back to School Law Despite "Weakening"', *New York Times*, 2 May 1969.

40. Ibid.

41. Interview with the Rev. C.H. Oliver, 21 May 1969 (in London).

42. Letter from David Spencer, 3 January 1969, mimeo.

2 Race, Class and Civil Rights

This chapter was first published in *Exploitation and Exclusion* and is reproduced with permission from Hans Zell Publishers, an imprint of Bowker-Saur, a division of Reed Elsevier (UK) Ltd. I wish to thank the Nuffield Foundation's Small Grants Scheme for the Social Sciences and the University of Manchester Committee on Staff Travel Funds for Research in the Humanities and Social Sciences for their financial assistance. I thank my colleagues at the Institute of Race Relations for their years of education and encouragement and also Benjamin P. Bowser, Pat Kushnick and Jacqueline Ould and the editors of this book for their comments and suggestions.

1. L. Kushnick, 'Racism and Class Consciousness in Modern Capitalism' in B.P. Bowser and R.G. Hunt, eds, *Impacts of Racism on White Americans*, Beverley Hills and London, Sage Publications, 1981, pp.191–216.

2. N. Murray, 'Anti-Racists and Other Demons: The Press and Ideology in Thatcher's Britain', *Race and Class*, vol.27, no.3, Winter 1986, pp.1–20; N. Murray, 'Reporting the Riots', ibid. pp.86–90; C. Searle, 'Your Daily Dose: Racism and the *Sun*', *Race and Class*, vol.29, no.1, Summer 1987, pp.55–72.

3. See, for example, D. Cluster, ed., *They Should Have Served That Cup of Coffee*, Boston, South End Press, 1979; S. Evans, *Personal Politics*, New York, Alfred Knopf, 1979.

4. See A. Alkalimat, et al., *Introduction to Afro-American Studies*, Chicago, Twenty-First Century Books, 1986.

5. R.A. Hill and B. Bair, eds, *Marcus Garvey: Life and Lessons*, Berkeley, University of California Press, 1987; T. Vincent, *Black Power and the Garvey Movement*, Berkeley, Ramparts Press, 1971.

6. M. Marable, *W.E.B. DuBois, Black Radical Democrat*, Boston, Twayne Publishers, 1986, p.171; see also M. Naison, *Communists in Harlem During the Depression*, Urbana, University of Illinois Press, 1983.

7. M. Marable, *Black American Politics*, London, Verso, 1985, pp.172–3.

8. J. Bloom, *Class, Race and the Civil Rights Movement*, Bloomington, Indiana University Press, 1987, p.120.

9. Ibid., p.218.

10. Marable, *Black American Politics*, op.cit., p.193.

11. Ibid., p.140.

12. L. Finkle, 'The Conservative Aims of Militant Rhetoric', *Journal of American History*, vol.60, 1973/4, p.701.
13. Ibid., pp.707–8.
14. Ibid., p.696.
15. G. Myrdal, *An American Dilemma: The Negro Problem and Modern Democracy*, New York, Harper and Row (1944), 1962, p.1004.
16. Ibid.
17. Ibid., pp.1006–7.
18. Ibid., p.1013.
19. Ibid., p.1015.
20. Ibid., p.1016.
21. Ibid., p.1018.
22. Bloom, op.cit., 1987, p.5.
23. Quoted in H. Zinn, *A People's History of the United States*, Harlow, Longman, 1980, p.440.
24. See L.C. Gardner, *Imperial America: American Foreign Policy Since 1898*, New York, Harcourt, Brace Jovanovich, 1976; G. Kolko, *The Politics of War: The World and United States Foreign Policy (1943-1945)*, New York, Vintage Books, 1968; W.A. Williams, *Tragedy of American Diplomacy*, New York, Delta, 1972.
25. G. Horne, *Black and Red: W.E.B. DuBois and the Afro-American Response to the Cold War (1944-1973)*, Albany, SUNY Press, 1986, p.64.
26. Ibid., p.208.
27. See P. Robeson Jr, 'Paul Robeson: Black Warrior', *Freedomways*, vol.11, First Quarter, 1971, pp.24–5 for a discussion of the processes involved in books about the theatre.
28. Ibid., p.23.
29. Horne, op.cit., p.280.
30. Ibid.
31. V.H. Bernstein, 'The Anti-Labor Front', The Antioch Review, vol.3, 1943, pp.337–8.
32. Congressional Record, 66th Congress, 1st Session, vol.58, Part V, 25 August-September 1919, 4303–5. Quoted in W.A. Clark, 'An Analysis of the Relationship Between Anti-Communism and Segregationist Thought in the Deep South (1948-1964)', PhD Thesis, University of North Carolina, Chapel Hill, 1976, p.9.
33. Bernstein, op.cit., p.330
34. *Baytown Employees Federation Bulletin*, nos 72 and 9 respectively, cited in ibid.
35. Clark, op.cit., p.87.
36. D.E. Carleton, *Red Scare: Right-Wing Hysteria and Fifties Fanaticism and their Legacy in Texas*, Austin, Texas Monthly Press, 1985, p.72.
37. L.K. Adler, 'The Red Image', PhD Thesis, University of California, 1970, pp.94–5.
38. Ibid., p.97.
39. See D. Caute, *The Great Fear*, New York, Simon and Schuster, 1978; C. Pomerantz, ed., *A Quarter Century of Un-Americana*, New York, Marzani and Munsell Publishers, 1963.
40. See, for example, R.A. Freeland, *The Truman Doctrine and the Origins of McCarthyism*, New York, Schocken Books, 1971; R. Griffith and A. Theoharis, eds, *The Specter*, New York, New Viewpoints, 1974.
41. Clark, op.cit., 1974.
42. A. Dunbar, *Against the Grain: Southern Radicals and Prophets (1929-1959)*, Charlottesville, University Press of Virginia, 1981, p.256.
43. S. Rosen, 'The CIO Era (1935-55)', in J.W. Jacobson, ed., *The Negro and the American Labor Movement*, Garden City, Anchor Books, 1969, pp.199-200.
44. R.O. Boyer and H.M. Morais, *Labor's Untold Story*, New York, Marzani and Munsell Publishers, 1965, p.361.

45. C.W. Cheng, 'The Cold War: Its Impact on the Black Liberation Struggle Within the United States, Part One', *Freedomways*, vol.13, Winter 1973, p.195.
46. Adler, op.cit., pp.427–8.
47. J.F. MacDonald, *Television and the Red Menace: The Video to Vietnam*, New York, Praeger, 1985, pp.11, 12.
48. C. Carson, *In Struggle: SNCC and the Black Awakening of the 1960s*, Cambridge MA, Harvard University Press, 1981.
49. Quoted in Horne, op.cit., pp.278–9.
50. Marable 1985, op.cit., p.90.
51. Robeson Jr, op.cit., p.28.
52. Quoted in Horne, op.cit., p.184.
53. Marable, 1986, op.cit., pp.184, 188.
54. Ibid., p.198.
55. Ibid.
56. M. Marable, *Race, Reform and Rebellion: The Second Reconstruction in America, 1945-1982*, London, Macmillan, 1983, pp.28–9.
57. H. Darby and M. Rowley, 'King on Vietnam and Beyond', *Phylon*, vol.47, no.1, March 1986, p.49.
58. C.W. Cheng, 'The Cold War: Its Impact on the Black Liberation Struggle Within the United States, Part Two', *Freedomways*, vol.13, Fourth Quarter, 1973, p.288.
59. J. Forman, *The Making of a Black Revolutionary*, New York, Macmillan, 1972, p.382.
60. Ibid., pp.383–4.
61. Marable, 1983, op.cit., p.75.
62. See Carson, op.cit.
63. H.H. Haines, 'Black Radicalization and the Funding of Civil Rights: 1957-1970', *Social Problems*, vol.32, no.1, October 1984, pp.41–2.
64. Quoted in Zinn, op.cit., p.449.
65. Ibid., p.450.
66. Marable, 1985, op.cit., pp.90–1.
67. Ibid. p.92.
68. Ibid.
69. Ibid., p.95.
70. See Chapter 4.
71. Horne, op.cit., p.224.
72. Ibid., p.225.
73. Marable, 1986, op.cit., p.207.
74. D.J. Garrow, *The FBI and Martin Luther King Jr*, Harmondsworth, Penguin Books, 1981, pp.214–15.

3 British Anti-discrimination Legislation

This chapter first appeared in *The Prevention of Racial Discrimination* published by the Institute of Race Relations, 1971, and is based on research made possible by grants from the Nuffield Small Grants Scheme for the Social Sciences and from the University of Manchester. The author wishes to thank them and all those who allowed themselves to be interviewed and consulted.

1. *The Sunday Times*, 28 January 1968. Italics added.
2. *The Times*, 8 April 1969.
3. *Jewish Chronicle*, 16 April 1965.
4. See, for example, *Glasgow Herald*, 8 April 1965; *Birmingham Evening Mail*, 8 April 1965; *Daily Telegraph*, 26 May 1965.
5. House of Commons, vol.711, 3 May 1965, cols 967-8.
6. Ibid., col.1021.

7. House of Commons, vol.711, 3 May 1965, col.990.
8. Ibid., col.928.
9. Ibid., col.929.
10. Ibid., col.948.
11. Ibid., col.950.
12. House of Commons, Sixth Sitting, vol.714, 23 June 1965, col.258.
13. House of Commons, vol.716, 16 July 1965, col.1056.
14. Italics added.
15. In an address by the Home Secretary to the Institute of Race Relations, published in *Race*, vol.VIII, no.3, January 1967, pp.216–21.
16. Race Relations Board, *Report of the Race Relations Board 1966-7*, London, HMSO, 1967, p.13.
17. Italics added.
18. House of Commons, vol.738, no.119, 16 December 1966, col.938.
19. Political and Economic Planning and Research Services Ltd., *Racial Discrimination*, London, PEP, 1967.
20. *The Sunday Times*, 23 April 1967.
21. *The Times*, 10 April 1968.
22. Including *The Times*, 27 July 1967.
23. *Yorkshire Post*, 27 July 1967.
24. Harry Street, Geoffrey Howe and Geoffrey Bindman, *Report on Anti-Discrimination Legislation*, London, Political and Economic Planning, 1967.
25. House of Commons, vol.763, no.102, 23 April 1968, col.62.
26. Street et al., op.cit., p.92.
27. Ibid., p.130.

4 Parameters of British and North American Racism

This chapter first appeared in *Race and Class*, vol.23, nos 2–3, 1981–2, published by the Institute of Race Relations.

1. A. Sivanandan, *Race, Class and the State*, Race and Class pamphlet no.1, London, 1978, reprinted in A. Sivanandan, ed., *A Different Hunger*, London, Pluto Press, 1982, pp.101–252; and *From Immigration Control to Induced Repatriation*, Race and Class pamphlet no.5, London, 1978, reprinted in ibid., pp.131–40.
2. Set up by President Johnson to investigate the riots of 1967.
3. Report of the National Advisory Commission on Civil Disorders, New York, 1968, p.304, hereafter referred to as the Kerner Commission.
4. Brixton Black Women's Group, 'The Brixton Uprising', *Spare Rib*, June 1981. See also, *The Thin End of the Wedge*, *Manchester Law Centre* Handbook no.5, Manchester, 1980; Islington 18 Defence Committee, *Under Heavy Manners: Report of the Labour Movement Inquiry into Police Brutality and the Position of Black Youth in Islington*, London, Islington 18 Defence Committee, 1972; S. Hall, C. Critcher, T. Jefferson, J. Clarke and B. Roberts, *Policing the Crisis: Mugging, the State, Law and Order*, London, Macmillan, 1978.
5. Section 4 has now been repealed after a sustained campaign led by black organisations — but has reappeared, in another guise, in the Criminal Attempts Act.
6. Institute of Race Relations, *Police Against Black People*, Race and Class pamphlet no.6, London, 1979, p.42; see also *The Thin End of the Wedge*, op.cit.
7. Ibid.
8. See A.S. Blumber, 'Court contingencies in the Right to the Assistance of Counsel', in R. Perrucci and M. Pilisuk, *The Triple Revolution Emerging: Social Problems in Depth*, Boston, Little Brown, 1971; J. Baldwin and M. McConville, *Negotiated Justice*, London, Martin Robertson, 1977.
9. Kerner Commission. op.cit., p.337.

232   *Race, Class & Struggle*

10. Ibid., p.340; see also Isaac D. Balbus, *The Dialectics of Legal Repression: Black Rebels before the American Criminal Courts*, New York, Russell Sage Foundation, 1973.
11. *LAG Bulletin, Legal Action* magazine, August 1981.
12. See Mike Phillips, 'Rage that Shattered Thatcher', *New Statesman*, 17 July 1981.
13. Tom Hayden, *Rebellion in Newark*, New York, Vintage Books, 1967, p.53.
14. See Gary Wills, *The Second Civil War: Arming for Armageddon*, New York, New American Library, 1968.
15. 'Toxteth's night of revenge', *The Sunday Times*, 2 August 1981.
16. Quoted in Phillips, op.cit.
17. Harold M. Baron, 'The Web of Urban Racism', in L. Knowles and K. Prewitt, eds, *Institutional Racism in America*, Englewood Cliffs, Prentice Hall, 1969.
18. Annie Stein, 'Strategies for Failure', in *Challenging the Myths: The Schools, the Blacks and the Poor*, Cambridge, Harvard Education Review, 1971, pp.133–4.
19. Malcolm X, *Autobiography of Malcolm X*, New York, Random House, 1964, p.36.
20. See L. Kushnick, 'Race, Class and Power: The New York Decentralization Controversy', *Journal of American Studies*, vol.3, no.2, 1969; chapter 1 in this volume.
21. Bernard Coard, *How the West Indian Child is Made Educationally Sub-normal in the British School System*, London, New Beacon Books, 1971.
22. Committee of Inquiry into the Education of Children from Ethnic Minority Groups, *Interim Report: West Indian Children in our Schools*, London, HMSO, 1981, p.12.
23. Center for Research on Criminal Justice, *The Iron Fist and the Velvet Glove: An Analysis of the US Police Force*, Berkeley, Center for Research on Criminal Justice, 1975, p.7.
24. Ibid., p.30.
25. Since the July uprisings in Britain, the Kerner Commission has been frequently cited politicians and the media as a source of ready-made solutions.
26. Kerner Commission, op.cit., p.336, and see also ch.12.
27. Center for Research on Criminal Justice, op.cit., p.32.
28. Kerner Commission, op.cit., p.315.
29. Ibid., p.318.
30. Pat Bryant, 'Justice vs. the movement', *Radical America*, vol.14, no.6, 1980.
31. Center for Research on Criminal Justice, op.cit., p.58.
32. Robert Allen, *Black Awakening in Capitalist America: An Analytic History*, Garden City, Anchor Books, 1969, pp.144, 147-8; Jon Frappier, 'Chase Goes to Harlem: Financing Black Capitalism', *Monthly Review*, vol.28, no.11, 1977.
33. Sivanandan, op.cit.
34. Daniel Moynihan, *The Negro Family: The Case for National Action*, 1965, in L. Rainwater and W. Yancy eds, *The Moynihan Report and the Politics of Controversy*, Cambridge, MA, and London, MIT Press, 1967.
35. E. Banfield, *The Unheavenly City*, Boston, Little Brown, 1990.
36. 'Will Whitelaw Pick a Dud?', *Daily Telegraph*, 27 July 1981.
37. See Jerry Hirsch, 'To "Unfrock the Charlatans" ', *Sage Race Relations Abstracts*, vol.6, no.2, 1981; Hilary Rose and Steven Rose, 'The IQ Myth', *Race and Class*, vol.XX, no.1, 1978.
38. Moynihan, op.cit.; Banfield, op.cit.; W. Shockley, 'A "Try Simplest Cases": Approach to the Heredity-Poverty-Crime Problem', *Proceedings of the National Academy of Sciences*, vol.57, 1967, pp.1767–74; A.R. Jensen, 'Reducing the Heredity-Environment Uncertainty', *Harvard Education Review*, vol.39, 1969, pp.449–83, R.J. Herrnstein, *I.Q. in the Meritocracy*, Boston, Atlantic/Little Brown, 1973; H.J. Eysenck, *Race, Intelligence and Education*, London, Temple Smith, 1971.

39. See City Bureau of Common Sense, 'Cities in crisis', *Radical Perspectives on the Economic Crisis of Monopoly Capitalism*, New York, Union for Radical Political Economies, 1975, p.158.

40. William Tabb, 'Civil Rights to Date: Now You Lose, Now You Lose', *Social Policy*, vol.10, no.3, 1979, p.48.

41. Ibid.

42. Frappier, op.cit., p.23.

43. Ibid., p.25.

44. See L. Kushnick, 'Racism and Class Consciousness in Modern Capitalism', in B. Bowser and R. Hunt, *The Impact of Racism on White Americans*, Beverley Hills and London, Sage Publications, 1981, pp.191–216

45. 'A Call to Action', *The Times*, 7 August 1981.

46. A. Sivanandan, 'Imperialism in the Silicon Age', London, *Race and Class*, pamphlet no.8, 1980, reprinted in A. Sivanandan, ed., *A Different Hunger*, London, Pluto Press, 1982, pp.143–200.

47. Ibid.

48. See David Edgar's 'Reagan's Hidden Agenda', *Race and Class*, vol.XXII, no.3, 1981, pp.221-38.

49. David Treadwell and Gaylord Shaw, 'Underclass: How One Family Copes', *Los Angeles Times*, 5 July 1981.

50. Ibid., and Richard E. Meyer and Mike Goodman, 'Marauders from Inner City Prey on LA's Suburbs', *Los Angeles Times*, 12 July 1981.

51. Meyer and Goodman, op.cit.

52. Ibid.

5 The United States: The Revocation of Civil Rights

This chapter first appeared in *Race and Class*, vol.32, no.1, 1990, published by the Institute of Race Relations. I would like to thank the Nuffield Foundation's Small Grants Scheme for the Social Sciences and the University of Manchester Committee on Staff Travel Funds for Research in the Humanities and Social Sciences for financial assistance.

1. One of the authors of the Fourteenth Amendment, Representative John A. Bingham, was 'later to admit that he had phrased it "word for word and syllable for syllable" to protect the rights of private property and corporations'. B.B. Ringer, *'We Are the People' and Others*, New York and London, Tavistock Publications, 1983, pp.217-18.

2. E.K. Hunt and H.J. Sherman, *Economics: An Introduction to Traditional and Radical Views*, 2nd edn, New York, Harper and Row, 1975, p.92.

3. A.P. Blaustein and R.L. Zangrando, eds, *Civil Rights and the Black American*, New York, Simon and Schuster, 1968, p.255.

4. Ringer, op.cit., p.220.

5. Ibid., p.221.

6. Ibid., p.223.

7. J.M. MacPherson, *The Negro's Civil War*, New York, Pantheon Books, 1965, p.300.

8. Where it could be shown that a set of employment practices had a differential impact on whites and blacks, the burden was on the employer to prove that these practices were justified on non-racial grounds.

9. See C. Ginsburg, *Race and the Media: The Enduring Life of the Moynihan Report*, New York, Institute for Media Analysis, 1989, pp.31-2.

10. See ibid.; *Education Week*, 30 March 1988; J. Kreiger, *Reagan, Thatcher and the Politics of Decline*, Cambridge, Polity Press, 1986, and D.H. Swinton 'Economic Status of Black Americans', National Urban League, *State of Black*

America 1, New York, 1989.
11. Interview with Frank Deale, 19 September 1989.
12. *New York Times*, 24 January 1989.
13. Ibid., 6 June 1989.
14. Ibid., 16 June and 23 June 1989.
15. D.R. Gordon, 'Last Hired ...' *The Nation*, vol.250, no.4, 29 January 1990.
16. *New York Times*, 24 June 1989.
17. Ibid., 7 August 1989.

6 Racism, the National Health Service, and the Health of Black People

This chapter first appeared in the *International Journal of Health Services*, vol.18, no.3, 1988. The author would like to thank Jackie Ould, Assistant Editor of Sage *Race Relations Abstracts*, and his colleagues at the Institute of Race Relations for their assistance, criticisms, and encouragement.

1. B. Beverly, S. Dadzie and S. Scafe, *The Heart of the Race: Black Women's Lives in Britain*, London, Virago, 1985.
2. P. Townsend and N. Davidson, eds, *Inequalities in Health: The Black Report*, Penguin Books, Harmondsworth, 1982, pp.58-60.
3. J. Bourne, 'Cheerleaders and Ombudsmen: The Sociology of Race Relations', *Race and Class*, vol.21, no.4, Spring 1980, pp.331–52; Brent Community Health Council, *Black People and the Health Service*, London, Brent Community Health Council, April 1981; J. Donovan, *We Don't Buy Sickness, It Just Comes: Health, Illness and Health Care in the Lives of Black People in London*, Aldershot, Gower Publishing Co., 1986; M. Pearson, 'The Politics of Ethnic Minority Health Studies', *Radical Community Medicine*, 16, 1983, pp.34–44.
4. S. Castles and G. Kosack, *Immigrant Workers and Class Structure in Western Europe*, 2nd Edition, Oxford University Press, Oxford, 1985; A. Sivanandan, *Race, Class and the State: The Black Experience in Britain*, reprinted in A. Sivanandan, ed., *A Different Hunger: Writings on Black Resistance*, London, Pluto Press, 1982, pp.106–26.
5. Commission for Racial Equality, *Ethnic Minority Hospital Staff*, London, 1983.
6. M. Anwar and A. Ali, *Overseas Doctors: Experience and Expectations. A Research Study*, Commission for Racial Equality, London, January 1987, p.73.
7. Ibid., p.74.
8. Ibid., p.75.
9. Sir Raymond Hoffenberg, *The Health Service and Race*, London, Centre for Contemporary Studies, London, 1985.
10. Ibid.
11. S. Watkins, 'Racialism in the National Health Service', *Radical Community Medicine*, vol.16, 1983, pp.55–60.
12. Ibid., pp.58–9.
13. Hoffenberg, op.cit., p.5.
14. Black Health Workers and Patients Group, *Bulletin no.1*, London, November 1981, pp.7–8.
15. L. Doyal et al., with the support of N. Parry, *Migrant Workers in the National Health Service: Report of a Preliminary Survey*, Polytechnic of North London, Department of Sociology, London, June 1980.
16. A. McNaught, *Race and Health Care in the United Kingdom*, Occasional Papers in Health Service Administration, Centre for Health Service Management Studies, Polytechnic of the South Bank, London, 1984.
17. Ibid.
18. Greater London Council Health Panel, *Ethnic Minorities and the National Health Service in London*, London, 1985.

19. P. Townsend and N. Davidson, eds, *Inequalities in Health: The Black Report*, Harmondsworth, Penguin Books, 1982, pp.58–60.

20. M. Whitehead, *The Health Divide: Inequalities in Health in the 1980s*, London, Health Education Council, March 1987, p.1.

21. A. McNaught, *Race and Health Care in the United Kingdom*, Occasional Papers in Health Service Administration, London, Centre for Health Service Management Studies, Polytechnic of the South Bank, 1984, p.26; see also M. Whitehead, *The Health Divide: Inequalities in Health in the 1980s*, London, Health Education Council, March 1987, pp.30–4.

22. *Guardian*, London, 8 November 1985.

23. M. Whitehead, op.cit., p.34.

24. Greater London Council Health Panel, op.cit., p.5.

25. Ibid., p.11.

26. N.P. Torkington, *The Racial Politics of Health — A Liverpool Profile*, Merseyside Area Profile Group, Liverpool, Department of Sociology, University of Liverpool, May 1983.

27. Ibid., pp.26–8.

28. C. Brown, *Black and White Britain: The Third PSI Survey*, London, Heinemann, 1984, p.256.

29. Greater London Council Health Panel, *Mental Health Services in London*, London, 1985, pp.18–19.

30. Hoffenberg, op.cit., p.8.

31. Brent Community Health Council, op.cit., p.13.

32. A. Henley, *Asian Patients in Hospital and at Home*, Oxford, Oxford University Press, 1982.

33. Brent Community Health Council, op.cit., p.14.

34. Torkington, op.cit., p.64.

35. A. Oakley and A. MacFarlane, 'A Poor Birth Right', *New Society*, vol.53, no.923, 24 July 1980, pp.172–3.

36. Ibid., p.173.

37. Greater London Council Health Panel, *Ethnic Minorities*, op.cit., p.13.

38. Ibid.

39. SUS refers to that part of a law dating from 1834 that makes it a criminal offence to be a suspicious person loitering with intent to commit a crime. This had been widely used against Afro-Caribbean youths; a major community campaign was conducted against it.

40. Brent Community Health Council, op.cit., p.18.

41. Greater London Council Health Panel, *Ethnic Minorities and the National Health Service in London*, London, 1985, p.6.

42. U. Prashar, E. Anionwu and M. Brozzovic, *Sickle Cell Anaemia-Who Cares? A Survey of Screening and Counselling Facilities in England*, The Runnymede Trust, London, 1985, p.38.

43. P. Foot, *Immigration and Race in British Politics*, Harmondsworth, Penguin Books, 1965, p.168.

44. Ibid., p.169.

45. *Pulse*, vol.41, no.6, 7 February 1981.

46. *Guardian*, London, 17 March 1980.

47. P. Gordon and A. Newnham, *Passport to Benefits? Racism in Social Security*, London, Child Poverty Action Group and The Runnymede Trust, 1985, pp.68–9; P. Gordon, *Policing Immigration: Britain's Internal Controls*, London, Pluto Press, 1985, pp.77–83.

48. Manchester Law Centre, *From Ill Treatment to No Treatment*, Law Centre Immigration Handbook no.6, Manchester, Manchester Law Centre, 1982, p.20.

49. Beverly, Dadzie and Scafe, op.cit., 1985, p.46.

7 The Political Economy of White Racism in Great Britain

This chapter was first published as Occasional Paper no.34, 1996 for the William Monroe Trotter Institute, University of Massachusetts. It was made possible by generous financial support from The Faculty of Arts, The University of Manchester; from the University of Manchester fund for Staff Travel for Research in the Humanities and Social Sciences; and from the Small Grants Scheme in the Social Sciences of the Nuffield Foundation. I would like to thank James Jennings and Gemima Remy and their colleagues at the William Monroe Trotter Institute; A. Sivanandan and my colleagues at the Institute of Race Relations for their years of dedicated and principled anti-racist practice; and Huw Beynon, Simon Katznellenbogen and Patricia Kushnick for their contributions and support.

1. W.E.B. Du Bois, *Black Reconstruction in America*, London, Frank Cass, 1966, p.30.
2. E. Williams, *Capitalism and Slavery*, London, André Deutsch, 1967. For a discussion on the role slavery and the economic system based on slavery had in funding the development of the New England economic system, see R. Bailey, 'The Slavery Trade and the development of Capitalism in the United States: The Textile Industry in New England', *Social Science History*, vol.14, no.3, 1990, pp.373–414.
3. J. Pope-Hennessy, *Sins of the Fathers: The Atlantic Slave Traders, 1441-1807*, London, Sphere, 1970, p.155.
4. Leo Huberman, *Man's Worldly Goods*, Monthly Review Press, New York and London, 1968, p.167.
5. P.Fryer, *Staying Power*, London, Pluto Press, 1984.
6. R. Drinnon, *Facing West*, New York, Schocken, 1980.
7. For a discussion on anti-Irish racism, see M. Hechter, *Internal Colonialism: The Celtic Fringe in British National Development, 1536-1966*, London, Routledge and Kegan Paul, 1975. Also see, M. Rai, 'Columbus in Ireland', *Race and Class*, vol.34, no.4, 1993, pp.25–34; and B. Rolston, 'The Training Ground: Ireland, Conquest and Colonization', *Race and Class*, vol.34, no.4, 1993, pp.13–24. For a discussion on anti-African racism, see P. Fryer, *Staying Power*, op.cit.
8. J. Foster, 'Nineteenth-Century Towns: A Class Dimension', in M.W. Flinn and T.C. Smout, eds, *Essays in Social History*, Oxford, Clarendon Press, 1974.
9. Ibid.
10. Richard Cobden, quoted in A. Briggs, 'The Language of "Class" in Early Nineteenth-Century England', in M.W. Flinn and T.C. Smout, eds, *Essays in Social History*, Oxford, Clarendon Press, 1974.
11. The London Working Men's Association, quoted in A. Briggs, op.cit.
12. W. Woodruff, 'The Emergence of an International Economy, 1700-1914', in C.M. Cipolla, ed., *The Fontana Economic History of Europe: The Emergence of Industrial Societies*, Part 2, London, Collins Fontana, 1973.
13. L.E. Davis, and R.A. Huttenback, *Mammon and the Pursuit of Empire: The Political Economy of British Imperialism, 1860-1912*, Cambridge, Cambridge University Press, 1986.
14. E. Hobsbawm, *Industry and Empire*, Harmondsworth, Penguin Books, 1968.
15. Ibid., pp.154-71.
16. M. Ellison, *Support for Secession: Lancashire and the American Civil War*, Chicago: University of Chicago Press, 1972.
17. V.G. Kiernan, *The Lords of Human Kind: European Attitudes Towards the Outside World in the Imperial Age*, London, Weidenfeld and Nicolson, 1969, pp.28-9.
18. P. Horn, 'Print Imperials', *Times Educational Supplement*, 1987, vol.3707, no.19, p.19.

19. Ibid.
20. J.A. Mangan, 'Images for Confident Control: Stereotypes in Imperial Discourse', in J.A. Mangan, ed., *The Imperial Curriculum*, London, Routledge, 1993, pp.6-22.
21. The Empire Day Movement was formed by Meath in 1903. Its first public celebrations were on 24 May 1904, which was also Queen Victoria's birthday. Government support came during World War I when there was general public enthusiasm. Support waned in the interior years but was revived by World War II. Interest waned in the post-war period and began to decline by 1959 when it became Commonwealth Day. J.M. MacKenzie, '"In Touch with the Infinite": The BBC and the Empire, 1923-53', in J.M. MacKenzie, ed, *Imperialism and Popular Culture*, Manchester, Manchester University Press, 1986, pp.168–81.
22. P. Horn, "Children of the Empire", *Times Educational Supplement*, vol.3648, no.19, 1986, p.19.
23. Roberts, quoted in Horn, ibid.
24. J.M. MacKenzie, *Propaganda and Empire*, Manchester, Manchester University Press, 1984, p.45.
25. K. Marx and F. Engels, *On Britain*, 2nd edn, Moscow, Foreign Languages Publishing House, 1962, pp.551, 552.
26. D. Nandy, 'Foreword', in J. McNeal and M. Rogers, eds, *The Multi-Racial School*, New York, Viking, 1971.
27. R. May and R. Cohen, 'The Interaction Between Race and Colonialism: A Case Study of the Liverpool Race Riots of 1919', *Race and Class*, vol.16, no.2, 1974, pp.111–26. Also see, Fryer, op.cit.; and N. Evans, 'Across the Universe: Racial Violence and the Post-War Crisis in Imperial Britain, 1919-25', *Immigrants and Minorities*, vol.13, nos 2 and 3, 1994, pp.59-88.
28. D. Byrne, 'The 1930 Arab Riot in South Shields', *Race and Class*, 1977, vol.18, no.3, pp.261–77. Also see, D. Byrne, 'Class, Race and Nation: The Politics of the "Arab Issue" in South Shields, 1919-39', *Immigrants and Minorities*, vol.13, nos 2 and 3, 1994, pp.89–104.
29. House of Commons, 4 December 1934, 1458.
30. N. Evans, op.cit.
31. See A. Sivanandan, 'Race, Class and the State', in A. Sivanandan, ed, *A Different Hunger*, London, Pluto Press, 1990, pp.101–25. Also see, L. Kushnick, 'Racism, the National Health Service and the Health of Black People', *International Journal of Health Services*, vol.18, no.3, 1988, pp.457–70; and C. Brown, *Black and White Britain: The Third PSI Survey*, London, Heinemann, 1984.
32. G. Smith, *When Jim Crow Met John Bull*, London, I.B. Tauris, 1987.
33. S. Joshi and B. Carter, 'The Role of Labour in the Creation of a Racist Britain', *Race and Class*, vol.25, no.3, 1984, pp.53–70. Also see, C. Harris, 'Configurations of Racism: The Civil Service, 1945-60', *Race and Class*, vol.33, no.1, 1991, pp.1–30.
34. Louis Kushnick, 'British Anti-Discrimination Legislation', in S. Abbott, ed, *The Prevention of Racial Discrimination in Britain*, Oxford, Oxford University Press for the United Nations Institute of Training and Research and the Institute of Race Relations, 1971, pp.223–68.
35. Fryer, op.cit., p.390.
36. J. Westegaard and H. Resler, *Class in a Capitalist Society: A Study of Contemporary Britain*, London, Heinemann Educational Books, 1975. Also see, P. Townsend and N. Davidson, eds, *Inequalities in Health: The Black Report*, Harmondsworth, Penguin Books, 1982; and C. Oppenheim, *Poverty: The Facts, Revised and Updated Edition*, London, Child Poverty Action Group, 1993.
37. Paul Foot, Immigration and Race in British Politics, Harmondsworth, Penguin Books, 1965.

38. See Louis Kushnick, 'Racism, the National Health Service and the Health of Black People', op.cit.
39. N. Murray, 'Anti-Racists and Other Demons: The Press and Ideology in Thatcher's Britain', *Race and Class*, vol.27, no.3, 1986, pp.1–20. Also see Searle, 'Your Daily Dose: Racism and the Sun', op.cit.
40. A. Sivanandan, 'A Different Hunger', op.cit., p.132.
41. See Murray, 'Anti-Racists and Other Demons', op.cit., and Searle, 'Your Daily Dose', op.cit.
42. *Daily Mail*, 7, 8, and 9 October, 1991.
43. Ibid.
44. *Daily Star*, 15 June 1991.
45. *Daily Star*, 25, 27 and 29 May 1991.
46. Searle, 'Your Daily Dose', op.cit.
47. *Daily Express*, 2, 7, 8 and 9 April 1992.
48. 'Paddy Puts Out the Welcome Mat for 4m from Hong Kong', *Daily Mail*, 7 April 1992.
49. 'Race and the Rapist: Cultural Differences are Behind Some Sex Attacks, says Expert', *Daily Mail*, 27 March 1992.
50. *Daily Mail* 7 April 1992.
51. Winston Churchill, MP, 28 May 1993, quoted in the *Daily Express*, 29 May 1993.
52. Paul Johnson, 'The Lying Game', *Daily Mail*, 13 February 1995.
53. See L. Fekete, 'Racist Violence: Meeting the New Challenges', *Race and Class*, vol.30, no.2, 1988, pp.71-6. Also see, N. Ginsburg, 'Racial Harassment Policy and Practice: The Denial of Citizenship', *Critical Social Policy*, vol.26, no.26, 1989, pp.66-81; Institute of Race Relations, *Policing Against Black People*, London, Institute of Race Relations (IRR), 1987; and K. Tompson, *Under Siege: Racism and Violence in Britain Today*, Harmondsworth, Penguin Books, 1988.
54. Home Office, *Racial Attacks: Report of Home Office Study*, London, HMSO, 1981.
55. Brown, op.cit.
56. Greater London Council, *Racial Harassment in London*, London, 1984.
57. Commission for Racial Equality, *Racial Attacks Survey of Eight Areas of Britain*, London, Commission for Racial Equality, 1987.
58. Sheffield Racial Harassment Project, *Because their Skin is Black*, Sheffield, Sheffield City Council, 1988.
59. Independent Committee of Inquiry into Racial Harassment, *Racial Harassment in Leeds 1985-6*, Leeds, Leeds Community Relations Council, 1987.
60. D. Walsh, *Racial Harassment in Glasgow*, Glasgow, Scottish Ethnic Minorities Research Unit, 1987.
61. G. Ford, *Fascist Europe: The Rise of Racism and Xenophobia*, London, Pluto Press, 1992.
62. R. Klein, 'Where Prejudice Still Flares in Violence', *Times Educational Supplement*, 6 January 1995, no.4097, p.9.
63. Home Affairs Committee, House of Commons, Session 1993-4, Third Report, *Racial Attacks*, vol.II, London, HMSO, 1994, 1.
64. Klein, op.cit.
65. *Guardian*, 14 March 1995.
66. See Louis Kushnick, 'Immigration and Asylum in the European Union', *Outsider*, no.42, April 1995, 3.
67. *Guardian*, 14 March 1995.
68. *Financial Times*, 8 March 1995.
69. *Financial Times*, 26 October 1995.
70. A similar process is in operation throughout Europe — see Kushnick 1995, op.cit.

71. *Guardian*, 20 March 1995.

72. J. Krieger, *Reagan, Thatcher and the Politics of Decline*, Cambridge, Polity Press, 1986.

8 Racism and Anti-Racism in Western Europe

This chapter first appeared in *Racism and Anti-racism in World Perspective*, Sage Publications, pp.181–202.

1. S.J. Gould, *The Mismeasure of Man*, New York, Norton, 1981. See also J.H. Stanfield, 'Racism in America and Other Race-centred Nation-states: Synchronic Considerations', *International Journal of Comparative Sociology*, vol.32, no.3-4, 1991, pp.243–61. H. Winant, and M. Omi, *Racial Formation in the United States: From the 1960s to the 1980s*, London, Routledge, 1986.

2. M. Hechter, *Internal Colonialism: The Celtic Fringe in British National Development, 1536-1966*, London, Routledge and Kegan Paul, 1975.

3. M. MacEwan and A. Prior, *Planning and Ethnic Minority Settlement in Europe: The Myth of Thresholds of Tolerance*, research Paper no.40, Edinburgh, Edinburgh College of Art/Heriot-Watt University School of Planning and Housing, 1992.

4. J.N. Pieterse, 'Myths and realities', *Race and Class*, vol.32 no.3, January-March 1991, pp.3–10.

5. A. Sivanandan, 'Editorial', *Race and Class*, vol.32, no.3, January-March 1991, pp.v-vi.

6. *Daily Mail*, 26 March 1992.

7. S. Castles and M.J. Miller, *The Age of Migration*, London, Macmillan, 1993. See also L.P. Moch, *Moving Europeans: Migration in Western Europe since 1650*, Bloomington, Indiana University Press, 1992; L. Potts *The World Labour Market: A History of Migration*, London, Zed Books, 1990.

8. G. Wallraff, *The Lowest of the Low*, London, Methuen, 1988.

9. J.P. Hollifield, *Immigrants, Markets and States: The Political Economy of Postwar Europe*, Cambridge, Harvard University Press, 1992.

10. E. Gaffiken and M. Morrisey, *The New Unemployed: Joblessness and Poverty in the Market Economy*, London, Zed Press, 1992. See also J. Michie and J.G. Smith, eds, *Unemployment in Europe*, London, Academic Press, 1994. See also J. Mitter, *Common Fate, Common Bond, Women in the Global Economy*, London, Pluto Press, 1986. See also S. Sassen, *The Mobility of Labour and Capital*, Cambridge, Cambridge University Press, 1988.

11. L. Fekete and F. Webber, *Inside Racist Europe*, London, Institute of Race Relations, 1994.

12. A. Sivanandan, 'Racism: The Road from Germany', *Race and Class*, vol.34, no.3, January-March 1993, pp.67–73.

13. A. Dummett, A. Nicol, *Subjects, Citizens, Aliens and Others: Nationality and Immigration Law*, London, Weidenfeld & Nicolson, 1990. See also P. Hainsworth, 'Introduction: The Cutting Edge: The Extreme Right in Post-war Western Europe and the USA' in P. Hainsworth, ed., *The Extreme Right in Europe and the USA*, London, Pinter, 1992. See also MacEwan and Prior, op.cit., 1992.

14. Refugee Forum and Migrant Rights Action Network, *The Walls of the Fortress: European Agreement against Immigrants, Migrants and Refugees*, London, Refugee Forum and Migrant Rights Action Network, 1991, p.16.

15. B. Carter, C. Harris and S. Joshi, *The 1951-55 Conservative Government and the Racialisation of Black Immigrants*, Policy Paper in Ethnic Relations, no.11, Coventry, University of Warwick, Centre for Research in Ethnic Relations, 1987. See also C. Harris, 'Configurations of Racism in the Civil Service', *Race and Class*, vol.33, no.1, July-September 1991, pp.1–30. See also S. Joshi and B. Carter, 'The

Role of Labour in the Creation of a Racist Britain, *Race and Class*, vol.25, no.3, winter 1984, pp.53–70.
16. *Guardian*, 2 March 1993.
17. S. Hall, C. Critcher, T. Jefferson, J. Clarke and B. Roberts, *Policing the Crisis: Mugging, the State, and Law and Order*, London, Macmillan, 1978. See also Institute of Race Relations. *Policing against Black People*, London, Institute of Race Relations, 1987. See also D.J. Smith, *Police and People in London*, 4 vols, London, Policy Studies Institute, 1983.
18. *Statewatch*, vol.3, no.2, March-April, 1993, p.3.
19. N. Rathzel, 'Germany: One Race, One Nation?', *Race and Class*, vol.32, no.3, pp.31–48.
20. Communities of Resistance Network, *Communities of Resistance*, first launch report, London, Communities of Resistance Network, 1992, p.11.
21. *Guardian*, 21 June 1991.
22. *Guardian*, 24 September 1991.
23. Hainsworth, op.cit., 1992.
24. *L'Humanité*, 17 February 1993. *Le Monde*, 18 February 1993.
25. *Le Monde*, 14 January 1993.
26. *L'Humanité*, 17 February 1993. Le Monde, 18 February 1993.
27. A. Simpson and M. Read, *Against a Rising Tide: Racism, Europe and 1992*, Nottingham, Spokesman Books, 1991, p.33.
28. F. Webber, 'From Ethnocentrism to Euro-racism', *Race and Class*, vol.32, no.3, January 1991, pp.11–18.
29. Rathzel, op.cit., p.38.
30. Ibid.
31. T. Bunyan, 'Toward an Authoritarian European State', *Race and Class*, vol.32, no.3, January-March 1991, pp.19–30. See also M. Baldwin-Edwards, 'Immigration after 1992', *Policy and Politics*, vol.19, no.3, 1991, pp.199–211. See also A. Cruz, *An Insight into Schengen, TREVI and other European Intergovernmental Bodies*, Briefing Paper no.1, 2nd edn, Brussels, Churches Committee for Migrants in Europe, 1991. See also Refugee Forum and the Migrants Rights Action Network, op.cit., 1991. See also M. Spencer, *1992 and All That: Civil Liberties in the Balance*, London, Civil Liberties Trust, 1990.
32. A. Sivanandan, *A Different Hunger*, London, Pluto Press, 1982. See also A. Sivanandan, *Communities of Resistance*, London, Verso, 1990.
33. Amnesty International, *Europe: Human Rights and the Need for a Fair Asylum Policy*, Geneva, Amnesty International, 1991.
34. Organisation for Economic Co-operation and Development, *SOPEMI: Trends in International Migration*, Paris, Organisation for Economic Co-operation and Development, 1992, p.13.
35. J. Toporowski, 'Fascist Spectre Looms over Stagnant Europe', *Observer*, 27 September 1992, p.24.
36. *Independent on Sunday*, Business Section, 10 January 1993.
37. J. Krieger, *Reagan, Thatcher and the Politics of Decline*, Cambridge, Polity Press, 1986.
38. *Searchlight*, May 1992, p.18.
39. Ibid., p.15.
40. *Independent*, 21 March 1993.
41. *Searchlight*, November 1994, p.21.
42. *Guardian*, 27 May 1993.
43. G. Ford, *Fascist Europe: The Rise of Racism and Xenophobia*, London, Pluto Press, 1992.
44. House of Commons, Home Affairs Committee, *Third Report: Racial Attacks and Harassment*, vol.III, London, House of Commons, 1994.

45. R. Klein, 'Where Prejudice Still Flares into Violence', *Times Educational Supplement*, no.4097, 6 January 1995, p.9. For a general discussion of racial violence, see C. Brown, *Black and White Britain: The Third PSI Survey*, London, Heinemann, 1984. Commission for Racial Equality, *Racial Attacks - Survey of Eight Areas of Britain*, London, Commission for Racial Equality, 1987. J. Cooper and T. Qureshi, *Through Patterns not our Own*, London, New Ethnicities Research and Education Group, 1993. L. Fekete, 'Racist Violence: Meeting the New Challenges', *Race and Class*, vol.30 no.2, 1988, pp.71-6, N. Ginsburg, 'Racial Harassment Policy and Practice: The Denial of Citizenship', *Critical Social Policy*, 26(26), 1989, pp.66–81. Greater London Council, *Racial Harassment in London*, London, London Commission for Racial Equality, 1984. Independent Committee of Inquiry into Racial Harassment, *Racial Harassment in Leeds, 1985-6*, Leeds, Leeds Community Relations Council/Institute of Race Relations, 1987. London Borough of Waltham Forest, *Beneath the Surface: An Inquiry into Racial Harassment in the London Borough of Waltham Forest*, London, London Borough of Waltham Forest, 1990. Sheffield Racial Harassment Project, *Because their Skin is Black*, Sheffield, Sheffield City Council, 1988. K. Tompson, *Under Siege: Racism and Violence in Britain Today*, Harmondsworth, Penguin, 1988. D. Walsh, *Racial Harassment in Glasgow*, Glasgow, Scottish Ethnic Minorities Research Unit, 1987.

46. L. Kushnick, 'Racism and Class Consciousness in Modern Capitalism', in B.P. Bowser and R.G. Hunt, eds, *Impacts of Racism on White Americans*, Beverly Hills, Sage, 1981, pp.191-216. See also L. Kushnick, 'Political Economy of White Racism in the United States and Great Britain' in B.P. Bowser ed., *Impacts of Racism on White Americans*, 2nd edn, Thousand Oaks, Sage, 1996.

47. *Campaign Against Racism and Fascism* (CARF), no.6, Jan./Feb. 1992, p.4.

48. Sivanandan, op.cit, 1993, p.69.

49. Reprinted in the *Guardian*, 5 February 1993.

50. CARF, no.2, April/May 1991, p.12.

51. CARF, no.8, May/June 1992, p.15.

9 The Political Economy of White Racism in the United States

This chapter first appeared in *Impacts of Racism on White Americans*, 2nd edition, ed. B.P. Bowser, Sage Publications, pp.48–67, 1996. Reprinted by permission of Sage Publications Inc.

1. E.J. Cornacchia and D.C. Nelson, 'Historical Differences in the Political Experiences of American Blacks and White Ethnics: Revisiting an Unresolved Controversy', *Ethnic and Racial Studies*, vol.15, no.1, 1992, pp.102–24. See also P. Horton, 'Testing the Limits of Class Politics in Postbellum Alabama: Agrarian Radicalism in Lawrence County', *Journal of Southern History*, vol.57, no.1, 1991, pp.63–84. J.H. Stanfield, 'Racism in America and Other Race-Centered Nation-States: Synchronic Considerations', *International Journal of Comparative Sociology*, vol.32, nos 3–4, 1991, pp.243–61.

2. L. Kushnick, 'Racism and Anti-Racism in Western Europe', in B.P. Bowser, ed., *Racism and Anti-Racism in World Perspectives*, Thousand Oaks and London, Sage Publications, 1995; chapter 8 in this volume. See also M. Marable 'Race and Class in the US Presidential Election', *Race and Class*, vol.34 no.3, January-March 1993, pp.75–85.

3. L. Kushnick 'Parameters of British and North American Racism', *Race and Class*, vol.23, nos 2–3, 1981–2, pp.187–206; chapter 4 in this volume.

4. W.E.B. DuBois, *Black Reconstruction in America*, London, Frank Cass, 1966, p.30.

5. H. Aptheker, 'Anti-Racism in the US: An Introduction', *Sage Race Relations Abstracts*, vol.12, no.4, November 1987, pp.3–32.

6. R. Bailey, 'The Slavery Trade and the Development of Capitalism in the United States: The Textile Industry in New England', *Social Science History*, vol.14, no.3, 1990, pp.373–414. See also E. Williams, *Capitalism and Slavery*, London, André Deutsch, 1967.

7. T. Allen, 'They Would Have Destroyed Me: Slavery and the Origins of Racism', *Radical America*, vol.9, no.3, 1975, p.42.

8. R. Drinnon, *Facing West*, New York, Schocken, 1980; see also B.B. Ringer, *We the People and Others*, New York, Norton, 1983; D.R. Roediger, *The Wages of Whiteness: Race and the Making of the American Working Class*, London, Verso, 1991; A. Saxton, *The Rise and Fall of the White Republic: Class Politics and Mass Culture in Nineteenth-Century America*, London, Verso, 1991; R.T. Takaki, *Iron Cages: Race and Culture in Nineteenth-Century America*, London, Athlone, 1980.

9. Du Bois, op.cit., pp.633–4.

10. Roediger, op.cit., 1991 pp.13, 14.

11. Ibid.

12. N. Glazer, 'Blacks and White Ethnics: The Difference and the Political Difference It Makes', *Social Problems*, vol.18, 1971. pp.444–61.

13. Cornacchia and Nelson, op.cit., p.103.

14. Ibid., p.120.

15. Du Bois, op.cit., pp.700-01; See also I. Katznelson and M. Weir, *Schooling for All: Class, Race and the Decline of the Democratic Ideal*, New York, Basic Books, 1985.

16. Aptheker, op.cit.

17. Saxton, op.cit.

18. Roediger, op.cit.

19. Du Bois, op.cit.

20. M. Davis, *Prisoners of the American Dream*, London, Verso, 1980.

21. Takaki, op.cit., p.238.

22. Ibid., p.239.

23. Horton, op.cit., p.65.

24. Ibid, pp.76, 77.

25. Ibid, p.83.

26. H. Braverman, *Labor and Monopoly Capital*, New York, Monthly Review Press, 1974.

27. A. Saxton, 'Race and the House of Labor', in G. Nash and R. Weiss, eds, *The Great Fear: Race in the Mind of Americans*, New York, Holt, Rinehart and Winston, 1970, p.115.

28. D. Noble, *America by Design*, Oxford, Oxford University Press, 1977.

29. W. Tuttle, *Race Riot, Chicago in the Red Summer of 1977*, Urbana, University of Illinois Press. See also S. Vittoz, 'World War I and the Political Accommodation of Transitional Market Forces: The Case of Immigration Restrictions', *Politics and Society*, vol.8, 1978, pp.49–78.

30. G. Gilder, *Wealth and Poverty*, New York, Bantam Books, 1982. See also C. Murray, *Losing Ground: American Social Policy 1950–1980*, New York, Basic Books, 1986. For a critique of these see T. Boston, *Race, Class and Conservatism*, Boston and London, Unwin Hyman, 1988. See also A. Reed, 'The Underclass as Myth and Symbol: The Poverty of Discourse about Poverty', *Radical America*, vol.24, no.1, 1992, pp.21–40.

31. L. Kushnick, 'Race, Class and Civil Rights', in A. Zegeye, L. Harris, J. Maxted, eds, *Exploitation and Exclusion: Race and Class in Contemporary US Society*, 1991, pp.158-9. Oxford, Hans Zell. Chapter 2 in this volume. See also M. Marable, *Race, Reform and Rebellion*, 2nd edition, London, Macmillan, 1991.

32. A. Hirsch, *Making the Second Ghetto: Race and Housing in Chicago*, Cambridge and New York, Cambridge University Press, 1983.

33. S. Bowles, D. Gordon and H. Gintis, *Beyond the Waste Land*, Garden City, Anchor Books, 1984.
34. A. Sivanandan, *A Different Hunger*, London, Pluto Press, 1990.
35. M. Marable, op.cit, 1993, p.76.
36. M. Mauer, *Young Black Men and the Criminal Justice System: A Growing National Problem*, Washington, DC, The Sentencing Project, 1990. See also C. Shine and M. Mauer, *Does the Punishment Fit the Crime? Drug Users and Drunk Drivers, Questions of Race and Class*, Washington, DC, The Sentencing Project, 1993.

Index

support for African independence 69
Robeson, Paul, Jr. 59, 229–30
Robinson, Jackie 70
Rockefeller, Governor Nelson 70
Roe v. Wade 140
Roediger, David 206, 207, 224, 242
Rogers, D. 26, 28, 29, 226, 227, 228
Rogers, Joel A. 52
Rogers, M. 237
Rolston, B. 2, 224, 236
Roma People 184
Roosevelt Administration 9
Rose, Paul, MP 92
Rosen, Sumner 63, 229
Rosenberg, E. 212
Rosenberg, J. 212
Rosenthal, R. 227
Rowan, Carl T. 70
Rowley, Margaret 70, 230
Runnymede Bulletin 201
Runnymede Trust 201

Sacco, N. 212
Safe Third Country rule 15
Sage Race Relations Abstracts (UK, US) 201, 224, 225, 226, 232, 241
Sassen, S. 239
Save the Children Fund in Scotland 201
Saxton, A. 242
Scafe, S. 234, 235
Schauble, Wolfgang (Christian Democratic Union, Germany) 197
Schengen: Agreement/Accord 12, 15, 192, 240; Information System 12
Schlesinger, Arthur, Jr 71, 74
Schleswig-Holstein (Germany) 197
Schmalz-Jacobsen, Cornelia (German Commissioner for Foreigners) 188
Schmidt, Emerson P. 62, 229
School for the Educationally Subnormal (UK) 123
Schuyler, George 52
Schwerner, George, 111
Scientific Management 214
Scientific racism 19, 129, 215–16, 226, 232
Scott, Nicholas, MP 105, 106, 108
Scottish Ethnic Minorities Research Unit (UK) 179, 241
Scribner's Monthly (US) 212
Searchlight (UK) 201, 240
Searle, C. 177, 228, 237, 238

Second Reconstruction 14, 22, 136, 140, 142, 143, 230
Second World War: and Africa 68; and black radicalism 52, 56; and industrialisation of South and Southwest 49; and Keynesian Accommodation 47; and origins of Civil Rights Movement 56; and post-Second World War period and anti-Communist purges 47
Selznick, G. 41
Senate Internal Affairs Committee, US 63
Seniority System 56
'Separate but Equal' 18, 55, 65, 102, 107, 213
Shanker, A. 35, 39, 40, 41, 43, 44
Shaw, G. 233
Sheffield: City Council (UK) 178, 238, 241; Racial Harassment Project 178, 238, 241
Sherman, H. J. 233
Shine, C. 242
Shockley, William 129, 232
Sickle Cell Anaemia 147, 159
Simpson, A. 192, 240
Sinclair, Sir George, MP 105, 106
Sivanandan, A. 128, 132, 225, 231–4, 236–7, 239–42
Skinheads 199
Slaughterhouse Cases of 1873 (US) 137
Slave uprisings 48, 209
Slavery 1, 3–6, 48, 138, 165–7, 185, 204–9, 224, 236, 241
Slough 86
Smaje, C. 226
Smedley, A. 225
Smethwick 81, 86
Smith, A. D. 225
Smith, D. J. 239
Smith, G. 237
Smith, J. G. 239
Smith, Susan J. 3, 224, 225
Smith, William French (Attorney General, US) 134
Smout, T. C. 225, 236
Social Democratic Party (Germany) 16, 186, 188, 195–6
Social dislocation 10, 15, 185
Social mobility 28
Social programmes 82, 134
Social Wage 10, 15, 115, 130, 142,